Milwaukee 150

"Greater Milwaukee's Enterprises"

by Dale Buss with Linda Duczman

Photo Researcher Carlen Hatala

Produced in cooperation with the City of Milwaukee
Department of City Development

Milwaukee Publishing Group
Milwaukee, Wisconsin

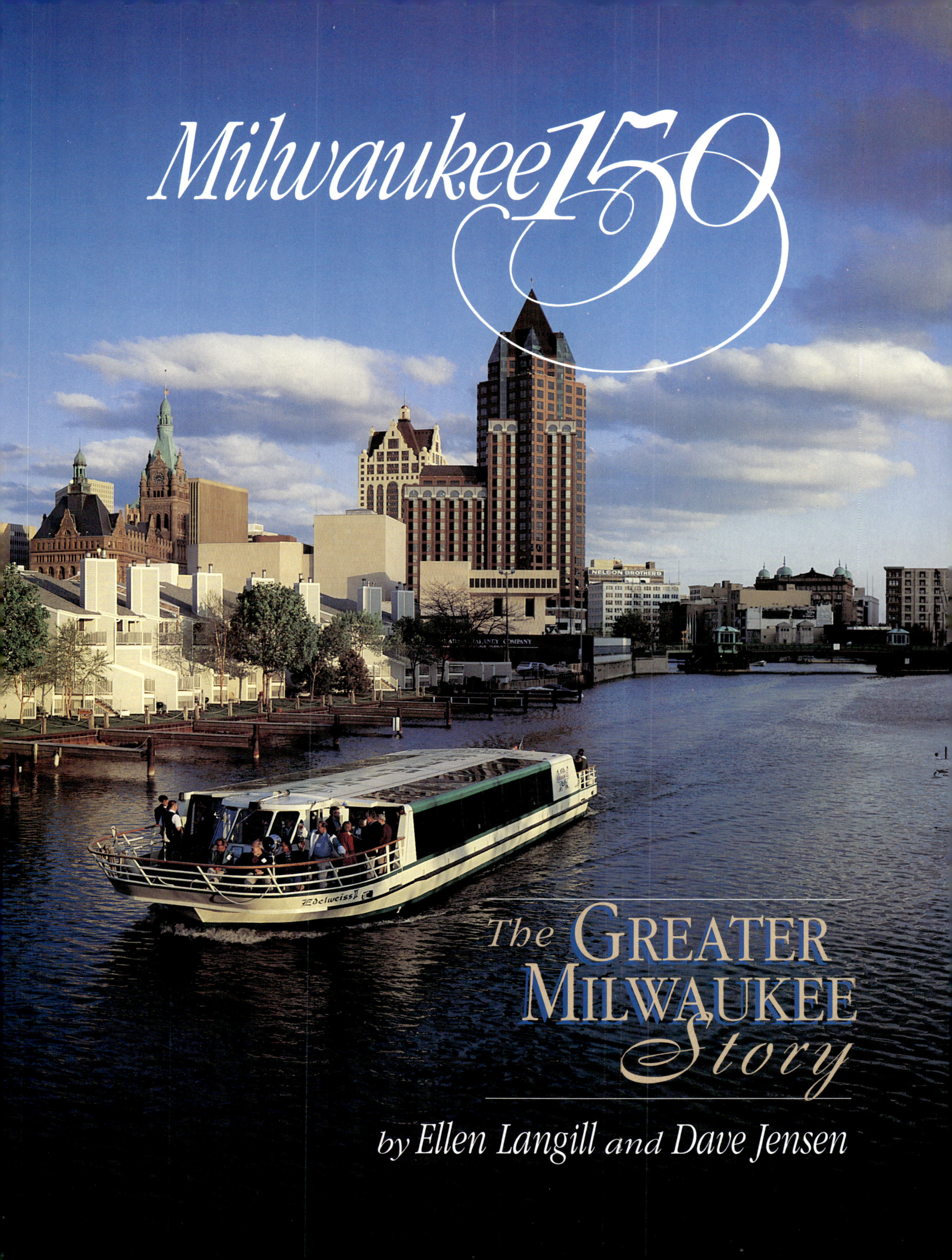

Milwaukee 150

The Greater Milwaukee Story

by Ellen Langill and Dave Jensen

Milwaukee Publishing Group
Book Division
EDITORIAL DIRECTOR
Karen Story
DESIGN DIRECTOR
Ellen Ifrah

♦

Staff for *Milwaukee 150*
EDITOR
K. Story
PHOTO EDITOR
Patty Salkeld
EDITORIAL ASSISTANT
Kathy B. Peyser
INDEXER
Teri Davis Greenberg
DESIGNER
E. Ifrah
PRODUCTION CONSULTANT
James Burke

MILWAUKEE PUBLISHING GROUP

PUBLISHERS
C. David Turner and Don Toohey

Library of Congress Catalog Card Number:
96-94439

ISBN: 0-9650759-0-7

Published 1996
Printed in the United States of America
First Edition

Frontispiece: Photo by Peter Saunders/Third Coast Stock Source

Page 5: Photo by Peter Saunders/Third Coast Stock Source

Page 6: Top photo by Milwaukee DCD/Dave La Haye; bottom photo by N.R. Rowan/Third Coast Stock Source

Page 7: Top photo by Milwaukee DCD/Dave La Haye; bottom left photo by William Meyer/Third Coast Stock Source; bottom right photo by Dale Guldan/Third Coast Stock Source

Pages 10/11: The Pabst Theater was built in 1895 by brewer Frederick Pabst. Its golden age flowered at the turn of the century, as this painting illustrates, but declined by World War I. The theater was restored in 1975-1976 and once again offers musical and theatrical performances. Painting by Lynn Casper

Endsheets: Photo by Eric Oxendorf

Milwaukee's architecture is one of its most enduring assets and the city abounds in remarkable historical specimens, which encompass an astonishing variety of styles. Showcasing this proud heritage, graceful renderings of some of the city's outstanding architectural details by noted Milwaukee artist/illustrator Steve Slaske appear throughout the book.

Contents

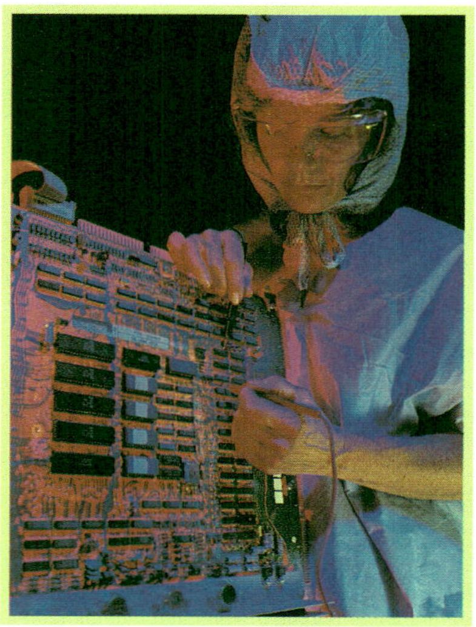

Foreword

It's a privilege to serve as mayor during Milwaukee's sesquicentennial, which is our opportunity to remember this city's proud history and to celebrate its rich cultural heritage. Milwaukee truly is an international city. You can see it in the design of our buildings, you can feel it at our ethnic festivals, and you can taste it in our German, Polish, Italian, Russian, Mideastern, and Asian restaurants. In many ways, we offer the best of both worlds—a city steeped in European traditions and a business community fortified with the best in American technological know-how.

Milwaukee Mayor John O. Norquist, who was elected to his third four-year term in 1996, stands in front of City Hall. Photo by Milwaukee DCD/Dave La Haye

Facing page: Milwaukee is aptly named the "City of Festivals," due in part to the beautiful Henry W. Maier Festival Park, which is located on the lakefront. Photo by Paul C. Butterbrodt/Third Coast Stock Source

Milwaukee 150: The Greater Milwaukee Story celebrates this great city's past and present. Its pictures and text paint a portrait of Milwaukee residents as hard-working, fun-loving people who have been leaders in commerce, strong supporters of the cultural arts, and visionaries committed to developing progressive policies that put people first.

Milwaukee today is a great city because of the many creative minds who envisioned new products or found better ways to make things, and the tens of thousands of workers who used their skills and sweat to hammer out Milwaukee's legacy as the "Toolbox of America." Because of their efforts, Milwaukee today is one of the nation's primary manufacturing centers, producing both the gears and motors that power huge earth-moving machinery and the delicate electronic circuitry used to detect the faintest of heartbeats. We also have a great service economy, with a vigorous financial sector that includes one of the country's leading insurance companies, two of the nation's largest banks, and several prominent mutual fund companies.

We offer a quality of life that many cities can only imagine. In addition to the major events that have earned Milwaukee the designation as the "City of Festivals," we enjoy a world-class zoo, a nationally acclaimed public museum, five professional sports teams, two opera companies, a ballet, a symphony, and more than a dozen theater groups offering everything from Shakespeare to the avant-garde. Then there is Lake Michigan, which is truly one of the greatest and most beautiful natural resources the world has to offer. We have been blessed not only with an ideal location on this greatest of lakes, but with the foresight and perseverance of the people who have fought to ensure that the public would always have access to miles of unobstructed shoreline.

Milwaukee has a lot to be proud of, but we cannot stand still. Everyday we must reinvent ourselves to address the challenges that face us. Everyday we must find new ways to make our streets both cleaner and safer, new ways to encourage businesses to create jobs where people live, and new ways to deliver city services more efficiently and at less cost. Many challenges await us, but we can meet them with the wisdom of our elders and a commitment to our children.

One hundred fifty years ago the citizens who founded Milwaukee set out to create the most beautiful city in the world. It was not enough to try to be like someplace else. We had to be the best. And we succeeded. We became the "Beer Capital of the World" and the "Toolbox of America." We shaped national debate by forging public policies that reinforce the dignity of human beings. At all times we have respected our history and the diversity of our ethnic heritage.

Our sesquicentennial observance is an opportunity to celebrate Milwaukee's founders and all of the people who, in the past and now, have made this city a great place to live and work. As we approach the next millennium, we owe the same effort to future generations, a commitment to building a peaceful, productive, and culturally significant city that will give joy and prosperity for hundreds and hundreds of years to come.

WSA

PART ONE

Milwaukee's Historical Heritage

BY ELLEN LANGILL

Café Pabst Theater Restau

Chapter ONE

From Fur-Trading Outpost to Busy Wheat Port

1830–1870

In the central area of what is now the city of Milwaukee, there was once only a tamarack swamp bounded by cliffs that overlooked several winding rivers and the great Lake Michigan into which they emptied. There were also abundant beavers, greatly valued for their fur, and fish and wildlife of many varieties. These plentiful resources supported settlements of Native American peoples who lived in the area, predominantly the Potawatomi, the Fox, and the Mescouten.

In pursuit of the rich supply of fur pelts and in cooperation with the indigenous peoples, French explorers first came to the mouth of the Milwaukee River in 1674. In that year Father Jacques Marquette, the renowned French Jesuit explorer, allegedly wrote of his first glimpse of these swamps on his return trip from the Mississippi River. Marquette thought that the site where the Milwaukee River met Lake Michigan was so marshy that it was completely uninhabitable. No doubt, his discomfort was increased by an illness that soon took his life and by the general miasma that greeted him. Fortunately, his prediction did not hold true as a general pursuit of beaver pelts brought many more Frenchmen to the area during the next four decades.

Created in 1944 on the walls of the Auditorium Building, this Thorston Lindberg painting depicts Solomon Juneau trading with Native Americans at his cabin along the Milwaukee River during the 1820s. Courtesy, Milwaukee County Historical Society

Jacques Vieau, a French Canadian trader who worked for the Northwest Fur Company, established a trading post in Milwaukee in 1795 on a hilltop overlooking the Menomonee River. Today this site is part of Mitchell Park. Vieau was active in Milwaukee until about 1825 and eventually retired to his farm in Green Bay. Courtesy, Department of City Development-City of Milwaukee

East Coast and European fashion had fallen in love with beaver hats and beaver coats and traders pursued this lucrative trade wherever native trappers harvested beavers.

However, none of these early explorers or fur traders stayed long in the region of the Milwaukee River, until the arrival of Jacques Vieau more than a century after Marquette. Vieau's trading post was located on the north bank of the Menomonee River near the site of the present-day Mitchell Park Domes. Vieau's wife, who was the daughter of a Green Bay fur trader and was part Indian, preferred to winter in Green Bay with their growing family. Vieau himself made many trips north from Milwaukee through Green Bay to Mackinac, delivering beaver pelts to the North American Fur Company for which he was an agent.

While Vieau was more rooted in the Milwaukee area than the other fur traders, he never dreamed of making it a permanent settlement. Rather, it was one of his young clerks who came to live on the banks of the Milwaukee River and to build a town. This young Frenchman, Solomon Juneau, who arrived in Milwaukee in 1818 and married Vieau's daughter, Josette, is therefore hailed as Milwaukee's first permanent European settler and the father of the city itself.

Juneau's trading post, on the east side of the Milwaukee River close to present-day Wisconsin Avenue, soon became a thriving fur center. The good relationship he established with the native peoples resulted in prosperity and caused Juneau to lay plans to drain the swamp and create town lots. Solomon Juneau was respected for his scrupulous fairness in keeping his account books and setting up a just system of rewards for each fur noted in his ledger. Standing at six foot, four inches tall, Juneau had learned to speak the Algonquin language and was able to dominate the entire fur-trading business in southeastern Wisconsin during the 1820s through his close ties to the indigenous peoples.

Along with his brother Peter, Juneau began to see the possibilities of great profits that could be gained by land speculation and particularly by town site development. The area's three rivers and its location near the lakeshore and between Chicago and Green Bay were ideal for their plans. Writing to a friend with enthusiasm, Juneau advised, "You ought to come here; it's going to be a big town!" A native French speaker, fluent in the Indian tongues, Juneau began to learn English in 1831, since Wisconsin was part of the United States and its future would be dictated by the Northwest Ordinance, which passed Congress in 1787.

By the fall of 1833 all of southeastern Wisconsin had been ceded to the United States by the treaties that followed the Indian defeats in the

Milwaukee's three founding fathers were of diverse backgrounds and temperaments, and each hoped that his settlement would become the center of the new community. Solomon Juneau (1793-1856) was a French Canadian known for his stalwart, honest character. He came to the region to pursue the fur trade and stayed on to develop the east side of the Milwaukee River when the territory was opened for settlement. Byron Kilbourn (1801-1870) was a shrewd, ambitious surveyor turned opportunist who saw the west side of the river as a place to make his fortune. George Walker (1811-1866) was a Virginia-born, Illinois-raised trader of genial disposition who saw the marshy south side as an area that could be transformed into a bustling, thriving village. Courtesy, Department of City Development-City of Milwaukee

Black Hawk Wars. The land on the Milwaukee, Menomonee, and Kinnickinnic rivers was open for purchase through preemption rights that allowed early settlers, or squatters, to press the first claims. Land speculation quickly replaced fur trading in profitability. Juneau succeeded in gaining the financial backing of Morgan Martin, a wealthy lawyer from New York and cousin to pioneer James Doty. Together they were able to purchase more than 500 acres of land east of the Milwaukee River stretching through the swamp to the lakeshore and its cliffs.

The growing interest in the area soon brought other speculators to the Milwaukee area. Ohio native Byron Kilbourn and George Walker, a Virginian, quickly bought land on the west and south sides of the Milwaukee River, respectively. By 1834 land that had been purchased by these three speculators for the government rate of $1.25 an acre was selling in divided town lots for $1,000 or more. Settlement fever became a strong magnet. Within the next two years Milwaukee's three separate sites boasted a population of more than 275 people.

However, the swampy area had to be drained and primitive streets laid out connecting the town lots into an organized pattern. Juneau hired teams of horses and wagons to carry dirt to work as quickly as possible so that the area would be attractive for settlement. Cliffs and hills were leveled, swamps were filled with dirt, trees were felled, and primitive docks were built to greet the lake steamers that brought hundreds of passengers to the "boomtown" on the lakeshore.

Because the mouth of the Milwaukee River met the lake in a marsh and a sizable sandbar blocked its entrance, the larger lake boats had to transfer passengers and all of their luggage to smaller crafts to enable them to come ashore in the new settlement. Often Lake Michigan's waves made this transfer very precarious and even on calm days it was a risky process at best. After more than one small boat capsized, the developers of Milwaukee's three town sites each attempted to make the landing (and the subsequent short boat ride to his location) much easier.

Smaller launches were purchased to meet each lake steamer and bring its passengers to whichever area its owner controlled. There was no give and take among the three developers. They competed for each arriving land purchaser. Whichever steamer arrived first alongside the larger boat was able to transfer the willing load of passengers to the docks of Juneau, Walker, or Kilbourn, whoever owned the respective steamer. Races actually took place to be the first to meet the incoming lake craft, full of eager investors.

Taking advantage of his southernmost location, George Walker benefited by being first on the route for those investors who arrived from Chicago along the road that terminated at what became known as "Walker's Point," south of the river. Not to be outdone, Kilbourn built a bridge crossing the Menomonee River that would allow travelers from Chicago to come to Kilbourntown, but not cross over to Juneautown. He also had a map printed and circulated around the Upper Midwest urging people to come to the area. His map showed no sketch of the rival town east of the river, only his own on the west side. Anyone reading it would think that the east side was completely undeveloped.

This 1940s painting by Willem de D. Van Langereis depicts the east end of Wisconsin Avenue as it looked between 1837 and 1855. The federal government approved funding for the construction of a lighthouse at the top of a 56-foot bluff about where Marshall Street intersects with Wisconsin Avenue. The lighthouse, seen here, was razed in 1855 after a new one was built in North Point. Courtesy, Milwaukee County Historical Society

Settlement Rivalry

Walker's Point, Kilbourntown, and Juneautown, as the three sites became known, also competed with each other by boasting of better streets or more town conveniences. Log hotels and boarding houses sprang up quickly to accommodate weary passengers while they invested their cash in town lots on one or the other side of the river. Only the national depression in 1837 slowed the steady growth of the area as many who had bought a town lot on credit faced bankruptcy and had to return to Chicago or the East. By late 1838, however, prospective settlers began to arrive again and Milwaukee's future brightened in the next two years.

Soon flour- and sawmills were built on the rivers, powered by new dams. Warehouses were erected to hold cargo and the building trades boomed as everyone who purchased a lot looked forward to moving into his own dwelling and out of the crude hotels as soon as possible. Carpenters and bricklayers arrived weekly to take advantage of the opportunities in the three rapidly rising settlements.

In 1836 Kilbourn began the area's first official newspaper, the *Milwaukee Advertiser*, which he used with great skill to promote the interests of his expanding west-side settlement. The following year Juneau established his own newspaper, the voice of the east side, the *Milwaukee Sentinel*. Juneau's paper was edited by several of his close associates until Rufus King arrived from Albany, New York, and took over its control eight years later. Under his skilled leadership, the *Sentinel* soon became the voice of not only Juneautown, but the entire Milwaukee area in its steady calls for urban improvements, better schools, and enhanced cultural opportunities.

In 1837 Juneau built a new courthouse on today's Cathedral Square. The white frame courthouse officially signaled that the east side had become the legal center of Milwaukee County, newly formed when Wisconsin separated from the Michigan Territory in 1836. Although Kilbourn had set aside a square on high ground for a courthouse site, Juneau and Martin were jubilant when their site was selected by the new territorial legislature. Martin's membership in the legislature was no doubt very helpful in this choice. It was an age of unabashed personal influence peddling in local, state, and national politics.

The stately new courthouse faced south onto the square between Jefferson and Jackson streets. Built of wood, it had two large courtrooms for the territorial court, four separate jury rooms, and an attached jail. Juneau and Martin chose a Greek-revival style with a cupola and columned portico. The building was used as the courthouse for the entire area until it was replaced by a stone structure on the same site in 1872. Its presence on the east side was a great boon to Juneau's dreams of dominating the other two developers.

Particularly fierce was the rivalry between Kilbourn and Juneau, whose streets intentionally reached the river at different points—allegedly to make unification by bridges very difficult. The area's first bridge, built in 1840, crossed the river at an angle from Chestnut Street (later Juneau Avenue) and was shortly followed by another angled bridge built at Wisconsin Avenue. Rivalry from west-side residents who feared that the bridges would lead new settlers out of their section and across the river to the east side brought violence in May 1845.

Marching en masse toward the hated bridges, rioters soon destroyed the structures hoping to once again cut off their east-side rivals. Responding in kind, east-siders are reported to have dragged a cannon to the shore and aimed it at Kilbourn's house on the west side. Cooler heads prevailed, however, and the lack of cannon balls also ended the standoff. An ordinance was passed making it illegal to destroy any more bridges, under penalty of a stiff $50 fine. The violence heightened public awareness of the harmful nature of town rivalry and pushed forward the growing movement for city unification.

In the rivalry between the three settlements, Juneautown took a decided lead when the first Milwaukee County Courthouse was built east of the river in 1836. Located on the north end of a public square donated by Juneau and his partner Morgan Martin, the Greek Revival-style structure included a courtroom and meeting rooms in the main building while the wings housed the jail and offices. It was replaced by a larger, more grandiose courthouse in 1872. Courtesy, Milwaukee County Historical Society

However, other aspects of the rivalry led to better facilities for immigrants. By the early 1840s Juneautown boasted the area's first "luxury" hotels for new arrivals: the Milwaukee House; the City Hotel, built by entrepreneur Daniel Wells; and the United States Hotel, developed by large landowner James Rogers. Juneau also made sure that the east side got its own land claim office (the area's first office was on the west side). Juneautown proudly claimed several drygoods stores to serve newcomers, and more than a few taverns and hostelries to feed and entertain them. It also had several livery stables and more than four dozen log or board buildings by the end of 1838.

That year most of the area's remaining tribal

Although they joined forces as a village in 1839, Juneautown and Kilbourntown retained autonomy over taxation and public improvements for their respective communities. However, disagreements raged over joint expenditures before the Territorial Legislature granted Milwaukee its city charter. In one instance, bridges over the Milwaukee River were dismantled by west-siders while east-siders threatened violence during the infamous Bridge War of May 1845. Courtesy, Milwaukee County Historical Society

peoples were forcibly removed by federal order and taken westward in wagons from the lakeshore area that had long been their home. It was Juneau's father-in-law, the aging Jacques Vieau, who helped to carry several of the oldest Potawatomi leaders west in his own wagon. The newly arriving Yankee settlers rejoiced at their departure, having stereotyped many native peoples, since the decline of the beaver trade had made a few Indians sadly dependent on charity. Most of Wisconsin's once-flourishing tribal peoples were pushed west of the Mississippi River to the Iowa Territory, leaving only a small remnant in the Milwaukee area. Local settlers gave food to these remaining native peoples but remained largely ignorant of their once-proud heritage.

Churches and the Public Spirit

Along with private charities, the city's earliest churches worked to assist needy immigrants who arrived at the port daily and helped to serve the many sailors who suffered from seasonal unemployment during the winter months. While the city's first Catholic church services were conducted in Solomon Juneau's east-side home during the 1830s, money was soon raised for three separate buildings. St. Mary's Church, established in 1846, St. John's, in 1847, and Holy Trinity, in 1849, worked among Catholic parishioners to raise money for people who had run out of luck even in the booming settlement.

Milwaukee's Protestants were first organized into congregations including the Methodists and Baptists, who met at halls or private homes. Between 1835 and 1837 the region's first four Protestant congregations were established and church building began in 1841 by the Methodists on a lot donated by Morgan Martin. Other early houses of worship such as the Plymouth Church (Presbyterian and Congregational) on the city's east side, or St. Paul's Episcopal Church on today's Knapp Street, were funded by member subscriptions. Plymouth Church, in particular, counted many of the city's earliest leaders among its members.

When the Presbyterians founded their own separate church in the early 1840s, Plymouth became Congregational. Unitarians held their first church meeting in the summer of 1841 and the first German Lutheran congregation was organized four years later on the west side. A Dutch Reformed congregation began worship in 1847, the same year Milwaukee's first Jewish service was held on Rosh Hashanah at a private home, the forerunner of Temple Emanu-El in 1850. Each of the three separate settlements had its own congregation in the first decade, meaning that even on Sunday, worshippers from Juneautown, Kilbourntown, and Walker's Point remained separated.

By the early 1840s the three settlements were enticed by promises of federal money for "internal improvements," such as harbor development, to straighten out the mud-filled mouth of the Milwaukee River. In 1843, after many broken pledges, the first grant of $30,000 allowed for a "straight cut" through the sandbar from Lake Michigan to the Milwaukee River. The cut allowed lake steamers to come directly to wharves along the river itself, and the old swampy mouth of the river 3,000 feet south was by-passed. In the process of this improvement, the land mass now known as Jones Island was created between the old and new mouths of the Milwaukee River.

Two years later, in 1845, another $25,000 grant further improved the harbor and guaranteed Milwaukee's rising status as a Great Lakes port. However, even more funding was needed to complete and maintain these improvements, but no additional federal money was allocated for another decade.

Harbor improvement brought increased traffic to Milwaukee and made better inland transportation a necessity. Roads to the western part of Milwaukee County were built by private enter-

Although this aerial photograph was taken in the 1920s, it serves to illustrate the "straight cut" made through the north end of Jones Island, as is seen here in the center of the picture between the two parallel breakwaters. By dredging a channel deep enough to allow easy ship access to the Milwaukee and Menomonee rivers, Juneautown, Kilbourntown, and Walker's Point benefited enormously. Courtesy, Department of City Development-City of Milwaukee

The rivers of Milwaukee were essential to the city's early commercial and industrial development and provided the means by which raw materials were exported and finished goods were imported. After the "straight cut" made the waterways more accessible, cargo ships, tugs, and even excursion vessels crowded the rivers, while their banks became lined with processing plants, grain elevators, shipbuilding yards, factories belching smoke, and commercial buildings. Painting by Lynn Casper

prises such as the Watertown Plank Road Company, created in 1846. The company laid flattened logs along the present route to Watertown and charged five cents for each wagon axle every five miles. Road companies became highly profitable as many small settlements developed west of Milwaukee. Travelers to present-day Waukesha, Delafield, Oconomowoc, and Watertown paid tolls that brought one road company a weekly income of $1,300. Tollkeepers' houses dotted the route and large, rimless wagon wheels, called turnpikes, controlled the payment of tolls, except on Sundays when travel was free.

Byron Kilbourn saw the profits from road companies and also knew about the success of eastern enterprises such as the Erie Canal in New York. Eager to attract trade to his west-side settlement, Kilbourn began to plan a grand canal leading west from Milwaukee to the Mississippi River. In 1838 he solicited investors for the Milwaukee and Rock River Canal Company and began to hire tradesmen who could dig such a "ditch." Even Solomon Juneau joined Kilbourn's company as an investor, hopeful that a successful duplication of the Erie Canal would benefit Juneautown as well. The company raised $100,000 very quickly, but needed $700,000 more to cover the anticipated cost of the long project.

However, before more than a mile of the canal could be dug, the enterprise went bankrupt, and the coming of the railroad to Wisconsin spelled the end of all such canal companies by the early 1850s. It was a time of boom and bust, and the day of successful canal enterprises was over. The canal continued to be utilized in its short span as an industrial waterway until it was filled in several decades later.

Politics, Statehood, and a New City Charter

As the steady stream of settlers came to Wisconsin and to the Milwaukee area, the territory began to prepare for admission to the union as a state in the mid-1840s. The politics of the rough-and-tumble settlement were fierce as Whigs vied with Jacksonian Democrats over territorial offices and also over local political questions. Each of the three separate Milwaukee sites ran its own affairs through a ward system of administration. However, the rivalry and divisiveness were soon to be ended for good. Wisconsin's pending statehood in 1848 forced the question of unification upon the residents of all three settlements.

By 1846 the three settlements—which soon united to form the city of Milwaukee—had a total population of more than 10,000, an overwhelming increase in only nine years. As the vote over uniting the three once-feuding settlements into one city neared, the advantages and disadvantages were weighed and debated. Foremost in many people's minds was the need to provide more urban services to a rapidly expanding population.

The three separate settlements had become unable to cope with such rapid growth and the increased demands for law and order, fire protection, health controls, garbage disposal, and many other remedies to urban problems. The separation

Right: Painted by G.J. Robertson in 1848, this image depicts how Milwaukee changed from a trading post to bustling metropolis with hundreds of buildings in just over a decade. In the foreground is the Eagle Brewery, established in 1847 at the corner of today's Eighth Street and Juneau Avenue. Courtesy, Milwaukee County Historical Society

of Waukesha County to the west in 1846 and the realization that unification would bring many advantages ultimately turned the tide. The victory for unification was a victory for the many new settlers who had forgotten what the old three-way feud was all about and just wanted a more livable urban environment.

The resulting official birth of the newly unified City of Milwaukee took place on January 31, 1846, as the Wisconsin territorial legislature signed its first city charter. The population of Yankees, and newly arriving Germans and Irish, celebrated the event with festivities such as torchlight parades and singing parties in the city's many hostelries and taverns. The four-year-old German newspaper, the *Wiskonsin Banner*, foretold of the arrival of many more immigrants from the homeland to the newly created city on the lake now that a city government could provide more civilized services.

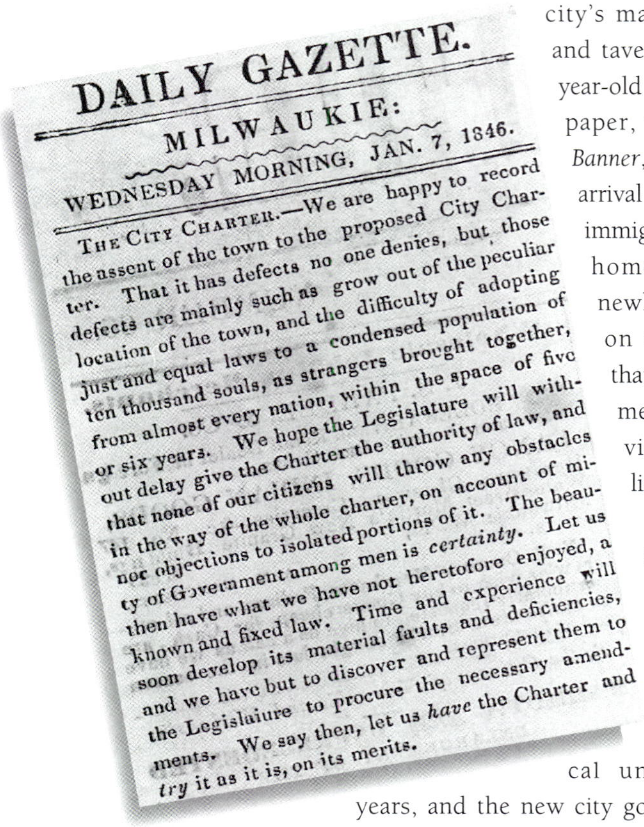

DAILY GAZETTE.

MILWAUKIE:

WEDNESDAY MORNING, JAN. 7, 1846.

THE CITY CHARTER.—We are happy to record the assent of the town to the proposed City Charter. That it has defects no one denies, but those defects are mainly such as grow out of the peculiar location of the town, and the difficulty of adopting just and equal laws to a condensed population of ten thousand souls, as strangers brought together, from almost every nation, within the space of five or six years. We hope the Legislature will without delay give the Charter the authority of law, and that none of our citizens will throw any obstacles in the way of the whole charter, on account of minor objections to isolated portions of it. The beauty of Government among men is *certainty*. Let us then have what we have not heretofore enjoyed, a known and fixed law. Time and experience will soon develop its material faults and deficiencies, and we have but to discover and represent them to the Legislature to procure the necessary amendments. We say then, let us *have* the Charter and *try* it as it is, on its merits.

Very little fanfare was devoted to the city charter in the English-language press, as is illustrated by this example, published by the Daily Milwaukie Gazette *the day after Milwaukeeans voted in the charter. Courtesy, Department of City Development-City of Milwaukee*

However, the ward system continued to serve as the city's most effective political unit for many years, and the new city government was not able to achieve many of the desired reforms overnight. The solution to sanitation, police, fire, building, commerce, health, and other issues would be worked out slowly and painfully over the next several decades.

Solomon Juneau, a Democrat, became the city's first mayor in 1846, wearing a cutaway jacket for the formal ceremony. He soon convened the city council in the basement of the Methodist Church at the corner of present-day Wisconsin and Plankinton avenues. City government was only a part-time matter in the 1840s and with a

new mayor each year and several new quarters for city meetings, there was little stability. No "official" city hall was designated until early in the 1860s, when two fires in the city's temporary offices destroyed many of the earliest records.

By 1848, when Wisconsin became a state, Milwaukee boasted a population of more than 16,000 and new business enterprises such as the first telegraph line, several lumber mills, large hardware and retail establishments, and a paper mill were growing rapidly. In 1851 the city's first rail connection was established with the opening of the Milwaukee and Mississippi Railroad and its new depot at the foot of Third Street and St. Paul Avenue. Within the next 10 years three other rail lines, with their own separate depots, were also completed.

The beginning of cityhood for Milwaukee coincided with the coming of the railroad to Wisconsin and the aldermen went overboard to use city funds to help finance construction. Along with expenditures for street paving and other municipal improvements, the city lent more than $230,000 to railroad companies beginning in 1849. The mounting debt and rising taxes frightened many citizens into passing a revision to the city charter in February 1852 that attempted to limit spending and tax increases. Conservative

mayors elected in the next several years on the "People's Ticket" cautioned against jeopardizing the good credit of the city to aid the railroads.

However, this conservative flavor was soon replaced by renewed railroad fever and the city once again began to lend money to underwrite railroad construction. Many citizens believed the speeches of ardent railroad promoters who argued that only with rail connections to the west and to outstate Wisconsin could Milwaukee hope to grow and prosper as a city. By 1858 the city's debt had grown to almost $700,000 and a second reform movement was born. The city's tax in 1857 was a staggering amount, larger than the previous five years combined.

The *Sentinel* and Rufus King accused the Democrats, once again in control of city government, of establishing a machine in Milwaukee, run by "Boss" Jackson Hadley. Meeting at Albany Hall on the corner of Michigan Street and Broadway, these new reformers gathered a wide representation of followers, including conservative Democrats, Whigs, and former People's Party adherents. The result was the Albany Hall Reform Movement, which finally achieved fiscal responsibility in city government through the election of one of its leaders, the attorney William Pitt Lynde as mayor in 1860. Under Lynde's leadership, a new Public Debt Commission was established that succeeded in retiring more than $890,000 of the city's mounting debt in the next five years.

Muddy Streets and City Smells

Along with cityhood came the call for other refinements such as paved streets and better sanitation measures. The original mud paths that were fringed by board sidewalks had proven too soggy on wet days for most wagons or pedestrians. Furthermore, the dirt that blew from the streets into shops and homes on windy days was mixed with the odor of horse manure and was a major public nuisance. Street-paving projects began in the early 1840s to civilize the settlement at last. The choice of paving materials was hotly debated. The flagstone pavement that Guido Pfister had paid for in front of his store was rejected as too costly and a pavement of crushed stone and brick was chosen instead.

Volunteer labor was used for most of the improvement projects; each male citizen was obligated to give two days each year (or the equivalent of one dollar) in labor for street or sidewalk construction. Finally, in 1852, the aldermen created the office of Street Commissioner and the city began to allocate public funds for planked (or wooden board) roads and even the construction of a costly limestone pavement for East Water Street.

That same year several ordinances were passed forbidding hogs and cattle to run wild in

Just a year after the city was incorporated, the Milwaukee and Waukesha was chartered as the state's first railroad and ran its first train on February 25, 1851. It was later renamed the Milwaukee and Mississippi and was eventually consolidated into the company known as the Milwaukee Road. This photo shows the company's original passenger depot at Third Street and St. Paul Avenue. Courtesy, Milwaukee County Historical Society

The Lake House Hotel, which burned in 1932, was built at the corner of Pittsburgh and Ferry streets in 1845. Courtesy, Milwaukee County Historical Society

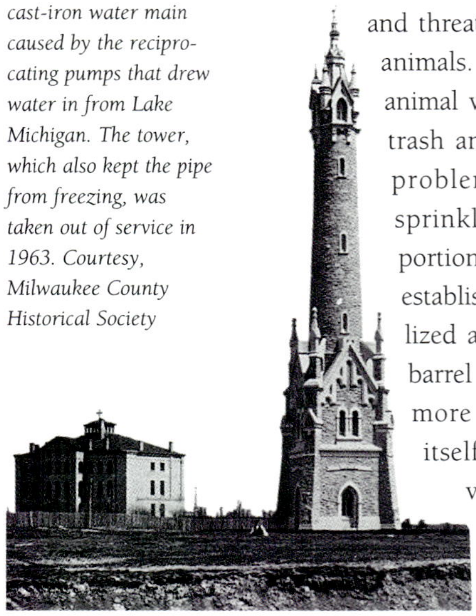

The North Point Water Tower was completed in 1874 and housed a standpipe that relieved the pulsations in the cast-iron water main caused by the reciprocating pumps that drew water in from Lake Michigan. The tower, which also kept the pipe from freezing, was taken out of service in 1963. Courtesy, Milwaukee County Historical Society

the streets, exacting penalties of two dollars and threatening the slaughter of any wanton animals. The removal of dead animals and animal waste, as well as casually discarded trash and garbage, also became a serious problem. In the early 1850s a private sprinkling company was hired to clean portions of the streets in front of specific establishments. At first, the company utilized a large tin watering pot, but later a barrel on wheels threw water streams in a more powerful arc. However, the city itself provided no street-cleaning services.

The problem of garbage grew with the city's population increases. Most people threw out their garbage as slop for the pigs that wandered the streets, but soon the problems of flies and odors became too noxious. Early attempts to thwart such casual disposal of refuse were largely ignored, but in 1866 the police department began to enforce storage and disposal ordinances and the city's smell noticeably improved.

Like the garbage problem, sewage disposal and the protection of a safe and clean water supply demanded public action in the early years of settlement. Suppliers of clean spring water were licensed, but many residents continued to use well water, even when its pollution contributed to disease and several deadly epidemics. Cholera swept the settlement for the first time in 1843 and smallpox in 1846. The many resultant deaths shocked leaders into action. Inadequate wooden sewers erected in several wards had to be replaced with tiled conduits until the "river of filth" that flowed down Wisconsin Avenue and other streets could be brought under control. With better tiling for the runoff, the city's health prospects brightened, but no underground sewer system was developed until the 1870s.

Guaranteeing a clean water supply was a more challenging task. The contamination of wells was widespread by 1846 and many families built private cisterns to collect rainwater. Throughout the 1850s several plans to build a city-financed pumping station for water from Lake Michigan failed to pass. Finally, under the leadership of banker Alexander Mitchell, the city's Board of Water Commissioners succeeded in bringing fresh water to Milwaukee residents in 1873.

Darkness was also a problem in the early settlement as nightfall brought with it the hazards of walking on uneven boardwalks, or driving a carriage through ill-lighted and potholed streets. A clear solution to this problem came in 1852, when the Milwaukee Gas Light Company was chartered to bring the benefits of gaslighting to the city for the first time. Within its first five years the company laid more than seven miles of gas pipe throughout the city's east side. Seven years later, in 1859, the Fifth Ward Gas and Light

Company brought the same benefits to the west side and the utter darkness of night vanished for good on the city's streets. Milwaukee's homes and business establishments could now switch from the dirty and dangerous kerosene lanterns to modern gaslights. Wood-burning cookstoves could be replaced by safer gas ovens.

Another kind of pollution, noise and nuisance, also became a concern as soon as Milwaukee's population reached into the thousands. The city passed restrictions upon the use of bells, drums, and other "disturbances of the peace." Cows were no longer allowed to roam through the streets on their way to a nearby pasture. Aldermen also tried to enforce ordinances against the danger caused by horses speeding down city streets. Only a "moderate trot" was acceptable and violators were faced with a stiff fine of five dollars. As an increasing number of carriages crowded the central city, accidents at busy intersections also multiplied, but there were as yet no traffic controls in place.

By the mid-1840s Milwaukee had grown beyond the dimensions of a "walking city" and the demand for some form of public transportation led to the beginnings of the first omnibus service, a large horse-drawn urban stagecoach. However, these vehicles had few springs and the bouncing ride was very uncomfortable. A large wagon that could be pulled along smooth rails would solve the problem and increase the comfort and speed of urban transit.

In 1859 the city licensed horse-drawn street railways on several main thoroughfares. The first two transit companies, the River and Lake Shore City Railway and the West Side Passenger Railway Company, began service in 1859 with large passenger streetcars, pulled on rails by teams of four horses each. The success of these two lines was so great that soon many other such companies with decorated horsecars and specific street routes were also chartered. Milwaukee had entered the era of mass transit.

Cows were no longer allowed to roam through the streets on their way to a nearby pasture.

Newcomers from Many Lands

As the city grew so did its ethnic diversity. By 1850 almost two-thirds of its population was foreign born with more than 60 percent coming from Germany. German residents clustered in several wards on Milwaukee's northwest side and new immigrants arrived at the port each week, lured by locally sponsored agents who worked in the eastern ports to bring German labor and talent to Wisconsin.

The skilled "48ers" from the unsuccessful social revolution in Germany soon filled Milwaukee with men and women of talent and vision who founded German newspapers, schools, singing societies, theaters, and a number of clubs and churches. As early as 1843 German musicians established the Beethoven Society. In May 1850 the Milwaukee Musical Society was established to perform classical concerts of the great Austrian and German composers. One year later its orchestra numbered more than 30 musicians and its chorus had swelled to 78 voices, which brought the music of Mozart, Mendelssohn, and Haydn to Milwaukee. Both Yankee and German settlers flocked to these concerts in large numbers; more than 800 attended concerts on several special occasions.

Facing page, bottom: Milwaukee had become a teeming metropolis by the mid-1870s. Wells Street is seen to the right and Jefferson Street crosses the image from right to left. The only buildings still standing today are the striking Italianate-style Matthew Keenan house, visible to the right below the church steeple, and two Greek Revival-style houses to its right and part of the rowhouse to its left. Courtesy, Milwaukee County Historical Society

Left: Gas streetlighting was introduced to Milwaukee in the early 1850s. Lamplighters came through at dusk and ignited the flame burner inside. The process was reversed at dawn. This view looks across East Wisconsin Avenue from Milwaukee Street to the Birchard and Follansbee Block. Courtesy, Milwaukee County Historical Society

This 1880s view of the busy intersection of Water Street and East Wisconsin Avenue features a horse-drawn streetcar of the West Side Street Railway Co., which was founded in 1874. The company electrified its route in 1890. The venerable Iron Block stands prominently at the center of the image. Courtesy, Milwaukee County Historical Society

German newspapers such as the *Wiskonsin Banner*, the *Volksfreund*, the *Humanist*, and the *Seebote* vied with each other to express the often diverse views of the city's growing German population. Religious distinctions between German Lutherans and Catholics sharpened lines in the community, as well as differences in politics that were carried over from the homeland. However, even with these internal differences, the German community remained insular in its "Dutch Athena" neighborhoods.

For many years there was very little intermarriage or social mixing by most Germans with their Yankee neighbors. Community leaders such as Fritz Anneke expounded on the glories of German culture and exulted in the great victory of their homeland over France in the Franco-Prussian War of 1871. Such sentiments alienated many Yankees, who ardently believed that the Germans should learn English and try to "melt in" to American culture instead of feeling superior to it.

One stimulus to German immigration was the establishment of a separate Catholic diocese in Milwaukee in 1844 with Bishop John Martin Henni, a German-Swiss, as its leader. Three years later Henni began to solicit funds to build the landmark St. John's Cathedral, on Juneau's courthouse square, which was consecrated in 1853. To supply the trained priests for other dioceses in the state, Henni also established the first seminary in 1855 headed by the Order of St. Francis and designed to train German-speaking clergy. The following year Henni purchased land on the city's west side as the site of what would become Marquette University, chartered in 1864 and opened 17 years later.

German schools were also established to

Established by the Jesuit Order, Marquette opened in 1881 as Milwaukee's first liberal arts college. Seen here at the northwest corner of 10th and State streets around 1888, the college relocated to a new building on Wisconsin Avenue in 1907. The original facility was used by St. Benedict the Moor parish until freeway construction necessitated its razing in the 1960s. Courtesy, Milwaukee County Historical Society preserve the language and cultural heritage of the homeland. One outstanding example was the German-American Academy, founded in 1851 and led by Peter Engelmann, who also helped to establish the collection that became the Milwaukee Public Museum. In addition to schools, the German community also believed in adult education. The popular exercise and social club, the "Turnverein," founded in 1853, became a political and intellectual center, as well as an active open-air gymnastics club.

Through this social activism and its political enthusiasm, the German community produced several outstanding leaders, such as journalist and politician Franz Huebschmann, mayor Emil Wallber, and statesman Carl Schurz. The German-American force in Milwaukee and Wisconsin politics became very powerful by 1850 and continued as a factor on major issues such as temperance and English-language education thereafter, even though Germans were both Democratic and Republican in party affiliation.

Second only to the Germans were the Irish, who comprised almost 25 percent of the city's population in 1850. The Irish were often more influential than the Germans in politics because they were solidly Democratic. Irish votes from the Third Ward on the city's south side contributed to the steady stream of Democratic victories in mayoral races and aldermanic contests throughout the 1850s and 1860s. Their leaders included Hans Crocker, an attorney who served as the first editor of the *Sentinel* and later as Milwaukee mayor, and Tim O'Brien, a colorful ward leader and strong opponent of any Yankee attempts to pass temperance reforms.

Very popular among both Irish and Germans were the military companies, founded largely as social clubs, which staged parades, worked in political causes, and acted as a citizen constabulary in their respective neighborhoods. The German troops included the Washington Guards and the Milwaukee Dragoons, while the Irish sponsored the Montgomery Guards. The loyal Yankees put together their paramilitary group known as the City Artillery, led by Rufus King.

One of the young city's worst disasters occurred when members of another Irish troop, the Union Guard, clashed with a Republican governor over the slavery issue in 1860. On a return trip from Chicago where they had traveled to raise money and buy arms, their lake steamer, the *Lady Elgin*, was rammed in the fog by a schooner and more than 300 Irish citizens were killed. Milwaukee Mayor William Pitt Lynde and his wife, Mary, led the city's all-out relief effort to aid bereaved families in the Irish community. Many children were orphaned by the disaster and the Irish community mourned its great loss for many years to come.

Other immigrants established a strong presence in the new city after 1846, including Czechs, Slovaks, Norwegians, and Poles. Like the earlier immigrant populations, these groups clumped

Architect Leonard Schmidtner patterned St. Stanislaus Church, erected from 1872 to 1894, after the dome-topped Baroque-era buildings of seventeenth- and eighteenth-century Poland. This contrasted with most of the city's German churches, which utilized the pointed forms of the Gothic Revival. Courtesy, Milwaukee County Historical Society

The Light Horse Squadron, shown here marching down West Kilbourn Avenue around 1900, had been organized as an escort for Ulysses S. Grant on the occasion of the Great Soldiers' Reunion, held in Milwaukee in June 1880. The group later saw active service during the 1886 labor riots and World War I. Courtesy, Milwaukee County Historical Society

As local breweries began to proliferate, reformers grew concerned about children going hungry and families torn asunder when the breadwinners squandered their paychecks on alcohol. The temperance movement never really caught on in Milwaukee, however, probably due to the large German-American population which relished its beer and beer gardens. This group was photographed in a southside saloon in 1912. Courtesy, Kwasniewski Collection, UWM

Horse-drawn wagons with steam engines were standard firefighting equipment for several decades before motorized vehicles came into regular use in the 1920s. These firemen are seen heading west on Becher Street at the intersection of South 14th Street. Courtesy, Kwasniewski Collection, UWM

together in identifiable neighborhoods, around parish churches, and only very slowly intermingled with the city's Yankee east-siders. The Poles succeeded in establishing their first Catholic parish in 1863 and erecting Saint Stanislaus Church. The Czechs followed in 1865 in a nearby parish and soon the area south of the former Walker's Point was dotted with many immigrant churches.

Civic Rowdiness and the Call for Reform

Along with this growing ethnic diversity, the atmosphere of Milwaukee was flavored by a variety of political and reform groups in the 1840s and early 1850s. Temperance, a growing cause nationwide, became an important reform in the city where an estimated one tavern for every 100 people meant that drinking had already become a problem. The city's first Temperance Society, founded in 1840 by attorneys Charles Lynde and Asahel Finch, met in private homes to further its crusade against the city's growing rate of drunkenness and public rowdiness. Even though the true frontier had moved westward with the California gold rush of 1848, gunshots and holdups still plagued the city as drunken brawls spilled out of taverns and into residential areas.

Complaints about drunken rowdiness multiplied until the city had to respond with a new constabulary force to police unruly residents and keep lawlessness to a minimum. In 1837 Juneau's first courthouse had also included a jail for miscreants but the matter of apprehension and incarceration still depended upon the volunteer efforts of law-abiding citizens. Although private watchmen and a nighttime constable patrolled the streets, the city remained largely unprotected even in the late 1840s.

In 1850 the police force consisted only of one marshal, several constables who patrolled the wards, and two or three watchmen for a city that had grown to more than 20,000 people. Finally, after serious problems with riots, a regular force of 15 policemen was established in 1852 to be paid out of the general fund. The first official police department was created three years later, consisting of one officer for every 3,000 inhabitants and a chief appointed by the mayor and city council. This ratio continued as patrolmen (many of whom were German or Irish) kept the peace by winning fistfights or using their sticks. Wearing badges but no uniforms, they met with limited success until a much larger force was established in 1866 that brought the ratio down to one policeman for every 1,700 citizens.

In a similar fashion, the new city's fire protection was in strictly volunteer hands for the first several years with all residents required to keep "two buckets handy" for fire emergencies. With the city's growth and its many wooden dwellings and office structures, the hazards of fire grew enormously during the 1840s. Finally, an ordinance was enacted forbidding the erection of any wooden business structures and the brickyards grew commensurately. The construction and maintenance of chimneys, hearths, ovens, and boilers were also supervised, but the peril of fire continued.

A "sack company" founded in 1851 included many of the city's most prominent citizens who agreed to bring white sacks to fires to hold valuables and prevent looting at the scene, but no professional firefighting department was established. Benefit concerts were held to support injured volunteers whose families would have borne a death or disability alone. Eager citizens also began to supply brandy to exhausted firefighters, until the results of too much imbibing by the volunteers were disastrous in an 1854 conflagration where the force failed to function at all.

Finally, the city began to support a more professional team of firefighters with public funds and ordered its first steam fire pumping engine in November 1861. Because of the city's major debt problems in the early 1860s, Mayor William Pitt Lynde had to make a substantial personal contribution to underwrite the $3,500 cost of the shining new engine, christened the "Solomon Juneau."

Other reform-minded citizens backed the establishment of the city's first charity in 1849 when public-spirited women, led by Mrs. A.D. Smith and Mrs. William Pitt Lynde, founded the Ladies' Benevolent Society. Collecting donations from many businesses and private citizens, the society organized relief efforts for the poor, soup kitchens for the hungry, and candle distribution and a firewood allocation for those suffering in winter.

Six years later, in 1855, the Milwaukee Relief Society was organized as public begging and problems with the homeless and hungry

Milwaukee Hospital, established in 1863, was popularly called the Passavant after founder Dr. W.A. Passavant, and took in critically ill indigents with infectious diseases as well as paying patients needing hospice care. It was located on West Kilbourn Avenue on the former estate of Asahel Finch. The institution underwent significant expansion after 1900 and the early structures shown here have all been razed. Courtesy, Milwaukee Public Library

Milwaukee's Music Hall, which opened on January 31, 1865, is said by local historians to have been the first in the country built exclusively for performances. Architect Edward Townsend Mix redrew existing plans and improved the acoustics, which were celebrated among such notable performers as Lillian Russell and Sarah Bernhardt. Its present facade at 625 North Milwaukee Street dates from a 1925 remodeling. Courtesy, Milwaukee Public Library

began to multiply. By the late 1850s more than 600 families were receiving aid each season, with as many as 200 people lining up at the soup kitchens daily. A more organized and stable answer for the city's poor was needed. Even assistance from Milwaukee County funds did little to address the growing social problems.

In 1848 the Sisters of Charity opened the area's first hospital, St. John's Infirmary, on the north side. When all forms of outdoor assistance for the sick and needy still proved inadequate, the Milwaukee County Board purchased more than 1,000 acres of land on the city's west side, in present Wauwatosa, and opened the area's first poor farm, or almshouse, in 1852.

However, this facility was not equipped to deal with sickness and the return of deadly cholera epidemics in several waves created an increasing health problem that had to be quickly addressed. In 1860 a 31-bed county hospital was established on the grounds in Wauwatosa, supervised by the county physician, Dr. Fisk H. Day. Also in the early 1860s the Relief Society helped to found the Milwaukee (or Passavant) Hospital and an orphan asylum, two privately funded shelters that supplemented the county-funded institutions.

Charitable work within the German community was carried out through separate efforts, and a Hebrew Relief Society was established in 1867. The Milwaukee Chamber of Commerce increased its subscriptions to alleviate the growing problem for all ethnic neighborhoods, but the majority of money disbursed by the city's charities came from private subscriptions for many more years. Even the creation of an office of Superintendent of the Poor in the 1850s did little to alleviate problems until substantially increased public funding could be obtained.

In addition to concern over public and private charity, Milwaukee citizens took action regarding the future of their youth. Public education came to the forefront as soon as the city was chartered in 1846, when it was noted that fewer than one-third of the city's 1,700 children attended any school. Private schools had served the three settlements since 1836, although even these were primitive log structures with few textbooks

The widened thoroughfare where Water Street joined Market Street formed an important plaza-like space where farmers sold their goods in Milwaukee's early years. After the market moved north to Juneau Avenue impressive hotels and commercial buildings came to line the square, housing merchants who sold everything from books to luggage and insurance. This 1880s image captures the bustle and energy of the era. Courtesy, Milwaukee County Historical Society

While every ward of the city had its designated market area, the best remembered was the so-called German Market, seen here along East Juneau Avenue between Water and Market streets circa 1890. Since so many of the patrons were of German descent, the area became unofficially known as the German Market. It drew scores of produce vendors, butchers, and florists as well as farmers who sold foodstuffs directly off their wagons. When this activity declined the Market Hall was razed and the Weinbrenner Shoe Co. built its factory on the site around 1910. Today the block is a surface parking lot. Courtesy, Milwaukee County Historical Society

and a single classroom for pupils from ages six to 16. With the leadership of Rufus King, Increase Lapham, and Edward Holton, Milwaukee finally took the education of its youth more seriously and included a mandate for free public schools in its city charter.

By the end of 1846 more than five free public schools had been established, one in each ward, and numerous other private seminaries for young men and women continued to spring up in the next decade. While these early public schools were only for younger children, the city finally established its first high school for older children in 1868, just before the state law of 1875 that mandated that advanced education be provided for children by all districts.

A growing concern about the city's culture, or lack of it, also came during the 1840s as public debates became the focus of a lyceum group that met regularly to promote learned discussion about the classics and even current political events. Two early lending libraries, one at the city's first bookstore in 1842 and the other at the *Sentinel* offices, revealed the settlers' thirst for information and entertainment. In music and drama, the German community continued to lead the way until the establishment of a Shakespearean theater company that gave performances beginning in the 1840s at an old warehouse at Third and Chestnut streets.

Even more popular than cultural events were the numerous balls held by the city's military societies throughout the social season. As early as 1836 a cotillion series attracted more than 60 couples from the area's three settlements, and New Year's dances also became popular. Each military company sponsored social events, the Irish gave their St. Patrick's Day parade and dance, while the Germans and Yankees danced to music at the Mai Fest and July Fourth celebrations. Ice-skating parties along the frozen rivers, horseracing along the beaches, and turkey shoots were also favorite pastimes.

With all of this gaiety, life in the first several decades of Milwaukee's cityhood developed its own cycle of entertainment and social celebration despite the continuing hardships of frontier existence. Even as mud streets gradually became paved and cow bells were silenced at night for restless sleepers, problems of contaminated food and overly competitive merchants plagued the citizens.

This mid-1870s image depicts the corner of North Milwaukee Street and East Wisconsin Avenue. Tenants in these buildings included tailors, grocers, physicians, lawyers, a china shop, and even a store selling trusses and artificial limbs. These buildings still stand today. Courtesy, Milwaukee County Historical Society

Another aspect of public reform faced by many new municipalities concerned the regulation of food and commodities sold within city markets. In 1847 Milwaukeeans constructed a "market house" on Market Square where the current city hall now stands. This centralizing of space for outdoor vendors and the provision of indoor booths was not only an early attempt at zoning, but was also designed to exert control over hours of operation, the quality of merchandise, and the standards of weights and measures. Produce was to be "fresh and wholesome" and bread loaves were to indicate exact weight and be stamped with the baker's initials to guarantee quality.

A Bustling Port and Economic Growth

Aware of its growing importance as a central marketplace for the state and expanding hinterland, Milwaukee citizens looked in earnest to develop the city's port facilities in the decades after cityhood. The initial harbor development began to prove inadequate as the first railroad lines reached west by 1851, bringing crops to the wharves for shipment east. Lines such as the Milwaukee and Mississippi, the Milwaukee and St. Paul, and the Chicago and North Western had absorbed smaller railroad companies by the close of the decade and were able to carry vast quantities of farm produce, particularly wheat, to the port terminus in Milwaukee.

City leaders lobbied Congress for further

Established in 1863, Spencerian College was noted for the thoroughness of the education it offered. Many of Milwaukee's late-nineteenth-century industrial leaders attended the college. Through 1925 the school was located in the Miller Building, shown here at the corner of Broadway and Wisconsin in the mid-1870s. Due to financial reverses, its modern facility closed in 1974, ending a long and successful career in Milwaukee. Courtesy, Milwaukee County Historical Society

This late-nineteenth-century photo shows the type of factory—with its jungle of overhead pulleys, machinery, stacks of materials and castings, and crowded work stations—where Milwaukee's working class produced the machines and metal tools that changed the world. Reform movements in the early twentieth century were responsible for an improvement in these factory conditions. Courtesy, Milwaukee County Historical Society

aid in developing the city's harbor and joined with other Great Lakes port cities in holding a River and Harbor Convention to discuss their problems. Finally, in 1857, the straight cut through to the Milwaukee River, begun 14 years earlier, was completed and Milwaukee became a major port facility almost overnight. Direct shipments of wheat to Europe began and the tonnage passing through the Port of Milwaukee doubled in the first year.

Among the commodities filling the docks, wheat was "king." Between 1846 and 1870 wheat exports from the city increased 75-fold from 213,448 bushels to 16,127,838. Milwaukee had become the nation's leading wheat port even before the Civil War in 1861 and continued as such for more than a decade after the war's end. By 1862 the city had become the largest wheat market in the world. This thriving enterprise created many fortunes in the city as storage bin owner Alanson Sweet worked with wheat broker Daniel Newhall in the shipping enterprise.

By the end of the Civil War, Newhall owned a fleet of 20 ships, the largest fleet on the Great Lakes, which carried wheat from Milwaukee to cities of the East and across the world. Newhall alone shipped more than 15,000 bushels daily on boats bound for Buffalo, New York, the eastern terminus where the Erie Canal began. Others active in the wheat business included George D. Dousman, Levi H. Kellogg, Philip D. Armour, and Edward D. Holton, who led the way in the establishment of Milwaukee's Board of Trade in 1849, which later became the Chamber of Commerce.

The laying of the transatlantic cable in 1866 brought orders from all over the world more swiftly to Milwaukee's grain traders, who often met in Newhall's grand hotel, the Newhall House built in 1856, to buy and sell grain contracts. In 1862 a more formal trading pit was established at the southwest corner of Michigan and Broadway, the former Albany Hall site. This was replaced in 1880 by the magnificent Chamber of Commerce Building, which still stands today. The luxurious Newhall House became a site to retire to for drinks and relaxation after the day's trading was completed and wheat contracts had been signed.

Although wheat led the way in Milwaukee's commercial boom, hog and cattle butchering became profitable by 1850. During the next two

While Milwaukee was no longer the center of the world's wheat trade by the time of this circa 1910 photo, the Grain Exchange, in the Chamber of Commerce Building, was still a bustling place as traders jostled one another to examine samples. Courtesy, Milwaukee County Historical Society

decades John Plankinton, Frederick Layton, Michael Cudahy, and Philip Armour developed packing houses that made Milwaukee rank fourth in the nation by 1871. An offshoot of the packing business, the tanning of hides, also developed during the same decades. In 1872 leather and tanning companies directed by men such as Guido Pfister, Fred Vogel, Albert Trostel, and A.F. Gallun made Milwaukee the largest tanning center in the world. The majority of the city's 30 tanneries in 1870 were owned by Germans who brought a special expertise to the business.

German expertise soon became important in another of the city's major productive enterprises, the breweries. At first operating only on a local level in neighborhood taverns, the city's breweries began to reach out to a national market by the early 1860s. The great Chicago Fire of October 1871 allowed the city's leading breweries to monopolize the national market for the first time, and ice-refrigerated railroad cars, developed in the same decade, provided for year-round shipping of Milwaukee beer.

The city's oldest brewery, founded in 1844 by Jacob Best, was renamed the Pabst Brewery when son-in-law Frederick Pabst assumed control. It increased its output from 7,000 barrels in 1860 to more than 100,000 by 1873. The August Krug Brewery was taken over by an employee, Joseph Schlitz, and prospered in a similar fashion. Valentin Blatz and Frederick Miller migrated to Milwaukee from Germany and also founded breweries that shared in the city's new booming export. Following the decline of the wheat trade in the 1870s, beer would become the city's major food export and production soared by the end of the century to heights unimaginable even in 1870.

The expanded port facilities also led to the growth of retail establishments such as Nazro Hardware, which supplied the ever-increasing hinterland with tools and general household products. By 1860 the city had 20 confectionery stores, 36 tobacco and snuff stores, 38 boot and shoe dealers, 52 shoemakers' shops, 64 drygoods establishments, 29 clothing stores, 27 millinery shops, 26 drugstores, more than 116 shops dealing in men's and women's ready-made clothing and hats, 18 jewelry stores, 70 meat markets, 20 cabinetmakers' shops, 28 wagon shops, and 224 retail grocery stores.

These stores and others served not only a local clientele, but also had their eye on the needs of the population in rural communities along the many rail lines that extended west from the city. In early 1861 leading merchants established the Milwaukee Merchants' Association to promote Milwaukee as a supply center for communities stretching as far west as Minnesota and Iowa.

As paperwork mounted and thousands of orders poured in, the city's merchants, as well as its tanneries and wheat traders, demanded more efficiency in office work and more skilled employees. Business colleges sprang up to train clerks, assistants, and secretaries for the demands of the new modern office of the 1850s and 1860s. Spencerian College was established on Wisconsin Avenue in 1863, preceded by the Mercantile Academy in 1849 and followed by many others that were short-lived. The invention and patenting of the typewriter in 1868 by Milwaukeeans Christopher Sholes, Carlos Glidden, and Samuel Soule brought about a significant advancement in office technology and efficiency, even though the machine itself could not be manufactured locally but was produced by the Remington Company of New York.

The lack of manufacturing capacity in the city became a concern to many even before the Civil War. Milwaukee's industrial growth came in the form of heavy industry, particularly iron foundries and machinery plants. After a slow start due to lack of capital, the city's manufacturing establishments began to flourish during the 1860s. Prior to that decade, Milwaukee listed only four iron foundries, with smaller shops producing wheelbarrows, millstones, boilers, and plows for shipment across the state. By 1869 iron castings and related manufactures had grown to fourth in the city's listing of products exported, behind wheat, leather, and clothing.

The establishment of the Reliance Iron Works in 1847 (taken over by E.P. Allis 10 years later), and the Milwaukee Iron Company during the 1860s by Alexander Mitchell and E.B. Ward, led the way in the growth of large-scale heavy manufacturing concerns. Using the new Bessemer

The Chamber of Commerce Building was constructed by Alexander Mitchell, who had the wealth and vision to commission a monument to trade from the city's foremost architect, Edward Townsend Mix. The facility features the bull and bear, symbols of the market, on the third story. Courtesy, Milwaukee County Historical Society

Left: Alexander Mitchell (1817-1887) has long been recognized as one of the most significant figures in Milwaukee's history. He left behind an architectural legacy including the Mitchell Bank Building, his own residence (the Wisconsin Club today), and the Chamber of Commerce Building. Courtesy, Milwaukee County Historical Society

Broadway was originally platted to be the chief thoroughfare of Juneautown. Substantial commercial buildings began to line the street in the 1850s. The three shown in this late 1860s image are particularly noteworthy for their exuberant sheet-metal cornices and elaborate hood molds above the windows. The Wisconsin Telephone Company now occupies the former Northwestern Mutual Life Insurance Co. building. Courtesy, Milwaukee County Historical Society

process, Milwaukee's iron industries pioneered in the production of all-steel rails in 1870. By 1873 the company employed more than 1,000 workers in its plant, leading to the construction of homes for workers adjacent to the foundry complex in a settlement that was named Bay View.

Other growing factories hired so many laborers that by 1872 more than one-third of Milwaukee's working population was employed in industry. Far-seeing bankers, among them Alexander Mitchell, may have realized that the city could not depend on wheat supremacy forever. A more diversified, industrialized economy would become vital as the center of the wheat trade began to shift westward away from Milwaukee after the Civil War.

Professionals led the way in banking, insurance, and the law throughout the city's first sever-

This mid-1860s view of East Wisconsin Avenue was taken from Broadway looking west toward Kilbourntown across the Milwaukee River. Milwaukee's prosperity is evidenced by the number of substantial brick buildings that replaced the crude frame structures that previously had lined Water Street and Wisconsin Avenue. Courtesy, Milwaukee County Historical Society

al decades. An immigrant from Scotland, Mitchell opened the city's first insurance company, the Wisconsin Marine and Fire Insurance Company in 1839. Supplanting the failing Bank of Milwaukee, the village's first such bank, Mitchell worked his way around the growing hostility to banks that led to a ban on banking in the state constitution of 1848. Mitchell was able to capitalize on a need for a sound currency and for a safe depository for citizens' savings and soon began conducting mostly banking business. He was backed in this venture by his promoter, George Smith of Chicago, who had set up the concern with an initial investment of $500,000.

The certificates of deposit of the Wisconsin Marine and Fire Insurance Company soon became the most trusted currency in the city in an era when few had faith in any paper money and prior to the Civil War when only the federal government could print dollar bills. Another banking venture, the Marshall & Ilsley Bank, was established in 1847 by Samuel Marshall a Quaker from Pennsylvania. This bank became the first state-chartered bank in 1852, when the state rescinded its prohibition against banking. The free banking law allowed bankers to stabilize the flow of deposits, engage in creative investments, and issue certificates that served the growing city's need for safe currency.

Mitchell's stubborn insistence on deposits to back the certificates he issued caused resentment among holders of paper money issued irresponsibly by "wildcat banks." In June 1861 an angry mob stormed Mitchell's bank at the corner of Water Street and Michigan Avenue because he had refused to accept their questionable notes issued by these unstable banks. Furniture and bank records were carried into the street and lighted into a large bonfire before the marshal arrived to disperse the mob.

Mitchell's staunch refusal and the reliability of his own certificates actually did a great deal to provide at least one stable currency in Milwaukee during its growing years. Soon other banks followed Mitchell's example, including the Farmers' and Millers' Bank (later the First Wisconsin or Firstar Bank).

Lawyers, Doctors, and Educational Interests

Banking and financial concerns, as well as land sales and wheat contracts, demanded the service of lawyers. In its very first years of settlement, Milwaukee had attracted several young attorneys from the East who came to the area to practice law and also engage in business and land investments. By 1839 the settlement listed a dozen lawyers among its growing population. The Panic of 1837 and resulting litigation involving land titles and bankruptcy claims provided more than adequate work for these attorneys, as did the need for contract settlements attendant upon the building trades in the growing area.

The failure of the Bank of Milwaukee brought further work as directors sued each other over their substantial financial losses. The earliest courthouse served Milwaukee County with cases heard weekly on matters relating to horse theft, debt payments, and assorted misdemeanors such as drunkenness or vandalism. Milwaukee County's first judge experienced his own difficulties with alcohol, and fortunately was replaced in 1838 by the eminent Andrew G. Miller who had come to Milwaukee from Pennsylvania.

In 1848 Lucy Parsons established what was originally known as the Female Seminary to provide secondary education to young women. A building was erected at the corner of Milwaukee and Juneau streets in 1852, and the school was renamed Milwaukee Female College. Classes included child care, teaching, nursing, and homemaking. Courtesy, Milwaukee County Historical Society

Most lawyers were trained by "reading the law" in these early decades, rather than by attendance at formal law schools. Among the city's earliest and most prominent attorneys were Hans Crocker, later mayor; Horatio Wells; Asahel Finch, a prominent Whig-Republican and later city attorney; and William Pitt Lynde, a graduate of Yale University Law School and later Milwaukee mayor and Wisconsin congressman. Lynde and Finch led the way in the establishment of the Milwaukee Bar Association next to their offices in the Albany Building in 1858, one of the first such law associations in the country.

Criminal cases, too, came before the courts, as Milwaukee's residents proved no more perfect in their behavior than settlers in any frontier area.

The bar association not only sponsored banquets and social events, it also started its own law library, which served as a reference resource for all of the city's attorneys and a valuable training place for those aspiring to the bar. The law library was moved to larger quarters in the newly erected Iron Block Building, at the corner of Wisconsin Avenue and Water Street in 1862, after a disastrous fire in the Albany Building destroyed part of the collection. Many new volumes were solicited successfully by the law firm of Finch and Lynde (forerunner of the present Foley & Lardner), also located in the Iron Block Building.

In small two-man partnerships, these men and other lawyers who soon came to the city served the economy's changing needs not only in continuing real estate development, banking, and the wheat trade, but also in the growth of industry and public utilities. Criminal cases, too, came before the courts, as Milwaukee's residents proved no more perfect in their behavior than settlers in any frontier area.

This growing urban population also required the services of physicians and pharmacists, as well as other professionals by the 1860s. In addition to its 73 lawyers, the city listed 7 architects, 12 civil engineers, and more than 50 physicians, many of whom also served as pharmacists or worked in other areas such as real estate or retailing. The city's first physician, Dr. Enoch

In March 1854 alleged fugitive slave Joshua Glover was captured while working in Racine, then transported to Milwaukee County Jail pending his return to his owner. Abolitionists led by Sherman Booth rushed the jail after the judge refused to release Glover, taking him to freedom in Canada. This 1930s painting by Monegar recreates the moment of Glover's rescue. Courtesy, Milwaukee County Historical Society

Chase, had supplemented his practice by working as a blacksmith, and it wasn't until after the Civil War that the practice of medicine achieved a regular financial footing in the nation as a whole.

Associations such as the Medical Society of Milwaukee County (1846) and the Milwaukee City Medical Association (1847) worked to promote professionalism and establish a fee structure for doctors, but there remained many questionable practitioners who peddled patent medicines for profit. The city's first female doctor, Laura J. Ross (Wolcott), opened her practice in 1857 and the establishment of the city's first hospitals over the next seven years also spurred the credibility and utility of the medical profession among residents.

Dr. Ross was not only an outstanding doctor, she was an outspoken advocate for women's equality, a growing movement across the East and Midwest in the 1850s. Prominent suffragist Lucy Stone addressed Milwaukee residents, male and female, in 1855 on her tour of the country in support of women's rights. The following year witnessed the founding of Wisconsin's foremost school for women, the Milwaukee Female Seminary. With an endowment from Catherine Beecher (sister of Harriet Beecher Stowe), the school attracted leading educator Mary Mortimer from New York who built the seminary into Milwaukee Female College (later Milwaukee Downer College), the city's first institution of higher education.

A comparable college for men, the University of Milwaukee, founded in 1855, folded in the national and local economic crisis of 1857. Although the state's public university in Madison provided higher education for male students, no such opportunity existed in Milwaukee for several more decades.

The Slavery Question and Sectional War

The decade of the Civil War and its aftermath brought many changes to the nation and to the city of Milwaukee. Although Democratic in its local elections, the city gave Republican candidate Abraham Lincoln a majority vote in 1860. The issues of anti-slavery and abolitionism had long been brewing in Milwaukee as it developed into a byway on the underground railway for slaves escaping to Canada. Assistance to escaped slaves had begun as early as 1842 in Milwaukee when lawyer Asahel Finch and a friend helped one fugitive on her path to freedom.

With the passage of the federal Fugitive Slave Law in 1850, many city residents became inflamed with fear that the city's free blacks might be entrapped by southern "slave catchers" who could now come north to seek runaways. One such incident, in 1854, centered around the fiery abolitionism of newspaper editor Sherman M. Booth. Booth was accused of inciting an angry mob to free a recaptured slave named Joshua Glover from the Milwaukee jail where he was held pending return to his southern owners.

As controversy and litigation swirled around Booth, the nation came closer to war over the issue of slavery's existence and states' rights. Lincoln's election in 1860 sealed the issue and the war began at Fort Sumter, South Carolina, on April 12, 1861.

With its new telegraph line, Milwaukee received the news of the war's beginning the following day and public meetings were held to recruit volunteers for the army. A recruiting station opened to sign up the first three-month volunteers and bands marched through the streets to stir up enthusiasm for the cause. Company A of the Milwaukee Light Guards was ready to march after a brief training period on the State Fairgrounds on the city's west side.

Soon the call for soldiers was renewed but many of the city's wealthier men preferred to pay for a substitute to fight in their place, a legal practice that began in 1861 with a fee of $50 and became considerably more expensive by war's end, rising as high as $800. War enthusiasm lessened as the conflict dragged on and casualties mounted with the many Union defeats. With the institution of a federal military draft in 1862, protests among many citizens grew angry and riots in the nearby cities of West Bend and Port

This is one of very few images taken of troops in Milwaukee during the Civil War. These soldiers are gathered in front of the old courthouse. The first troops departed for the war from Milwaukee on June 9, 1861. To house and drill the enlistees, three encampments were established here—Camp Scott on West Wisconsin Avenue, Camp Reno/Sigel at Prospect Avenue and Royall Place, and Camp Washburn on today's McKinley Boulevard. Courtesy, Milwaukee County Historical Society

When the numbers of wounded soldiers exceeded the capacity of institutional care, Congress enacted a bill in March 1865 to create a national asylum for veterans of the Civil War. Designed by Milwaukee architect Edward Townsend Mix, the distinctive Victorian Gothic-style structure housed patients and included a chapel, lounges, and recreational and dining areas. Now known as the Clement J. Zablocki Veterans Administration Medical Center, it is the only one still standing of the three original sites in the nation to be chosen as veterans' hospitals. Courtesy, Milwaukee County Historical Society

Washington had to be forcibly ended.

Military regiments such as the 17th Wisconsin, composed largely of Milwaukee Irishmen, and the 14th and 16th Wisconsin participated in the slow progress of victories in the western campaigns under General U.S. Grant, including the bloody battle of Shiloh in 1862. The election of 1864 found Lincoln far from popular among war-weary Milwaukeeans who gave his opponent, George McClellan, a substantial majority in the hope that the war would soon end.

However, news of Northern victories brought parades and celebrations, as well as the crowning of several Milwaukee heroes. At war's end in April 1865, the euphoria lasted all day and all night as bands led parades that became torchlight processions after dark. An effigy of Robert E. Lee was torn apart in front of the Newhall House and the black crepe that had hung from many buildings during the war was pulled down in jubilation.

Milwaukee citizens led the way in the care of wounded veterans with the establishment of the state's first hospital for soldiers located on the city's west side. News of Lincoln's assassination only days later brought the celebrations to a halt as the city and the nation prepared for the difficulties of healing and restoring the country at war's end. On April 19, the day of Lincoln's funeral, Milwaukee once again dressed in black crepe and held a somber procession of mourning.

War's end brought the first Negro citizens to the polls in the city in the 1866 mayoral election, when a Democrat lost for the first time in many years. While the nation faced the enormous problems of Republican Reconstruction, Milwaukeeans looked ahead with enthusiasm to the promise of ever-greater commercial and industrial prosperity in the postwar decades.

Left: Edward Townsend Mix (1831-1890) owned the most successful design firm in nineteenth-century Milwaukee. Mix's engineering skills, design expertise, and large corps of draftsmen enabled him to obtain the most prestigious commissions of the day, including the Mitchell Building, Chamber of Commerce Building, Milwaukee Road Depot, Exposition Building, Plankinton Hotel, National Soldier's Home, and the YMCA. Courtesy, Milwaukee County Historical Society

The DEVIL DOGS are
Crashing through to Berlin
ENLISTMENT OPENS OCT. 1st
U.S. MARINE RECRUITING STATION
PATTON BUILDING
ESPENHAINS
THE PEOPLES STORE
Food will win the wa

Chapter TWO

Prosperity, Politics, and the War to End All Wars

1870–1920

Even before 1870 Milwaukee's great urban rivalry with Chicago had proven to be a stimulus to the development of the former's industry, harbor improvements, and railroad service. Although the population of Milwaukee had almost doubled between 1860 and 1870 from 45,000 to 71,000, that of Chicago had almost tripled in the same period, from 109,000 to 298,000. However, the competition between the two cities provided incentives for the growth of new businesses and the great Chicago Fire of October 1871 opened up unexpected new opportunities for her urban rival up Lake Michigan's shore to the north.

Urban rivalries blossomed in the 1870s and 1880s throughout the United States as new immigration brought vast population growth to many cities and competition for industrial dominance became fierce. Newspapers became shameless vehicles of "boosterism" as each city touted its advantages over nearby rivals. In 1879 a group of leading Milwaukee businessmen in the Merchants' Association and the Chamber of Commerce developed a plan to exhibit the achievements of their city in commerce and industry and put Milwaukee on the map. Pooling their financial resources, the groups subscribed to a $300,000 stock issue and erected Milwaukee's Exposition Hall on

The excitement of a parade drew thousands of residents to downtown Milwaukee in support of efforts to end World War I. This view, taken September 28, 1918, looks west on Wisconsin Avenue from Fourth Street. Courtesy, Milwaukee Public Library

Kilbourn Avenue at Sixth Street.

Patterned after the Philadelphia Hall used for the national centennial in 1876, Exposition Hall opened with a great gala of Milwaukee's achievements in September 1881 and continued to be used for such exhibits for the next 24 years, until the hall was destroyed by fire in 1905 and the State Fairgrounds took over its purpose. Four years later the Milwaukee Auditorium was built on the same site to serve the city's residents as an entertainment and exposition center for the next century. Milwaukeeans were thus able to continue showing off their commercial and industrial achievements and boasting with pride of their city's economic and civic health.

Milwaukee's Exposition Building was a large enclosed exhibit hall constructed to promote the latest in science and technology. The Queen Anne-style structure was designed by Edward Townsend Mix with a central domed space and towered wings and contained an art gallery, museum, library, offices, ballroom, and concert hall, and even a glassed-in conservatory. The facility, located between Fifth and Sixth and Kilbourn and State streets, hosted regular conventions until it burned in 1905. Courtesy, Milwaukee County Historical Society

One area in which Milwaukee could claim superiority over Chicago was in the field of public health. As the disastrous cholera epidemics swept through cities such as St. Louis and Chicago, Milwaukee's population was less affected than in earlier decades. Its worst epidemics occurred in the pre-Civil War years, prior to the decision to install a fresh-water pumping station and begin a massive sewer-building project. In 1869 the Board of Public Works undertook the plan of providing the entire city with sewage disposal.

By 1879 more than 93 miles of sewer had been constructed leading to the pumping station on Jones Island, and seven years later an intercepting system was completed with its own flushing tunnel. However, the cleanup of the sewers and of the rivers resulted in the pollution of Lake Michigan. Finally, in 1913, the new Sewerage Commission created a plan to treat the sewerage waste at a plant on Jones Island before emptying it into the bottom of the lake.

Milwaukee thus became a city where clean water and efficient sewers led to a healthier population. Even the nearby dairies, such as the Nutricia Milk Company of Thiensville, advertised that their products were "tuberculin tested and perfectly pasteurized." The attractiveness of the growing resorts in Waukesha County to the west of Milwaukee proved a boon to the city as well. Thousands of people from southern cities and from Chicago flocked each summer on trains through Milwaukee to these resorts on lakes including Pewaukee, Oconomowoc, and Lac LaBelle. The city of Waukesha, too, attracted hundreds of summer visitors who came to drink its pure spring waters and take part in the social season of balls and talley hos, or carriage rides.

Not to be outdone by the resorts to the west, Milwaukeeans pressed for a free public bath and swimming pool as a "promotion of public health" and recreation. In 1889 the first public natatorium was built and Milwaukee citizens lobbied further for "healthy breathing spots" in the form of public parks, similar to Hyde Park in London or the Bois de Boulogne in Paris. Mayor Emil Wallber, a prominent German citizen, supported the public park movement and secured the passage of a $100,000 allocation by the city council in 1884 for the creation of parks and the establishment of the city's first Board of Park Commissioners.

Led by public-spirited citizens such as Christian Wahl, the commission created today's Lake, Washington, Mitchell, Kosciuszko, and Humboldt parks out of a number of acres of land purchased by the city and other acreage donated by several private citizens. A number of parks featured landscaped gardens or a band shell where public concerts could be given on balmy summer nights. In addition to these large open parks, the city had 11 public squares and small green spaces, including Juneau, Kilbourn, and others scattered throughout its many neighborhoods. The recreational aspect of these parks was enhanced when the commission invited the prominent planner Frederick Law Olmstead to landscape both Washington and Lake parks with walkways, foliage and flowers, and lagoons.

Washington Park, in particular, benefited from its close proximity to the west-side homes of many wealthy German residents, including several of Milwaukee's "beer barons." In 1893 Gustave Pabst donated some deer to the park and encouraged the development of a small zoo there, the forerunner of today's Milwaukee County Zoo. The newly developed electric trolleys brought citizens to the zoo and to the other parks for picnics, band concerts, and sporting events or boat rentals.

In addition to these public parks, Milwaukee had a strong tradition of private parks and recreation areas, including beer gardens. Schlitz Park was equipped by the brewery with fountains, cricket fields, and a summer opera. The Schlitz Brewery also built the elegant downtown Palm Garden on Wisconsin Avenue west of the river, with its vaulted ceiling and many indoor plants for the pleasurable repast of the beer-drinking public.

The Whitefish Bay resort, on the northern outskirts of the city, had its own special interurban trolley that carried visitors to enjoy its views of Lake Michigan and its beer garden and entertainment. A special lake steamer, the *Bloomer Girl* also carried summer passengers to the resort from downtown Milwaukee. National Park on the city's southwest side featured a baseball field, race track, and a popular roller coaster.

As baseball grew in popularity and gained prominence as a national pastime, Milwaukee and neighboring cities began to organize clubs. In 1878 the Cream City Club of Milwaukee joined the National Baseball League, but later switched to membership in the American League. Manager Connie Mack brought prominence to the club with pennant-contending teams in the late 1890s and baseball became firmly established in popularity in the "Cream City."

Both boxing and golf were growing in popularity in Milwaukee as well as across the country. At first, boxing contests featured bare-knuckled contenders and resulted in many permanent injuries, although that did not diminish the

Facing page, top: The prosperity of the 1880s ushered in an era of building unparalleled in the city's past for sheer volume and exuberance. The Milwaukee County Jail, shown here, was constructed in 1885 at the southeast corner of Broadway and Wells. Local architect Charles Gombert designed the stone edifice with whimsical turrets and gables that Walt Disney himself would have admired. Sadly, the building was razed in the 1930s. Photo by A.J. Breitwish; courtesy, Milwaukee County Historical Society

This rare photo of men working to construct a sewer tunnel, believed taken in the 1920s, illustrates the difficult and hazardous nature of the job when sewers were built piece by piece rather than by assembling pre-formed components. Initially, sewage was discharged into the rivers and out into Lake Michigan. But the stench and contamination of the city's drinking water, which came from the lake, led to the construction of the Jones Island Treatment Facility.Courtesy, Kwasniewski Collection, UWM

One can almost hear the laughter and feel the excitement of the young girls racing in Kosciuszko Park on the city's south side nearly 90 years ago. The park, located between Lincoln Avenue and Becher Street, is a block from St. Josephat's Basilica, whose dome appears in the distance. Courtesy, Kwasniewski Collection, UWM

Baseball is the sport most often associated with our nostalgic remembrances of the nineteenth century. Milwaukee's Cream City Baseball 9, seen here in 1869, included E.C. Wells, W.H. Dodsworth, Archie McFadden, J.H. Wood, M. Larkin, Jr., F.A. Smith, C. Smith, C.S. Harris, and George Redlington. Courtesy, Milwaukee County Historical Society

sport's popularity. The safer sport of golf developed as the leisure pursuit of Milwaukee's wealthier class and became established as a social outlet with the founding of the Milwaukee Country Club in 1895.

Of Culture and Temples of Learning

In addition to athletics, the decades of the late nineteenth century witnessed the continuing love affair of many Milwaukeeans for fine choral and orchestral music. In 1875 the German Musical Society celebrated its 25th season of monthly concerts. In 1886 Milwaukee was selected as the host city for the national "Saengerbund" and John Plankinton offered a $1,000 prize for the German singing group that offered the best cantata. The festival featured choruses of children 1,000 strong, and also celebrated the rich heritage of Milwaukee music. A Yankee singing society, the Arion Club, was allowed to perform along with ethnic singing groups from across the country.

While singing societies filled the city's air with songs, both English and German, it was the newly arriving Italian community that gave Milwaukee its first professional opera company, Maretzeks' Italian Opera, in the 1880s. The company performed in various city parks throughout the summer, particularly in Schlitz Park, and then traveled to New Orleans for the winter season.

Instrumental music was also popular with Milwaukeeans as prosperity and growth continued well into the 1870s and 1880s. In 1893 prominent civic leaders, along with the German Musical Society, began to encourage patronage for a local symphony orchestra. In the 1880s or 1890s many American cities sought the help of a few wealthy individuals in establishing professional orchestras. In Boston, one music-loving individual paid the entire bill for the Boston Symphony orchestra during its first several seasons!

As the idea of a professional orchestra gained in popularity in Milwaukee, rivalry with Chicago again became an issue. A traveling orchestra from Chicago, which played several concerts each season in Wisconsin, seemed to meet the need for a professional orchestra and therefore slowed the establishment of a separate Milwaukee symphony. In addition, the abundance of talented volunteer musicians in the city lulled the citizenry into complacency because of the luxury of its free local talent. As a result of both factors, the creation of a separate professional orchestra for Milwaukee did not occur for many decades.

In celebrating the talents of its homegrown artists in the visual arts, Milwaukee was more successful. Immediately following the Civil War several leading citizens pushed for the establishment of an Academy of Fine Arts for the city. Milwaukee Female College sponsored art classes and exhibitions each year, under the leadership first of Mary Mortimer, and later (as it became Milwaukee Downer College) of Ellen Clara Sabin. Other women's groups attempted to stimulate citizen interest in painting exhibitions, but the support for an organized museum of fine arts was tabled until the late 1880s.

Finally, in 1888, meat-packing tycoon Frederick Layton gave the city a building in which to house his art collection, valued at $50,000, and established an endowment fund of $100,000 to support the purchase of other works of art. Local painters were encouraged by his example and organized the Milwaukee Art Association in 1901, a league that supported local artists and sponsored their further education at the Layton School and other training institutes. The Layton School and Gallery served as the genesis of the later art museum in Milwaukee to which passed the heritage of the city's first substantial collection of fine art.

More popular than traditional art in Milwaukee was the phenomenon known as "panorama painting," brought to the city in the 1880s by German immigrants. Housed in their own panorama studio at the corner of Fifth and Wells, these German painters created a series of 360 degree art panoramas that toured the country as a form of early motion pictures. A large elevated platform, built in the center of the exhibition hall, allowed viewers (for a fee) to witness the full circle of a historic battle scene or religious spectacle, painted on canvas more than 30 feet tall and surrounding them in a full circle. The success of these panorama exhibitions brought fame to Milwaukee as the home of this art genre and further stimulated interest within the city's artistic community to continue to press for more gallery space and local art training programs.

Not only art and music benefited from Milwaukee's abundant local talent and its spirit of civic volunteerism. The city's public library and museum developed in a similar fashion. From its founding by the Young Men's Association in the 1840s, the library collection had grown to more than 10,000 volumes by 1867, too large a collection to be managed solely by volunteers. In 1878 the city assumed responsibility for the library collection and the Milwaukee Public Library came into being as a civic institution.

With the city's strong financial support, the collection continued to grow until the city council purchased land on Grand Avenue (present-day Wisconsin Avenue), adjacent to the splendid home of Alexander Mitchell. The Beaux Arts library building was designed by architects George Ferry and Alfred Clas in 1895 after similar buildings at the Chicago World's Fair. It was completed three years later at a cost of $630,000, a temple to the city's love of books and learning. The library's design included rooms for public lectures and study groups and also for a history museum.

The museum collection (which was housed in the public library building until the current Milwaukee Public Museum was completed in the early 1960s) had been initiated by pioneer German educator Peter Engelmann in the early 1850s as he collected biological and archeological specimens for use in his classroom at the German American Academy. Engelmann's collection was transferred to the city in 1881 and kept in the

The Layton Gallery was Milwaukee's first museum designed and built specifically to view works of art. In 1883 wealthy meatpacker and patron of the arts Frederick Layton began planning the museum to which he would donate 38 paintings. Opened in 1888 at the corner of Jefferson and Mason streets, the gallery later began a prestigious school, the Layton School of Art, whose faculty eventually formed today's Milwaukee Institute of Art and Design. This building was razed in the 1960s to make way for the new Jefferson Street shop developments. Courtesy, Milwaukee Public Library

By the 1890s, when these bird's-eye depictions were made as advertisements, the Uihleins and the Pabsts were building their breweries to reflect picturesque, Old World German-style architecture. Courtesy, Milwaukee Public Library

Exposition Center on Kilbourn Avenue, until the new library building was completed. Exhibits about the region's natural history, its earliest native inhabitants, and many other artifacts were added until it became one of the outstanding such museums in the country.

The interest in cultural institutions and the ability to support them grew in Milwaukee in the decades following the Civil War as the city thrived. However, Milwaukee's post-Civil War prosperity was founded on a different basis than in earlier decades. As the nation's leading wheat port before the Civil War, Milwaukee had enjoyed the blessings of a booming commerce, with its granaries full and its port bustling with grain ships. However, the high point of the city's wheat export business was reached in 1873, when a total of 32.5 million bushels of grain passed through the Port of Milwaukee. Thereafter, the trade began to decline as Minneapolis and Duluth, Minnesota, entered the race and gained primacy by the 1880s.

A New Economic Base

With the wheat trade declining and wheat farming moving westward to the Dakotas, Wisconsin farmers looked for other cash crops to replace their lost revenues. Soon milk and cheese production took over, but these dairy commodities were initially produced for local consumption and did not contribute substantially to the commercial profits of Milwaukee entrepreneurs. The city needed a new commercial and industrial base to recover from the loss of the wheat trade and to continue its development as a prosperous urban center.

The decline in wheat trade was partially offset by a continuing flow of commodities defined as "coarse grains" (including corn, oats, and barley), as well as an increase in milled wheat, or flour. A 1909 merchants' book listed 20 commission merchants in the grain trade and 23 in the produce trade, including E.R. Godfrey & Sons on Broadway. The Roundy, Peckham & Dexter Company led the way in the wholesale grocery import and distribution business in the city by 1902.

As late as 1909 Milwaukee ranked third in the nation in the export of flour, although even in that commodity Minneapolis gradually took over by the outbreak of World War I in 1914. In 1892 a city brochure touted Milwaukee's 22 miles of port dockage and boasted that shipping charges from the Port of Milwaukee to eastern lake ports were four cents a ton lower than from Chicago, a fact that made "the enormous manufacture of flour possible" in those decades.

More promising than the grain and flour trade, the growth of the city's breweries signaled the turn away from commerce to manufacturing and productive enterprises after the Civil War. Between 1871 and 1910 Milwaukee's annual beer production and export rose from 142,000 to 3.7 million barrels, a 26-fold increase. The great Chicago Fire in October 1871, which burned out many of that city's breweries, proved to be a boon for Milwaukee's beer industry. Without the nearby rivals, and with the invention of refrigerated (ice-cooled) rail cars, beer could be safely shipped from Milwaukee to markets across the Midwest and the country.

Aggressive marketing techniques also contributed to the rising fame of Milwaukee beer. The Pabst Brewery (formerly the Best Brewery) led the way in marketing innovations under the leadership of Captain Frederick Pabst. Between 1873 and 1893 the company's production soared to more than a million barrels annually, placing it first among the nation's breweries. A "blue ribbon" award in the beer competition at a World Exposition gave the Pabst Brewery its logo for many decades thereafter. Actual ribbons of blue were attached by hand to Pabst premium bottles during the 1880s as the symbol of this excellence.

Not to be outdone by Pabst, the up-and-coming Schlitz Brewery, led by August Uihlein after 1875, competed in seeking national markets and in licensing taverns to sell its products exclusively. By 1902 Schlitz had surpassed the million-barrel output at Pabst and remained the nation's leading brewery (with Pabst still in second place) until Prohibition.

Other major breweries, the Val Blatz Company, the Miller Brewery, and the Gettelman Company (later purchased by Miller), added to the city's image in the profession of high-quality beer production. Brew masters, trained in Germany, used only the best yeast, hops, and barley in the production process. As Milwaukee's breweries prospered, so did its related producers of malt, such as the Froedtert Company, and yeast, including the Red Star Yeast Company at 79 Buffalo Street. A whiff of Milwaukee air, even in those years, told of the abundance of yeast and malt that would soon be used to produce the city's finest brewed beer.

Breweries utilized many innovations in their production and shipping processes. The Pabst Brewery pioneered in the use of refrigeration in its plants to cool the wort and underground vats to store the liquor. Bottling soon replaced barrels as the container of choice and Schlitz introduced the famous "brown bottle" after studying the effect of sunlight upon bottled beer.

West Wisconsin was known as Grand Avenue when this photo was taken and the lacy iron bridge decorated with urns and griffins had recently replaced the old wooden truss bridge that connected Juneautown and Kilbourntown. The towered structure on the right is the Empire Building, which was later remodeled into a castellated fantasy by Otto Strack for the Pabst Brewing Co. It stood until replaced by the current building, which houses the Riverside Theater. Courtesy, Milwaukee County Historical Society

Advertising campaigns turned to effective gimmickry as a Pabst beer bottle was "found" at the North Pole by explorer Admiral Edwin Peary and former President Teddy Roosevelt took a supply of Schlitz beer with him to Africa on one of his big game hunting expeditions. The American fleet that captured Manila and occupied the Philippines during the Spanish-American War received a reward of 3,600 bottles of Schlitz beer for their conquest. Milwaukee's beer-selling competition had become global and the result was worldwide recognition. The name "Milwaukee" soon became synonymous with beer, and the gaiety of competing beer gardens and the German atmosphere of good spirits, or "gemutlichkeit," became a hallmark of the city's national and international image.

Patrick Cudahy Incorporated started its meat-packing/processing plant in 1888 as Cudahy Brothers. The Cudahys assisted their employees in buying houses by offering low-cost home loans through the Locust Street Branch Bank, as is seen here advertised on the company's truckbeds. Courtesy, Patrick Cudahy Incorporated

The beer barons also diversified their interests by investing in banks, real estate, and commercial enterprises both in Milwaukee and in eastern cities. The ownership of New York hotels and restaurants (which served only their brew) was one measure of the national success and the immense profits that flowed from the beer industry before the turn of the century. In 1898 Schlitz won a slogan battle against Pabst and gained the exclusive right to use the phrase that would solidify Milwaukee's image for many decades to come: "the beer that made Milwaukee famous."

Although beer attained greater national popularity and visibility for the city in these post-Civil War decades, many other productive enterprises contributed to Milwaukee's manufacturing prosperity. The meat-packing industry, led by companies such as Cudahy and Plankinton, made the city the fourth-largest slaughtering and packing center in the nation as early as 1871. Once again the growth of refrigeration technology was a significant part of this boom, as it had been for the breweries. Refrigerated rail cars could carry meat products across the country with relative safety from spoilage.

Even before the turn of the century, Milwaukee rivaled nearby Chicago as a "hog-butchering" center. One of the favorite uses of this meat was in the famous German "wurst," or sausages, which local butchers made in abundance. Beer and sausage became twin hallmarks of the good life in Milwaukee as companies, such as Usinger's, became famous for the quality of spices used in their bratwurst and other sausages. In 1898 alone, more than one million hogs were butchered and packed in local plants. However, the move by Philip Armour from Milwaukee to start his own company in Chicago later tipped the scales in favor of Milwaukee's rival.

Ancillary to meat packing, the tanning business also continued to thrive as firms such as Pfister & Vogel and Gallun led the way in hide curing and leather production. The giant Albert Trostel & Sons Tannery, and its neighbor the Star Tannery, helped to place Milwaukee on the map as a national tanning center. A Chamber of Commerce report for 1908 listed leather goods second only to metalworking products in total industrial output at $39.664 million to $77.36 million.

Shoe and leather goods factories grew up alongside the tanneries. A book touting "commercial Milwaukee" published in 1909 listed the F. Mayer Boot & Shoe Company, which had a production capacity of 9,000 pairs of boots a day. The Weyenberg Shoe Manufacturing Company specialized in "heavy service shoes" for "loggers, lumberjacks, farmers, and prospectors." More stylish footwear came from the Bradley & Metcalf Company, founded in 1843, which produced and sold "high-grade men's shoes" for four dollars a pair. Other successful leather goods enterprises included the V. Schoenecker Boot & Shoe Company on North Seventh Street and the Mahler Albenberg Leather Coat Company on East Broadway.

Third in line, behind metal goods and tanning, was "clothing and kindred goods" at $27.85 million, followed by beer and tonics at $25.7 million and meat products at $25.4 million. The Blumenfeld, Locher & Brown Company, on Broadway, engaged in wholesale millinery, as did its neighbor, the Miller-Genz Company. Broadway, in fact, soon became the hub of the city's rapidly growing millinery and fashion business. The Holeproof Hosiery Company had two six-story factory buildings on the south side of the city that produced both men's and women's hosiery at the turn of the century. And the Everwear Hosiery Company on Fifth Street advertised a "six months' guarantee" on its men's socks.

Perhaps most significant of all of Milwaukee's growing manufacturing prowess in this post-Civil War period was the rapid development of the metalworking industry.

Perhaps most significant of all of Milwaukee's growing manufacturing prowess in this post-Civil War period was the rapid development of the metalworking industry. Led by the giant Bay View Iron and Steel Works, Milwaukee established a reputation for skilled machining and high-quality metal products by the early 1890s. Established in 1866, just at the war's end, as the Milwaukee Iron Company, the Bay View Mills prospered from the great demand for rails for the westward expansion of the railroads after the war. After a merger with the North Chicago Rolling Mills Company and the Minerva Furnace, the Bay View Works dominated iron and steel output in the Upper Midwest, outside of Chicago itself. In 1892 the Bay View Works alone employed 2,000 workers to labor in its plant's six blast furnaces and two rolling mills.

Milwaukee's ideal location, between the iron fields of Minnesota and the coal mines of Pennsylvania, resulted in the establishment of other rolling mills and foundries before the turn of the century. In the 1870s alone, the output from these shops increased more than 500 percent from $402,000 to more than $2.2 million. The Reliance Iron Works, directed by E.P. Allis, produced some $3 million by the end of 1889. Allis had displayed great business acumen in his bid to manufacture the pipes and pump engines for Milwaukee's sewer system in the 1870s and in hiring engineers to design a new milling process for flour that utilized rollers, as well as a new all-iron band saw for the lumber industry.

Such innovations put the newly renamed Edward P. Allis Company in a competitive position in the national market and resulted in the creation in 1901 of the consolidated corporation of Allis-Chalmers Company, which helped to put the name of Milwaukee on the national map for more than just its production of beer. Other machine shops that contributed to the city's reputation for finely tooled iron and steel equipment were the Geuder and Paeschke Manufacturing Company and the Pawling and Harnischfeger Company, established in the early 1880s. From his beginning in the machine and pattern business, Henry Harnischfeger soon began to specialize in the manufacture of large cranes and established his own separate corporation for this purpose.

Other companies engaged in iron and steel castings included the Vilter Manufacturing Com-

Foundries were essential to Milwaukee's transformation into an industrial giant in the late nineteenth and early twentieth centuries. Foundries like the one shown here in the 1920s produced castings that went into finished goods or into machinery that produced finished goods. Courtesy, Kwasniewski Collection, UWM

German immigrant Henry Harnischfeger came to Milwaukee in 1881 and three years later founded the P&H Machine & Pattern Shop with pattern maker Alonzo Pawling. This 1920s machine shop interior is equipped with Harnischfeger's traveling cranes, which enabled the lifting and transporting of raw materials and equipment throughout the plant. Harnischfeger is still a world leader, building cranes with up to an 800-ton lifting capacity. Courtesy, Milwaukee County Historical Society

pany, Schwaab & Sons, and the Crucible Steel Casting Company, all on Clinton Street. Specializing in hardware and related metal products were the Chain Belt Company, the Milwaukee Malleable Iron Works, and the Shadbolt & Boyd Iron Company. The Nordberg Company at Oklahoma and Chicago avenues built many different kinds of engines, and the Johnson Service Company produced "humidostats, pressure governors, and pneumatic tower clocks" in its building at Jefferson and Michigan streets, described as the "largest reinforced concrete factory building in the Northwest."

Widening Boundaries and Workers' Settlements

By 1908 the city's metalworking industries had surpassed beer, tanning, and leather production with a total output of $77.36 million. Two years later a new industry benefited from the city's steel and fine-machining trades when the Milwaukee Motor and Manufacturing Company opened its doors in 1910 to produce and market automobiles, the vehicle that would change the face of American cities within the next two decades. The P.H. Brodesser Company, at Burleigh and Weil streets, manufactured a "motor delivery wagon" that would "carry up to 2,000 lbs. and go anywhere where horses cannot go!" Soon the Milwaukee commercial landscape would be dotted with motor car companies and sales showrooms, such as the elegantly appointed Kopmeier Motor Car Company on North Summit Avenue.

Many of these large industrial companies located their plants on the perimeter or outside of the city itself. The resulting loss of tax revenues caused problems for the city budget. Conversely, Milwaukee County enjoyed greater revenues from its tenfold increase in industry between 1890 and 1900. The great influx of workers, who came to labor in these iron and steel plants and other factories, sought affordable housing in neighborhood clusters close to their factories, often outside the city limits.

Bay View grew up near the southern lakeshore around the developing iron works operated by Eber Brock Ward, who actually dug his own harbor to serve the needs of his Milwaukee Iron Company just south of the city limits. By early 1879 the area numbered more than 2,000 residents, mostly workers in the iron company, which had been purchased by the North Chicago Rolling Mills. The Village of Bay View was incorporated that year, becoming the first official suburb of the city, but its independent existence was short-lived. Just eight years later, in 1887, residents voted for annexation to the city in order to receive vitally needed services.

Another industrial suburb, West Allis, was a farming community until the extension of a street railway line in 1887, and the official sanctioning of the State Fairgrounds there in 1892. It became a desirable industrial site as the Kearney and Trecker Company, the Rosenthal Cornhusker Company, and finally the Edward P. Allis Company located there by 1900 and workers soon followed. The area's population grew so quickly that it was chartered as a village in 1902 and as a city only four years later.

In a similar fashion, South Milwaukee grew up around the Bucyrus Steam Shovel and Dredge Co., which moved to the area from Bucyrus, Ohio, lured by real estate promoters who platted and improved the area beginning in 1890. After severe financial setbacks that slowed the growth of the area, Bucyrus was able to secure important contracts to make large steam shovels for the Panama Canal project being developed by the U.S. government under the leadership of President Teddy Roosevelt.

A later industrial suburb, West Milwaukee (incorporated in 1906), had first been developed as the site of the National Soldier's Home just after the Civil War in 1867. With the coming of the street rail line along western National Avenue, many large homesites were platted in the area. The settlement grew dramatically after 1905, when the Pawling and Harnischfeger Company located there.

Packing plants also sought open spaces in the county outside the city limits. Patrick Cudahy moved his meat-packing plant south to an area once known as Buckhorn, because he feared city restrictions against meat packing. An 1892 publication by the Association for the Advancement of Milwaukee predicted that "it is expected there will be a large village at Cudahy, as the new plant will employ a large number of men, most of whom, of course, will reside near the works." The prediction was accurate and the city of Cudahy was chartered in 1906. Elsewhere, as in Cudahy, workers' houses seemed to spring up almost overnight in the industrial and immigration boom of the 1880s and 1890s.

The city's population, which had been slightly over 71,000 in 1870, more than doubled to 204,468 twenty years later in 1890. In each of the next three decades the number increased by more than 80,000, totaling 285,315 in 1900, 373,857 in 1910, and 457,147 in 1920. Much of this growth was reflected in the many new neighborhoods that developed north, west, and south of the central city. Workers flocked from rural areas and from Europe to find employment in the many growing factories of Milwaukee.

Throughout the nation, the relationship between workers and factory owners became increasingly stormy during the 1870s, 1880s, and 1890s as labor unions began to stage strikes and walkouts, demanding workers' rights and better wages. Milwaukee experienced its share of labor unrest during these decades as strikes against the transit company, breweries, and tanneries erupted. Tailors, sailors, ship carpenters, cigar makers, printers,

Awesome in scale and complexity, machines like this press were commonplace in the scores of manufacturing plants throughout Milwaukee and enabled the production of precision parts and equipment. While today much of this type of work is automated, men were still needed to set gauges and place materials at the time this photo was taken after World War I. Courtesy, Kwasniewski Collection, UWM

pipelayers, coal heavers, and even bellboys at the city's luxury hotels began to demand fewer hours and higher wages.

Compared to many American cities of the same time period, however, Milwaukee's labor troubles were of shorter duration and less costly in property damage or loss of life. On May 5, 1886, striking workers at the North Chicago Rolling Mill Company were fired upon by militia, resulting in five deaths and a number of wounded. It was Milwaukee's worst labor confrontation in the century. In Chicago, the violence of the bombing at Haymarket Square on May 4, 1886, illustrated what a combination of anarchist terrorist tactics and labor unrest could produce. Milwaukee's unrest, while turbulent, paled by comparison with strikes across the country where hundreds were injured and many lives were lost before troops arrived to control angry mobs.

Although more than 12,000 Milwaukee workers went on strike in the spring of 1886, several protest parades ended up in social gatherings at the Schlitz Beer Garden. Even though the militia was present, only a few incidents occurred and injuries were slight. Paul Grottkau, Milwaukee's leading labor organizer, was fined and the city's labor movement turned to politics instead of strikes to answer its demands. The Knights of Labor agreed to abide by Mayor Emil Wallber's policy that while they had a right to strike, they should not threaten property or nonstriking workers.

Eugene V. Debs is shown here at left with Milwaukee's premier Socialist, Victor Berger, in a photo taken by a local studio, Klein & Guttenstein, between 1896 and 1898. Debs and Berger created the Social Democratic Party in 1898. Both men were indicted for conspiracy due to their outspoken advocacy of neutrality during World War I. Courtesy, Milwaukee County Historical Society

Partisan Issues and Party Politics

During the 1880s and subsequent decades the effect of the great number of industrial workers and the many new immigrants upon Milwaukee city government and upon the flavor of local politics was dramatic. An earlier mayor, Harrison Ludington, who espoused the cause of responsible government, had been elected on the Citizens' Ticket (or Reform Republicans) in 1871, 1873, 1874, and 1875. Ludington, a wealthy lumberman, was popular with German voters in the city as well as with the old-time Yankee residents, but received few working-class votes. He attempted to overcome problems of corruption, which existed in Milwaukee government although on a smaller scale than in many big cities during the late nineteenth century.

In response to these Republican victories, the city's Democrats organized Catholic, Polish, and Irish voters and campaigned to recruit new adherents from the immigrants arriving to work in Milwaukee's breweries, foundries, and machine shops during the 1870s and thereafter. By 1900 the workers' vote was a significant factor in Milwaukee politics with the rise of the national Social Democratic Party and its popular candidate, Eugene V. Debs. Milwaukee County gave Debs 7 percent of its vote in the presidential election of 1900 and 26 percent in 1904.

In local party politics, the Democrats organized the People's Reform Party (their answer to the Republicans' inclusive title, the Citizens' Party) and won several mayoral elections by the late 1870s. However, the Republican tide on the national level following the Civil War was hard to beat, and workers in Milwaukee were often angered at the Democrats' reputation for graft and corruption. By the turn of the century many immigrants and workers in the city, as well as many old-line Germans, turned to a third organization, the Socialist Party.

Milwaukee's brand of socialism, while it resembled the national Socialist Party in some respects, was considered by many to be more responsible and less radical. Prominent German leaders endorsed Milwaukee socialism, while shying away from the more extreme platforms of Eugene Debs. In 1882 Milwaukee newspapers began to herald a new day in city politics, based on the voting power of the independent labor element.

In 1886 Milwaukee's chapter of the national Knights of Labor had an estimated 50 lodges with more than 16,000 members, which advocated not only higher wages, but more social advantages for the working classes. They also pushed for controls on child labor, for equal pay regardless of gender, for an eight-hour day, and for the establishment of a bureau of labor statistics. By the late 1880s

Parochial schools were most typically associated with Catholic and Lutheran congregations who deemed it appropriate for their children to be educated in a religious setting and in a language familiar to their membership. This classroom at St. Joseph Orphanage was photographed in 1924. The inscription on the blackboard is in Polish, indicating that teaching in a foreign language was still typical in religious-run schools. Courtesy, Kwasniewski Collection, UWM

labor's candidates were winning many countywide elections, both for city offices and even for judicial positions. The old political battles had taken a dramatically new turn.

In 1888 many labor leaders helped to nominate a "Union Labor Party" candidate for mayor who ran on a ticket that called for public ownership of municipal improvements, more control of basic urban utilities, the building of public baths, and lower taxes. Only a split between rival labor candidates that divided the working-class vote brought defeat on election day. Milwaukee socialism had begun its climb to political prominence, but the establishment politicians reacted strongly to what they perceived as the dangers of working-class rule.

German newspapers in the city, such as *Der Sozialist*, published the cries for urban reform and for improvements for the working men and women of Milwaukee. Calling for workers of all nationalities to join with the Socialists, the paper led the way in the growth of the Socialist Party in Milwaukee during the 1890s. In Milwaukee, the Socialists gradually drew into their ranks many Germans who had previously supported one of the two main parties, but became disaffected over the issue of temperance or of German language instruction in the schools.

In 1872 the passage of the Graham Law (a temperance measure) by the Wisconsin legislature alienated many Germans from the Republican Party, which they had supported for at least two decades. A second factor that cost the Republicans many longtime ethnic followers was the passage of the Bennett Law in 1889, which mandated that the English language be used in all Wisconsin schools. Outraged at this perceived attack upon their parochial schools, their language, and their culture, German voters deserted the Republicans in the elections of 1890, demonstrating that no one party could blindly count on Milwaukee's ethnic vote.

During the 1890s many reforms became popular with American voters, as a general cleanup of city and state governments was accomplished through the adoption of civil service programs. Control of fire and police departments was handed over to professionals instead of political appointees, and a general movement toward honesty and professionalism was in the making. Spearheading this reform thrust in Milwaukee were the German Socialists, led after 1892 by schoolteacher Victor L. Berger, who realized that as America's foremost German city, Milwaukee could successfully elect candidates who supported Socialist and working-class reforms akin to reforms tried earlier in the German homeland.

The platform of the Milwaukee Socialists (while conservative by national Socialist standards) centered around a call for control of all public utilities, the use of eight-hour days for city workers, public jobs for the city's unemployed, pure milk for babies, free public toilets, fair taxation of large corporations, free legal and medical service for the poor, free schoolbooks for children, better housing control of slum dwellings, and at least one symphony concert each month at public expense! By 1910 Milwaukee socialism would begin its domination of Milwaukee politics, which would last for several decades. But the Socialists' day did not come until two last old-line politicians had enjoyed center stage.

Democratic Mayor David G. Rose, the free-wheeling spirit of Milwaukee politics, won victories in 1898 and four times thereafter, even though he staunchly opposed most of the reforms. Rose unabashedly favored private enterprise and even drew up a sweetheart deal highly favorable to the street railway company. His lavish gifts to ethnic churches and his advocacy of a free-flowing liquor policy for the city increased his popularity for a time. During the first decade of the 1900s many ferries from Chicago arrived each afternoon in Milwaukee to enjoy the gaiety of River Street (on the east bank of the Milwaukee River) with its saloons, music, and redlight district. A round-trip ferry ride cost only $1.50 on the Goodrich Transit line and a passenger could choose from three convenient runs each day. With its growing reputation as an open "sin city," Milwaukee seemed further away from reform than ever.

However, the jollity of the Rose years brought scandal to the city's reputation across the country. More than 70 aldermen and supervisors were indicted for graft in a grand jury probe in 1903. Licenses for illegal gambling houses had been bought for $1,000 bribes to city officials, and aldermen were found guilty of accepting hundreds of dollars to fix transit contracts, make deals with saloon owners, or establish special utilities programs. The extent of the corruption was so widespread that it brought substantial numbers of reform-minded Germans into the fold of Milwaukee socialism, along with working-class voters. The time was ripe for change.

This spirit of reform and optimism that prevailed at the turn of the century was not marred by America's entrance into the Spanish-American War in 1898. Few Milwaukeeans actually served in Cuba or the Philippines since recruiting officers eliminated men who had foreign accents from their lists. One outcome of the war was the discovery of marching music and the pleasure of listening to bands drilling to tunes written by the newly popular John Phillip Sousa. Milwaukee, a city that had long loved bands, reawoke with a fervor to parades, brass bands, and the thrill of victory in 1899 at war's end.

Milwaukee, a city that had long loved bands, reawoke with a fervor to parades, brass bands, and the thrill of victory in 1899 at war's end.

Ethnic Diversity and Socialist Reform

A further sign that the reform spirit would soon prevail was the groundswell of public support for a revision in the city charter in 1908, which passed in a referendum only to be defeated in the state legislature. Socialists had supported the proposed charter revisions that would have given Milwaukee more control over its financial matters. In elections in 1906 and 1908, many Social Democrats were elected aldermen as Milwaukee's brand of socialism began to convert even many formerly conservative businessmen. Dropping its insistence on public ownership of utilities while keeping its demand for municipal supervision of their operations, Milwaukee's Socialists were poised to sweep the municipal elections in 1910 with a vast coalition of former Democrats and former Republicans, now solidly behind the Social Democratic Party.

Even the 1906 election of Republican Sherburn M. Becker, "boy mayor," who represented the last hurrah of traditional party politics in the city, could not dislodge the growing Socialist coalition, now led by Alderman Emil Seidel as well as Berger. In 1910 Seidel was elected mayor of Milwaukee on the Social Democratic ticket, by the largest margin ever in the city's mayoral history. The Socialists also won in 16 of the city's 23 wards, and carried the aldermanic races to dominate the city council with 21 Social Democrats, to 10 Democrats, and only 4 Republicans. Even the county's congressional delegation changed hands as Victor Berger was elected to Congress as a Socialist in 1910. Milwaukee was the first large American city to elect both a Socialist mayor and Socialist city council. The heyday of Milwaukee socialism in municipal politics was at hand.

In 1914 another outstanding Socialist and former city attorney, Daniel W. Hoan, won election as mayor, a position he held until 1940, making Milwaukee not only the first, but also the most enduring, Socialist city in the country. The cleanup of corrupt city politics began in full force. During the years of Socialist dominance, many civic improvements placed Milwaukee in the forefront of America's most honest and progressive cities. Significant reforms were achieved, including workmen's compensation, health clinics for children, a technical school with evening classes, public safety programs such as traffic signs, safety islands for pedestrians, city gardens, and arboretums. Civil service exams were instituted for office seekers, which helped to end the corrupt spoils system, and immunizations against typhoid and diphtheria were made available. The city began full-scale inspections of food products and the regulation of gasoline storage tanks that serviced automobiles.

By 1920 the success of the Socialists in Milwaukee was measured in clean government, many new civic services, regulations (but not public ownership) of utilities, and progressive reforms such as a municipal reference bureau. The Socialists also succeeded in providing chlorination of water; classes for teaching English; trash collection; control of liquor, prostitution, and gambling; the use of voting machines to eliminate ballot fraud; tuberculosis control; and even the use of sand for icy intersections in winter. Only the emotional anti-Germanism of World War I, from

Electric-powered streetcars became commonplace in Milwaukee by the mid-1890s. By 1893 the Milwaukee Street Railway Company had acquired all of its competitors and had completed the electrification of its routes, making Milwaukee the first city in the country to have a city-wide, completely interconnected, and unified electric streetcar system. This late 1890s scene looks north up Water Street to City Hall. Painting by Lynn Casper

Merchant Frank Bzdawka, shown here at his shop at 1112-1114 West Lincoln Avenue, had a large clientele judging from the number of Toledo scales lined up at his counter. The exterior of Bzdawka's store, which was built in 1919, reflects his pride in his Polish ethnicity and displays the boldly profiled gable that was patterned after traditional Polish architecture. The family operated the meat market through the 1960s. Courtesy, Kwasniewski Collection, UWM

1914 to 1918, brought disaffection with the Socialists, despite their many significant achievements in the betterment of Milwaukee's urban environment.

Although German immigrants had dominated Milwaukee society for many decades, by 1910 most of the newly arriving settlers in the city were from Poland, Czechoslovakia, and Italy. In 1850 fully 38 percent of the city's population had been German-born; five decades later, in 1900, German natives comprised only 19 percent, and the number of Poles had risen to 6 percent.

The Polish community, which was almost completely Roman Catholic, grouped itself around the significant Polish parish churches, such as the original St. Stanislaus, St. Hedwig (built in 1871 on the city's east side), and St. Hyacinth (built in 1883 on the southwest side). One of the most outstanding examples of church architecture from this period is the St. Josephat Basilica on the corner of Lincoln Avenue and Sixth Street, completed in 1901 by Polish residents on Milwaukee's south side. Using materials salvaged from two Chicago buildings, the parishioners helped to erect this shrine to their faith, designed in a Neo-Renaissance style, with a dome patterned directly after that of St. Peter's Basilica in Rome. Besides the parish churches, other important groups included the Kosciuszko Guard, with its meeting place, Kosciuszko Hall, built in the mid-1880s as a center of activities within the Polish community.

This diminutive cottage is typical of the hundreds that can be found in the working-class Polish neighborhoods of the city, especially on the south side. Popularly called the "Polish flat," this type of cottage is a unique architectural manifestation of immigrant culture in Milwaukee and was built almost exclusively by immigrant Poles. Courtesy, Kwasniewski Collection, UWM

The Polish press, just as its German counterpart, played an important role in uniting Polish voters and stirring ethnic and working-class issues in the turmoil of Milwaukee politics between the 1880s and 1920. Newspapers such as the *Krytyka* (the critic) urged support for Polish candidates for alderman and supported the Democratic Party in the early years. However, after the turn of the century they endorsed many of the Socialists' programs to clean up city government and bring justice to all classes.

Clustered in dense neighborhoods on the south side of the city, the Polish population filled the need of Milwaukee's growing industries for labor. They also saved their wages to erect small, one-story private homes near each parish church. Reflecting the German traditions already established in the city, the Polish founded their own singing societies, such as the Harmonia Male Choir, and their own theater, the "Teatr Polski." They also agitated for instruction to be given in Polish in the city's grammar schools, a measure that finally succeeded in 1896.

Third and fourth in percentage of immigrants were the Czechoslovakians and the Russians, who arrived in large numbers after the 1890s. The former group were often political refugees from troubles in Central Europe and the latter included many Jewish families, pushed out of western Russia by pogroms of the czar. These newer Jewish congregations, and many of Milwaukee's original German Jewish settlers, built Temple Emanu-El at Broadway and State streets in 1872 and Temple Emanu-El B'ne Jeshurun on East Kenwood 50 years later.

Many other immigrant groups from Central and Southern Europe, including Italians, Austro-Hungarians, Greeks, and Serbs, were also fleeing from Europe's growing unrest that would result in the outbreak of World War I in 1914. Milwaukee's rich ethnic heritage included a representation from all of the countries of Southern and Eastern Europe, as well as its initial pattern of German, British, Irish, Dutch, and Scandinavian peoples from Northern Europe.

Transportation and Telephones

As each new wave of immigration arrived, new neighborhoods were established in clusters around specific churches, or near the large industries that employed these workers. Milwaukee's older residential neighborhoods, on the east side and on the German west side, continued to expand outward. The expansion was made possible by the growth and development of the older street railway, where horses pulled cars on tracks, into the modern mass transit system of interurban rail lines and trolleys.

As the city grew in population and expanded horizontally over an ever-greater area, the slow pace of the horse-drawn railway became inefficient. The demands of a city with a population (in 1890) of 204,468 were vastly different than 20 years earlier when there were only 71,440 people and most still lived within a few miles of the central district. In 1890 Milwaukee's first electric trolley issued a challenge to a horse-drawn omnibus that proved to be no real contest at all. The horse conveyance could take as long as an hour, even in

The cultural life of Milwaukee's Poles paralleled that of the city's German community and there were numerous choirs, singing societies, and theatrical groups active from the 1870s to the 1940s. This 1939 photograph documents a social gathering of the Kalina Singing Society in an unidentified hall. Courtesy, Kwasniewski Collection, UWM

Wagons, carriages, and trolleys—not to mention hundreds of pedestrians—crowd onto Wisconsin Avenue just east of Water Street in this view taken shortly after 1901. The Wells Building, at the corner of East Wisconsin Avenue and Milwaukee Street, was completed in 1902 and is just visible in the upper right of the photograph. While this scene certainly appears congested, the activity lent an undeniable vibrancy and excitement to downtown that we can only imagine today. Courtesy, State Historical Society of Wisconsin

good weather, to make a one-way run through the city, whereas the electrified trolley could complete the journey in less than half that time. In bad weather, the difference in speed and dependability was even more extreme. The 1890s witnessed the demise of the horse-drawn rail cars and the rapid rise of electrified mass transit.

Even with its superior speed and reliability, the potential danger of electric wires hanging over Milwaukee's streets alarmed some citizens who feared the electrocution of passengers or pedestrians. However, despite these fears, the city chartered its first electric railway line, the West Side Street Railway along Wells Street, in April 1890. This venture was soon renamed The Milwaukee Electric Railway and Light Company and became a large conglomerate, known as TMER&L, which dominated mass transit in the city for the next several decades. Although the city began to light its streets with electric lights as early as 1880, the transit conglomerate swallowed up several small lighting companies and served both the transit and lighting needs of the city for many years. In 1919 an electric utility company, Wisconsin Electric Power, evolved from TMER&L as a separate entity.

Led by John I. Beggs, Henry C. Payne, and Henry Villard, the TMER&L became a power to be reckoned with in city politics, lobbying for favorable rates from city hall and gradually merging with competing lines to form a virtual monopoly within the city. In several key court battles, fought for TMER&L by the law firm of Miller, Noyes, Miller, & Wahl (later Foley & Lardner), the company defeated attempts to roll back its fares or force it to use expensive paving material in the spaces between the rails. The company's political power was so enormous that it won a favorable rate and franchise agreement in 1899, which was designed to last until 1934.

Like the electric company and its predecessor the electric street railway, the gaslight company experienced a significant period of growth in the post-Civil War decades. Chartered originally in 1852, the Milwaukee Gas Light Company soon expanded to control most of the city's miles of gas piping and its residential and commercial gaslight fixtures. However, the era of gaslights was ultimately eclipsed by the growing public confidence

The advent of the electrified streetcar immediately made the horse-drawn trolley obsolete as conductors could better regulate the vehicle's speed and avoid the delays necessitated by changing horses. Car #61, shown here, is believed to have been the first electric streetcar to run for the West Side Street Railway in 1890. The company eventually consolidated into the transit monopoly known as TMER&L, The Milwaukee Electric Railway & Light. By the time this photo was taken in 1910, car #61 was being used for maintenance on the power lines. Courtesy, Milwaukee County Historical Society

in the safety of electric lighting. By the early 1920s many Milwaukee homes and businesses were converting to the newer electric lights and using gas purely as a cooking or heating fuel.

Another utility that was chartered in this post-Civil War period was the telephone company. Following the patent by Alexander Graham Bell in 1876, telephone technology and telephone service in large American cities developed at a rapid rate. By 1879 Charles H. Haskins had become the Milwaukee representative of the National Bell Telephone Company, with its first formally organized switchboard and exchanges. By 1881 there were more than 600 individual and personal subscribers in the city and by 1896, more than 3,000. Formally incorporated in 1882 as the Milwaukee Telephone Company, the local utility established long-distance linkages with the American Telephone and Telegraph Company for nationwide service.

Women Take a Role

One of the results of the growing telephone exchange business was the need for switchboard workers. At first young boys were used to change the wire plugs with each incoming call, but soon a pool of young women became the city's first telephone operators. In many other industries as well, women entered the work force in ever-increasing numbers during the late nineteenth century. Department stores such as T.A. Chapman and the Boston Store, as well as Woolworth's and Gimbels, employed "shop girls" to wait on customers. The visibility of women in the growing work force was echoed by their presence in the labor movement and the establishment of several all-women labor unions before 1890.

In education and in the professions as well, women were a more visible part of the city's horizon by 1900. The city's first female doctor, Dr.

Dr. Laura Ross Wolcott was one of nineteenth-century Milwaukee's more remarkable women. As a female pioneer in the medical field, she met with opposition and ridicule from her male colleagues but managed to overcome numerous obstacles to complete her studies and establish her own successful practice. Dr. Wolcott was also active in the Woman's Suffrage Association, the State Academy of the Arts, and the Humane Society. Courtesy, Milwaukee County Historical Society

tion of Women's Clubs brought more than 4,000 women from all over the country to Milwaukee, where they gathered at the elegant Pfister Hotel. Matters of concern to those in attendance included questions about the status of women, such as the welfare of working women, the issues of women and economics, and the call for clubwomen to take responsibility to make the world a better place.

Milwaukee's tradition of women's activism was a long and honored one, beginning with the earliest endeavors of leaders such as Mary Blanchard Lynde, wife of attorney William Pitt Lynde, to establish the city's first orphan's home. In 1871

Above: The plight of African-American residents in Milwaukee is poignantly caught in this image taken in the late 1930s or early 1940s. Confined to the oldest and most derelict housing in the city between Sixth and Eighth streets north of State Street by racial prejudice, blacks found it impossible to relocate to better neighborhoods. Courtesy, Milwaukee Public Library

Right: One of Milwaukee's most venerable institutions was the outdoor beer garden where patrons could enjoy beer, sandwiches, and entertainment. The beer garden began to appear in Milwaukee in the late 1840s, coinciding with the first great influx of German middle-class and professional immigrants. Pabst's Whitefish Bay Resort, shown here circa 1905, is one of the most fondly remembered. It closed in 1914 and was subdivided for development. Courtesy, Milwaukee County Historical Society

Laura Ross, pioneered in medicine and married General Erastus B. Wolcott, surgeon general of Wisconsin and a Civil War hero. Dr. Ross was active in the post-Civil War women's suffrage movement, serving as the first president of the newly reorganized Wisconsin Woman's Suffrage Association in 1882. Ross had kept the Wisconsin suffrage movement alive almost single-handedly, since its informal beginnings in 1869 when Susan B. Anthony and Elizabeth Cady Stanton came to the state to elicit support for women's suffrage.

Also active in the early cause of women's rights were Mathilde Fransziska Anneke, a German "48er," and Meta Berger, wife of Socialist leader Victor Berger. While economic issues remained of crucial importance to many immigrant women and their families, a growing call for legal rights and for the ballot began to pull even Milwaukee clubwomen into the suffrage movement. A 1900 convention of the General Federa-

she became the first Wisconsin woman to be appointed to a state position, as she led the Wisconsin Board of Charities and Reform in its efforts to change prison conditions, to help women without work or support, and to humanize many other institutions, asylums, and orphan's homes. Several other Milwaukee women worked for the establishment in 1894 of the city's first hospital to serve only children, today's Milwaukee Children's Hospital. Located at first on Brady Street in a small home rented for $30 a month, the hospital moved several times to new locations until it settled in 1922 at its long-term site at 17th Street and Wisconsin Avenue. Children's Hospital is now located at the Southeastern Wisconsin Regional Medical Center in Wauwatosa.

Mary Lynde also was instrumental in the organization of the nation's first chartered and joint-stock woman's club, the Women's Club of Wisconsin, in 1876. Meeting at the home of Mrs.

Alexander Mitchell, wife of the prominent banker, several Milwaukee women contacted Bostonian Julia Ward Howe for assistance in forming their own club. Howe agreed to come to Milwaukee and meet with a group of 30 prominent women, led by Mary Lynde and Mary Mortimer (president of Milwaukee Female College).

Announcing that they had heard "to weariness of the 'Sphere of Woman,'" club members vowed in their statement of purpose that they had grown "not only weary but rebellious" of such pronouncements and that they desired to be heard "as much as our brother man." With this call to social activism, the club began its long history of sponsoring educational lectures, working for social welfare causes, and of providing a haven for women of Milwaukee to meet and debate current issues. One such lecture series was given by Major Henry Roberts, on the topic of parliamentary procedure, which he was studying for his forthcoming book, *Roberts' Rules of Order*.

All of these diverse elements of the women's movement in Milwaukee worked for improved social institutions and for the betterment of women. The passage of laws raising the age of consent, limiting prostitution, and eventually granting women the right to vote, all came prior to 1920 as many Milwaukee women joined in league with Waukesha's Theodora W. Yeomans, president of the Wisconsin Woman's Suffrage Association. Women's hard work during the war years from 1917 to 1918 also furthered the cause of equal rights.

One unfortunate by-product of these decades at the turn of the century was the continuation of Northern racial attitudes and the persistence of the "color line" in social institutions and in economic opportunities. Just after the Civil War in 1866, when Negroes had political rights for the first time, Milwaukee listed only two dozen Negro males among its voting residents. The city's black population, which numbered only 996 in 1910, was represented in many of the trades and service occupations, but was not fully integrated into the life of the city or its institutions.

Typical of many Northern cities that looked south at the evils of racism, Milwaukee was often blind to the problems under its own roof in regard to prejudice. Even the Women's Club faced this color barrier at its 1900 convention, when the Pfister Hotel refused to admit a prominent Negro woman delegate from Boston, and the convention itself voted against seating any members from Negro women's clubs. As the twentieth century dawned, the nation as a whole became more aware of racial issues. The founding of the NAACP in the early twentieth century heightened the call for equity and social justice in the North as well as in the South. (The Milwaukee chapter of the NAACP was chartered in 1915.)

The number of Negro residents in Milwaukee more than doubled during the World War I years with the migration of many Southern Negroes seeking work in industry. However, their true integration into the city's social and economic life would be the story of many decades of continuing struggle long after the close of that war and a second world war as well.

The New Urban Landscape

As Milwaukee's population grew and diversified, the city continued to expand geographically outward. The development of more efficient electric street trolleys made this horizontal growth possible, as residents of "streetcar suburbs" could now commute to the heart of the city for work or for shopping.

In addition to the industrial suburbs of Bay View and Cudahy, residential suburbs developed before the turn of the century. One of the first and most prosperous, Wauwatosa, had its beginnings as Hart's Mills, a grist- and sawmill center in the 1830s. It was incorporated in 1892 as a separate village, and a city in 1897, on Milwaukee's western limits. Used as a country retreat by wealthy beer barons such as Fred Pabst, Wauwatosa was also the site of the county's first institutions, including a home for disabled soldiers on its southeast corner.

Similarly, both Shorewood and Whitefish Bay grew up around distinct commercial institutions, but quickly developed into residential suburbs during the streetcar era of the 1890s. Shorewood was first known in the 1870s as "Cementville" because of the riverside location of the Milwaukee Cement Company on its western perimeter. The area also had its own resort parks,

Clubhouses were important architectural projects in the nineteenth and early twentieth centuries and great care was taken to make them as distinctive as possible. The Turn Verein Milwaukee, or Turners as they are commonly known, were established in 1853 as a social organization devoted to the training of the mind and body. Turner Hall is the only one of the group's clubhouses to survive in Milwaukee; it is currently being restored. Courtesy, Milwaukee County Historical Society

Above right: Fortunately for us today, nineteenth-century photographers often climbed out onto ledges and hung over rooftops to document the city's changing skyline. This image looks northwest from the intersection of Milwaukee Street and East Wisconsin Avenue in the mid-1890s. All of the buildings shown along Wisconsin Avenue are gone today, but Milwaukee Street, to the right, still retains a majority of the structures from this time period. Courtesy, Milwaukee Public Library/Department of City Development-City of Milwaukee

including Lueddemann's, renamed Coney Island in 1900 shortly before it folded. In 1886 and 1898, respectively, the Whitefish Bay Railway Company and an electric trolley line were built to serve the resort clientele. As the settlement expanded eastward from the Milwaukee River toward the lakeshore, large homesites were developed for prosperous Milwaukeeans who wished to move just north of the city's boundary at Edgewood Avenue. In 1900 the village of East Milwaukee (renamed Shorewood in 1919) was officially incorporated.

Whitefish Bay developed around the resort built by the Philip Best Brewing Company at the foot of Henry Clay Street in 1888 to serve Milwaukeeans who wanted a convenient getaway spot not too far from the city. Renamed the Whitefish Bay Resort and purchased by the Pabst Company, the park became a popular summer picnic spot for city residents. With the development of Lake Drive and the building of a street rail line to the resort park, the settlement began to attract residential development. It was incorporated as the small village of Whitefish Bay in 1892, and grew very slowly thereafter. In 1895 it had a total population of only 464 year-round residents.

Horizontal growth was made possible by the expansion of electric street railways, but vertical growth in Milwaukee was the result of other important design and engineering innovations. Most significant was the breakthrough in the use of iron as a structural material in office buildings, brought to Milwaukee in 1860 when James Martin erected the Iron Block Building at the southeast corner of Wisconsin and Water streets. This building housed one of Milwaukee's earlier elevators, added in 1879, an invention that also made the vertical growth of cities more feasible.

The 1880s and 1890s witnessed a building boom in the city beyond all the dreams of earlier decades. Companies that supplied building materials, and the makers of fine furniture, enjoyed a booming business as homes and public edifices filled once-vacant city lots. The Bayley Structural Iron Company supplied ironwork for bridges and buildings, including fire escapes, and steel roof construction. The Steinman Lumber Company, established in 1872, sold boards of pine, hemlock, and hardwoods from its two lumberyards in

the city, one on Eighth Street and another at 35th and Chestnut. Tews Brothers, at Humboldt and Commerce, supplied a vast assortment of building supplies for many of the city's newly rising structures. Furniture companies, such as Paul Weise on Farwell Avenue, manufactured and sold fine furniture of all kinds, which it delivered in its elegant wagon with a two-horse team.

In addition to many private homes, other new buildings dotted the city's horizon by 1900. The Milwaukee Turners Club erected an elegant Italianate-style hall on North Fourth Street in 1883. One year later members of Milwaukee's business elite built their dark brick Milwaukee Club in a Queen Anne style on the corner of Wisconsin and North Jefferson streets. Across from the Milwaukee Club, the city's new hotel, the Pfister, was built in the Richardsonian Romanesque style in 1893 on the northwest corner of Jefferson and Wisconsin. Designed by Milwaukee architect Henry C. Koch, the Pfister featured limestone and brick with terra cotta ornamentation and became the city's finest hotel in the Victorian era. The slightly older Plankinton House Hotel, on the west side, still welcomed visitors to its more than 450 rooms, which opened onto a large central atrium.

An earlier hotel of equal elegance and prominence, the Newhall House, had been destroyed a decade earlier on January 10, 1883, in one of the city's worst fires. The inability of the city's fire department to fight the blaze resulted in the deaths of 43 people and the complete loss of the hotel. Aspiring newspaperman Lucius W. Nieman, in sleuthing for a story about the fire, wrote an exposé that blamed the hotel's owners for negligence (if not arson), and faulted the fire department for its tragically inadequate response. Nieman's paper, the *Milwaukee Journal*, sold so many copies of the story that it quickly rose to prominence as the rival of the long-established *Sentinel*.

Other disastrous fires had destroyed several of the city's older neighborhoods where dwellings of frame were tinderboxes waiting to ignite. An 1892 fire in the Third Ward destroyed almost 2,000 homes and changed the character of the neighborhood entirely, as the old Irish population was burned out and newly arriving Italian immigrants moved in and rebuilt the area. Erecting new structures of brick and stone to replace older wooden buildings became common in the 1880s and 1890s as the city literally grew up and reshaped itself in just 20 years.

Many public school facilities, primarily of red brick, had been built in the 1840s and 1850s during the city's first phase of school construction. However, high-style architecture prevailed in the erection of new grammar and high schools in the post-Civil War decades. Queen Anne, Italianate, and Romanesque schools of stature and craftsmanship were erected on Fourth Street, Hubbard, and elsewhere across Milwaukee before 1900. In the city's enthusiasm for education, schools were not to be cheaply built structures, but rather elegant temples of learning.

The private German-English Academy celebrated the completion of its cream city brick structure on North Broadway in 1891. A new building for the Milwaukee State Teachers' College on Wells Street between 18th and 19th streets opened its doors in 1885 to offer a specific normal training course for future teachers in the city's public schools. Similarly, the city's first Catholic college, Marquette University, which opened in 1881, selected Wisconsin Avenue for its first college building, Johnston Hall. It was completed in 1905 near the Church of the Gesu, an elegant Gothic cathedral constructed 11 years earlier.

Both the City and County of Milwaukee entered the building boom of these decades. The elegant new city hall, completed in 1895 in the Flemish Renaissance style by Henry C. Koch, dominated the old Market Square area where its predecessor had stood since 1860. The building's clock tower and spire became a symbol of the city's aspirations, just as its large granite arches at the southern entry symbolized openness to the city's people.

Even the many new fire stations built during these decades revealed a city that took pride in its civic structures. Engine House Number 3, for example, located at 100 West Virginia Street in Walker's Point, was a twin-towered facility of Italianate style, with two engine doors on either

The most devastating conflagration in Milwaukee's history occurred on October 28, 1892. In the district known as the Third Ward, south of East Wisconsin Avenue, the Union Oil Company on Water Street caught fire around 5:30 p.m. and before the night ended more than 300 buildings in a 15-block area burned. Rebuilding took place almost immediately and today the Third Ward is designated a historic district. Photo by J. Goeloner; courtesy, Milwaukee County Historical Society

People of all ages filled Market Square to celebrate the 50th anniversary of Wisconsin statehood in 1898. The new City Hall was draped in bunting and flags bedecked neighboring buildings during the festivities, which included demonstrations by firefighters and a carnival. Courtesy, Milwaukee County Historical Society

side. Milwaukee County erected monumental new buildings as well, including two new Classical revival-style courthouses—the first, on the old courthouse square bounded by Jefferson and Jackson, and the second on the west side on Kilbourn.

Commercial structures also reflected the city's aspirations in building style and elegance. The John Pritzlaff Hardware Company, founded in 1853, constructed its four-story central store and warehouse on North Third Street in 1874, using an Italianate style and cream city brick. Alexander Mitchell, a leading banker and railroad tycoon, commissioned architect Edward Townsend Mix to design the five-story Mitchell Bank Building in the Second Empire style of granite and limestone. Mix, one of the city's leading architects, also designed homes for many of Milwaukee's most prominent citizens, as well as the towering Victorian Gothic National Soldiers' Home for Civil War Veterans.

Milwaukee's insurance companies also built new high-style office structures along and near Wisconsin Avenue. The 1885 Northwestern Mutual Life Insurance Co. headquarters featured a central courtyard rising eight stories to a rooftop skylight. The Northwestern National Insurance Company building, several blocks west on Wisconsin Avenue, was designed in 1906 by architects Ferry and Clas, out of limestone in the Greek revival style with a French Renaissance influence. Similar in appearance was the Second Ward Savings Bank, built in 1913 on North Third Street; it was once called the "Brewers' Bank" since so many of the German brewery owners were officers of the bank.

Monuments to the city's rail commerce were also significant. New railroad depots symbolized both passenger service and Milwaukee's era of growing tourism. Most prominent among these depots was the Chicago and North Western Building at the east end of Wisconsin Avenue, erected in 1889. Its clock tower crowned the red brick and granite structure designed in a

Romanesque style. Less elegant, but equally large, was the Milwaukee Road's Union Depot, which was completed in 1866 between North Third and North Fourth streets along West Everett Street. By 1873 Milwaukee could boast that 10 major railroad lines, with 14 branches, served its population of 70,000 people. Even the TMER&L erected its Milwaukee Interurban Terminal Building in 1903 on West Michigan Avenue, with wide doors to which rail lines brought cars for passenger service. There were even extra rooms above the transit area that could be used as hotel accommodations in case the electricity of the transit cars failed.

General office buildings lifted the city's skyline, including the 12-story Railway Exchange Building, 1899; the 15-story skyscraper monument, the Wells Building, 1901; and the towering Pabst Building (later the Wisconsin National Bank) at the northwest corner of Water and Wisconsin, 1892. More unique was the elegant Pabst Theater on Wells Street, built in 1895 on the site where the old German Stadt Theater had entertained Milwaukeeans for many decades. Also a landmark was the Germania Building, erected in 1896 by George Brumder, banker and publisher of the prominent *Germania* newspaper. Located on West Wells Street, the building featured turrets that were said to resemble Prussian helmets.

The stately new federal building, erected in 1892 on Wisconsin Avenue of granite in the Romanesque style, joined the parade of commercial and civic structures on the city's main thoroughfare. In these decades prior to World War I, the entire face of both residential and commercial Milwaukee was changed. The last vestiges of the frontier city were gone, replaced by brick, stone, and granite structures that spoke of permanence and prosperity.

As the commercial center developed between 1890 and 1920, many large private homes dotted Milwaukee's landscaped boule-

Left: City Hall, shown here in 1918, is probably Milwaukee's best-loved building and the one that most embodies the city's Old World character. Courtesy, Milwaukee Public Library

Below: The unusual site dictated City Hall's trapezoidal shape, which is evident in this early view of the interior atrium space. Courtesy, Milwaukee County Historical Society

The rapid expansion of county government necessitated the replacement of the original Greek Revival-style courthouse with this more imposing domed structure in 1872. Leonard Schmidtner, the architect of St. Stanislaus Church, designed the building, which took its inspiration from the Renaissance architecture of Europe. When the county outgrew this facility a new courthouse was erected on 10th Street in 1930. Despite protests from local groups who wanted to see the building adapted as a museum and veterans' memorial, it was razed in 1939. The site is now part of Cathedral Square. This circa 1905 image looks northwest from Jefferson Street. Courtesy, Milwaukee County Historical Society

vards, reaching north along Lake Drive and Sherman Boulevard, and west along Wisconsin Avenue and Highland Boulevard. Designed by the city's most prominent architects, including Edward Townsend Mix, Henry Koch, Eugene Liebert, George Ferry, Alfred Clas, and Alexander Eschweiler & Sons, many of these grand dwellings survive today.

These elegant homes have become the city's visual hallmark of the era of the 1880s and 1890s, once labeled the "gilded age" for its abundant display of wealth. Frank Lloyd Wright designed the stately Bogk House on the east side in 1905, although it wasn't actually built until 1916. Most of Wright's architectural influence in the city came through the designs of his followers, the Prairie School architects. Wright's only entry into multifamily structures, four duplexes, still stand today on West Burnham Street.

Specifically planned residential communities such as Highland Park, begun in 1900, and the Hi-Mount subdivision in the Washington Park area, 1909-1920, on the city's western perimeter,

featured spacious homesites and landscaped boulevards. The coming of the first automobiles in the years before the war made these newer areas both accessible and desirable to residents who sought an escape from an increasingly crowded central city.

Other residential neighborhoods were more modest, but still of architectural interest today. Merrill Park, on St. Paul Avenue between North 33rd and North 35th streets, grew up between 1890 and 1910 as a workers' subdivision filled with single-family homes. Workers' cottages and modest frame houses also filled the area known as Piggsville, on the upper Menomonee River between North 39th and North 44th streets. Many German workers first settled in the area in the 1890s, and other immigrant groups followed before it was annexed to the city in 1925.

As the gilded age came to an end in the early twentieth century, both progressive politics and the onset of World War I changed the nature of American life. National politics brought office seekers to Milwaukee, particularly in the lively presidential campaign of 1912. Running on a third-party Progressive ticket that year, former President Teddy Roosevelt visited Milwaukee for a campaign speech, only to be met by a bullet from a would-be assassin. Luckily, the thick folds of the speech in his pocket stopped the bullet from penetrating his chest and he was able to deliver his talk before seeking medical attention for his surface wound.

Milwaukee Faces the Great War

However, it was the Democratic candidate, Woodrow Wilson, and not Roosevelt, who was elected to the presidency in 1912 and accelerated the country's march toward reform and ultimately toward world war. Wilson's brand of progressivism brought many political and economic reforms, similar to the ongoing Socialist efforts in Milwaukee itself. One change in particular slowed the growth of the massive personal fortunes accumulated during the gilded age. A new progressive income tax, passed in 1913, brought a percentage scale of taxation with a formula that taxed the wealthy at a higher rate than those of more modest income. This change, more than any other, marked the close of the gilded age and the new economic realities of the twentieth century.

More significant, however, than any progressive reforms were the many drastic changes brought to Milwaukee by the outbreak of the world war in Europe in 1914. The city's German flavor was forever altered by the growth of anti-German sentiment during the next four years, particularly after America entered the conflict in 1917. A tragic tide of hatred and anti-German bigotry swept the country, leaving once-proud German settlements, like Milwaukee, quivering in its wake.

The German language, once the most popular in all of the city's schools, became odious to many people who insisted that their children enroll in French classes instead. From a high point of 30,000 students enrolled in German in Milwaukee schools in 1916, the number fell to only 400 two years later. German merchants, who once had to post signs in their stores saying "English spoken here," found that speaking German was seen as a sign of disloyalty to the Allied cause. German words and phrases, which had entered

This view of Milwaukee from City Hall tower was created in 1898 by Gugler Lithographic Co. The Pabst Building, the Germania Building, the second County Courthouse, and the County Jail on Broadway are among the recognizable landmarks. Courtesy, Milwaukee County Historical Society

Situated on the lakefront, the Chicago and North Western Depot was built in the Romanesque style in 1889-1890. Like railways across the country, the Chicago and North Western experienced a dramatic decline in rail use following World War II and discontinued its line here in the 1960s. Despite valiant efforts to save the landmark depot, it was razed in the 1960s. O'Donnell Park has since been built on the site. Painting by Lynn Casper

into common usage, were changed. Sauerkraut was christened "Liberty cabbage" and the German-English Academy was renamed the Milwaukee Academy and later the Milwaukee University School.

Most difficult were the war's early years when Milwaukee's Socialists ardently opposed America's entry and many of the city's German citizens raised money for the homeland or sent aid to relatives fighting with the kaiser. With President Wilson's pronouncements of official neutrality, many German-Americans believed that their Old World loyalties could be safely expressed. "Germans for the Fatherland," a group formed at the outset of the war, and the national German-American Alliance recruited many thousands of members from Milwaukee, where more than 50 percent of the surnames were still German. Almost 175,000 Milwaukeeans, including many prominent German businessmen and their wives, made donations in 1916, which were sent to war victims in Austria and Germany. One year later such activities were viewed as treason when America's entry into the war made Germany an enemy power.

Even though such pro-German activities were canceled upon America's declaration of war, Milwaukee was seen by many as a turncoat city filled with lovers of the now-hated kaiser. The *Milwaukee Journal* went so far in trying to correct this impression that it stirred up anti-German sentiment to a fever pitch in the city, a campaign that earned the paper a Pulitzer Prize. This suspicion lingered despite the loyal efforts of most Milwaukeeans, German and non-German, to support the Allied cause after April 1917. Thousands of Milwaukee citizens signed up for overseas duty in the army or the Red Cross. Milwaukee's Home Council of Defense helped to plant victory gardens, organized book donations to soldiers in the trenches, and set up other programs of self-sacrifice to help those in the front lines. Milwaukee distinguished itself in all of these pro-war efforts, but the taint of suspicion still remained.

An organization known as the Loyalty Legion, formed in 1918, spearheaded a drive to find disloyal citizens in the city. Boycotts of the German press, persecution of known Socialists, pressure to buy Liberty Bonds, even demands to drop German music from concerts or to give theater performances only in English were examples of the group's efforts. This intense loyalist pressure forced further changes as the Germania Bank became the Commercial National Bank and the Deutscher Club was rechristened The Wisconsin Club. By June 1919 the teaching of German in Milwaukee's elementary schools was completely discontinued.

Armistice Day, November 11, 1918, brought jubilation across the country and in Milwaukee too. Parades, celebrations at taverns and corner bars, and the ringing of church bells filled the city. War's end brought a new world both in Europe and in the United States. However, the flavor of Milwaukee was changed forever by the hatred of the war years. While some of its ethnic richness remained and was revived six decades later in city festivals, the once-powerful Germanism of Milwaukee was gone for good.

The 1920s, after the war's end, brought automobiles, the radio age, the Americanization of mass culture, and the era of Prohibition to the city. Milwaukee entered the decade with courage, but was clearly shaken by the many drastic changes brought about in the previous few years. Not only was it suspect to toast anything German, it became illegal on July 1, 1919, to toast with alcohol at all. The attempt to "dry out" Milwaukee was an enormously challenging campaign in the exciting decade to come. The years from 1920 to the 1980s reshaped Milwaukee into a modern American city built upon its rich ethnic and industrial heritage.

Theodore Roosevelt made a return visit to Milwaukee in 1918 and was welcomed by a group that included his old friend General F.C. Winkler, shown here sporting a bowler hat and cane. On an earlier stop here in 1912 while campaigning for president, Roosevelt became the victim of an assassination attempt. He suffered a flesh wound but went on to deliver his speech before seeking medical attention. Courtesy, Milwaukee County Historical Society

News of the Armistice on November 11, 1918, brought about spontaneous celebrations throughout the country, including Milwaukee where residents thronged downtown streets to participate in the festivities. Courtesy, Milwaukee Public Library

LAWTONS
$18.50
CLOTHES
WARNER
RICHMANS
RIVERSIDE
GIMBELS
NO LEFT TURN

Chapter THREE

From the Roaring Twenties to Henry Maier

1920–1988

Not only did 1920 bring women the vote with passage of the Nineteenth Amendment at war's end, but it also ushered in the era of Prohibition through the passage of the Volstead Act and the Eighteenth Amendment. Many voices in Milwaukee and in Wisconsin had been raised in protest against a complete ban on alcohol, urging measures for moderation or temperance instead. However, the country seemed determined to go completely dry in July 1919, at least on paper, and Wisconsin had to try to follow.

Flashy signage, scurrying pedestrians, cars, trolleys, and the new rubber-tired buses all contributed to the liveliness of the urban streetscape, seen here at Third Street and Wisconsin Avenue in 1941. Courtesy, Milwaukee County Historical Society

Complying with a rule for the complete abstinence from any alcoholic consumption seemed a radical step in Milwaukee, where beer and spirits had flowed freely even when the French fur traders roamed the area in their colorful red hats. Drying out Milwaukee seemed to many observers to be an impossible task, and the next 14 years (until Prohibition was canceled by the Twenty-First Amendment in 1933) proved just how impractical it was.

At the dawn of the "dry era," Milwaukee had almost 2,000 saloons that

This unidentified officer posed for a photographer while confiscating an illegal still housed in somewhat decrepit surroundings. Scenes like this 1920s image were common during Prohibition. Old-time Milwaukeeans still delight in relating how their otherwise quiet and law-abiding neighbors were rousted in the middle of the night by police coming to confiscate their brewing apparatus. Others tell of transporting liquor in baby or doll carriages. Courtesy, Milwaukee County Historical Society

served its population of 457,000, a ratio of roughly one to every 225 people. Moreover, as the beer capital of America, the city faced double jeopardy. Milwaukee's nine breweries employed more than 6,000 people who would lose their jobs, in addition to the crisis facing its tavern owners and their employees. Furthermore, the tide of anti-Germanism that had helped to pass Prohibition left a lingering bitterness among the city's once-proud population. The happy brew that flowed throughout the city had been labeled not only undesirable, but also unpatriotic.

On the evening of June 30, 1919, the last night of legal consumption, Milwaukee conducted rituals of farewell. One group gathered to hold a funeral service for "John Barleycorn." A parade of mourning, led by the Elks' Club band, wound its way down Wisconsin Avenue to the Schlitz Palm Garden where midnight celebrants sang "How Dry I Am," followed by a solemn rendition of "Taps." Many of those present doubted whether the newly posted "closed" signs on the taverns would truly bring an end to alcohol consumption. As Robert W. Wells noted regarding Milwaukee's record on temperance: "The prohibition against selling liquor lasted for fourteen years, five months and five days. Milwaukee's willingness to abide by this new law lasted less than twenty-four hours."

Any law that does not have public support is virtually impossible to enforce. No matter how many federal agents were posted to Wisconsin, ice cream parlors secretly sold beer, calling it an ice cream soda because it had white froth on top. Saloons reopened their front doors, calling themselves drugstores or "soft drink parlors," and speakeasies opened their back doors all over town. Violators who were apprehended saw no shame in disobeying such an unpopular law. Producers of home brew became heroes and smuggling liquor from Canada down the shore of Lake Michigan became big business, particularly for mobsters who made great profits during the decade.

Even officials who were commissioned to catch violators often found it too tempting to accept an illegal drink, or a hefty bribe, themselves. Milwaukee set a national record for the number of its Prohibition officials who were sent to jail during the 1920s. Police often looked the other way as boxcars of "medicinal liquor" arrived in Milwaukee, supposedly to help its citizens fight some dreaded disease. Every doctor was given 400 allotments of liquor each year to help patients who had colds or respiratory ailments. According to one commentator, the number of Milwaukeeans afflicted with colds expanded so rapidly that every physician in town had a long waiting list of people who required "medicinal" treatment.

Most of the illegal beer consumed in Milwaukee, however, was of the home-brewed variety and the citizens' ingenuity extended to vast purchases of malt and hops from local outlets and the circulation of books and pamphlets with the best recipes. It was impossible for federal or local officials to police this vast production network, so the city settled in for the duration of the Prohibition period to enjoy a new approach to alcohol consumption.

The breweries themselves tried a variety of creative measures to stay in business. Schlitz produced candy and malt syrup, others made cheese, chewing gum, or "near beer." Even though the tight scrutiny of the breweries made illegal operations difficult, there were ways around the law. "Near beer" was produced by making beer and then taking the alcohol out. No one had an accurate record of how many barrels left the plant before the second stage of the process was completed.

Even these creative approaches did little to salvage the tremendous financial losses experienced by both breweries and taverns during the 1920s. By 1921 the value of the city's total production of beverages dropped to only $2.6 million, less than 10 percent of the $35-million value of only three years earlier. Fewer than 550 employees worked in the city's industry compared to more than 6,000 in 1918.

While the larger breweries such as Schlitz, Pabst, and Miller were able to weather the dry years, even with great losses, many of the city's smaller breweries closed their doors forever before Prohibition was repealed in 1933. When liquor was legalized by the Twenty-First Amendment, on April 7, 1933, only eight breweries reopened of the more than two dozen that had flourished in the state 15 years earlier.

As the day of reopening approached, an estimated 50,000 people gathered around the breweries. At 12:01 a.m. on April 7, 1933, whistles sounded throughout the city, from factories to tugboats, and the crowds danced as the American Legion Band at the Schlitz Brewery blared out "Happy Days Are Here Again." Not caught unprepared for legalization, Milwaukee's breweries had been allowed to prepare beer for shipment, and on April 7 more than 15 million bottles were ready to quench the "long thirst" of Americans across the country. By the end of 1933 recovery was well under way as total sales equaled $30 million, very close to the pre-1918 record. Seven years later, even during the midst of the Great Depression, the value had jumped 33 percent to $40 million. Brewing was once again one of the city's premier industries.

The Roaring Twenties

It wasn't just the rage of speakeasies, roadhouses, and illegal stills that gave the nickname "roaring" to the decade of the 1920s. Americans embraced new technology that made life faster, louder, and more entertaining. The postwar decade brought airplanes, radio, mass entertainment, and sports. It also ushered in the age of the automobile. Milwaukeeans, like the rest of the country, fell in love with cars. The first known appearance of an automobile had actually occurred in Milwaukee in

While at first glance this may look like an experimental lab with its banks of lights and menacing machines, it in fact is the interior of a successful south-side beauty salon, circa 1928. As hemlines crept upward and long tresses were shorn in favor of wavy bobs, salons became increasingly popular. They were generally staffed—if not owned—by women, providing employment opportunities. Courtesy, Kwasniewski Collection, UWM

The large arena in the Auditorium Building, adorned with a reflecting globe, was a fitting setting for the 1929 Auto Show. Once they became affordable for the average family, the public fell in love with automobiles—which provided a freedom and mobility unknown before. Courtesy, Milwaukee Public Library

1899. Seven years later advertisements for automobiles of many styles appeared in various newspapers, but cars were not a common sight. It wasn't until 1913, when cars were first in evidence on the city's streets in measurable numbers and thereafter, with the interruption of the war, that the volume multiplied dramatically.

By 1920 Henry Ford managed to produce enough Model Ts in his assembly line to provide affordable transportation to even middle- and working-class families. The price of a Model T in 1920 was only $600, less than a third what many cars had cost before the war in 1916. The sole stipulation, as Ford himself commented, was that a Model T could be ordered in any color, "as long as it was black!"

Twenty years later, despite the hard years of the 1930s, the number of cars in the city had increased by 45 percent. Many of Milwaukee's industries shared in the automobile boom as well. During World War I the Ford Motor Company built a production plant in Milwaukee that was later converted to the Delco Electronics Division. Formerly a fine tool machine manufacturer of bicycle and buggy frames, the A.O. Smith Company developed an automated assembly line for the production of automobile chassis in 1921, producing as many as 10,000 a day. Producers of batteries, such as Globe Union, flourished as did Briggs and Stratton, which made small gasoline engines and

An entire service industry grew up around the automobile. Oil companies developed signature trademark buildings and pump design. This Standard Oil station with its crown-topped pumps even had a uniformed attendant giving service with a smile as he fills the tank of a shiny new 1939 Ford. Courtesy, Hugh Swofford Collection automobile locks.

Another craze that accompanied the automobile age was the invention of the motorized bicycle, or the motorcycle. Milwaukee led the country in the production of these popular two-wheel vehicles after three Davidson brothers, William, Walter, and Arthur, joined with William Harley in 1903 to create the Harley-Davidson Company. By 1917, when the war began for the United States, the company was producing more than 18,000 motorcycles to be used each month for the war effort. As the soldiers returned home, the popularity of these vehicles soared and the 1920s witnessed a continuation of the motorcycle craze, along with the desire for automobiles. America was "on wheels" once and for all, and Milwaukee manufacturers were instrumental in many aspects of vehicle production.

In the matter of public safety and traffic control, Milwaukee led the way with the installation of traffic lights at key intersections as early as 1922 and traffic police in 1926. Using the latest technology of radio, the Milwaukee police were able to communicate with their patrol cars by radio in 1930 and even with policemen on motorcycle patrol by 1931.

Industries related to the automobile, from service garages to gas and oil production companies, also expanded during these years. Road building and gas station construction were added to the city's agenda throughout the decade. One popular design used in many gasoline stations across the city was the pagoda style with its red tile roof tilting upward at the gables. One of the city's most elaborate stations in this style was the Wadham Oil

South-siders Ig and John Urbanski were photographed clowning around with their new Harley-Davidson on Christmas Day, 1915. Young men in particular found the motorcycle appealing for its ease of maintenance, reasonable cost, and improved mobility over automobiles. Harley-Davidson promoted this enthusiasm not only through traditional advertising but by sponsoring clubs, rallies, races, and special publications, much as the firm does today. Courtesy, Kwasniewski Collection, UWM

Company's three-tiered pagoda filling station at 27th and Wisconsin, designed by Alexander C. Eshweiler, which also featured slanting pagoda roofs over each separate pump. Other gasoline companies tried to compete by using Egyptian pyramids, windmills, or lighthouse designs for their filling stations.

The automobile also contributed to the continuing horizontal spread of the city as the former "streetcar suburbs" grew in population and previously undeveloped areas were brought into the city even though they were not on the trolley lines. Between 1910 and 1940 Milwaukee's physical size doubled from 22 to 44 square miles through the annexation of surrounding residential communities. The city's total population of 457,147 in 1920, however, increased by its lowest percentage ever to 578,249 in 1930 and 587,472 in 1940. This slower population growth was due to many factors.

The primary cause was the ending of mass immigration. During the war itself, very few people were able to leave Europe and come to the United States. At war's end, Congress acted to establish a quota on all immigration and after 1924 only a few new immigrants arrived in Milwaukee each year. Another reason for the slower growth between 1930 and 1940 was the great economic crisis of the Depression. Americans could not afford to have large families while jobs were scarce.

While the birth rate declined during the

The Milwaukee corporate headquarters for Mack Truck was constructed in 1926 by Bentley Brothers, Inc., and designed by S. Scott Joy of Chicago. Mack Truck's heavy utility trucks were known for durability and symbolized by the Mack bulldog logo. After a period of occupancy by UPS from 1938 to the early 1970s, Milwaukee Mack has resumed tenancy of its old building. Courtesy, Bentley & Son

Tuberculosis was a scourge that affected the poorest and most densely populated sections of the city. Public health nurses instructed families on how to prevent the spread of TB. This 1920s display at the Auditorium Building was set up as part of the Tuberculosis Commission's educational mission. Courtesy, Milwaukee Public Library

1930s due to the Great Depression, Milwaukee's outstanding health care programs brought the city continued fame for having one of the nation's lowest death rates. The average age of death, which had been 38.7 years in 1920, rose markedly, even during hard times, to 58.4 in 1940. Even more spectacular was the fact that persons over the age of 5 had a life expectancy in the city of 60.8 years for men, and 64.6 for women, one of the highest in the nation.

This outstanding record of public health, long a tradition in Milwaukee, was furthered during the 1920s and 1930s by many Socialist programs. As early as 1919, the city hired a team of public health nurses to work with schools and families, and one year later, in 1920, it provided immunization against typhoid and diphtheria. The next year a dental clinic was established at low cost and special obstetrical nurses were trained to help in families where hospital costs for giving birth were still too steep. Four years later the city established a program whereby all-day nurseries for child care were to be inspected and regulated, particularly in terms of healthy conditions and disease control. By 1928 home hygiene nurses from the city were available to any resident and free home hygiene classes were offered.

The Depression saw no decrease in these city health services. In 1931 an eye, ear, nose, and throat clinic was established at public expense and the next year a series of community health centers were built in high-need areas around the city. In 1934 residents could receive subsidized scarlet fever inoculations, and the next year Milwaukee established tight controls over the sale of all produce within its city limits, as well as inspections of dishwashing methods in all public eating places. Before the end of the 1930s, as infantile paralysis became an increasing plague, the city established the first iron lung facility and continued its inspection efforts in the area of housing standards and industrial hygiene to halt the spread of polio and other diseases.

Airplanes and Commuter Rails

More exciting than the abundant automobiles in the postwar decade was the arrival of the air age. World War I had proved to be a testing ground for air technology and the next two decades saw airplane travel become increasingly accepted by the public. In 1927, the same year as the first talking motion pictures, Milwaukeeans, along with the rest of the world, thrilled to the first transatlantic flight of Charles A. Lindbergh. On May 20 Lindbergh's solo journey in his plane, *The Spirit of St. Louis*, from Newfoundland to Paris, ushered in a new age in flight. On a tour of the country following his success, Lindbergh visited Milwaukee and was treated to a tumultuous parade down Wisconsin Avenue on August 20, 1927. Milwaukeeans had witnessed other pioneering aviation feats that had not ended so happily.

One of the country's first passenger flights was orchestrated in 1919 by flight enthusiast Albert W. Lawson, who established the Lawson Air Line and carried a small group of 11 brave citizens in his two-engine, 26-passenger plane from the county airport at Curry Park to Chicago in 58 minutes. The rest of the trip was not as smooth, but the journey continued to Cleveland, Buffalo, New York City, and finally Washington, D.C. In the capital, Lawson persuaded several senators and cabinet members to take a short trip to Pennsylvania before he finally headed home to Milwaukee. The trip lasted 78 days in all (due to many delays and mechanical failures) and covered more than 3,000 miles.

Lawson's experimental flight put Milwaukee on the map as a pioneering city and the love affair of Wisconsinites with experimental aircraft has continued ever since. After this first flight, Lawson developed an even larger passenger plane prototype, with bunks and showers, but it crashed on its first flight and Lawson was forced out of business. More successful, for a time, was entrepreneur Thomas F. Hamilton, who founded the Hamilton Aero Manufacturing Company and created his own test landing strip on South Howell Avenue, near Layton. Hamilton airplanes, two-seaters with a single motor, were popular during the mid-1920s, until larger aviation production companies forced Hamilton to close in 1930.

By that time, his private airstrip had become the home of the new municipal airport for the city, purchased in 1926 by the Milwaukee County Park Commission, today's General

Milwaukee's contribution to the fledgling aviation industry included the experimental passenger planes of Albert W. Lawson and the single-engine planes of Thomas F. Hamilton (bottom). More significant was Milwaukee's General William "Billy" Mitchell (below), whose outspoken advocacy of air power for the military led to his court-martial. Loyal supporters saw him proved right in World War II. Both photos courtesy, Milwaukee County Historical Society

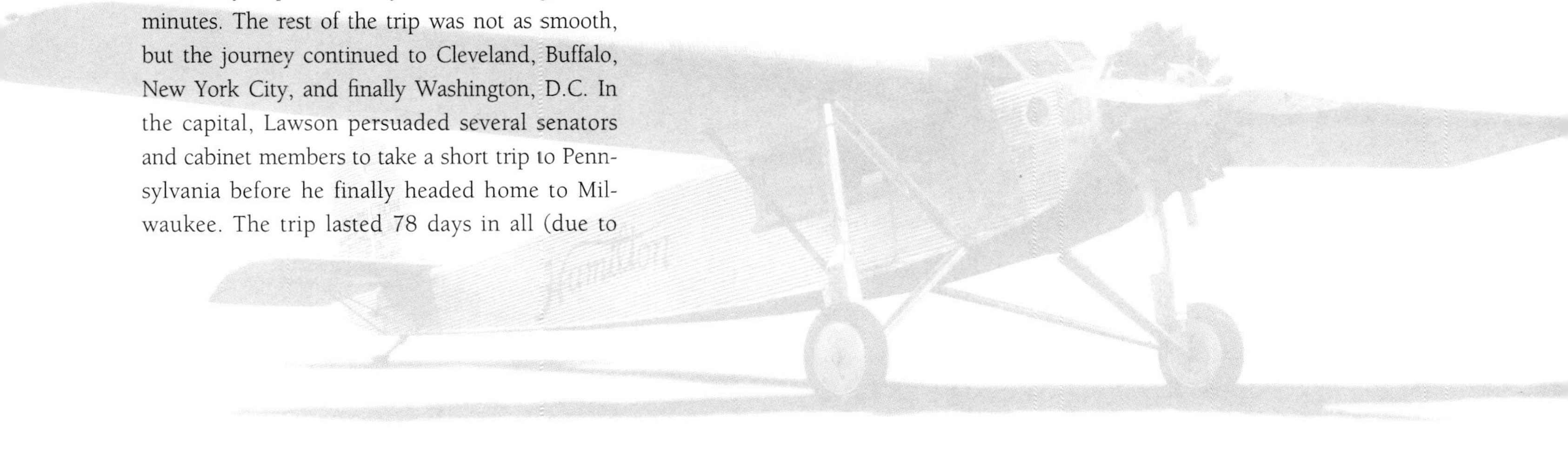

Mitchell Field (officially Milwaukee International Airport). Even air traffic controls were established very early in the city by 1928.

The pioneering commercial airline, Northwest Airways, began passenger service to Milwaukee on July 5, 1927, carrying passengers to Chicago and later to both coasts. In December 1928 passengers could fly to Green Bay from Milwaukee for a $15 fare and soon Northwest flew daily trips to Minneapolis and even Seattle.

Another Milwaukeean who had fallen in love with airplanes was William Mitchell, grandson of Alexander Mitchell whose Wisconsin Marine and Fire Insurance Company had fueled much of the city's early growth. During World War I "Billy" Mitchell was named to lead the army's aviation section and he became an astute observer of the role of air power in military supremacy. However, his ardent advocacy of air power, and his demonstration in 1921 of how easily a bomber plane could destroy even a large warship, proved to be too far ahead of his time. He was ultimately court-martialed for overt criticism of his superiors, and resigned his military commission. Continuing his call for the development of an American air force, Mitchell remained a hero to Milwaukeeans who saw his theories vindicated at Pearl Harbor in 1941, five years after his death in 1936.

Bowling was tremendously popular in the 1930s and virtually every Milwaukee church and place of business had a team; women even had their own leagues. Bowling alleys could be found in such fashionable locations as the lower level of the Plankinton Arcade as well as scattered throughout the neighborhoods in local taverns. Courtesy, Kwasniewski Collection, UWM

Although Milwaukee failed to become an industrial center for aviation factories, the spirit of experimental flight remained strong in the city and in Wisconsin. Pioneer aviators the Crites brothers (Dean and Daryl) turned a Waukesha farm field into the area's premier landing strip for small planes of all kinds, and barnstormers made both Curry Park and other small airstrips into landing sites for their popular aerial shows.

Along with highway building, street paving, and airport construction, the expanding city needed even better facilities for mass transit. The interurban rail line continued to serve Milwaukee and its western suburbs during the 1920s and 1930s. A new Northshore commuter rail line was established before World War II to serve Milwaukee citizens who commuted south to Chicago or to villages along the way.

Equally as popular as baseball or football was the sport of bowling, which had come to Milwaukee even before the twentieth century when it was played outdoors at beer gardens.

The Age of Entertainments

Prosperity and an increase in leisure time brought new forms of entertainment to the American public during the 1920s. Radios became standard equipment in many homes, bringing comedy, sports, and music shows. Milwaukee's first radio station, WTMJ, licensed in 1927, developed from the Marquette University station begun five years earlier. Local broadcasts included music of the bands from the roof of the Wisconsin Hotel, as well as shows from the Wisconsin Theatre.

Broadcasts occurred only when there was material to fill the time, so on some nights the radios were silent. The first national hookup, through what became NBC, also came to Milwaukee in January 1927, bringing news and sports broadcasts from around the country and around the world. Listeners could hear the static-filled progress reports four months later, as Lindbergh's flight was broadcast into many American living rooms. By 1935 fully 95 percent of the city's households had a radio, and the broadcast of presidential "fireside chats" by Franklin D. Roosevelt reached into almost every home.

The increased popularity of professional sports resulted from radio broadcasts, as the 1920s witnessed the phenomenon of mass audiences through the air waves. Horse races, featuring steeds such as Man of War, fascinated listeners, as did Gertrude Ederle's famous swim across the English Channel in 1926. Milwaukee's baseball team, the Brewers, continued to attract a loyal following, but their games were played in the Minor Leagues, and radio was rapidly contributing to the star quality of key Major League players such as Babe Ruth and Ty Cobb.

It wasn't until 1953 that Milwaukee finally got its own Major League team, the Milwaukee Braves, formerly the Boston Braves. One commentator noted that on the day the announcement was made more than 10,000 people came to the stadium just to celebrate even though there was no game scheduled. Presumably they sat there dreaming of the innings to come.

Professional football came to Milwaukee during the 1930s, as the state's rugged team, the Green Bay Packers, began to play several games each season in the city to try to stay solvent. Soon Packer football fans equaled the number of baseball fans and the city's love affair with the green and gold jerseys has continued ever since.

Equally as popular as baseball or football was the sport of bowling, which had come to Milwaukee even before the twentieth century when it was played outdoors at beer gardens. Moving indoors to large bowling halls, it continued its association with good fellowship and beer. In 1905 the national tournament of the American Bowling Congress was held in Milwaukee with a prize purse of more than $11,000. The next year the headquarters of the American Bowling Congress was moved to Milwaukee as a key center of bowling in the country.

Movies, too, swept the country during the 1920s and subsequent decades. In Milwaukee, movie palaces built during the 1920s included the lavish Oriental Theatre on the east side, and the Riverside, Wisconsin, and Palace theaters in the downtown area. Favorite films of Milwaukeeans were *The Sheik* with Rudolph Valentino, *It* featuring Clara Bow, and Walt Disney's *Mickey Mouse*. So popular did movies become in the city, as well as across the nation, that by 1940 Milwaukee could boast of eight large downtown movie

Movie going in the 1920s was a novel adventure to be savored, and some theater owners changed their lobby fixtures with each new performance so that patrons could experience for themselves the setting of the feature they were about to see. The Alhambra Theatre, seen here in April 1920, was transformed into the exotic and foreign world of The Virgin of Stamboul, *starring Priscilla Dean. Courtesy, Milwaukee County Historical Society*

The stepped-back upper stories of the Wisconsin Gas building are clearly visible in the steel framing shown in this circa 1930 photo. The 22-story Art Deco-style structure was built as the headquarters for the firm, the state's oldest utility, and remains its home office today. An impressive flame-shaped light installed on the roof in the 1950s changes color to signal changes in the weather and has made the building one of the most popular on the city's skyline. Courtesy, Milwaukee County Historical Society

palaces, and more than 60 smaller theaters in the surrounding areas. In 1927 the Garden Theatre made history with the showing of the first sound film in the city, *When A Man Loves*, on September 3, 1927.

Home-Grown Clubs and Culture

Even though electronic forms of entertainment, from radio to movies, grew in popularity during the 1920s and 1930s, Milwaukeeans continued to cherish their own musical clubs and societies. The Milwaukee Civic Orchestra, founded in 1921, played for several seasons, to be succeeded by the Milwaukee Philharmonic Orchestra during the 1930s. The tradition of outdoor concerts continued in popularity with the erection in 1938 of the Emil Blatz Temple of Music in Washington Park. Outdoor festivals with fireworks, small theatrical productions, and band music also became a feature of summers in the city. However, the fate of professional theater was less successful. Even the "little theater movement," established in Milwaukee in 1909 with Laura Sherry's Wisconsin Players, did not last through the 1920s. Opera continued to be overshadowed by Milwaukee's proximity to Chicago and its grand Lyric Opera Company.

Club membership grew also with the prosperity of the 1920s. In 1921 the University Club of Milwaukee completed its Georgian-style brick building on Wells Street near the lake bluff. The stately structure was designed by nationally renowned architect John Russell Pope (who also designed the Jefferson Memorial and the National Gallery of Art in Washington, D.C.). The Milwaukee Country Club moved north to more spacious green acres in River Hills in 1929, leaving behind its original six-hole course and rambling Greek-revival home in Shorewood where it had been housed since its beginning in 1895.

The most exotic fraternal club building in the city, the Tripoli Temple, was completed in 1928 at 30th Street and West Wisconsin Avenue, designed by Milwaukee architects Clas, Sheperd, and Clas. The temple was built in the mosque style of Indian and Saracenic architecture, inspired by the Taj Mahal of India. One of Milwaukee's most expensive private structures at the time, the building cost one million dollars and featured sculpted stone camels, a large onion-shaped dome, and four minarets.

One of the city's most remarkable new office towers was the Art Deco-style Wisconsin Gas Company headquarters, designed by architects Eschweiler and Eschweiler in 1929. As the site on Wisconsin Avenue was being prepared and excavated, an old hotel had to be wrecked and the contractors encountered an unusual problem. The Lincoln Hotel's tavern and liquor room annex had been padlocked during Prohibition by order of a federal judge. Permission to unlock the structure and relocate its contents so that it could be demolished took so long that the contractors needed to improvise. To avoid further delay, they simply wrecked the rest of the hotel, propped the padlocked structure up on large stakes, and proceeded to excavate the entire site for the basement while the annex hovered in mid-air above them. Finally, just as the foundation had to be laid, the federal judge lifted the order, and the annex could be demolished at last. Where its supply of liquor went is unrecorded, but perhaps members of the company and construction crew used it to celebrate.

The hallmarks of prosperity, from onion domes to high-rise office buildings, continued to raise the city's skyline even when the prosperity itself had faded. After the terrible stock market crash of 1929 and the Depression that followed, few buildings were constructed in Milwaukee unless they were subsidized by some sort of public funding. School construction led the way during the early 1930s, as a bond issue for $11 million paved the way for the construction of 27 new elementary, junior high, high, and vocational schools in the city.

Milwaukee's schoolchildren were just as ethnically diverse as ever, but a lower percentage were foreign born. Rather than the European immigrant arrivals of previous decades, many children new to the local schools came from southern states as thousands of Negro citizens flocked northward during World War I seeking jobs. Milwaukee's black population, which had numbered fewer than 1,000 in 1910, grew to twice that size 10 years later and to eight times that number, or 8,821, by 1939. The Milwaukee black community enjoyed the establishment of its own Urban League Charter in 1919 and the publication of its own community newspaper, *The Wisconsin Enterprise-Blade*, founded in 1916. Similarly, a newly arriving Hispanic population in the early 1920s increased in number as industries actively recruited workers throughout the decade. To celebrate the richness of its ethnic heritage, Milwaukee's International Institute was established in 1923, sponsoring folk events. Its annual Folk Fair continues to this day.

Good Government and Good Business

Milwaukee's politics were as colorful as the rest of life in the uproarious 1920s and 1930s. Mayor Daniel Webster Hoan carried the mantle of Socialist leadership alone after Victor Berger was struck and killed by a Milwaukee streetcar in 1929. Holding to the motto of clean government, the so-called "sewer Socialism," Hoan reminded voters, including the newly enfranchised women, that the city's great gains in honesty, civic beautification, and health were due to Socialist leadership. Hoan's popularity was due to the public faith in his honesty and to the recognition that Milwaukee was "a city that works." Hoan defeated ex-Mayor David Rose in 1924, even though Rose promised voters to "bring a little more life" to the city.

A well-run police force free of outside influence was an important part of Mayor Daniel Hoan's social reforms. The patronage system in effect earlier led to chaos and corruption as police chief and officers were hired and fired with each new change in administration. Jacob Laubenheimer, Hoan's new chief of police (who would serve from 1921 to 1936), is shown standing at right; Mayor Hoan is standing second from right. Standing at left are Laubenheimer's father and Secretary Foley. Members of the Police Commission are seated in front. Courtesy, Milwaukee County Historical Society

With graft and corruption a problem of the past and with Milwaukee basking in its national reputation as an honest and well-run city, Hoan experienced many other challenges to his leadership in the years before 1940, but he outpaced them all, making Milwaukee the premier Socialist city in the nation. The *Milwaukee Journal* wrote of him: "The city has rather got into the habit of reelecting him." Known for his great integrity, Hoan worked valiantly to pull the city through the many changes of the 1920s and the trials of the 1930s.

During the 1920s, when mobsters turned many city governments into tools for their control, Hoan and many Milwaukee leaders remained scrupulously honest. As he noted in an early speech, "Ours is a city of liberal and progressive-minded people and it behooves us to administer the affairs of government in the spirit of her citizenship." Avoiding outright municipal ownership of major utilities, Hoan's brand of socialism led to the city's purchasing of several concerns, such as a limestone quarry and a repair shop, which lowered the price of street paving by 50 percent. Similarly, ownership of a streetlighting system reduced the cost of city lights by almost one-half.

Hoan advocated good business, both for

The onset of the Great Depression took its toll on the citizens and businesses of Milwaukee. This scene outside the Klitsner Brothers store at Lincoln Avenue and South 13th Street was one repeated all over the city as layoffs resulted in reduced consumer spending—especially of nonessential goods like furniture, expensive clothing, and automobiles. Crowds lined up to take advantage of bargains, however. Winter coats may have been the draw here as the sale took place on a cold February 2, 1932. Courtesy, Kwasniewski Collection, UWM

honest private enterprises and for the city as a whole. He worked tirelessly for programs such as harbor improvement to help Milwaukee commerce, and he was the first to enroll Milwaukee in an active plan to support a St. Lawrence Seaway. This latter dream did not become a reality in the city until July 1959, when Milwaukee staged a great celebration to hail the new era. According to one commentator, England's Queen Elizabeth had agreed to land in Chicago, and therefore Milwaukeeans were only able to wave at the yacht *Britannia* as it sailed close to shore. However, the military exhibition of marines landing on McKinley Beach, despite foul-ups with the crowd that at first prevented the landing, made the festivities a sufficient success.

Hoan's government was similarly farsighted in its attempts to assist Milwaukee citizens during the hard times of the 1930s. Even before Roosevelt's New Deal brought relief money to the region, Hoan had established a successful program for cooperative housing, called the Garden Homes project, which provided both work and housing at significant savings. This first effort was followed by a model partnership program in 1937, called Parklawn, which used federal dollars through the Public Works Administration to create homes and jobs in a housing project on the city's northwest side.

A Socialist City in Depression and War

With the onset of the national Depression, many believed that the diversity of Milwaukee's industrial base would protect the city's economy. However, by 1932-1933, the facts showed otherwise. The number of wage earners declined that year by 75 percent and less than 50 percent of the property taxes could be collected. A building slump of major proportions also accompanied the shattering effect upon heavy industry. Scarcely 12 percent of the pre-Depression construction occurred during the Depression years.

The rest of the decade witnessed an uneven record of vicissitudes, as the legalization of alcohol lifted the city's economy temporarily and New Deal programs brought some public works jobs and construction to the unemployed. By 1939 the total output of the city's economy was only $437 million, slightly more than half that of 1929. Recovery was slow and painful.

By 1930 more than 140,000 city residents—approximately 20 percent of the total population—needed aid. Although most official relief efforts came through county government, the city government also responded to the increased need for soup kitchens and relief. A Committee on the Homeless was established in 1931 and Mayor Hoan allowed a vacant armory to be used for a soup kitchen and relief center for the thousands of jobless and homeless. In trying to hire the jobless, Hoan used every device at his disposal, once bringing more than 12,000 men to day "pick-and-shovel" work at parks and playgrounds for 60 cents an hour.

Hoan was also active as a lobbyist on the federal level, organizing the United States Conference of Mayors to put pressure on Congress for urban relief. Gradually the burden of public relief was switched from city and county to federal programs as Roosevelt's New Deal brought vast sums to cities across the country. In Milwaukee, the public relief rolls of the county's budget dropped steadily throughout the 1930s, as federal assistance increased from $2 million in 1935 to $18 million between 1935 and 1936 alone. Three years later the outbreak of the war in Europe brought an upturn in orders for Milwaukee's heavy industries and jobs were again available. The city's dependence on a limited number of industries remained a problem, however. Even in 1940, just one year before the bombing of Pearl Harbor, almost 50 percent of the city's workers were engaged in the manufacture of iron and steel products.

One of the more unique innovations of the Depression era and of New Deal policy was the program to create "greenbelt" cities. Milwaukee was chosen as one of three sites for the experiment and a whole new town was planned and constructed on its southwestern perimeter, the present city of Greendale. By 1938 more than 500 homes were ready for families who were interviewed for occupancy according to both need and their readiness to contribute to the community in areas such as joining a community band. The community featured a New England-style village green at its center, and a winding system of bike and pedestrian paths meant that children crossed a minimum of streets to walk to school. While initially greeted with enthusiasm, the experiment ultimately was returned to private hands, the homes were sold, and the city government became as independent as other Milwaukee suburbs.

Federal programs, which benefited Milwaukee citizens during the Depression years, included sewer construction and repair, street paving, and the creation of new parks and playgrounds. Between 1934 and 1937 all of the city's greenways and parks were merged into a single unified County Park System for more efficient planning

As part of President Roosevelt's "Second New Deal," in which he called upon Congress to redress some of the judicial reversals of his earlier programs, the National Labor Relations Act of 1935 was passed and restored to workers the right to bargain collectively. With their right to strike protected, many labor groups chose to lobby for better wages and conditions. Here members of CIO Local 99 picket the Majestic Restaurant on Water Street not far from City Hall. Courtesy, Hugh Swofford Collection

With his good looks, infectious smile, and beautiful voice, young Carl Zeidler unseated veteran Daniel Hoan, whose steady hand and scrupulous honesty had led Milwaukee through rough times. Mayor Zeidler is seen here presenting a doll to an unidentified young girl in 1940, the year of his victory. While his term of office was too brief to assess critically, many observers believed Zeidler could have gone on to Congress or a governorship had he not died at sea in 1942. Courtesy, Milwaukee Public Library

and management. Other New Deal programs, such as the Civilian Conservation Corps and the Works Progress Administration, brought the construction of the city's new Pulaski High School, an entirely new water filtration plant, and also a community-based theater project.

A significant aspect of Hoan's leadership was his ability to bring a calm voice to bitter disputes, even during many crises of the Depression. In 1934 alone, there were more than 100 separate strikes in the city and fears of a workers' rebellion grew. Empowered by the city council to work against open destruction, Hoan acted to shut down plants where violence was threatened.

Hoan's voice for moderation and calm was valuable throughout labor difficulties. The passage of the federal Wagner Act in 1935 further fortified labor's right to organize and strike and the mayor had to cope with keeping the peace in the city even during one week when more than 27,000 workers were out on strike. Only the slurs of a renewed "red scare," which labeled Hoan a Communist, and the power of a new nonpartisan coalition brought his 24-year tenure as mayor to an end in 1940.

The young and charismatic city attorney, Carl Zeidler, who replaced Hoan as mayor in 1940, inherited one of the nation's best-run cities. During his predecessor's years, Milwaukee had not only been awarded the gold ribbon first prizes for being the nation's healthiest and safest city, it was also fiscally sound. Known for his good looks and great singing voice, Zeidler was supported by many businessmen who hoped for lower taxes and fewer Socialist programs. His personal popularity was enhanced by the fact that he sang regularly on city radio programs and was a member of more than 25 clubs. His victory brought an end to the long Socialist era, and the beginning of a new style in politics in the 1940s.

All of Milwaukee's heavy industries geared up for the war effort to make jeeps, explosives, bomb casings, parts for tanks, and other war materials.

As the country's youngest mayor at age 42 in 1940, Carl Zeidler brought a new flair to Milwaukee politics. He also succeeded in attracting the national convention of World War I veterans to the city in September 1941, with his rendition of "God Bless America." The convention sang its way through the city that autumn with impromptu street choruses, piano sing-a-longs on Wisconsin Avenue, and a record-length parade of 12 hours. The decade of the 1940s dawned with optimism at home but the somber reality of another war in Europe and many unanswered questions about this country's potential involvement.

Those questions were answered only two months later at Pearl Harbor on December 7, 1941. Unlike the war declaration in 1917, Pearl Harbor and America's entry into World War II found Milwaukee a united city. A few fringe groups, such as the "Volksbund," had supported Hitler and the Nazis before Pearl Harbor, even establishing a small training camp called Camp Hindenburg on the Milwaukee River near Grafton. However, the "day of infamy" ended such overt support and Milwaukee Germans were determined not to suffer from questions of disloyalty again.

Only four months after Pearl Harbor, Milwaukee's new mayor left his post and joined the navy as a commissioned lieutenant. By the end of 1942, less than 12 months later, Carl Zeidler and the ship on which he served went down at sea, presumably torpedoed by a German submarine. Milwaukee lost its popular young mayor and his youthful baritone voice full of hope and enthusiasm. An acting mayor, John L. Bohn, managed the city throughout the war and was even elected to a term in his own right in 1944, defeating Carl Zeidler's brother, Frank.

The war brought many sacrifices to Milwaukee citizens as had the first war, but it did not result in the internal turmoil of anti-German persecution. Milwaukeeans loyally bought war bonds, followed rationing guidelines, planted Victory Gardens, and signed up to serve in record numbers. More than 90 acres of Milwaukee parks were set aside for Victory Gardens. Gas rationing meant that even horse-drawn vehicles were once again seen on city streets and the use of the interurban mass transit lines skyrocketed. The Milwaukee County Transit Company, which had converted to buses after the streetcar strike of 1934, had to rely upon the electric trolleys during the period of gas rationing.

All of Milwaukee's heavy industries geared up for the war effort to make jeeps, explosives, bomb casings, parts for tanks, and other war materials. By 1942 Cutler-Hammer was making controls for naval ships, increasing its production by 400 percent in the next year alone. Airplanes too used these motor controls, including the notoriously successful B-29 models built by The Boeing Aircraft Company of Seattle. More than 70 local manufacturing companies were involved in making parts for the atomic bomb that helped to end the war almost four years after Pearl Harbor.

Many women entered the service of their country, signing up as part of the navy (WAVES) or army (WACS). Women also enlisted in the corps of industrial workers who built war materials. Fully 29 percent of Milwaukee's work force was women in 1940 and the number grew to almost twice that figure by war's end. Many women also helped through work in the USO, which provided entertainment and many other services to soldiers stationed nearby. Milwaukee County Parks joined the effort by making all park facilities available to the USO in its entertainment efforts.

The sailors who were stationed at the Great Lakes training base in northern Illinois came by bus to Milwaukee for relief from their duties. The city outdid itself in expressing its gratitude to the soldiers and in showing its loyalty. The Wisconsin Federation of German-American Societies sponsored an anti-Nazi rally at the Auditorium on Kilbourn Avenue and many thousands of Milwaukee Germans attended. The city was united as it had not been in the earlier war.

Part of the Milwaukee airport, renamed

General Douglas MacArthur came from an illustrious family with ties to Milwaukee. He was in charge of the Pacific Campaign in World War II and was placed in command of United Nations troops during the Korean Conflict. MacArthur was removed from his command by President Harry Truman in 1951 when he openly criticized the president's policies toward Communism in Asia. Despite his dismissal, MacArthur returned to the states and made a triumphal tour of cities across the nation, including Milwaukee, where he was welcomed at the County Courthouse. Courtesy, Lyle Oberwise Photography Archive

General Mitchell Field in 1941, was used by the U.S. Army Air Force to train pilots for Air Transport Command in C-47 aircraft. Other parts of the airport were used by the civil defense force, which also trained at Waukesha's airport and throughout Milwaukee County. Close to the airport, a prisoner-of-war camp was opened in 1944. It housed up to 1,000 captured German soldiers, who were put to work there making batteries. Other German prisoner camps were also established throughout the area, and in Waukesha County. Many of the prisoners were relieved to be in an area where people spoke their language. Several relocated to make Milwaukee their permanent home at war's end.

War's end in Europe in May 1945, and in Japan in August, brought victory parades and the celebration of local heroes. One famous Milwaukeean, General Douglas MacArthur, was claimed by the city as a local hero even though he chose to relocate to New York as his permanent home. Returning veterans were met with jubilant welcomes at the two stately train stations as Milwaukeeans looked forward to a return of peacetime and prosperity.

Almost 3,000 Milwaukee County citizens had given their lives in the war. To commemorate the sacrifice of its servicemen and -women, a war memorial was planned for the lakefront. After much debate about its form, the decision was made to construct a combined veterans' center, public center, and art museum. Designed by architect Eero Saarinen, the Milwaukee War Memorial and Art Museum was completed in 1957 at the eastern end of the downtown area, overlooking Lake Michigan. A separate fund-raising campaign for a music hall and theater building began the next year and was finally completed in 1969 as the current Marcus Center for the Performing Arts in the heart of downtown east of the Milwaukee River.

The Milwaukee Repertory Theatre, founded in 1954, had given a variety of dramas and musical comedies from its home base on Oakland Avenue at the Fred Miller Theatre. In 1969 it welcomed the construction of a permanent new home and moved into its quarters at the completed Performing Arts Center (now the Marcus Center for the Performing Arts). One of the city's oldest cultural groups, the Florentine Opera, was established in 1933 as the Italian Opera Chorus. The group changed its name during the war years, and moved into the "PAC" in 1969. Another long-awaited cultural institution, the Milwaukee Symphony Orchestra, established in 1959, also became part of the new PAC. Its concerts in the spacious Uihlein Hall continued the city's strong musical traditions dating back more than eight decades.

Postwar Politics

The turbulence of the 1950s brought fear of the

One of the more pleasurable events enjoyed by war-weary residents after the war was Milwaukee's year-long celebration of the 100th anniversary of its incorporation on January 31, 1846. Various events were scheduled as Milwaukeeans took a long nostalgic look at their past before throwing themselves into the work of "modernizing" the city. Courtesy, Lyle Oberwise Photography Archive

WTMJ, the city's pioneer television station, had news photographers on the scene ready to chronicle the events of the day since the late 1940s. The heavy cameras, requiring tripods and a stationary location, did not allow for the spontaneity we expect of today's news footage. The camera here is poised to record a Men's Club event in August 1969. Courtesy, Lyle Oberwise Photography Archive

Cold War to every American city, where civil defense routes had to be posted to alert citizens in case of an atomic attack. Milwaukeeans, like other Americans, saw signs denoting public fallout shelters, and many families built their own private shelters. Other tensions during the decade brought Milwaukee and Wisconsin to the forefront as Senator Joseph McCarthy, once a student at Marquette University, began his career of Communist witch hunting in late 1950. Many Wisconsinites supported the cries of McCarthyism against suspected traitors, but the *Milwaukee Journal* took an anti-McCarthy stance in its issue of September 10, 1952, urging the election of his opponent and the end of his red-baiting terrorism. It took two more years before the United States Senate officially repudiated McCarthy and ended his enormous power through censure. By that time the televised "Army-McCarthy Hearings," aired in May 1954, had seriously eroded the senator's hold over the public imagination.

The postwar years brought the new technology of television into American homes. In 1947 Milwaukee's first licensed station, WTMJ-TV, went on the air December 3. Many television sets were in taverns or youth centers, but within the next decade most homes had sets as well. Milwaukeeans could watch news reports of the Cold War, the Berlin Airlift of 1948, or the conflict in Korea in 1950-1953. The hero of that war, General Douglas MacArthur, finally paid a visit to the city where his ancestors had lived for three generations. The parade in April 1951 took place after he was fired by President Truman but before he "faded away." Milwaukeeans turned out in record numbers for a view of MacArthur's motorcade as it wound down Wisconsin Avenue for a rally at Marquette Stadium.

Politics in the postwar era also took center stage. In 1948 Carl Zeidler's younger brother defeated John Bohn in the mayoral race. Frank Zeidler served as Milwaukee's mayor throughout the next decade until the election of 1960, contin-

With the U.S. entry into World War II, passenger car production ceased between 1942 and 1945. Since most vehicles in the country were at least 10 years old by the war's end, the public went into a buying frenzy from 1947 to 1950, when cars like these were targeted for the average middle-class family. This 1948 image was taken at the old Fruit Boat Market located at the south end of the Water Street bridge. Courtesy, Lyle Oberwise Photography Archive

The current debate over the new Brewers stadium has many of the same arguments over location that were put forth in the decades before the present ball field was built. County Stadium was intended for the Minor League Milwaukee Brewers but the Boston Braves relocated here in 1953. The Braves moved to Atlanta in 1965 and the Seattle Pilots moved here to become the Milwaukee Brewers in 1970. Courtesy, Lyle Oberwise Photography Archive

The Housing Authority of the City of Milwaukee was established in 1944 to eliminate slum areas and develop subsidized housing for the poor. Hillside Terrace, proposed in 1947 and opened in December 1948, was located in the most blighted section of the city, a two-block site bordered by Sixth, Seventh, Galena, and Vliet streets. Courtesy, Lyle Oberwise Photography Archive

uing the city's record of long-tenured mayors and able leadership. One of the most significant aspects of the Zeidler years was his emphasis on planning. By 1950 Milwaukee residents owned 172,000 automobiles, or one for every 4.45 people. Zeidler and others recognized that express highways would be necessary to control the flow of traffic and began elaborate planning to build an extensive freeway system. In 1952 formal plans for an expressway system were drawn up in city hall, but the next year the planning function was transferred to a County Expressway Commission, which opened the first part of the highway system in 1962. Federal funds also became available through the passage of the Federal Interstate Highway Act of 1956, pushed forward by President Dwight Eisenhower who had been impressed by Hitler's autobahn during the war years.

By 1970, 10 years after he had left office, Zeidler's foresight was proven correct. There were more than 406,000 cars in Milwaukee County, or one for every 2.6 people, and the growth of the outlying suburbs justified all of the expenses of road-building efforts. Between 1950 and 1957 eight new suburbs were incorporated in the area surrounding Milwaukee on three sides—including Mequon, Menomonee Falls, Brookfield, Butler, Elm Grove, New Berlin, Glendale, and Muskego. Zeidler realized the vital importance of keeping all of these communities tied to jobs and to commerce in the city's center through the ease of highway travel.

Unfortunately, in many American cities including Milwaukee, expressway construction in the 1950s and 1960s often cut through urban neighborhoods, forcing the removal of many residents and the loss of identity. In this area of ethnic changes, Frank Zeidler proved to be a farsighted leader. Whereas the Milwaukee of the first half of the twentieth century was dominated by a patchwork quilt of European neighborhoods, the city was again changed by the wartime years of 1941 to 1945. Milwaukee's African-American population, once a very small minority, had grown as industry reached out to new labor pools. In 1950 African-Americans numbered more than

21,000, an increase of 13,000 since 1940. In the next 10 years the trend continued, with African-Americans numbering 62,458 in 1960, and 105,088 in 1970.

Similarly, the Hispanic population of Milwaukee grew dramatically during the war years and the 1950s. By 1980 the number rose to more than 26,000, or 4.1 percent of the city's total population. Native American residents of the city increased to more than 3,300 by 1970. Mayor Zeidler established a special committee to study potential social problems due to newer ethnic mixes in the city. The report of the committee was completed before Zeidler left office in 1960, paving the way for Milwaukee's responses to the urban challenges of the 1960s.

Arising from these many population shifts, Zeidler and others realized that the City of Milwaukee had to work more closely than ever before with its surrounding communities and with Milwaukee County itself. An unwieldy entity, the county—which had overlapping boundaries but extended farther than the city—had accrued an ever-increasing set of responsibilities through state mandates in the early twentieth century. Finally, in 1959, the responsibility for running county government and its various departments was put into the hands of its first county executive, John Doyne. Joint county-city planning soon became one measurement of efficient government in Milwaukee.

One area in which joint planning was vital was in the growth of schools. While public school enrollment in Milwaukee had leveled off during World War II, the 1950s brought a baby boom and a tremendous increase in the school-age population. Some 44 new schools were constructed across the county during the 1950s alone. Higher education also took on new importance at war's end. The county assumed the responsibility for the operation of vocational schools, which trained returning veterans in many trades.

The GI Bill of Rights, passed before the end of the war, also meant that the city's institutions of higher learning would be flooded with returning veterans. The State Teachers' College, or Normal School, in Milwaukee merged with the Milwaukee Center of the University in Madison in 1956, and became the present University of Wisconsin-Milwaukee. Marquette University expanded its facilities with several large building programs during the 1950s and 1960s, and other area colleges, such as Alverno, Cardinal Stritch, and Mount Mary, began ambitious programs to expand their campus facilities. The Milwaukee School of Engineering, founded in 1903, expanded its downtown facilities during the 1950s and 1960s to become a nationally recognized institution. Similarly, the medical program of Marquette University, founded in the 1890s, became a separate school, the Medical College of Wisconsin, in 1967.

Other accomplishments of Milwaukee's

This 1948 view looks down onto the 100 block of East Wisconsin Avenue. At the left is the Pabst Building, and at right is the Mack Block, built in 1883. In just 12 years the Mack Block and its neighbors to the south would fall to the wrecking ball to make way for the new Marine Plaza. Courtesy, Lyle Oberwise Photography Archive

third Socialist mayor included the establishment of a non-partisan Public Enterprise Committee to keep Milwaukee's economy flexible enough to meet the new challenges of the 1950s. This group soon became known as the Greater Milwaukee Committee and provided valuable leadership for the city's continued revitalization in the postwar decades. Along with new industries, Milwaukee needed low-cost housing for both workers and the returning veterans. It also needed to attract new industries. Zeidler urged the expansion of the library, the creation of a new building for the Milwaukee Public Museum (completed in 1963), and the erection of a new sports stadium.

The stadium project, completed in 1953, assured the city's attractiveness to the new Milwaukee Braves Major League Baseball club, which arrived that year. Four years later, in 1957, the team brought a frenzy of excitement to town with a victory in the World Series. The next year a pennant victory kept hopes alive, but the Braves lost the series itself. The success of the team put the names of Eddie Mathews, Warren Spahn, Hank Aaron, and Lew Burdette in the roster of Milwaukee stars. Unfortunately, the team could not repeat its stunning victories and was traded to Atlanta in 1965, despite extensive lawsuits to keep it in town. Major League Baseball didn't return to Milwaukee until five years later, in 1970, when the Brewers arrived from Seattle to rekindle the city's enthusiasm for the sport.

Other recreational projects of the 1950s included plans for an entirely new zoo, under the auspices of Milwaukee County. The Washington Park location of the old zoo was too small for the projected expansion and so, in 1947, the county began to purchase land west of the city along Bluemound Road. By 1964 more than 175 acres had been acquired, allowing an expansion of eight times the size of the old zoo. Construction began in 1958 with the monkey house and continued with the reptile house, the aviary, and other buildings until the old zoo was permanently vacated in 1963. The joint support of the county and the Zoological Society has meant that the Milwaukee Zoo has earned an outstanding reputation nationwide for its diversity and its quality care of animals.

Renovating and preserving existing historic structures became part of downtown's growing excitement during the 1960s and 1970s.

Another highlight for the city, the geodesic domes were built in Mitchell Park in 1964. Traditionally the site of Milwaukee's horticultural conservatory, Mitchell Park had exhibited a variety of vegetation since its establishment in 1898. The three modern domes, inspired by the work of architect Buckminster Fuller and designed by Donald Grieb, each featured a different climate, highlighted by the Tropical Dome's 25-foot waterfall. Another nature center was established in Whitnall Park at the Todd Wehr Nature Center in 1974. The famous rose garden nearby, in the Boerner Botanical Gardens, became a perennial favorite. Throughout the 1960s and 1970s many additional park features were added throughout the city and county, including 130 tennis courts, a winter sports area, bicycle trails, and many golf courses, particularly the golf course in Brown Deer Park, where an annual national tournament—the Greater Milwaukee Open—began in 1977.

A commitment to the revitalization of the downtown area was another Zeidler program. In 1959 the Marine Bank began construction on a 22-story building on Water Street and Wisconsin Avenue, the first such structure erected downtown since the Depression. Soon thereafter, the construction of a new train station and federal post office on St. Paul Avenue in 1965 continued the pattern. The MECCA auditorium and convention center followed in 1974, and the city's hotels and restaurants, from the venerable Schroeder (Milwaukee Hilton) to the new Hyatt and Wyndham, were remodeled or developed to support convention business. The Pfister Hotel added a 23-story round tower of additional rooms to accommodate Milwaukee's growing needs. Many other new buildings began to lift the downtown

Magnificent train stations were symbols of a railway company's prestige and importance. Designed by Edward Townsend Mix, the Milwaukee Road Depot was built in 1886 on Everett Street near what was then called Fourth Ward Park between Third and Fourth streets. By the time this photo was taken in 1965, the depot's tower had been removed and the building was awaiting demolition. Courtesy, Lyle Oberwise Photography Archive

landscape, including the new Marshall & Ilsley Bank Building in 1968, the Mortgage Guaranty Insurance Corporation Building in 1972, the 42-story First Wisconsin Center in 1974, and the expanded Northwestern Mutual Life Insurance Building in 1979. By 1980 the once-stagnant urban center was attracting many other building projects and companies were looking favorably at locating in the city. The remodeling of the west-side commercial district into a new mall, The Grand Avenue, in 1982 also contributed to downtown's redevelopment as did the nearby Henry Reuss Federal Plaza on Wisconsin Avenue.

Renovating and preserving existing historic structures became part of downtown's growing excitement during the 1960s and 1970s. One of the first successful efforts in this cause was the conversion of the former Second Ward Savings Bank to the Milwaukee County Historical Society in 1965. Other preservation efforts followed as the stately old Mitchell and Mackie buildings on Michigan Avenue, dating from the nineteenth-century era of Milwaukee's dominance in the grain trade, were renovated and preserved. Another outstanding structure, Milwaukee's Iron Block Building at the corner of Wisconsin and Water streets, was restored and saved in the early 1980s, when it was threatened with destruction. Milwaukee's landscape thus became a blend of new skyscrapers and classic old structures that symbolized both progress and stability

The City of Festivals

As the energy of revitalization contributed to the prosperity of Milwaukee's city center, so the changing tide of urban politics brought a new personality to the forefront in 1960, with the election of a new mayor to succeed Frank Zeidler. Henry Maier, a graduate of the University of Wisconsin, was only 42 years old when he moved from a seat in the state assembly to take the post of Milwaukee mayor in 1960. A solid Democrat, Maier was able to continue many of the enlightened programs of Zeidler and the Socialists, but also to stress the need for the city to attract visitors and more leading businesses.

The Maier years, which stretched until his retirement in 1988, set a record of longevity that exceeded even the 24-year tenure of Daniel Hoan. Maier combined the ingenuity of Hoan with the song and ebullience of Carl Zeidler and the level-headed city boosterism of Frank Zeidler. One of Maier's favorite projects grew out of the idea of a circus parade in the early 1960s. In 1962 the director of the Circus World Museum in Baraboo, Chappie Fox, persuaded the Uihlein family, owners of the Schlitz Brewery, to sponsor a parade where authentic circus wagons pulled by draft horses would carry a display of circus animals through the streets of the city. The first parade

Long hair, beads, bell bottoms, peace signs, and guitars were all part of the Brady Street scene in the late 1960s and early 1970s. The nineteenth-century commercial thoroughfare, home to Polish and then Italian immigrants, took on a new life as it became the center of Milwaukee's hippie culture. To celebrate the street's unique character, the Brady Street Festival became an annual event in the 1970s, featuring crafts, food, and music. Courtesy, Lyle Oberwise Photography Archive

was so successful that it was decided to make it an annual event.

Another successful idea that Maier supported brought Milwaukee fame as a city of festivals. Beginning in 1968 a "Summerfest" of music, food, polka dancing, and other activities was sponsored in a lakefront park. For the occasion, Maier himself wrote and sang a new song, "The Milwaukee Summerfest Polka," which was very popular with festival-goers. This first festival became the impetus for the great series that expanded to include numerous ethnic festivals, including German Fest, Fiesta Mexicana, Polish Fest, Festa Italiana, Irish Fest, African World Festival, Asian Moon Festival, and Indian Summer, as well as Summerfest itself. Another popular outdoor event, sponsored every June by the Friends of Art, was the annual Lakefront Festival of the Arts, which featured artists from across the state and the country.

However, festivals and polka bands were not the only story of the 1960s as the city's ethnic and racial diversity and the growing problems of its poor population began to surface. Racial tensions in most American cities had escalated and Milwaukee's protesters, many led by Father James E. Groppi, rightly pointed out the practices of discrimination, particularly in the area of housing. Marches for open housing began as early as 1965, and a rising tide of frustration followed from the sluggishness of racial progress.

Across the country, rising expectations from federal programs for the poor, a long history of neglect of the inner cities, and opposition to the Vietnam War erupted into race riots in 1965-1968. Milwaukee's police force, one of the targets of racial tension, was alerted to the potential danger of a race riot. On July 30, 1967, the inner city witnessed a rampage of destruction that forced Mayor Maier to call out the National Guard. Within 72 hours the danger was over, although it took several weeks for the city to settle back into a routine and a curfew to be lifted.

When the riot ended, many people wondered whether new policies regarding integrated housing, open neighborhoods, and more equitable hiring policies in the police department and other municipal agencies would be a result. How-

Henry Maier was Milwaukee's longest-serving mayor, holding that post from 1960 until his retirement in 1988. Maier had a high profile with the Democratic Party and is shown here with Hubert Humphrey (under the umbrella) and Congressman Clement Zablocki (to Humphrey's right). Henry Maier died on July 17, 1994, at the age of 76. Courtesy, Milwaukee Public Library

ever, such changes came only gradually over the next two decades. By 1970 Milwaukee remained a highly segregated city, with its minorities clustered in separate urban neighborhoods. The push for school integration became one solution to the lack of progress in the area of housing.

School districts across the North had begun to face in the 1960s and 1970s the court-ordered integration that many southern schools had complied with in the 1950s. In 1965 the Milwaukee United School Integration Committee was formed to provide a workable plan for an equitable racial mixture in the city's schools. As a court battle was being waged, the Milwaukee School Board adopted a plan to create specialty schools as magnets, and to allow busing of students to the school of their choice. By the time the lawsuit was settled in 1979, many adjacent suburban schools were also included in the integration program. The implementation of these school integration programs began immediately and occurred without the violence that erupted in several other cities.

Milwaukee's leadership in these troubled times came under fire for moving too slowly in the cause of social justice. However, one of Henry Maier's lasting gifts to the city he served for 28 years was his tireless work to highlight city problems in the national political arena. Maier led the U.S. Conference of Mayors and the National League of Cities as a lobbyist on behalf of federal aid to cities. He also organized the Wisconsin Alliance of Cities to lobby state government on behalf of urban needs. A booster for his adopted city, Maier never tired of calling it "Old Mother Milwaukee," and kept the city's bond rating at the top AAA level to facilitate development dollars. He created an industrial land bank to attract new factories and jobs and he established the first municipal economic development division of city

These bathing beauties with Queen Sharon Hatzky were chosen to preside over the 1965 South Shore Water Frolics. Begun in 1948, the event has grown into a two-day celebration with parades, music, entertainment, and a fireworks display in addition to the beauty pageant. Courtesy, Lyle Oberwise Photography Archive

Roman Catholic priest James Groppi was born and raised in Milwaukee where his family ran an Italian grocery store in the Bay View neighborhood. Civil injustice, especially in the area of housing discrimination, propelled Father Groppi into activism. He is seen here leading a protest march to Madison against cuts in welfare benefits in September 1969. He remained active in civil issues until his death in 1985. Courtesy, Milwaukee Public Library

government in the country. For many people who had not known Dan Hoan, and knew Frank Zeidler only a little, "Maier was Milwaukee."

The mayor's ardent love affair with Milwaukee continued throughout his seven terms in office, from 1960 to 1988. His popularity seemed limitless as he won one election, in 1968, with a record 86 percent of the vote. Nevertheless, much remained to be done for the city as the Maier era came to an end. It still had a great need to improve its inner-city housing stock and to facilitate open housing measures. The school district remained in financial and philosophical trouble. And also, like many big cities, Milwaukee was plagued with a rising crime rate and inadequate resources to meet all of its needs. Even Maier's creation of the National Conference of Democratic Mayors as another pro-city lobbying group could not bring enough resources to solve all of Milwaukee's ills.

However, after his retirement to a university professorship and then to private life in 1988, until his death in 1994 Maier was still revered as one of Milwaukee's most successful leaders. The Summerfest grounds were renamed Henry W. Maier Festival Park, and many still remembered his love of public ceremonies, such as the annual Christmas tree lighting party, where he personally led most of the carol singing. Even with the unrest of the 1970s Milwaukee emerged from the decade a far stronger place than when Maier took office in 1960.

By the close of Maier's last term, Milwaukee was served by more than 82 miles of freeway and the suburbs remained tightly linked to a vital central city. Even with the end of rail transit, the local bus system provided linkage of neighborhoods with industry and with the city center. Milwaukee was not yet clogged in a commuter's nightmare and downtown was both a usable and enjoyable success. The opening of a new sports arena on the west side, the Bradley Center, endowed by Jane and Lloyd Pettit in 1988, sealed this success. Both the professional basketball team, the Milwaukee Bucks, and the ice hockey team, the Admirals, enjoyed the new facility as did hundreds of thousands of citizens who attended events of all kinds there from gold medal ice-skating shows to the visiting circus each year.

One of the darkest days in Milwaukee's history occurred on July 30, 1967, when the tensions in the city's black community erupted into rioting. Racism, segregation, and job loss were recognized as contributing factors. Picketing and marches led by Father James Groppi took place in the preceding months but violence broke out nonetheless. Three persons were killed, 100 were injured, and 1,000 were arrested. Burned-out houses on Center Street, seen here, stood as reminders of the outbreak of violence. Courtesy, Lyle Oberwise Photography Archive

Milwaukee's businesses and industry were prospering as well. The city continued to be one of the nation's largest users of steel for finely machined products, and a world leader in the production of gasoline engines, motorcycles, tractors, and road-building equipment. The Square D Company's production of microprocessors, Johnson Controls' innovations in building automation systems, The Falk Corporation's production of

Bradley Center is a major sports arena that is home to a number of collegiate and professional teams. One of several recent investments in Milwaukee's infrastructure, it was a gift to the city from local philanthropists Jane and Lloyd Pettit. Photo by Milwaukee DCD

power transmission machinery, and the Allen-Bradley Company's manufacturing of electromechanical industrial controls were illustrations of the city's highly skilled manufacturing concerns. The use of skilled labor in the Milwaukee market remained a hallmark of the highly trained work force present in the city's labor pool.

While its nineteenth-century commercial origins rested in agriculture and commerce, Milwaukee had become an industrial center in the twentieth century. In 1980 a number of the city's manufacturing companies were ranked on the list of the *Fortune* 500. Among these were the Briggs and Stratton Corporation; the Pabst and Schlitz breweries; Rexnord, Inc.; the Clark Oil and Refining Corporation; the A.O. Smith Corporation; Johnson Controls Inc.; Allis-Chalmers Corporation; Harnischfeger Industries; and the Bucyrus-Erie Company (now Bucyrus International). Throughout the twentieth century Milwaukee's tanneries remained strong, even though the shoe and harness business had faded. By the end of the 1980s the city still had tanneries, led by Pfister & Vogel and Gallun. Although the wheat trade had left Milwaukee, malting industries such as Froedtert, Kurth, and Ladish were thriving as were its wholesale food businesses, notably Universal Foods, Roundy's, and Godfrey and Company.

Milwaukee's cultural institutions had come of age with the inauguration of the Performing Arts Center, and the establishment of the Milwaukee Ballet Company and a variety of other smaller dance companies and theater groups. The city also led the country in the consumption of brandy and beer and in the still-notable spirit of welcome and good fellowship, first christened "gemutlichkeit" more than a century before.

From Mader's, Ratzsch's, and John Ernst's fine German restaurants to the diversity of other ethnic dining places, the Old World atmosphere of the city still flavored its nightlife, as well as its summer festivals. With all of the fun and celebrations, the thrifty German soul of the city remained in its city hall, which kept the highest bond rating among American cities, and continued its ingrained habits of conservative good government. By the close of the 1980s Milwaukee enjoyed the double virtues of prosperity and progress, while retaining its historic soul of cultural diversity and harmony.

Dialogue

Mayor John Norquist and Former Mayor Frank Zeidler Reflect on Milwaukee's Legacy and Its Future

Who could be more qualified to serve as co-chair of the Milwaukee Sesquicentennial Celebration than former Mayor Frank Zeidler and current Mayor John Norquist? Both are passionate in their support of urban living and the future of Milwaukee. And both have worked hard to make it a better place to live—Zeidler as mayor from 1948 to 1960; and Norquist who was first elected mayor in 1988 and is now entering his third term. Co-author Dave Jensen recently sat down with both men to ask them how Milwaukee has helped to shape the state and the nation, and the challenges and opportunities that they see in Milwaukee's future.

Dave Jensen: When a city celebrates its sesquicentennial, it's only natural to talk about its heritage. What do you think have been Milwaukee's most significant contributions—socially, politically, and economically—to the people of Wisconsin and the nation?

Frank Zeidler: Socially, Milwaukee has been a city in which people from about 50 different nationalities and ethnic origins have lived together fairly harmoniously. Politically, Milwaukee has a reputation as being one of the best-governed cities in the nation. The Social Democrats, who were elected in 1910, passed the first legislation that provided protection for women, protection for children, and workers' compensation. It was legislation that was especially helpful to people in the early days of the Industrial Revolution. Economically, Milwaukee's greatest contribution has been industrial manufacturing, which has always been a critical component of our economy. We didn't make things that were bought off the shelf. We made the machinery that made things that were bought off the shelf. Perhaps our single greatest contribution to the world was the invention of the typewriter, the forerunner of all of our communication systems and one of the real seminal inventions of all time.

Jensen: Mayor Norquist, what do you consider Milwaukee's most significant contributions?

John Norquist: I would agree with much of what Mayor Zeidler said. I believe Milwaukee has been the "Toolbox of America." Allen-Bradley makes electronic controls that are used in machines all over the world. Astronautics Corp. of America makes the black boxes that monitor the controls of every airplane in the western world. Then you take a company like Cerac Inc., which makes the material used in the space shuttle's heat shield. That is the secret to Milwaukee's economic success—knowing how to make things and knowing how to invent things.

Socially, Milwaukee has always been known for innovation and experimentation. The Central Europeans brought to Milwaukee a lot of the things that were happening in Germany in the nineteenth and early twentieth centuries. The union movement has always been big here. And the concept of school choice, which is now a big social issue in America, came out of Milwaukee's central city.

Jensen: Mayor Norquist, how do you think Milwaukee compares with other metropolitan areas of similar size?

Norquist: Milwaukee has a higher percentage of its metropolitan area living in the city than other midwestern cities because we suburbanized later. Most people don't realize it, but the city of Milwaukee is bigger than Minneapolis and St. Paul combined. It is also bigger than Boston. But urban sprawl is accelerating, and even though the city's population isn't declining, the suburbs are growing much faster. In that respect, we are like all of the other midwestern cities. The successful cities, like Milwaukee, Cleveland, or Cincinnati, are holding their own. Their economies are growing at about the rate of inflation. The unsuccessful cities—Detroit, for example—have seen their economy decline.

metropolitan form of government.

Jensen: Mayor Norquist?

Norquist: The American suburb is dependent on the heavy subsidization of the automobile, cheap gasoline prices, and a preference for highways. In 1956 author Lewis Mumford predicted that interstate highways would do more damage to American cities than all the bombing did to European cities during World War II. If anything, I think that was an understatement. The grossest example is Detroit, which actually looks like it was target bombed. Half of the buildings in the downtown are empty and I really think it's because of this almost cancerous overinvestment in roads and the destruction of transit systems. But now that suburbs are here, we've got to do more than just regret them. There are suburbs like Port Washington, which has a beautiful little downtown and a very coherent nature. I think Port Washington, Shorewood, Wauwatosa, Waukesha, and other suburbs, which have a sense of community, live in concert with Milwaukee. They're like little brothers and sisters. On the other hand, you have the sprawl suburbs, like Brookfield or New Berlin, which really have no center and no sense of community. There are no sidewalks, there is no place to walk. They're just places with big lots and houses on

"Perhaps our single greatest contribution to the world was the invention of the typewriter, the forerunner of all of our communication systems and one of the real seminal inventions of all time."

Jensen: How do you think we compare to similar-size cities, Mr. Zeidler?

Zeidler: Every metropolitan area has an economic purpose. Minneapolis, for instance, is a great financial center as well as a distribution center for the Northwest. St. Paul is like Madison because it makes its living off of state government. Milwaukee is more like Cleveland. It's an industrial town. Cleveland and Milwaukee were the machine shops of the country and Milwaukee, I think, has maintained itself better. We diversified our industries here and it helped a great deal.

Jensen: Both of you have been strong advocates of the City of Milwaukee and have been discouraged by urban sprawl. Yet the suburbs appear here to stay. What role do you see them playing in the future of the metropolitan area?

Zeidler: You open a very difficult door for me. As mayor, I was opposed to the formation of suburbs. In many cases, they were formed imperfect and then demanded that the City of Milwaukee provide them with water services, sewer services, library services, and so on. The desire of some people to move out of the city so they don't have to meet its general burdens while at the same time enjoying the city's advantages has never sat well with me. If I were in the state legislature I would advocate a

them, lots of parking lots with strip malls. I think that kind of development is a fundamental threat to American civilization and we need to challenge it.

Jensen: This is a very exciting time in the city's history. A building boom in the late 1980s dramatically changed the city's skyline. We're just completing several downtown projects, including the Riverwalk. And we're embarking on more than $400 million in new construction projects, including a new convention center, a new baseball stadium, and a major addition to the Milwaukee Art Museum. How do you think these developments will affect the city?

Norquist: The Wisconsin Center will enhance the community and the businesses around it. We believe there will be a substantial spinoff in terms of economic development, as is always the hope with any of these projects. There also are some encouraging things happening that aren't associated with government. Developers are turning old factories into offices and apartments. This bodes well for the city. Twenty years ago people were somehow repelled by the urban form. Everyone wanted to turn the city into something that looked like a suburb. But now, the urban form is coming back into style. We are seeing developers who, instead of looking at the city as some place to feel sorry for, are seeing that you can develop the city in an urban way and make money.

Jensen: Mr. Zeidler, what do you think the impact of these developments will be?

Zeidler: I am not as familiar with these projects as the mayor. I can only tell you that in the past, there was a much greater reliance on city planning. And the future that I see would require a considerable amount of city planning to determine how the city should evolve. Whether the city will do that, or whether it will rely on private developers to do that, remains to be seen. But I do feel that an overall plan is necessary.

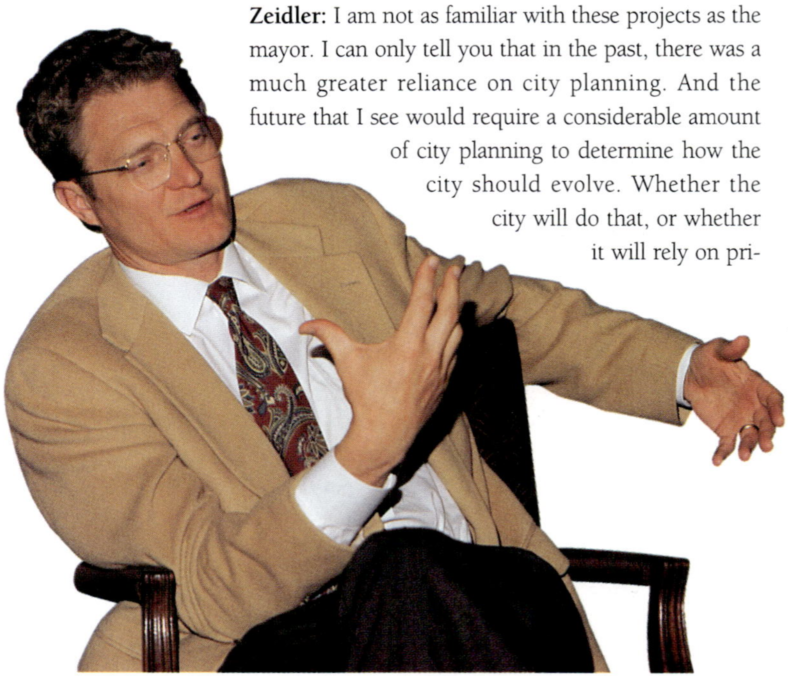

Norquist: I would agree with that. I think we need to use our zoning tools to create an overall vision of an area, whether it's a big area like downtown, or a street like Brady Street. At the same time, we need to encourage private developers to share a positive vision toward urban life.

Jensen: Mayor Zeidler, in your speech at the city's Sesquicentennial Celebration, you stated that "in today's world, where so much is uncertain about the survivability of any city, our goals should be to make Milwaukee an example of human comity and friendly human interaction." Could you elaborate?

Zeidler: One of the greatest tests of any big city is its human relations—its ethnic and race relations. As some of the older population moves out into the suburbs, Milwaukee will look less like the old Yankee, German, and Polish settlers of the early 1900s and it will be critical to develop some social harmony among the people who will be living here. That will be the task of the mayor and the common council. In my opinion, their policies should include integrated education and the development of a community spirit so that people of different cultures will feel comfortable living together. That is going to be very hard to achieve.

Jensen: Why is that?

Zeidler: Because there always has been in the history of Milwaukee, and probably will be in the future, people who trumpet the leadership of their ethnic community over everything else. The old Socialist idea was that we don't want any hyphenated Americans. I don't want to subordinate peoples' ethnic heritage, but at the same time I don't want it to become a source of friction.

Jensen: Mayor Norquist?

Norquist: Milwaukee clearly is a collection of peoples. There are more American Indians in the city of Milwaukee than there are anywhere in the state, including Menominee County, which is an Indian

Photos by Milwaukee DCD/Dave La Haye

reservation. Over 80 percent of the state's African-Americans, and half of the state's Hispanics, live in Milwaukee. All of the major European groups have their greatest concentration of people here. These ethnic groups have identities that they are proud to promote and we want to encourage that. But I think we need to get people to rally around being citizens of Milwaukee as opposed to being hyphenated Americans.

Jensen: What is the state of the city and what do you see as the major challenges and opportunities facing it?

Norquist: Economically, our city is strong relative to other large cities in America. We have a AA+ bond rating, which is one notch below the absolute highest. We have very low unemployment and companies that are constantly advertising for workers. But we still have poverty and we have unemployment rates that are extremely high in the central city. We have a structural gap in our economy and we have to deal with it comprehensively. We must continue to drive crime down. Our educational system has to dramatically improve. There has to be a transformation in the way people who have money and other resources look at the city. We want to encourage the notion that people can invest in Milwaukee and put their businesses where jobs are needed most and still make money. That's our strategy and I think it will pay off. I think Milwaukee also has a real challenge in that we are going to continue to decentralize and emulsify unless we change our transportation priorities.

Jensen: What do you think is the greatest opportunity facing the city?

Norquist: I think a lot of other cities are locked into an old, declining economy. Milwaukee, on the other hand, has a very diverse economy—a big service sector, a financial sector, and a large manufacturing sector. We have the ability to adapt to a changing economy because we don't have any one employer or sector that is dominant.

Today the economy is spread out over different sectors and there are a lot more small businesses than big ones. I think that is our real opportunity.

Jensen: Mr. Zeidler, what do you see as the city's greatest challenges and opportunities?

Zeidler: Milwaukee has certain basic advantages and one of them is its water supply. Many industries in the future, particularly manufacturing industries, are going to require a fresh water supply, which you can't get except around the Great Lakes. We have a potential in the harbor. Great Lakes shipping has gone through a series of setbacks, but I think that in the long run, the harbor will play an important role again. I think another advantage is that you don't have to pay graft to conduct business. A businessman recently told me just how much he liked to do business here because in cities like New York, he had to pay somebody off at every turn. We don't have these appendages, which can seriously drain a business.

I agree with the mayor that among the city's great strengths are the industrial skills that are inherent in the community. The school systems need to develop people who are not only skilled in the arts, but also have marketable skills that will enable them to get a job when they graduate. Finally, I think the city needs to go all out in an effort to attract high science and technological industries. We were, and still are, pretty far advanced in electrical industries and we do have a chemical industry. We ought to be more involved in the life sciences, particularly those that are related to health care, and we need to do something more in the communications field.

"Milwaukee...has a very diverse economy—a big service sector, a financial sector, and a large manufacturing sector."

Lake Michigan, one of Milwaukee's greatest natural assets, has played an instrumental role in the city's development as a trading and entertainment center. Photo by Peter Saunders/Third Coast Stock Source

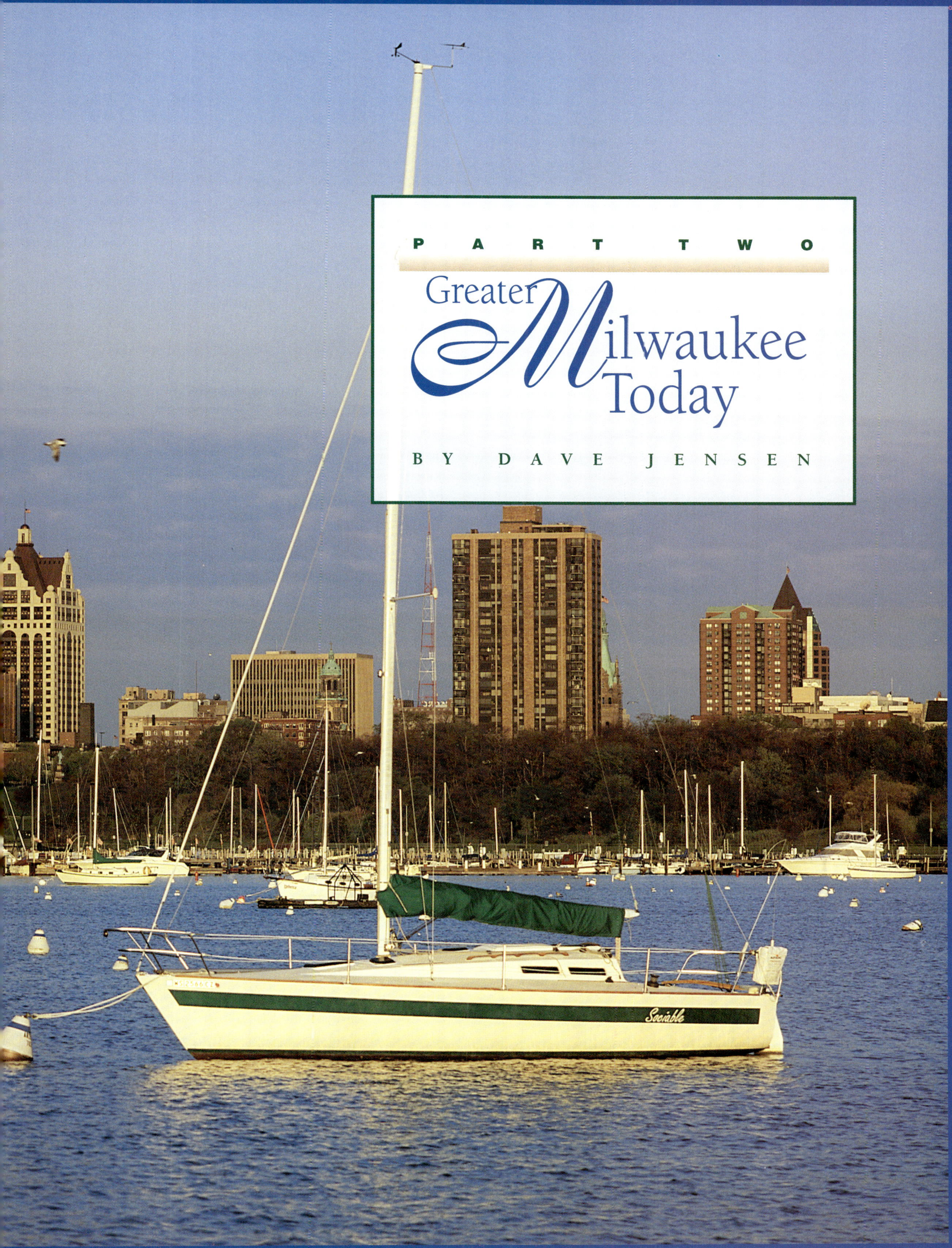

PART TWO

Greater Milwaukee Today

BY DAVE JENSEN

RAŁ I POŚWIĘCIŁ TO MIEJSCE ABY TAM IMIĘ MOJE BYŁO NA WIEKI A ŻEBY TAM TRWAŁY OCZY MOJE I SERCE MOJE PO WSZYSTKIE DNI KS. KRÓL

Chapter FOUR

A Big City Bubbling with Small-Town Neighborhoods

St. Josaphat's Basilica was built at the turn of the century by Polish immigrants and craftsmen who used marble, limestone, granite columns, and woodwork from a Chicago federal building demolished in the 1890s. Photo by Ralph Antczak/Crystal Studio

On a clear day the sun's rays bounce off the copper globe at the top of the 100 East building, spreading golden rays throughout the blue sky for as far as the eye can see. Like a beacon guiding sailors to shore, it proclaims your arrival to Milwaukee, a hidden jewel on the shores of Lake Michigan.

For many, Milwaukee remains a land of beer and brats, of "Laverne and Shirley," of bowling, cheese, and "The Fonz." Few people outside of the Midwest can correctly place the city in the right state. But for those who have lived or visited here for any extended length of time, Milwaukee is teeming with excitement, a city of restaurants, theaters, concerts, and sports, a city where there is always something to do—no matter how hot or cold the weather. It is the home of Summerfest, the nation's largest music festival, and the home of Winterfest, one of the nation's few celebrations of winter.

In fact, Milwaukeeans are known to celebrate just about anything—from circuses to the French Revolution. We celebrate summer with Summerfest and the Milwaukee River with RiverSplash! We honor the anniversary of the creation of the Harley-Davidson motorcycle by shutting down the expressways and letting tens of thousands of Harley-Davidson enthusiasts

roar through the downtown on their Hawgs. And we celebrate our ethnic heritages with close to a dozen festivals, earning us the uncontested title of "City of Festivals."

Milwaukee is also a city that invests in itself. In the past 10 years more than $250 million worth of construction has been completed in the downtown area, including several new office buildings, the $71-million Bradley Center, an 18,000-seat sports arena, and the $100-million Milwaukee Center, which includes a 220-room hotel, a 28-story office building, and a suite of performing arts venues. Down the street, construction crews have completed a multistory Humphrey IMAX Theater and the new home of Discovery World, a science and technology museum. At the east end of Wisconsin Avenue, where the roadway curves north to avoid Lake Michigan, children are learning about the wonders of life in the new Betty Brinn Children's Museum, which is located in the lakefront O'Donnell Park.

It truly is an exciting time to be living in Milwaukee. In addition to the city's already full social calendar and the recent building boom,

Spectators welcome the 60,000 motorcyclists who rode into Milwaukee from around the nation in 1993 to celebrate the 90th anniversary of Harley-Davidson's founding. Photos by Joann Miller and Todd Dacquisto/Third Coast Stock Source

Milwaukee is poised to benefit from close to $450 million worth of new construction projects just getting under way, including the Wisconsin Center, an expansive, state-of-the-art convention center, and Miller Park, the soon-to-be-home of the Milwaukee Brewers Major League Baseball team.

The Wisconsin Center

The $170-million Wisconsin Center promises to be a catalyst for additional downtown development. The three-story facility will span four city blocks and will include a 200,000-square-foot exhibition hall, 42,000 square feet of meeting rooms, and a 38,000-square-foot ballroom. It will be equipped with the latest in technology to accommodate computers, modems, and multimedia presentations and to provide Internet access.

To allow continuous operations, the Wisconsin Center is being built in phases. The first phase, which is scheduled for completion in 1998, will be bordered by Wisconsin Avenue on the south, Wells Street on the north, Fourth Street on the east, and Sixth Street on the west. The second phase will be completed in 1999 and will be located on the site of the current convention and exposition hall, which will be razed. More than two dozen meeting rooms will be located on the center's first and second floors. The third-floor exhibition area, which will be large enough to accommodate three football fields, will span Wells Street, allowing traffic to pass underneath. A series of skywalks will connect the Wisconsin Center to the Hyatt Regency, the Milwaukee Hilton, and The Grand Avenue shopping mall.

Even though the Wisconsin Center will be three stories high and span four city blocks, its design team took great care to ensure that the structure would not dominate downtown. The main public facades of the building will consist of alternating sections of precast concrete and brick to create a rhythm that will blend the building into the surrounding architecture. Its gables, spires, and cinnamon-colored brick pay respect to City Hall, the Flemish Renaissance landmark designed and built slightly more than a century ago. But the Wisconsin Center's skylights and massive expanses of glass will give it a distinctively contemporary character and will visually connect conventioneers with the hustle and bustle of downtown.

Milwaukee already is a treasured convention location because of its central location and its affordability. In October 1995 the Runzheimer Meal and Lodging Index rated Milwaukee as the least-expensive convention destination of 74 areas surveyed. According to Runzheimer, the average cost of first-class lodging, which includes meals, was $125.80 a day in Milwaukee. That compares to $289.40 in Manhattan (the most expensive city in the survey), $233.05 in Chicago, $174.45 in

Facing page: Milwaukee is proud of its heritage. Some of the city's newer structures, including the 100 East office building, enhance its European feel. Photo by Eric Oxendorf/Third Coast Stock Source

I HAVE LIVED IN MILWAUKEE VIRTUALLY ALL OF MY LIFE. I HAVE BEEN offered positions around the country but I never moved because I love this city. It is a wonderful place with a good work atmosphere and very friendly people. It is also easy to get around. You can get anywhere you want to go in just a matter of minutes. One of my greatest disappointments today is that too many people are moving from the city to the suburbs. My home is in downtown Milwaukee overlooking Lake Michigan. I can walk to work when the weather is pleasant and my house guests are awed by my views of the lake and marina. Too many people who live here fail to realize how wonderful this community is. We need to realize how fortunate we are to live here, and then take the responsibility to make this community a stronger and better place—for people of all colors and religions.

BEN BARKIN

Public relations consultant and founder of the Great Circus Parade

PABST THEATER

Cleveland, $156.95 in Minneapolis, and $129.40 in Madison. The new Wisconsin Center will build on these benefits by offering a state-of-the-art facility that can accommodate large conventions.

It's hard to overestimate the importance of the new center. In 1995 the city's largest convention was the National Conference of State Legislators, which drew 5,000 delegates. Because of the new Wisconsin Center, Milwaukee was selected to host the American Legion Convention, which will bring 20,000 delegates and family members to the city in the year 2000, and the International Association of Chiefs of Police, which will bring more than 9,000 delegates to the city in 2001. In addition to attracting larger conventions, the Wisconsin Center will provide more room for current events including the Holiday Folk Fair, the Milwaukee Journal Sentinel Sports Show, the Milwaukee Auto Show, and the Milwaukee Boat Show.

When completed, the Wisconsin Center is expected to add more than 2,000 permanent jobs to the Milwaukee-area economy and is likely to spawn additional economic development, just as The Grand Avenue shopping mall did when it was completed in 1982. "The Wisconsin Center is going to bring a lot of activity to the heart of the city," says Charles Engberg, a principal with Engberg Anderson, the project's architect of record. "It is going to become a centerpoint of civic energy that will renew and refocus development interest on the west side of downtown."

Two downtown hotels—the Hyatt Regency and the Milwaukee Hilton—have already announced plans to add 250 rooms each and the city has committed to spend $8 million to renovate the 46-year-old Arena, which will continue to host concerts and special events. In addition, a new downtown apartment project, which could eventually include up to 300 apartments, has been planned for just east of the main Milwaukee Public Library on Wisconsin Avenue.

Play Ball! Going to Bat for Miller Park

West of the downtown, crews have broken ground in the Menomonee Valley for the largest building project in the state's history—Miller Park, the new $250-million home for the Milwaukee Brewers Major League Baseball team. The park will seat 42,500 people, include more than 70 luxury skyboxes, and feature natural grass and a convertible roof that can be closed during

Above: The new Wisconsin Center, which will span four city blocks, will allow the city to host large conventions and could act as a catalyst for additional downtown development. Courtesy, Engberg Anderson Inc.

Facing page: Milwaukee's downtown is a blend of old and new designs. The modern Milwaukee Center office building towers over the 100-year-old Pabst Theater, but its design pays respect to the Pabst's German Baroque style. Photo by Peter Saunders/Third Coast Stock Source

Miller Park, the new home of the Milwaukee Brewers, will feature a natural grass field and a convertible roof that can be closed during inclement weather. Courtesy, Eppstein Uhen Architects

inclement weather. Slated to open in the year 2000, Miller Park has been the decade-long dream of Milwaukee Brewers owner Bud Selig, who brought the team to the city in the 1970s.

The stadium project is a unique public-private partnership that includes $160 million in public money, $21 million in low-interest loans from area foundations, and a $49-million commitment from the Brewers, the largest team contribution of its kind in the history of professional baseball. Although Milwaukee is among the smallest professional baseball markets, the Brewers' pledge far exceeds the $15 million pledged by the Chicago White Sox for the new Comiskey Park and the $34 million contributed by the Cleveland Indians for Jacobs Field.

Milwaukee's business community also came to bat for the Brewers. Miller Brewing Company contributed $40 million for naming rights to the new stadium and area businesses are lending the Brewers $14 million to ensure that the park becomes a reality.

Construction of Miller Park is being overseen by the Southeast Wisconsin Professional Baseball Park District, a 13-member board that includes representatives from the state, the City of Milwaukee, Milwaukee County, and four surrounding counties. Design and engineering is being handled by HKS Inc. of Dallas and Eppstein Uhen Architects, Milwaukee, and construction is being coordinated by Huber Hunt Nichols, Chicago, and Hunzinger Construction, Milwaukee, which served as the general contractor on the County Stadium Project in 1953 and has been a consultant to the Brewers since late 1993. The Hammes Company,

Brookfield, is the project manager.

Miller Park is expected to have a tremendous impact on the city and the Brewers. Construction of the ballpark will create more than 1,000 jobs, many of them for minorities, and the new park will preserve the hundreds of jobs needed to keep a ballpark operating. The Brewers' fans will benefit from a state-of-the-art ballpark that will offer the newest amenities in a turn-of-the-century atmosphere. The convertible roof will ensure the fans' comfort, especially during the cold and rainy months of April and May.

Downtown Development

On the city's lakefront, the Milwaukee Art Museum has unveiled plans for a stunning new addition that will increase the museum's exhibition space by 25 percent and create a dramatic link between the lakefront and downtown when it is completed in the year 2000. Designed by Santiago Calatrava, a Spanish-born architect who has won several international design awards, the addition will stretch along the lakefront, just south of the existing museum. Visitors will enter the museum through a grand 60-foot-tall entry pavilion that will be connected to O'Donnell Park by a pedestrian bridge with a distinctive 100-foot angled mast and cables reminiscent of a suspension bridge. Towering over the pavilion will be a dramatic wing-like sunscreen that can be opened to

A new, $27-million addition to the Milwaukee Art Museum will increase the museum's exhibition space and create an impressive lakefront sculpture that will change with the weather. Courtesy, Milwaukee Art Museum

control the pavilion's light and temperature. When fully extended, the elegant sunscreen will resemble a seagull gracefully taking flight.

"The museum will be not only a place to view fine art, but a piece of art in itself," says Milwaukee Art Museum director Russell Bowman. "We believe the museum will become as well known as other cities' architectural icons, such as St. Louis' arch or Sydney's opera house, because of its bold futuristic design and its practical usage."

Also planned for downtown are two major residential developments—Westown Village, which will be located just west of the Milwaukee River, and City Hall Square. The first phase of Westown Village will include 73 apartments and is slated to be completed by the end of 1998. The four-story building will also include underground parking and at least 5,000 square feet of street-level retail space. Ultimately, the project could add 300 apartments to the downtown area. City Hall Square is a $22-million development that will rehabilitate several riverfront buildings and add more than 150 apartments and 19,700 square

The Riverwalk, a public-private development that features boat docks, pavilions, and promenades, is drawing residents back to the Milwaukee River. Thanks to the $10-million project, the river could once again become a center of activity, as it was in the 1800s when it served as downtown's main thoroughfare. Photos by Dave La Haye

Right: Constructed in the 1870s, the Mitchell Building is among the city's oldest standing commercial buildings and is an excellent example of the French Second Empire architectural style. Photo by Eric Oxendorf/Third Coast Stock Source

Far right: There are still many houses from the earliest days of the city, including this Gothic home in suburban Wauwatosa. Photo by Eric Oxendorf/Third Coast Stock Source

feet of commercial space.

Then there's the Riverwalk, the $10-million walkway and entertainment area that meanders along both sides of the Milwaukee River. "The Riverwalk is a truly unique opportunity for the city because it allows us to take a resource that the city had turned its back on for many decades and transform it into something that will draw people back to the water in downtown Milwaukee," says Robert Cooper, an architect with Eppstein Uhen Architects, which has played a lead role in the Riverwalk development, including the design of the Pere Marquette Pavilion and the Riverwalk.

There are plenty of private downtown developments as well. Sinai Samaritan Medical Center is spending $55 million to expand its East Campus by adding 250,000 square feet to its inpatient facilities, erecting a new parking structure and renovating two buildings. In addition, Johnson Controls plans to build a new $6-million administration and engineering facility next to the original structure that founder Warren Johnson built in 1885.

There's little doubt about it: Milwaukee is a city on the move.

Milwaukee is the nation's 17th-largest city with a population of 629,296, based on 1994 estimates. It is the largest city in Wisconsin and the fourth-largest city in the Midwest. The metropolitan area, which includes Waukesha, Ozaukee, and Washington counties, is home to 1.5 million people, making it the 35th-largest urban area in the country and comparable in size to the metropolitan areas of Cincinnati, Indianapolis, Kansas City, Orlando, Sacramento, and San Antonio.

Lake Michigan tempers the city during the cold and cloudy winter months and has a moderating effect on snowfall, which averages 45 inches a year. That's about the same amount of snow that

falls in the Twin Cities and half the 90 inches of snow that is dumped each year on Buffalo, New York. On steamy summer days, the "local ocean" has a cooling effect, keeping the downtown between 6 and 10 degrees cooler than the outlying areas.

Because of its age and rapid development during the late 1800s and early 1900s, Milwaukee is one of the more densely populated cities in the country, giving it a vibrancy that many urban areas lack. This is especially true on the city's near north and near south sides, where bungalows, taverns, and bakeries are tucked in together along tree-lined streets.

Walker's Point is one of the city's oldest neighborhoods. Located on the near south side, it includes a mix of residential, commercial, and industrial properties. Much of the neighborhood has been listed on the National Register of Historic Places because of the area's nineteenth-century charm. Photo by Scott Witte/Third Coast Stock Source

Milwaukee's month-long Winterfest is one of the nation's only urban celebrations of winter. Photo by Milwaukee DCD/Dave La Haye

Not even the blustery winds of winter can keep Milwaukee residents from enjoying the outdoors. Photo by Ken Wardius/Third Coast Stock Source

"In many ways, Milwaukee is much like the cities of Central Europe," says Milwaukee Mayor John O. Norquist. "Many of the buildings have an architecture similar to those of European cities. They help create an atmosphere that can't be found in many cities. It's an atmosphere that is also in our homes and in the many ways we celebrate our ethnic traditions."

The metropolitan area... is home to 1.5 million people, making it the 35th-largest urban area in the country and comparable in size to the metropolitan areas of Cincinnati, Indianapolis, Kansas City, Orlando, Sacramento, and San Antonio.

Milwaukee's architecture is one of the city's most enduring assets. The city abounds in remarkable historic specimens, including St. Josaphat's Basilica, which was built at the turn of the century by Polish immigrants and local craftsmen, and City Hall, a Flemish Renaissance masterpiece that was built on a pie-shaped lot. "Milwaukee's City Hall is the only American city hall remotely resembling the town halls of Europe," says H. Russell Zimmermann, a Milwaukee architect and historian. "It is really remarkable that the city spent that kind of money to build something so spectacular."

Zimmermann says Milwaukee's "practicality" is the main reason its architectural heritage has been preserved. "In retrospect, it seems Milwaukee has been more conservative and frugal than other cities of its size," he says. "It has, accordingly, resisted temptation to run roughshod over its history in an effort to grow too fast. From an architectural standpoint, this has been good news. While there have been some tragic losses due to civic shortsightedness and personal greed, the city's predominant approach followed the European tendency to use buildings until they could no longer be used."

The People of Milwaukee

Milwaukee's ties to Europe are no accident. In 1890 the city was considered the most "foreign" city in the nation because of its huge immigrant population. By the early 1900s immigrant families accounted for 75 percent of Milwaukee's population. The area's primary "ancestral" influence is German. In the 1990 Census approximately 40 percent of the metropolitan area's residents listed German as their primary ancestry. Other major ancestral origins include African-American (13 percent), Polish (10 percent), Irish (5.4 percent), English (3.4 percent), and Italian (2.9 percent).

But who are we? What do we like and what do we do? To get an idea, the *Milwaukee Journal Sentinel*, the area's major daily newspaper, conducts a consumer analysis of metropolitan Milwaukee residents. Each year it surveys more than 2,500 randomly selected homes to develop a profile of the people who live here.

Who's in the typical metropolitan Milwaukee home? According to the 1996 survey, odds are good that it's a two-person household with no children. Both are probably residents 35 to 49 years of age who have a household income of between $25,000 and $75,000. Odds are 50-50 that there's a pet in the house, and if there is,

chances are strong it's a dog. Families are small, even in the homes where there are children. Less than 8 percent of the households surveyed reported having three or more kids.

Men are the primary wage earners in half of the homes, and they're most likely to be employed as executives, administrators, and managers (21 percent), professionals (17 percent), and precision skilled workers and craftsmen (16 percent). Women are more likely to be employed in clerical and other administrative support functions (30 percent), professional specialty occupations (21 percent), or as executives, administrators, and managers (15 percent).

When we shop, we're just as likely to spend $30 as we would $150, but we almost always go to two food stores a week. What do we put in the shopping cart? According to the *Journal Sentinel* analysis, our favorite items (in order of importance) are milk, toilet paper, toothpaste, paper towels, facial tissues, ice cream, laundry detergent, margarine, frozen vegetables, women's deodorant, spaghetti, candy bars, sliced lunch meat, fresh chicken, potato chips, white bread, sliced cheese, salad dressing, and cookies.

We're more likely to buy beer than wine, and when we do buy beer we favor locally brewed brands such as Miller and Pabst. Miller Lite is our favorite brand, followed by Miller Genuine Draft. And while we're just as likely to buy light beer as anything else, we shy away from imported beers and beers that don't contain alcohol.

Almost all of us own a VCR and a remote control, but only half of us subscribe to a cable service. We're not big on sending flowers either; fewer than half of us sent someone a bouquet in the past 12 months. Almost half of us went to a gambling facility within the past year, and when

Above: The Wisconsin Dells, with its natural rock formations, water parks, and the Tommy Bartlett Water Show, is one of the most popular tourist destinations of area residents. Photo by Phil Moughmer/Third Coast Stock Source

Facing page: Usinger's, a downtown establishment since 1880, has made Milwaukee one of the nation's leading producers of brats and sausage. Photo by Dale Guldan/Third Coast Stock Source

Thanks to creative planning and the foresight of civic leaders, Milwaukee is blessed with many parks and waterways, including this one near St. Josaphat's Basilica on the city's south side. Photo by Milwaukee DCD/Dave La Haye

There are more than a half dozen farmers' markets that offer fresh flowers and produce throughout the Milwaukee area during the summer. Photo by Milwaukee DCD/Dave La Haye

we did, odds were 2 to 1 that it was an Indian casino. When we vacation, we're likely to stay in Wisconsin. Door County, the Wisconsin Dells, and north-central Wisconsin are our favorite destinations. If we do get on a plane, we're more likely to fly to Disney World or Las Vegas than anywhere else. When we do venture outside the United States, our favorite destinations are Canada and the Caribbean.

Why We Live Here

Why do we live in Milwaukee? For many residents, it's the only place they know as home. But many others have moved to Milwaukee from other cities. Once here, they have been captivated by the city's charm and the people who live here. What makes Milwaukee such a great place to live? It depends on who you ask.

"The quality of life here is one of Milwaukee's greatest assets," says Bill Lacy, president and CEO of MGIC Investment Corporation, one of the nation's leading providers of private mortgage insurance. "The people really love the community, the ease of commuting, and the abundance of recreational activities."

As part of its sesquicentennial celebration, the city asked residents what they liked about Milwaukee. Approximately 3,000 people responded and their "Top 10" reasons, in order of importance, were: 1) The caring and friendly people; 2) The diversity of the people who live here; 3) The city's lakefront and beautiful beaches; 4) The lively ethnic festivals; 5) The city's small-town feel and big-city appeal; 6) The area's four distinct seasons; 7) The area's *great* parks; 8) The city's hometown feel; 9) Summerfest; and 10) The city's accessibility and convenience.

Converse Smith, a regional vice president for the Newark Group, is one of the many "transplants" who quickly fell in love with Milwaukee. He first came to the city in 1986 as general manager of Wisconsin Paperboard. "In the two years that we were here, my wife and I became thoroughly enchanted with Milwaukee," he says. "Like everyone else who moves here, we had heard that Milwaukee was a very industrial city—the land of beer, brats, and baseball. That's all true, but we

Milwaukee's festivals are family events, with plenty of things to do for both children and adults. Photo by Milwaukee DCD/Dave La Haye

discovered that there is so much more. There is the symphony, ballet, live theater, professional sports, museums, and fine dining."

In 1988 Smith was promoted to a corporate position at the Newark Group's headquarters in Cranford, New Jersey. Both he and his wife were sad to leave. "My wife told me she wanted to move back here if we ever had the opportunity," he says.

That opportunity came in 1992, when the Newark Group decided to establish a regional office to oversee its Midwest mills. Smith was given the job and was told he could be located anywhere he wanted. He chose Milwaukee. "The people here are so warm and friendly," he says. "It is a very easy place to be accepted and there is so much to do. When we lived in New Jersey, we found that we were lucky if there was something we wanted to do once a month. In Milwaukee, there can be two or three things that you want to do in one day. It is a very social town."

People who call Milwaukee home say there are three things that make the metropolitan area a wonderful place to live—its accessibility, affordability, and variety. Milwaukee has an average one-way commute time of less than 22 minutes and you can get from downtown to the city's farthest edge in 15 minutes or less. Milwaukee also is affordable. According to a 1991 study done by Runzheimer International, Milwaukee was ranked the third-most-affordable city in a comparison of 12 urban areas. According to the study, Milwaukee's cost of living was 3 percent below Minneapolis, 13 percent below Chicago, and 26 percent below New York City. Another Runzheimer study demonstrated that Milwau-

I FIRST CAME TO MILWAUKEE IN 1948 TO ATTEND A YWCA MEETING.

It was wintertime and beautiful. The snow was so white and pure. I thought everything about Milwaukee would be just like the weather, but that was not to be true. When I came here, the black community was quite isolated, as were other ethnic groups. Walnut Street was our commercial district and North Avenue was as far north as blacks lived or worked. I have seen the expansion of housing. It hasn't always been good, but it has been a rich experience. I like Milwaukee. It is a clean city and all of us together are trying to keep it well-managed. Unfortunately, there is too much crime, too much joblessness, a disregard for education and personal hatred that is eating at the souls of some people. Only in believing that we can learn to live together in one world will our life's mission be fulfilled.

ERNESTINE OBEE
President, Northwest Funeral Chapel

Right and below: Strong neighborhoods are the keys to Milwaukee's exceptional quality of life. Also critical are the many nonprofit organizations, including the Boys & Girls Clubs of Greater Milwaukee, which offers guidance, educational programs, and recreational activities for more than 45,000 youths. Photos by Milwaukee DCD/Dave La Haye and the Boys & Girls Clubs of Greater Milwaukee

kee's housing costs are among the best in the nation.

Clean and Safe

Milwaukee is also a safe—and clean—city. Over the past four years it has consistently been rated as one of the 10 safest urban areas of its size in the United States. "A lot of people who come to Milwaukee remark on how clean and safe the city is," says Robert Milbourne, executive director of the Greater Milwaukee Committee, a group of 175 civic leaders. "They are really amazed that a city this size is so clean."

Visitors also are impressed with the honesty and integrity of the people who live here. "We're not a phony city with phony people," says Mayor John Norquist. "The people here are real. That is one of the reasons the Greater Mil-

waukee Convention & Visitors Bureau settled on "Milwaukee: Genuine American" as the theme to promote the city. There are real people here making real products. And there is a friendliness here that you don't find in other cities. The people really do want to know how they can help you."

Milwaukee-area residents are also very hard working. Milwaukee boasts the lowest worker absentee rate in the country. And even when they're tempted to do otherwise, Milwaukeeans watch out for each other.

In early 1993 the editors of the *Sentinel*, which was then Milwaukee's morning newspaper, decided to test the honesty of the city's residents. Borrowing an idea from a popular travel magazine, the news staff placed brightly colored backpacks at six busy locations throughout the city, including shopping malls and the local airport. In the magazine experiment, the backpacks were stolen 70 percent of the time. But in Milwaukee, *none* of the backpacks was taken—even though more than 500 people passed them by. People did pick up the backpacks, but only to put them in safer locations.

"We did the experiment to confirm that there is a real sense of community in Milwaukee and that people watch out for each other," says Keith Spore, who was the *Sentinel* editor and is now president of Journal/Sentinel Inc. and publisher of the *Milwaukee Journal Sentinel*. "And still, we were surprised at just how incredibly friendly and honest the people are."

A City That Cares

Milwaukeeans are also very caring. Over the years many public-private partnerships have been formed to bring about social good. The Milwaukee Foundation, for instance, was formed in 1915 to fund local charities. Today it is one of the fastest-growing community foundations in the

Several new upscale developments have made downtown Milwaukee an exciting place to live. Photo by Milwaukee DCD/Dave La Haye

Prospect Avenue, located on the bluff overlooking Lake Michigan, has always been one of the most prestigious places to live in the city as can be attested by the Victorian mansions and modern apartment buildings that stand side by side. Photo by Ralph Antczak/Crystal Studio

country, managing more than $170 million in 370 different funds. Each year the foundation pumps $7 million into the community to fund a variety of projects. In 1995, for example, it helped fund the Discovery World Museum, the YWCA Women's Enterprise Center, the Bruce Guadalupe School, and the New Hope Project, which helps low-income families find meaningful work in the Milwaukee area. The Lynde and Harry Bradley Foundation, which contributes generously to local organizations, provided a $20-million low-interest loan to help fund a new baseball stadium for the Milwaukee Brewers.

Partners Advancing Values in Education (PAVE) is an independent, nonprofit organization that offers partial scholarships for low-income students attending private nonsectarian and religious schools. PAVE provided $3.54 million in scholarships to 4,305 students during the 1995-1996 academic year. The Metropolitan Milwaukee Association of Commerce's $13-million scholarship fund helps deserving Milwaukee high school graduates attend college.

The United Performing Arts Fund is a national leader in fund raising for the cultural arts. In 1995 it raised $7.5 million for the Milwaukee Symphony, Milwaukee Repertory Theater, Milwaukee Ballet, Florentine Opera Company, Skylight Opera Theatre, and other groups. Only one other city—Los Angeles—raises more money for the arts. The Greater Milwaukee Initiative, which was formed by the Greater Milwaukee Committee in 1984, encourages businesses to donate at least 2 percent of their pretax domestic earnings to charity. More than 350 businesses have heeded that call, making it one of the most successful such efforts in the country.

Urban Living

Among the most treasured aspects of living in Milwaukee is the diversity of neighborhoods in which you can live—from downtown condominiums to quiet south-side bungalows, from 100-year-old lakefront mansions to new suburban homes.

In the past 10 years there has been a flurry of new apartments and condominium projects in downtown Milwaukee. Young professionals and empty nesters are moving into apartment high rises that feature spectacular views of Lake Michigan and are within walking distance of the city's restaurants, festivals, and sporting activities. The former Blatz brewery has been turned into an upscale apartment building featuring loft and bilevel apartments. Newer apartment projects include Yankee Hill, Landmark on the Lake, and East Pointe Commons. The Mandel Group is building a new 109-unit apartment complex on Prospect Avenue overlooking Lake Michigan, and there are plans for new apartments on both sides of the Milwaukee River. In addition, several new condominium projects have been developed in the downtown area, including the River Houses along the Milwaukee River and Astor Court. The Cudahy condominiums, which overlook Lake Michigan, are among the most prestigious places to live in Milwaukee.

There are plenty of residential neighborhoods in Milwaukee as well. Among the most established and well-known are the lower east side, Brewer's Hill, Bay View, Sherman Park, Story Hill, and Jackson Park.

The lower east side is Milwaukee's "hippest" neighborhood. Located near downtown and the University of Wisconsin-Milwaukee, it is home to

many students and young professionals. Specialty shops and boutiques are scattered throughout the neighborhood and in clusters along Brady Street and Downer and Oakland avenues. Within just a few blocks of each other are restaurants offering Greek, Mideastern, Mexican, Italian, and Serbian cuisine. Prospect Avenue, which runs along the bluff of Lake Michigan, has been one of the city's premier residential addresses since before the turn of the century. Many beautiful Victorian mansions remain as homes but others have been converted into offices, museums, and schools. Today they stand elegantly next to the upscale apartment buildings and condominiums that offer commanding views of Lake Michigan and easy access to downtown Milwaukee.

West of the Milwaukee River and north of North Avenue is the neighborhood known as Riverwest. First developed in 1850 to provide homes to the people who worked in the paper mills along the Milwaukee River, Riverwest today is home to the city's growing arts community. Small shops and eateries line the main thoroughfares that led to the summer homes of the city's early beer barons and the modest flats of Polish immigrants.

Brewer's Hill, located just north of downtown near the Milwaukee River, is named after the beer barons who developed the area so they could live close to the breweries that were making Milwaukee famous. Perched on high ground with a commanding view of downtown, Brewer's Hill was the heart of Milwaukee's German community at the turn of the century. Bordered by North

The east side of Milwaukee offers an abundance of older and tastefully designed homes and is close to downtown, Lake Michigan, and the University of Wisconsin-Milwaukee. Photo by Eric Oxendorf/Third Coast Stock Source

Brady Street, which has a long and colorful history, is currently undergoing a major facelift to enhance its charm. Photo by Milwaukee DCD/Dave La Haye

Avenue, Holton Street, Walnut Street, and Martin Luther King Jr. Drive, Brewer's Hill was developed between 1850 and 1920 and offers many fine examples of nineteenth-century architecture, including Greek Revival, Italianate, and Queen Anne styles. The city took an active interest in reviving the area in the 1970s by selling vacant land and making low-interest loans available to homeowners. Today young people are renovating many of the older houses, restoring them to their original grandeur. Their efforts have resulted in some of the most rapidly appreciating home values in the metropolitan area. Commercial developments have further enhanced the area. The former Schlitz Brewery has been turned into a modern office park along the Milwaukee River. In addition, developers have been working on plans to convert other riverfront offices and factories into upscale condominiums and apartments.

Milwaukee's Third Ward, located just south of downtown between the Milwaukee River and Lake Michigan, is emerging as one of the trendiest office and residential locations in the city. In 1892 a fire devastated this warehouse district, destroying nearly all of the buildings. Developers quickly rebuilt the area, which is now listed on the National Register of Historic Places as having the largest collection of turn-of-the-century warehouses in the

MILWAUKEE IS A GOOD-SIZE CITY TO GET TO KNOW PEOPLE IN.

It is not so small that you feel like you're in a little town, but it also is not so big that you can't get your arms around it. I came from a very homogenous community where almost all of the people were white. One of the things that I have always really liked about Milwaukee is its diversity. Milwaukee has its problems, but I have found that if you are willing to reach out and be fair, then other people will reach out too. I have some very strong friendships with people from a lot of different backgrounds and I think that is a real key to Milwaukee.

JULIA TAYLOR
Executive director, YWCA

country. The city spent several million dollars in the early 1990s to install decorative streetlights and streetscaping to enhance the architectural flavor of the area. Today the warehouses in the Third Ward house galleries, offices, apartments, restaurants, and condominiums.

Bay View, nestled along the Lake Michigan shoreline south of the Hoan Bridge and east of South Sixth Street, offers one of the best views of the Milwaukee skyline. Formed as a company town by the Milwaukee Iron Company in 1867, the community became home to hundreds of immigrants from England, Scotland, and Wales. Although Bay View has been part of Milwaukee since the turn of the century, it has maintained a distinct sense of community because of its isolation from the rest of the city by the Menomonee River. In recent years many young professionals have flocked to Bay View to renovate some of the older Milwaukee bungalows. And every summer residents from throughout Milwaukee head to Bay View's South Shore Park to celebrate the South Shore Water Frolics, the city's largest neighborhood celebration.

Sherman Park is located just north and west of downtown. Bordered by 60th Street on the west, Capitol Drive on the north, 31st Street on the east, and North Avenue on the south, this well-established neighborhood is a melting pot of ethnic diversity with 40,000 Germans, Jews, and African-Americans calling it home. Developed between 1900 and 1950, this was the first Milwaukee neighborhood to feature the wider lots and larger homes that today have become the staple of suburban living. Designed for what was then the city's emerging middle class, Sherman Park maintains a distinctively suburban atmosphere. Zoning regulations have restricted businesses on the main thoroughfares and the area's setback requirements give the neighborhood a spacious feel.

Story Hill, which sits on a bluff overlooking County Stadium and the Menomonee Valley, is at the geographic center of Milwaukee County. Although hemmed in by some of the city's busiest arteries—I-94 to the south and Wisconsin Avenue to the north—this is a quiet neighborhood of winding streets and beautiful brick and stone homes. Named after Hiram Story, who helped settle the area, this neighborhood developed rapidly in the 1920s and 1930s. The oldest houses date back to World War I and feature the gently sloped roofs of the Prairie School style and the oversize bungalows that are characteristic of the

Even though sometimes it means snowdrifts and stuck cars, winter can be one of Wisconsin's most beautiful seasons. Photo by Eric Oxendorf/Third Coast Stock Source

Craftsman movement. There are also many Milwaukee bungalows and Period Revival homes, which feature half-timbered facades and leaded-glass windows. Cape Cods and ranch-style homes, which were built after World War II, line the outskirts of the neighborhood.

Mitchell Street, located on the city's near south side, has been a commercial center for more than 100 years. Once dubbed "The Polish Grand Avenue," it was the primary shopping center for the south side, which was then home to the thousands of Polish immigrants who were flooding into the area. In the 1920s Mitchell Street was a center for Milwaukee nightlife and featured several theaters, including the Modjeska, which boasted one of the largest vaudeville stages in the state. The street fell on hard times in the 1960s and 1970s with the emergence of shopping malls, but in recent years the city has sought to renew the neighborhood by removing the culs-de-sac and wide sidewalks that restricted traffic. Today Mitchell Street is a blend of the old and new. There is Goldmann's, a department store that opened in 1896, and Kunzelmann-Esser, a furniture store that opened in 1900. There also are many new bridal shops, restaurants, and stores. The neighborhoods surrounding Mitchell Street are still home to many of the original Polish descendants as well as Hispanics and African-Americans.

The Jackson Park neighborhood is considered one of the most desirable places to live on the city's south side. Named after the 117-acre park located at Forest Home Avenue and South 43rd Street, the neighborhood was developed after World War II. It is the heart of the city's predominantly working-class south side and home to many of its German and Polish descendants. Jackson Park is an area known for its impeccably kept yards and beautiful flower gardens. The major thoroughfare in the area is Forest Home Avenue, which stretches diagonally from the Mitchell Street shopping district on the northeast to Highway 100 on the southwest. Forest Home is named after the Victorian-style cemetery located at Forest Home Avenue and South 27th Street, which is the final resting place for many of the city's rich and famous, including beer barons Valentine Blatz, Joseph Schlitz, and Frederick Pabst.

Also located here is Alverno College, a women's school that has been nationally acclaimed for its innovative approach to educa-

Above: Funky offices and loft apartments are springing up in the warehouses of the historic Third Ward, which is located just south of the city's downtown. Photo by Milwaukee DCD/Dave La Haye

Facing page: Brewer's Hill, located just north of downtown, is currently undergoing a major renovation as young people fix up homes once owned by beer barons and brewery workers. Photo by Milwaukee DCD/Dave La Haye

Residential neighborhoods are known for their tree-lined streets and well-kept lawns. Photo by Bruce Buchanan/Third Coast Stock Source

tion. A sizable percentage of its 2,500 students attend "weekend college," a program Alverno designed to serve working women and homemakers. In addition to providing a complete liberal arts curriculum, Alverno offers Jackson Park residents a full calendar of social and cultural events, including concerts, plays, and traveling shows.

The Metropolitan Area

Milwaukee is the heart and soul of the four-county metropolitan Milwaukee area, which includes Milwaukee, Waukesha, Ozaukee, and Washington counties. The city accounts for two-thirds of Milwaukee County's population and almost half of the population for the entire four-county area. Only three other cities in the metropolitan area have populations greater than 45,000—West Allis (63,379), Waukesha (58,428), and Wauwatosa (49,434).

Of the surrounding counties, Waukesha County has the strongest ties to Milwaukee. It is the second-most-populated county in the metropolitan area with more than 323,000 residents, and many of them work in Milwaukee. According to the state Department of Industry, Labor and Human Relations, 57,500 people, or about one-third of the Waukesha County work force, commute to Milwaukee County. Washington and Ozaukee counties are more rural in nature, with populations of 105,105 and 76,320, respectively.

Each county has its own distinct flavor. Milwaukee County is the most urban with cities, villages, and towns woven together in an urban fabric. There are the prestigious North Shore communities of Shorewood, Whitefish Bay, Fox Point, and Bayside, where some turn-of-the century lakefront mansions command sales prices in excess of one million dollars. Just west of I-43 and north of Good Hope Road is River Hills, the only village in the metropolitan area that is zoned entirely residential and where homes are built on five-acre estates. West Allis, located south of I-94 and west of 43rd Street, is primarily a blue-collar town. It was the home of Allis-Chalmers, which was the state's largest private employer until it went bankrupt in the early 1980s. Wauwatosa, located just north of West Allis, is primarily a white-collar community. It is home to the Milwaukee Regional Medical Center, one of the largest medical centers in the nation. It includes the Children's Hospital of Wisconsin, Froedtert Memorial Lutheran Hospital, the Medical College of Wisconsin, and the Curative Rehabilitation Center, the nation's largest treatment facility with more than 40 specialty clinics. Greendale, located in southern Milwaukee County, is one of three "Greenbelt" communities developed by the federal government in the 1930s as an experiment in suburban planning. Parks, gardens, and recreational areas completely surround its downtown.

Waukesha County is a blend of urban and rural living. There are the well-established communities along its eastern edge, including Menomonee Falls, Brookfield, Elm Grove, and New Berlin. Bluemound Road, which parallels I-94 as it cuts through Elm Grove and Brookfield, is one of the area's busiest commercial and business districts. Western Waukesha County, known for its many lakes and the rolling topography of the kettle moraine, has become one of the fastest-growing

Wauwatosa is one of the older communities in the metropolitan area with many 100-year-old homes. Photo by Tony Casper/Third Coast Stock Source

YOU CAN'T SEPARATE MILWAUKEE FROM ITS PEOPLE. THE REASON I live in Milwaukee is because I have faith, or perhaps hope, in the people who live here. One of the challenges we face is to do a better job of celebrating the multicultural fabric that makes Milwaukee so rich. We must focus on the positive aspects of our ethnic diversity rather than the pettiness and misunderstanding and lack of trust that diversity can also bring. Of course, we treasure our own ethnic identity so we cannot expect others to abandon their identity and values and culture. We should never cease to reach out and investigate the beauty and wonder that other cultures offer, but at the same time we must seek out ways to develop our commonality. We must think of Milwaukee's people as being as rich a human resource as our Lake Michigan is a rich natural resource and devote equal time and energy to developing each of them. This is both our challenge and our opportunity.

VEL PHILLIPS

Attorney, former Milwaukee alderwoman, and secretary of state

areas in the state. Upscale homes and condominiums are cropping up throughout the county, especially in the communities of Pewaukee, Dousman, Delafield, Oconomowoc, and Wales.

Ozaukee and Washington counties maintain a distinctively rural flavor, although they have experienced considerable development along their borders with Milwaukee County. Ozaukee County, which stretches vertically along Lake Michigan north of Milwaukee County, features many

The historic village of Cedarburg is especially charming during the holidays. Photo by Susan Lina Ruggles/Third Coast Stock Source

With more than two dozen public courses and several private country clubs, including the scenic Westmoor Country Club in Waukesha County, the Milwaukee area offers a variety of challenges and scenic panoramas for golfers. Photo by Eric Oxendorf/Third Coast Stock Source

charming small towns and quaint country inns. Its county seat, Port Washington, is a fishing village of about 10,000 residents. The city of Cedarburg features buildings dating back to the 1800s. Its downtown is listed on the National Register of Historic Places and its many specialty stores, antique shops, and restaurants make it a popular tourist destination. Mequon, located along the Milwaukee County border, has become a mecca for new residential development.

Washington County, located northwest of Milwaukee, boasts some of the most beautiful topography in the metropolitan area. The many rolling hills and lakes were carved out by two glaciers that collided here during the Ice Age. One of the most spectacular views in the county is from Holy Hill, the National Shrine of Mary. Hundreds of pilgrims come each year to pray at this twin-spired church. The county's largest city is West Bend, the county seat, but the fastest-developing community is Germantown, which abuts the city of Milwaukee.

The communities and counties that surround Milwaukee owe their vibrancy and viability to Milwaukee, the economic engine of southeastern Wisconsin. In return, these cities, towns, and villages offer their residents alternatives to urban living.

For decades, people have been making the pilgrimage to Washington County's Holy Hill, the National Shrine of Mary, to pray for good health. It is also a popular destination in the fall, when the church's observation towers offer breathtaking views of autumn colors in the Kettle Moraine countryside. Photo by Bruce Buchanan

Chapter FIVE

The City of Celebrations

Bo Black was apprehensive.

It was 4 p.m. on the final day of Summerfest and somewhere out there among 90,000 revelers was Pearl Jam's Eddie Vedder—perhaps the most celebrated singer of the college crowd—walking around the grounds with just a baseball cap for a disguise. What would happen if the crowd suddenly realized that the singing superstar was in their midst? Bo didn't want to know.

Instead, Summerfest's executive director grabbed a walkie-talkie, adjusted the laces on her hiking boots, and headed out of her office. "Eddie's good friends with Collective Soul and they're playing at the Leinie Stage so we're pretty sure that's where he's headed," Bo explained between garbled exchanges on her walkie-talkie.

That's how the Sunday afternoon was unfolding for the chief troubleshooter of the nation's largest music festival, which was concluding its 28th year with a record attendance of more than 864,000 people. Bo gently nudged her way through the moving wall of people, pausing only to

The African World Festival is one of eight ethnic celebrations held at the city's lakefront festival park. More than 600,000 people attend the events, which are held almost every weekend throughout the summer. Photo by Susan Lina Ruggles/Third Coast Stock Source

Right: Summerfest, the nation's largest music festival, is held on Milwaukee's lakefront and attracts more than 800,000 people during its 11-day stand. Photo by Susan Lina Ruggles/Third Coast Stock Source

Far right: Irish Fest, a major celebration of Irish music and culture, features many activities for children. Photo by Milwaukee DCD/Dave La Haye

acknowledge someone shouting her name or thanking her for another year of fun in the sun.

The mobs of people and the throbbing musical din on this final day stood in sharp contrast to the festival's opening 11 days earlier when fewer than 1,000 people were on hand at the opening ceremonies to hear Milwaukee Mayor John Norquist sing along with the local band, Mrs. Fun. Back then, Bo didn't have to worry about whether the crowds would recognize the mayor. At 6 foot, 7 inches he's hard to hide. Besides, a singing mayor is as commonplace at Summerfest as cold beer and good music. Milwaukee mayors have been performing their unique version of karaoke at almost every Summerfest since the event began in 1967.

Summerfest was the brainchild of former Milwaukee Mayor Henry Maier, who was captivated by Munich's Oktoberfest celebrations on a visit to Germany. He sought to celebrate Milwaukee's diverse ethnic heritage with a similar event, but Summerfest quickly grew into a major music festival that now attracts more than 800,000 people each year. The festival is held on a 90-acre lakefront park, which has been named the Henry W. Maier Festival Park in honor of the late mayor's vision. It features 11 permanent stages and a continual lineup of jazz, rock, zydeco, blues, big band, and golden oldies music. The 24,000-seat

Marcus Amphitheater draws top acts from around the country. Featured entertainers in 1995 included Bonnie Raitt, Vince Gill, Luther Vandross, Randy Travis, Hootie & the Blowfish, Boyz II Men, Michael Bolton, and Milwaukee's own band, the BoDeans. Then, of course, there was Pearl Jam.

The crowd's intensity surged as Bo approached the Leinie Stage, and she wondered aloud whether Eddie Vedder had been spotted. Suddenly, there was a piercing cry of "Bo! Bo!" Bo turned instinctively, coming face to face with the person who had shouted her name: a young man in his late twenties who was sporting colorful, knee-length shorts and a new Summerfest T-shirt. One of his arms was draped around his smiling girlfriend. In his free hand he grasped a cold beer. "Hey Bo," he said, with a widening smile. "Thanks again for a good time!"

Bo sighed, then smiled back. "Thanks for coming," she replied. Just then the walkie-talkie cackled the news that Eddie Vedder was safely back in his dressing room. Bo acknowledged the message and smiled again. "Oh well," she said. It was just another day at Summerfest.

Ethnic Celebrations

Summerfest isn't the only event that keeps Milwaukee's lakefront bustling with excitement. When Pearl Jam, Jimmy Buffet, John Mellencamp, the BoDeans, and Hootie & the Blowfish aren't playing their respective brands of music, the lakefront park is alive with celebrations of Polish, German, Italian, African-American, Native American, Asian, Mexican, and Irish cultures. Many of these three-day celebrations, including Irish Fest, Festa Italiana, and German Fest, are the largest celebrations of their kind in the nation. All told, these eight summer festivals attract more than 600,000 people a year who come to sample the food, music, and culture of the many ethnic groups that comprise Milwaukee.

Festa Italiana is the most popular ethnic festival, attracting more than 150,000 people during its four-day run. The first Festa Italiana was held in 1978 to bring together the Italian families that had been displaced by local urban renewal and freeway construction in the 1960s. Festa Italiana truly is a celebration of Italy and its culture. The music stages attract major stars such as Dick Contino, The Four Aces, Danny and the Juniors, and Renato, an Italian tenor currently living in England. Gondoliers rekindle romances in the channel that separates the main festival park from Summerfest Island. Sicilian brass bands, costumed Sbandieratori Casventum flag-throwers, and folk groups provide entertainment throughout the grounds.

The festival features an impressive exhibit of sacred art from many of Milwaukee's Catholic churches. Also on view are many vin-

Festa Italiana is the largest of the city's ethnic festivals, offering dancing, music, and lots of delicious Italian specialties. Photo by Milwaukee DCD/Dave La Haye

The Folklorico Dancers energize the Mexican Fiesta with color and dance. Photo by Susan Lina Ruggles/Third Coast Stock Source

Balloon hats are popular among children attending the African World Festival. Photo by Susan Lina Ruggles/Third Coast Stock Source

tage photos of Milwaukee's early Italian immigrants and their communities. Festa Italiana is a celebration for the tastebuds as well. In addition to the many delicious sauces, sausages, and pastas that can be enjoyed at the "Pasta Palace," there are dozens of booths selling cannoli, amaretto puffs, cappuccino, and cassata cakes. Each night, at the conclusion of the day's festivities, an impressive display of fireworks illuminates the shoreline. On Sunday, hundreds of worshippers attend an outdoor Mass that features a colorful religious procession reminiscent of ancient Sicily.

German Fest, which was started in 1981, is coordinated by 33 different German-American societies. Here you will find oompah bands, dachshund shows, tuba players, chess tournaments, yodeling contests, and the always-popular Hummel contest, in which judges look for children who most closely resemble the famous figurines. The festival attracts approximately 100,000 people each year and features more than 40 beer and wine booths, 10 musical stages, and two dozen restaurants offering bratwurst, rollbraten, Wiener schnitzel, and other German favorites.

Irish Fest has been named one of the top 10 attractions in North Amer-

ica by the American Bus Association and is considered one of the best festivals for children because it features a large children's area, storytellers, wandering jugglers, and magicians. The festival, which attracts more than 95,000 people annually, also lures some of the biggest names in Irish music. It features 14 stages with music, dance, and theater, plus daily parades, cultural exhibits, and contests. People come to enjoy the soothing sounds of bagpipes and to admire the work of Irish weavers, knitters, and artists. In addition, those interested in Irish culture can attend a week-long "summer school" that is held the week before Irish Fest. It offers folks the rare opportunity to meet and work with notable Irish scholars and musicians in classes and lectures on Irish music, dance, culture, and history.

Polish Fest was started in 1982 by the Polish National Alliance and today is one of the city's more colorful ethnic festivals. Bright red-and-white banners add an air of vibrancy to the festival grounds, while traditionally dressed dancers perform polkas and other ethnic dances. Polanki, the Polish Women's Cultural Club of Milwaukee, creates educational displays of the kings and queens of Poland, Milwaukee's immigrant neighborhoods, and the country's contribution to the Allied cause in World War II. Also not to be missed are the hand-painted Easter eggs, the charming Christmas tree decorations, and the food, which includes polish sausages, pierogies, czarnina, roast chicken, and roast pig.

Milwaukee's African-American community started African World Festival in 1983 to showcase the culture of their home continent and to promote the achievements of the modern African-American scene. The festival begins with the ritualistic pouring of water and a blessing offered by African shamans. In the thatched-roof village set up in the center of the grounds, African-American artisans demonstrate basketmaking and weaving and storytellers recreate important myths and legends while the tribal chief holds court. Colorful clothing and musical recordings are available in a tented marketplace. Here you can find soul-stirring gospel music, riveting blues, rap, and reggae selections. And when it comes time to eat you can dine on such traditional favorites as sweet potato pie, fried chicken, and corn on the cob. Or, you can sample peanut soup and other truly African dishes.

Mexican Fiesta celebrates life south of the border, featuring souvenirs and artwork from El Salvador, Guatemala, and other Central American countries. The festival attracts more than 60,000 people who come to munch on tacos and tostadas and to dance to the rhythms of mariachi bands and Tex-Mex music. The brave at heart can participate in the jalapeño pepper-eating contest, which is arguably the hottest contest held on the festival grounds!

Indian Summer is one of the last festivals of the year, held just as Milwaukeeans enjoy those last warm rays of summer. Started in 1987, Indian Summer celebrates the spirit of Native America and specifically the Oneida, Menominee, Potowatomi, Ho-Chunk, Chippewa, Stockbridge-Munsee, and other nations. At Indian Summer, many traditional crafts are on display, including basketweaving, wood and stone carving, finger weaving, horsehair art, beadwork, and bow and arrow making. There also is a wide selection of work by modern artists. In keeping with Native

All told, these eight summer festivals attract more than 600,000 people a year who come to sample the food, music, and culture of the many ethnic groups that comprise Milwaukee.

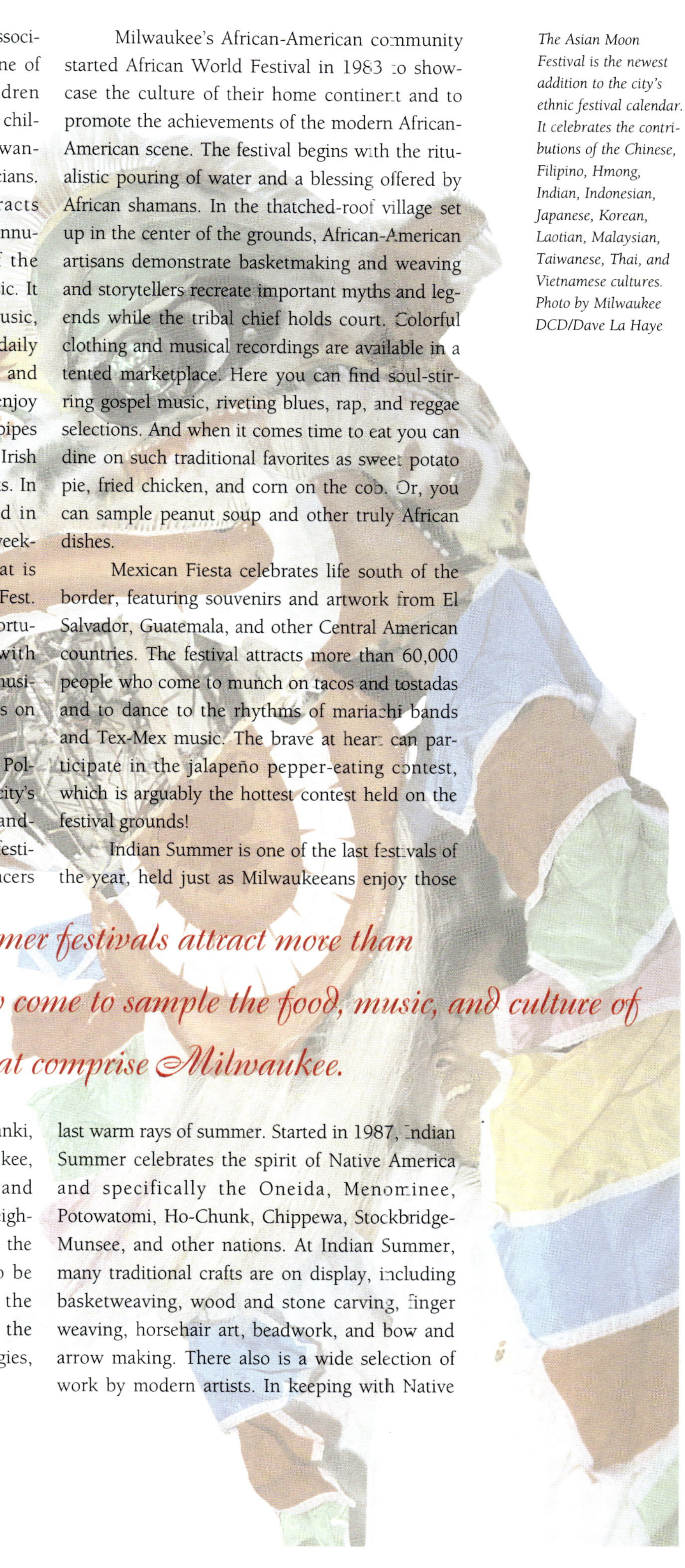

The Asian Moon Festival is the newest addition to the city's ethnic festival calendar. It celebrates the contributions of the Chinese, Filipino, Hmong, Indian, Indonesian, Japanese, Korean, Laotian, Malaysian, Taiwanese, Thai, and Vietnamese cultures. Photo by Milwaukee DCD/Dave La Haye

Americans' reverence for the earth, Indian Summer features an environmental area that promotes the importance of protecting our planet and its resources.

The Asian Moon Festival is Milwaukee's newest lakefront ethnic festival, celebrating Chinese, Filipino, Hmong, Indian, Indonesian, Japanese, Korean, Laotian, Malaysian, Taiwanese, Thai, Vietnamese, and other Asian cultures. Started in 1994 by more than 20 of the city's Asian-American communities, Asian Moon is easily one of the city's most enchanting festivals. The Summerfest grounds explode with bursts of yellow, crimson, and white satin and silk. Among the more popular attractions at the three-day event are calligraphy, kite making, storytelling, origami, and martial arts. Chefs from Milwaukee's noted Asian restaurants serve up tasty dishes and provide cooking demonstrations and tips for at-home cooking.

While there's no question that Milwaukee's lakefront roars with energy during the summer festival season, the streets of downtown Milwaukee boast their own celebrations.

Every July, The Great Circus Parade winds its way through downtown Milwaukee, entertaining tens of thousands of people with its more than 600 horses, 132 clowns, 10 marching bands, and 56 antique circus wagons carrying elephants, tigers, bears, and snakes.

Also in July is Milwaukee's Bastille Days, the largest celebration of the French Revolution in North America. Downtown streets are closed off as people take to the streets to dance to accordions and zydeco music, and to sample French cuisine. The festival begins with the popular "Storm the Bastille" run, a nighttime event that attracts hundreds of joggers and walkers.

In June, the city celebrates its riverfront with RiverSplash! a three-day festival that features music and food along the Milwaukee River. In January, city and suburban residents gather at Cathedral Square for the city's annual Winterfest, which includes a lighted skating rink and an ice-sculpting contest.

Other major Milwaukee area events include the Wisconsin State Fair, which attracts more than 800,000 people to suburban West Allis every

In addition to the many ethnic festivals held on the city's lakefront, Milwaukee hosts numerous street festivals, including Bastille Days, the largest celebration of the French Revolution held in America. Photo by Milwaukee DCD/Dave La Haye

Facing page: Indian Summer, which is held in September, honors the spirit of Native America. Photo by Susan Lina Ruggles/Third Coast Stock Source

FOR A BIG CITY, MILWAUKEE HAS A SMALL-TOWN ATTITUDE.

People are not afraid to talk to you, to help you, and to give you directions. I think that means a lot. I really like everything about Milwaukee. One of the city's greatest assets is Lake Michigan. Our lakefront is both beautiful and calming. If you ever have problems you can go down to the lake, walk along the shore, and see how insignificant your problems are in the grand scheme of things. The ethnic festivals have been a great help in promoting diversity in this city. I never used to know much about the German people or the Polish people. The same was true for the Hmong and the Africans. I knew very little about their cultures. I think the ethnic festivals have helped a lot by opening up whole new worlds to people.

MARLENE WEISROCK

Owner, Four Winds Native American Gift Shop

The Great Circus Parade, started in 1963 by the Jos. Schlitz Brewing Company, features a wide variety of stiltwalkers (opposite) and clowns (above), as well as hundreds of animals and antique circus wagons. Photo on facing page by Alan Magayne-Roshak/Third Coast Stock Source; top photo by Ralph Antczak/Crystal Studio

Left: Juneteenth Day, which celebrates the end of slavery, has been a major summertime event in Milwaukee for 25 years. Photo by Milwaukee DCD/Dave La Haye

RiverSplash! is held in early June along the Milwaukee River and is the city's first summer festival. It features live music, jugglers, and wandering street entertainers. Photos by Milwaukee DCD/Dave La Haye

summer; the Holiday Folk Fair, the nation's oldest and largest indoor ethnic festival, which is held around Thanksgiving; and the Lakefront Festival of the Arts, one of the largest juried art shows in the Midwest, which is held in June.

Museums

There is plenty to do in Milwaukee even when there isn't a festival or parade. The city has a wealth of museums for both children and adults, and recent investments will ensure that this legacy will continue for some time to come. More than $16 million is being spent on three museum projects located on the same city block: the renovation of the Milwaukee Public Museum; the building of a new 40,000-square-foot facility for Discovery World, a science, economics, and technology museum; and the construction of a 260-seat, multistory Humphrey IMAX Theater.

These investments will further enhance Milwaukee's reputation for excellent museums. The Milwaukee Art Museum, located in a spectacular lakefront setting designed by internationally acclaimed architect Eero Saarinen, houses 25,000 works of art spanning several centuries of European and American painting, sculpture, prints, drawings, photography, and decorative arts. It includes masterpieces by Rembrandt, Dürer, Picasso, and Warhol, as well as its famed American and Haitian folk art collections. A new $27-million addition, slated to be completed by the year 2000, will increase the museum's exhibit space by 25 percent and add a 300-seat auditorium. Other Milwaukee art museums of note are the Patrick and Beatrice Haggerty Museum of Art at Marquette University; the University of Wisconsin-Milwaukee Art Museum; the Villa Terrace Decorative Arts Museum, which is located in a

There are plenty of places along the Milwaukee River to sit and enjoy the music, especially near Pere Marquette Park. Photo by Milwaukee DCD/ Dave La Haye

There's always time for art in Milwaukee, whether it's an international ice-sculpting contest (above) or the Lakefront Festival of the Arts (right), one of the largest juried art shows in the Midwest. Photos by Milwaukee DCD/Dave La Haye

Facing page: The Wisconsin State Fair, held every August, is one of the region's most popular events. Photo by Dale Guldan/Third Coast Stock Source

38
Drink
Milk
in the
Shade
and
get
in a
Cool
Mooo-d

beautiful Italian-style villa on a bluff overlooking Lake Michigan; the outdoor Bradley Sculpture Garden; and the Charles Allis Art Museum, which houses a breathtaking collection of paintings and priceless *objets d'art* in the city's most elegant historical mansion of the Edwardian period.

The Milwaukee Institute of Art and Design will soon open an advertising and design museum that will celebrate the city's rich marketing communications heritage. The 22,000-square-foot Eisner Museum, named after William F. Eisner, Sr., founder of local advertising agency William Eisner & Associates, will be located on two floors of a MIAD-owned building at North Water and East Chicago streets in the historic Third Ward.

The Milwaukee Public Museum is considered one of the best natural history museums in the country and enriches the lives of approximately 450,000 patrons each year. Home to more than 4.3 million specimens, the museum also conducts nationally recognized field work and research. Its most popular attractions include the world's largest dinosaur skull, in Dinosaur Hall; "The Streets of Old Milwaukee," which depicts life in the city at the turn of the century; "The Rain Forest: Exploring Life on Earth," a two-story exhibit that features five video theaters and a working waterfall; "A Tribute to Survival," which provides an overview of Native American history and culture; and "Temples, Tells & Tombs," which features Egyptian mummies.

The Milwaukee Art Museum contains 25,000 works spanning several centuries of European and American art. Photo by Ralph Antczak/Crystal Studio

Milwaukee boasts two museums dedicated to children. Discovery World, which is geared for children six years and older, features more than 140 exhibits, including "The Great Electric Show," "The Light Waves & Laser Beam Show," and "Health is Wealth."

The Betty Brinn Children's Museum, which opened in March 1995, offers stimulating interactive exhibits and activities for inquiring young

The Bradley Sculpture Garden showcases an impressive collection of contemporary sculptures in a beautifully landscaped setting. Photo by Joanne K. Peterson/Third Coast Stock Source

minds and their families. One of its more popular attractions is the "Trading Place," a play area designed to give children a hands-on feel for work, economics, and commerce. Here they can "manage" a restaurant or a produce stand, operate an apple juice factory, or work in a bank that features a vault, a security camera, and a "drive-up" window.

Nature lovers flock toward the Boerner Botanical Gardens—40 acres of formal gardens that showcase more than 3,000 perennials, 35,000 tulips, 350 peonies, and one of the largest flowering crab tree collections in the country. Boerner's annual Rose Festival, a major summertime event, pays tribute to the more than 350 varieties of roses grown there. Another popular attraction is the Mitchell Park Horticultural Conservatory. Known locally as "The Domes," it showcases three different environments, each housed in its own glass dome. One dome is dedicated to desert plants, another to tropical fauna; the third dome features seasonal displays.

The 200-acre Milwaukee County Zoo was designed so that the animals could live in their natural surroundings. In many of the exhibits, only a hidden moat separates predators and their prey. The zoo features 4,000 different types of animals and attracts approximately 1.4 million

The new Discovery World museum and Humphrey IMAX large-screen theater are slated to open in late 1996, bringing more family-type entertainment to downtown Milwaukee. Courtesy, Discovery World Museum

visitors each year. Recently the zoo has invested $26 million in a new primate building, a new penguin exhibit, and a renovated aviary. In 1995 the zoo opened a refurbished aquatic and reptile center, which includes sharks, octopuses, alligators, and several displays of fish that are native to Wisconsin lakes.

Milwaukee County also oversees more than 15,000 acres of parkland, encompassing 150 parks and parkways, 16 public golf courses, 100 tennis courts, and more than a dozen indoor and outdoor swimming pools. The county's beaches offer several miles of unobstructed Lake Michigan shoreline, giving the public easy access to the

I MOVED TO MILWAUKEE TO GET CLOSER TO CHICAGO INITIALLY, and I've had some opportunities to leave the city, but the city has grown on my family. It's a great place to raise a family and we've become involved with many community events, including Juneteenth Day, which is celebrating its 25th anniversary. What would I tell friends who were thinking about moving to Milwaukee? I would tell them that it's becoming a lot more progressive. The rap against Milwaukee when I first got here was that it was 20 years behind the rest of the country in fashion, music, trends, and culture. But I think Milwaukee has changed quite a bit over the years. I see a lot of signs that Milwaukee is growing, due in large part to all of the ethnic festivals it has. Almost every ethnic group has a festival and behind that festival is an enormous amount of pride. That is something that Milwaukee has over other cities. A lot of cities aspire to have that kind of close-knittedness and that kind of celebration, but they just can't start it or sustain it.

BILL TAYLOR
Anchor, WTMJ-TV

area's most valuable natural resource. With one acre of land for every 60 residents, it is no wonder that the parks department is an important part of county government.

Theaters and Music

Many believe that the emerald in Milwaukee's cultural crown is its acclaimed theater scene, which boasts well over a dozen professional companies and numerous community theater groups. Fueled by the proven successes of the University of Wisconsin-Milwaukee's renowned Professional Theater Training Program and the irrepressible arts advocacy of the Milwaukee Repertory Theater's Sara O'Connor, who served as the theater's managing director for 20 years, the city boasts one of the most vibrant theater communities in the country.

"Other than New York, there's no city for theater like Milwaukee," says former *Sentinel* drama critic Jay Joslyn. "Neither Boston, San Diego, nor Los Angeles has half as much. Milwaukee is truly exceptional."

With newly established leadership by artistic director Joseph Hanreddy and managing director Dan Fallon, the nationally acclaimed Milwaukee Repertory Theater continues its tradition of excellence in its downtown, three-stage complex. The 1995-1996 season's final show, Larry Shue's "The Nerd," was of considerable significance for Milwaukee. Created when Shue was in residence with the Rep, the sparkling comedy has gone on to become a standard repertory piece for theater companies on virtually every level from amateur to professional.

The Rep recently established an endowment fund to provide the theater with greater financial stability in an era of shrinking government budgets. "We refer to our endowment as a campaign to create the future," Fallon says. "It is enabling us to be sure of the fact that we will be here and will continue to grow."

A variety of smaller companies contribute in an equally important way to the city's theater

With more than 11,000 tulips on display, the Boerner Botanical Gardens is an ideal place for a leisurely Mother's Day stroll. Photo by Milwaukee DCD/Dave La Haye

The Mitchell Park Horticultural Conservatory, locally known as "The Domes," consists of three geodesic domes showcasing different environments. One features tropical fauna; another houses cacti, palm trees, and other desert plants. The third dome features spectacular seasonal displays. Photo on facing page by Tony Casper/Third Coast Stock Source; top photo by Peter Saunders/ Third Coast Stock Source

community. The adventuresome Theatre X specializes in the innovative and the avant-garde, blending theater with performance art under the astute guidance of artistic director and recent Pulitzer Prize nominee John Schneider. The "X" in Theatre X stands for the company's quest to explore, experience, and examine the unknown factor in the human equation. For 27 years Theatre X has been "doing its own thing" and every year that thing changes, because in the span of just one year that new thing becomes an old thing. Along the way, the group has developed and produced plays in New York, Seattle, Chicago, Baltimore, Amsterdam, London, Sweden, and Japan.

Also on the cutting edge of contemporary theater is David Cecsarini's Next Act Theatre. "Every show I've seen has knocked my socks off," says the Skylight Opera Theatre's marketing director Marietta Hedges, a big fan of theater in all forms. "It's the kind of thing that moves you, and that's what theater should do."

At the other end of the spectrum is Montgomery Davis' Milwaukee Chamber Theatre, a strong literature-based company that puts great emphasis on the spoken word. With a repertoire ranging from classical through contemporary, its mission is to challenge, involve, and entertain. One of its major attractions is its annual Shaw Festival, an event that regularly attracts national attention.

The African-American community has several theater companies of its own. Among them are the African-American Children's Theatre, the Hansberry-Sands Theatre Company, and the new Andre Ellis Company.

Milwaukee offers a rich theatrical experience for children as well as adults. The Great American Children's Theater, led by producer Teri Mitze, entertains more than 50,000 Milwaukee children each year. The 1995-1996 season included performances by the Peking Acrobats, the American Indian Dance Theater, the Preservation Hall Jazz Band, and Milwaukee's own Ko-Thi Dance Company. "Children learn best about children when they know about each other's culture," Mitze says. There are several other children's theaters as well. M&W Productions specializes in such favorites as *The Princess and the Pea*, *The Story of the Nutcracker*, and *The Reluctant Dragon*, while First Stage Milwaukee presents six innovative shows annually. Under the direction of artistic director Rob Goodman, First Stage Milwaukee was named "the outstanding new children's theater company in America" in 1991 by the American Alliance for Theatre and Education. Also of note is the Milwaukee Public Theatre, an outgrowth of the street theater concept for children.

It incorporates circus-based techniques such as juggling, parades, and masques into its performances.

The metropolitan area is fortunate to have an extensive network of community theaters as well, including the Sunset Playhouse, Acacia Theatre Company, the Boulevard Ensemble, and a host of smaller groups such as the Bay Players, the Brookfield Players, Amethyst, the Evergreen Theater, and the Falls Patio Players.

Milwaukee is a city that knows how to dance. It is among only a handful of cities that can boast a full-scale ballet company. The Milwaukee Ballet, under the direction of artistic director Basil Thompson, features 28 company dancers and another 14 dancers who perform on occasion. Its 1995-1996 slate of productions was representative of the diverse repertoire the company promotes. It included *Virgin Forest*, a hometown original that was commissioned by the Milwaukee Ballet. It featured the jungle paintings of Henri Rousseau, which were literally brought to life on stage; *The Tempest*, a visual extravaganza with choreography by Michael Smuin and music by Paul Chihara, based on a score by Henry Purcell; and the classic *Beauty and the Beast*.

Dancecircus is a modern dance troupe and folk music group that performs throughout Wisconsin and the Midwest. Under the direction of dancer Betty Salamun and her husband, folksinger David Drake, Dancecircus mounts more than 200 concert-level dance and folk music productions annually. The Milwaukee Dance Theatre, led by artistic director Isabelle Kralj, appeals to a wide audience through its celebration of stylistic and theatrical diversity—from baroque to flamenco to modern—with a prominent emphasis on the expressive elements of dance. The Ko-Thi Dance Company celebrates the spirit and vitality of African dance and drumming with two major productions annually—Kuumba, which takes place every summer, and the Harvest Celebration, held in the fall. "In the Spirit," the 1995 Harvest Celebration performance, paid tribute to the

The Milwaukee Repertory Theater (opposite) presents a variety of classical, contemporary, and holiday offerings, including the always-popular "Christmas Carol." Courtesy, Milwaukee Repertory Theater

Milwaukee is one of only a few cities that can boast a ballet with its own symphony orchestra. During the Christmas season, it gives two dozen performances of the "Nutcracker Suite," which has become a Milwaukee holiday tradition. Photo by Ralph Antczak/Crystal Studio

The Ko-Thi Dance Company has earned an international reputation for innovation and excellence in African dance. Courtesy, Ko-Thi Dance Company

Right: The Milwaukee Dance Theatre appeals to a wide audience through its celebration of stylistic and theatrical diversity. Courtesy, Milwaukee Dance Theatre

influence of artistic director Ferne Caulker, who recently spent three months in Tanzania on a sabbatical. Other dance companies of note include Debra Loewen's Wild Space Dance Company, which specializes in improvisational dance styles; and Yves deBouteiller's Et toi, tu danses?, which continues to nurture local talent.

Unique to the Milwaukee community is the three-year-old Danceworks, a dance service organization that provides instruction and outreach, and coordinates the presentation of local and national dance artists. "They're really revitalizing the dance community," says Chris Segedy, who has managed various Milwaukee arts organizations.

Milwaukee has a rich musical heritage. It attracts many major popular concerts, which are held at the Riverside Theater, the Marcus Amphitheater, or the Bradley Center. The city also boasts several smaller venues. The performing arts are typically staged at one of three major venues: the Marcus Center for the Performing Arts (formerly the Performing Arts Center), the Broadway Theatre Center, and the Milwaukee Center, which includes the Pabst Theater, the Stackner Cabaret, and the Powerhouse Theater. The three performing areas share a common foyer that also connects them with a 28-story office building.

The elegant Pabst Theater, which celebrated its centennial in 1995, was built by beer baron Captain Frederick Pabst. Designed in the German Baroque Revival style, the 1,400-seat theater escaped destruction by developers in the 1960s and is now listed on the National Register of Historic Places.

The Pabst Theater is well known for its performing arts series, which encompasses world music, big bands, comedy, and dance, along with pianist Jeffrey Siegel's enduringly popular Keyboard Conversations. The Pabst's Artist Series has a long tradition of presenting the finest in chamber music on an international level. Its 1995-1996 season included pianists Andre Watts and Awadagin Pratt, along with the Leipzig Chamber Orchestra. The Pabst's Hal Leonard Jazz Series is studded with names on the order of Benny Carter, Wayne Shorter, and Horace Silver.

Another major venue is the Marcus Center, which includes several venues for performing artists, including the 2,300-seat Uihlein Hall and the outdoor Peck Pavilion, which is home to a popular series of summer lunchtime concerts. The Marcus Center also recently began hosting a number of touring Broadway musicals.

The city's newest venue is the Broadway Theatre Center, located in the city's Third Ward. It includes the new homes of the Skylight Opera, the Milwaukee Chamber Theatre, and Theatre X.

Milwaukee's colleges and universities contribute significantly to the city's strong musical tradition. The University of Wisconsin-Milwaukee's Great Artist Series features a diverse lineup focusing on some of the country's most exciting names in jazz and dance. The internationally acclaimed Fine Arts Quartet offers a series of several concerts annually while Judit Jaimes' Piano Chamber Concerts and Jeffry Peterson's Vocal Arts Series both showcase outstanding events including guest performers of international stature.

Alverno Presents, sponsored by Alverno College, has established itself as an indispensable performing arts series that ranges from "Sweet Honey in the Rock" (in 1995) to famed author and poet Maya Angelou. Additionally, the Wisconsin Conservatory of Music's Concert Series annually showcases its fine faculty, while Mount Mary College

The Milwaukee community has always shown strong support for the arts. One of the city's major venues, the Marcus Center for the Performing Arts (above), is undergoing a $22-million interior and exterior renovation. The city's largest theater company, the Milwaukee Repertory Theater (left), performs at its new home at the Milwaukee Center. Top photo by Eric Oxendorf/ Third Coast Stock Source; photo at left by Jay Westhauser/ Milwaukee Repertory Theater

Facing page: The 1,400-seat Pabst Theater recently underwent a major renovation to restore its century-old splendor. Photo by Dale Guldan/Third Coast Stock Source

has developed a popular two-concert recital series featuring guest artists of national renown.

The Milwaukee Symphony Orchestra is one of the nation's busiest orchestras, performing approximately 200 concerts annually in its classical and pops subscription series, along with a wide variety of educational programs for children of all ages. The orchestra has attained national acclaim for its innovative educational ideas including the Arts in Community Education project, a collaborative venture with selected area schools; the beloved Kinderkonzerts, which are designed to kindle musical appreciation in young children; the popular high school concerts; Sound Generations, a series of performances geared to families; and the consistently sold-out Classical Conversations with resident conductor Neal Gittleman.

The Milwaukee Chamber Orchestra, which is close to celebrating its silver anniversary, presents works for small orchestras under the baton of Stephen Colburn. Its late-winter choral concert in the Cathedral of St. John, which featured the Milwaukee Symphony Chamber Singers and Milwaukee Children's Chorus, is fast becoming an indispensable Milwaukee tradition.

Now comfortably ensconced in its sterling Baroque-style space in the new Broadway Theatre Center, the Skylight Opera Theatre rests firmly on its established reputation for intriguing, sparkling, and stimulating productions of opera and musical theater. The troupe is known for its wide-ranging repertoire, which includes everything from Mozart to Gilbert & Sullivan. *The Atlanta Journal and Constitution* called it "one of the country's most extraordinary music theatre companies." Its 1995-1996 season included Mozart's *Marriage of Figaro*, a Gilbert & Sullivan revue, and *Die Fledermaus*, which closed the season in June.

The Florentine Opera Company, now in its seventh decade, is the fifth-oldest opera company in the nation. It lavishly produces three grand operas annually in conjunction with the Milwaukee Symphony Orchestra. Great Lakes Opera produces first-rate operatic works, particularly from the earlier part of this century, on a modest budget using reductions of the musical score for synthesizer or piano. Milwaukee Musical Theatre contributes notably as well to the medium of operatic performance on a smaller scale.

Present Music, guided by artistic director Kevin Stalheim, has established itself as the city's premier new music ensemble. Its burgeoning audiences can attest to its proven formula for

MILWAUKEE IS A BIG CITY WITH A SMALL-TOWN ATTITUDE. IT IS FILLED with people who understand and appreciate hard work and its rewards. Milwaukeeans are the most accepting people I have ever met. They treat you like family, rejoicing in your triumphs and helping you through the tough times. It's also a city that looks out for its own. You can be sure that your family, and especially your children, can grow up safely with small-town values in a big city. I was born and raised in Wisconsin and I would never want to leave the Midwest. —CAROLE

Milwaukee is a great place to raise a family. I have a wife and three kids and I like the school systems and I like the values—good midwestern values. I am from Pittsburgh and I love the Midwest. Milwaukee is like Pittsburgh in many respects. They are both filled with people who are very devoted to their families. They work very hard, but they also know how to have a good time. —DAVE

CAROLE CAINE and DAVE LUCZAK
Radio personalities at WKLH-FM

making new music educational, enlightening, and consummately entertaining. While Present Music unveils exciting new musical visions of the future, other Milwaukee groups celebrate music's rich heritage. Joan Parsley's Historical Keyboard Society of Wisconsin combines the talents of some of the world's greatest period-instrument virtuosi with those of local gifted artists, while Early Music Now presents a slate of internationally renowned early music ensembles.

Sports

Milwaukee is a city of sports. Local sporting events attract close to 3 million people annually. The city boasts two new sporting complexes, the Bradley Center, which is used for basketball,

The Pettit National Ice Center (left) is both a training ground for U.S. Olympians and a recreational facility for families. Amal McGaskill (above) led the Marquette University Golden Eagles to the second round of the 1996 NCAA Tournament. Photo at left by Milwaukee DCD/Dave La Haye; top photo courtesy, Marquette University

The Lake Park Bistro, one of Milwaukee's newest restaurants, offers exquisite French cuisine in a setting that overlooks Lake Michigan. Photo by Bruce Buchanan

Sanford D'Amato, chef and co-owner of Sanford Restaurant, was recently named the best Midwest chef by the nation's leading chefs, restaurateurs, and food writers. Photo by Bruce Buchanan

hockey, soccer, and arena football, and the Pettit National Ice Center, one of only three facilities of its kind in the world. It contains two international-size hockey rinks and a 400-meter speed-skating oval that is used to train Olympic athletes for competition.

City, county, and state officials are working with the Milwaukee Brewers on a new $250-million stadium for the professional baseball team. The new stadium will feature natural grass and a convertible roof that can be closed in inclement weather.

Frozen custard is one of Milwaukee's favorite foods. Even in the depths of winter, lines will form at custard stands such as Leon's Frozen Custard Drive-In on South 27th Street. Photo by Milwaukee DCD/Dave La Haye

In addition to the Brewers, Milwaukee is home to the Milwaukee Bucks, a professional basketball team; the Milwaukee Admirals, which belong to the International Hockey League; the Milwaukee Wave, a professional indoor soccer team; and the Milwaukee Mustangs arena football team. Fans of collegiate-level sports can watch the home games of the Marquette Golden Eagles and the University of Wisconsin-Milwaukee Panthers, both of which competed in the NCAA Division I.

Race car enthusiasts head to the Milwaukee Mile at the State Fair Park, which is the nation's oldest continuously operated raceway. It hosts several major events, including the Miller Genuine Draft 200 Indy Car Race in early June and the NASCAR Busch Grand National Series Stock Car Race on the Fourth of July weekend.

Milwaukee is home to the Greater Milwaukee Open, which attracts more than 13,000 spectators and some of the best talent on the PGA circuit. The event is held at the Milwaukee County-owned Brown Deer Park golf course, ranked as one of the five best public courses in the nation.

Eating Out

As a melting pot of nationalities, Milwaukee can dish up for the tastebuds a wealth of savory meals from around the world and at a value that amazes many people.

"People are keeping their cultures alive through flavors and that's what makes Milwaukee's restaurant scene so magical," says Willard Romantini, a well-known food enthusiast whose restaurant reviews are regularly featured in *Milwaukee Magazine* and on WKTI-FM radio.

"Milwaukee is a celebration of diversity," Romantini says. "People enjoy showcasing their culture through food, whether it be Polish, German, French, Japanese, or Middle Eastern. Because of that, you can literally go in and take a tour of the world just by visiting some of Milwaukee's restaurants."

For many years, Milwaukee was best known for its German and Polish restaurants, which served hearty portions at "workingman's prices." Those who ventured off the beaten path, however, could also relish the delicacies of French, Serbian, Greek, and Italian cuisines at small restaurants tucked away in quiet neighborhoods.

Knut Apitz, executive chef and owner of Grenadier's restaurant, a downtown dining landmark, says that 20 years ago Milwaukee's restaurant scene was dominated by Europeans. Today, he says, it's wide open.

Thanks to the influx of recent immigrants and more adventuresome diners, restaurants featuring Russian, Vietnamese, Middle Eastern, and Thai food have opened in recent years. In addition, the advent of overnight delivery services has made the finest fruits, fish, and truffles the world has to offer accessible to even the smallest establishments.

"There are a lot of young people who are putting their own unique stamp on Milwaukee's palate," says Apitz, who recently received the President's Medal from the American Culinary Federation for his lifelong contributions to the culinary arts.

Milwaukee's blossoming dining scene has not gone unnoticed. *Nation's Restaurant News*, a leading restaurant publication, featured the Milwaukee market in a recent issue. "Milwaukee has become a popular town because it has so many good places to eat at a relatively good bargain compared to places like Chicago and New York City," Romantini says.

Some restaurants serve a delicious mixture of ethnic flavors. Take Sanford Restaurant, a nationally acclaimed downtown neighborhood restaurant that has been owned and operated by chef Sanford D'Amato and his wife, Angela, since 1989. "He takes a multi-ethnic approach to classical French," Romantini explains. "His food is French with an American twist, but it also has Asian influences."

Born in Milwaukee, D'Amato studied and worked in New York before returning here. In 1996 he was named the best Midwest Chef in the Sixth Annual James Beard Awards, which are judged by the nation's leading chefs, restaurateurs, cookbook authors, and journalists.

D'Amato says he enjoys operating a restaurant in Milwaukee because the city allows him and his wife to fully enjoy their work. "We're making a good living and we have a great lifestyle," he says. "And there is a tremendous amount of great ethnic food here—which is wonderful." Angela D'Amato says Milwaukee's fine dining scene is supported by "very loyal" patrons. "We have a very wonderful and gracious clientele who appreciate fine dining," she says.

Grenadier's Apitz says Milwaukee dining is special because of the attention to detail and service each customer receives. "In Milwaukee, you have to serve every customer as well as you possibly can because they live here for life," he says. "They're not transients."

In addition to Grenadier's and Sanford Restaurant, there are many other acclaimed dining establishments in the Milwaukee area, including Steven Wade's Cafe, Bartolotta's Lake Park Bistro, The English Room at the Pfister Hotel, Bartolotta Ristorante, Osteria del Mondo, Mike & Anna's, and Heaven City, which specializes in offering local specialties, such as pheasant, rabbit, and other game.

Friday nights are for fish fries. There are few restaurants in the Milwaukee area that don't serve up heaping portions of Atlantic cod or lake perch to satisfy the city's almost insatiable hunger

I CAME HERE FROM LAOS FOUR YEARS AGO TO LIVE WITH MY UNCLE.

I did not know anything about Milwaukee, but I am very glad I came here. There are so many jobs and so many educational opportunities. Young people can find work here if they look around. I came from a small village of 300 people and it took me awhile to get used to living in the city. I think there is too much crime. I see too many young Hmong people in jail because their parents don't know how to help them. Because the English language is very hard, sometimes the Hmong and the police cannot work well together. But Milwaukee has been very good to me. I have been treated with respect and given many opportunities. I have studied very hard in school. During the summer I have worked at a factory to make money. Right now, I think I would like to go to college and return home to help the people in my country.

YOUA VANG
1996 graduate of Washington High School
Martin Luther King, Jr., Scholarship winner

Carriage rides offer a romantic tour of downtown Milwaukee. Photo by Milwaukee DCD/ Dave La Haye

for these low-priced meals. In fact, demand is so great for these fish fries that many restaurants offer carry-outs. One of the city's best-known places for fish fries is historic Turner Restaurant, a downtown landmark that has been a major gathering place since the late 1800s. In 1995 the restaurant underwent a major renovation. Stained-glass windows, dark trim, and polished wooden floors have recreated its Old World charm.

Milwaukee can boast some unique flavors. It is one of a handful of cities in the nation where you can buy frozen custard, a delicious alternative to ice cream. Dozens of frozen custard stands are sprinkled throughout the metropolitan area, the most famous of which are Leon's Frozen Custard Drive-In, which boasts a 1950s "Happy Days" motif, and Kopp's, which has three custard stands, each of them architecturally distinct.

Also unique to Milwaukee is George Webb's, a locally owned chain of more than three dozen diners that dish up inexpensive meals to everyone from blue-collar workers to chief executive officers. Although George Webb's may be the standard-bearer for family-style diners, there are hundreds of other restaurants serving great meals at affordable prices to Milwaukee families. Whether you're looking for gourmet dining experience or a hearty hamburger, Milwaukee's restaurants have a menu selection for you. "If you're planning to visit Milwaukee, come here hungry," says Romantini. "You're going to get fed very well."

From rock and roll to opera, from museums to sports and fine dining, Milwaukee is a city that is alive with activity.

"There is never a shortage of things to do in Milwaukee, especially in the summertime," says Maribeth Lynch, president of MB Publications, a Milwaukee company that publishes *The Greater Milwaukee Relocation Handbook*, which helps new people become accustomed to the area. "People who have lived here all of their lives assume this is what life is like in any city, but the people who move here are just amazed at all the things there are to do."

ESAB

Chapter SIX

The Heartbeat of the Midwest

On September 22, 1995, Milwaukee-based Midwest Express Airlines took to the air for the first time as a publicly traded company. Even before the first trade was made, the stock's price had surged from $18 to $21.50 per share—and demand still outstripped supply. More than one million shares changed hands within the first 90 minutes of trading on the New York Stock Exchange.

This was no high-flying, high-tech stock that speculative investors were snapping up in order to rake in profits. The demand for Midwest Express stock ran much deeper. It was based on real value: the airline's commitment to quality and its reputation for providing "the best care in the air." In many ways, Midwest Express is like the city it calls home. Both are known for their strong work ethic and have a reputation for value. Neither is given to glitz or self-aggrandizement.

After suffering severely in the manufacturing recession of the early 1980s, area businesses retooled and retrained. Since then, Milwaukee has become a leader in exports and manufacturing, consistently outperforming the national economy over the past decade. Photo by Scott Witte/Third Coast Stock Source

Started as a corporate shuttle service for Kimberly-Clark executives, Midwest Express has evolved into one of the world's most highly regarded airlines. It's not big. With 23 jets, Midwest Express isn't even ranked with Delta, United, TWA, Continental, or the other commercial airline giants. Nor is it flashy. Many people outside of the Midwest have never heard of the airline.

MIDWEST Express
N700ME
N600ME
MIDWEST Express

And Midwest Express is not out to conquer the world.

"We're not trying to become something we're not," Midwest Express president Timothy Hoeksema told Peter S. Greenberg, The Savvy Traveler, in a 1992 interview. "We just want to grow slow enough to maintain our culture and service ... We have no illusions about being a big airline. We just want to be the best."

And for many people, Midwest Express is the best. It is continually praised for its service, wide seats, gourmet food, and chocolate chip cookies, which are baked on board and served fresh to passengers.

The Consumer Reports Traveler Letter has named Midwest Express the best domestic airline four years in a row. The readers of *Condé Nast Traveler*, a New York-based travel magazine, bestowed an identical honor on the airline in 1992, 1993, 1994, and 1995. And Midwest Express was the only U.S. airline to be ranked among the Top 10 airlines worldwide by the prestigious *Zagat Airline Survey*, which polls 9,400 frequent flyers and travel industry professionals. The inclusion of Midwest Express—dubbed the "Rolls Royce of Regionals"—marked the first time an American airline had made the survey's Top 10.

Like Midwest Express, Milwaukee has had to build its reputation on quality, not size. As the 17th-largest city and 35th-largest metropolitan area in the country, Milwaukee is seldom compared to New York, Los Angeles, or Chicago. Many people outside of the Midwest have a hard time placing it geographically. But Milwaukee is known—both nationally and internationally—for quality products, competitive prices, and a labor force that understands what it means to put in an honest day's work.

This commitment to quality and service has paid off. Both Midwest Express and the Milwaukee metropolitan area have outperformed the nation in key economic areas. Midwest Express has been consistently profitable since 1986, during a time when the airline industry as a whole was losing billions of dollars. During that same period, metro Milwaukee's job growth, unemployment rate, business start-ups, and residential construction have outperformed national averages.

In 1992 the *Kiplinger Washington Letter* noted Milwaukee was "growing as a world leader in exports and manufacturing (with) everything from medical instruments, controls, small engines, and gears to aviation electronics, ceramics, padlocks, and construction equipment. ... Milwaukee avoided the recession that hit most of the U.S. While top sprinters take a breather—San Diego, Los Angeles, Portland, Seattle, Washington, D.C.—workhorse cities such as Milwaukee will carry the nation's economy."

But Milwaukee is known—both nationally and internationally—for quality products, competitive prices, and a labor force that understands what it means to put in an honest day's work.

In 1994 the metropolitan area was ranked as the sixth-best place to start a business, and the *1995 Corporate Almanac* reported that Milwaukee has the second-best business survival rate among the nation's major metropolitan areas and the 10th best jobs-generation rate.

Both Milwaukee and Midwest Express can trace their current fortune back to 1984. Back then, Milwaukee was grappling with the worst recession it had endured since the Great Depression. Manufacturers were boarding up their foundries and factories, throwing tens of thousands of people out of work. Executives were looking for ways to restructure their companies so they could compete and grow in a marketplace that had seemingly changed overnight. Nineteen eighty-four also was the year that Midwest Express officially became an airline.

Both Midwest Express and Milwaukee faced an uphill battle. Many analysts doubted whether the airline's gourmet meals, personal service, and

Facing page: Midwest Express, which is based in Milwaukee, is the only U.S. airline to be ranked among the top 10 airlines worldwide by frequent flyers and travel industry professionals. Courtesy, Midwest Express Airlines

Federal Plaza, which was built in 1983, features an airy, 13-story atrium. Photo by Eric Oxendorf/Third Coast Stock Source

roomy airplanes could survive in a marketplace that was increasingly dominated by discounted tickets and rate wars. Economic pundits, meanwhile, had already written off Milwaukee as another casualty of "The Rustbelt."

But both Milwaukee and Midwest Express stuck to their values—and it paid off. Today Midwest Express employs more than 1,500 people, provides direct service to 24 cities, and serves more than one million passengers annually from its hubs in Milwaukee and Omaha, Nebraska. Milwaukee's economy, meanwhile, has created more than 130,000 jobs since 1983. The metro area's unemployment rate has dropped from 10.4 percent in 1983 to 3.2 percent in September 1995, the lowest rate in 25 years.

"Milwaukee companies have successfully realigned their activities to become cost-effective producers of quality capital goods," says Clare Zempel, chief economist for Robert W. Baird & Co. Incorporated, a large regional brokerage firm based in Milwaukee. "In addition, the Milwaukee labor force has demonstrated that it is skilled and much more flexible than many might have thought in the early 1980s."

Milwaukee may be best known for its breweries, but in reality it has a diverse economy that features strong manufacturing and service sectors. Milwaukee-area businesses generate more than $60 billion in sales annually, two-thirds of which comes from manufacturers and wholesalers. The government sector is conspicuously small. Less than 12 percent of the work force is employed in public-sector jobs, almost a third less than the national average. "Milwaukee is a private-sector city," says Milwaukee Mayor John Norquist. "We are not the state capital, so we don't have a lot of government employees. And we don't have military bases. As a result, the economic tide of the city rises and falls with commerce."

Flower stands blossom throughout the Milwaukee area in early summer, when residents begin sprucing up their yards and neighborhoods. Photo by Bruce Buchanan

I HAVE LIVED IN MILWAUKEE ALL OF MY LIFE, AND I TALK IT UP wherever I go. It is one of the cleanest cities I have ever been in and it is also a city of opportunities. You can get a nice job here. All you've got to do is have the know-how, push yourself, and keep moving. We lost a lot of jobs when Schlitz, Blatz, and American Motors left town and we need some companies to come into the city and create more jobs. But we are starting to see some development along Martin Luther King Jr. Drive and I think the Wisconsin Center is really going to help the city. We've got to police the politicians. If they don't do what they promise, you get them out of office. I think Milwaukee is a great place to live. People might leave Milwaukee, but a lot of them come back.

EVERETT "BOOBIE" MOORE

Owner of Boobie's Place cocktail lounge and restaurant

PLAZA EAST GARAGE

Plaza East, one of several office buildings constructed in downtown Milwaukee since 1984, is located just down the street from City Hall and the Marcus Center for the Performing Arts. Photo by Milwaukee DCD/ Dave La Haye

There are close to 38,000 businesses in the metropolitan area, which includes Milwaukee, Ozaukee, Washington, and Waukesha counties. Sixty percent of area businesses are located in Milwaukee County and another 28 percent have set up shop in Waukesha County.

All told, Milwaukee businesses employ more than 780,000 people, 96 percent of whom live in the four-county area. The vast majority of these companies—93 percent—are small businesses with fewer than 50 employees. However, the Milwaukee area is home to several large national and international companies, including Allen-Bradley, A.O. Smith, Briggs & Stratton, GE Medical Systems, Harley-Davidson, Johnson Controls, Manpower, Marquette Electronics, Master Lock, Miller Brewing Company, Northwestern Mutual Life Insurance Co., Quad/Graphics, Universal Foods, and W.H. Brady Co.

Since 1986 the service sector has been the primary source of local jobs. Today service firms provide about 30 percent of the area's employment. Another 16 percent is employed by retailers. Milwaukee's manufacturing base remains strong, however, accounting for 22 percent of the work force.

Tourism is also important to Milwaukee. The city's summer festivals, museums, art galleries, professional sports teams, and theaters act as magnets to attract people to the area. Approximately 5 million tourists visit Milwaukee each year, spending an estimated $1.9 billion that employs more than 40,000 people in tourism-related jobs.

Why does Milwaukee have such a strong economy? It is partly because of the city's central location in the Upper Midwest. More than 65 million people and one-third of the nation's manufacturing volume is located within 600 miles of Milwaukee. The city has its own international airport, which serves 5 million passengers annually, and it is one of the few urban areas that can boast a shipping port on the Great Lakes. In addition, Milwaukee is just 90 miles north of Chicago, the major rail hub for the Midwest.

Another reason for Milwaukee's success is the quality of its work force. The city is known for having employees who are educated, highly skilled, and productive. Close to half of the area's adult population has attended college. Twenty percent have college degrees. In addition, Milwaukee has a strong work ethic. According to a recent study conducted by the National Center for Health Statistics, Milwaukee workers call in sick just three days a year, the lowest absentee rate among all of the cities surveyed. Workers in other cities, such as Chicago, and San Bernardino, California, typically miss between six and nine days of work annually.

Milwaukee manufacturers have prospered because they were quick to realize the importance

Milwaukee workers call in sick just three days a year, the lowest absentee rate among all of the cities surveyed.

of exports. Since 1987 Wisconsin exports have more than doubled—to $10.1 billion. In 1995 alone, the state's exports increased 16 percent. A sizable portion of those exports originate from Milwaukee-area manufacturers, which account for about one-fourth of the state's manufacturing volume.

Another reason Milwaukee has a strong economy is because it has a government that works with business and not against it. When Pennsylvania was looking for ways to improve that state's business climate, a Blue Ribbon Commission selected Wisconsin as one of six states to study. The commission praised Wisconsin's state and local governments for cutting personal and corporate taxes, streamlining regulatory processes, revamping workers' compensation laws to reduce rates and litigation, and for forging strong partnerships between business, government, and labor.

Mayor Norquist has been a strong advocate of business development. Almost immediately after being elected mayor in 1988, he established the Committee for the Future of Milwaukee, which recommended making city government more efficient.

"One of the goals was to raise the confidence level of business that Milwaukee is a good place to do business," Norquist says. "The committee felt it was important to demonstrate both fiscal stability and fiscal restraint, and to adopt policies to help businesses grow."

Norquist has followed the commission's recommendations. He cut taxes and city expenditures and implemented programs to make it easier for small businesses to raise capital.

"We are committed to doing what we can to encourage the development of businesses that benefit the city," Norquist explains. "I try to use every strategy that works, especially if it is market oriented."

In 1995 the business newspaper *The Economist* dubbed Norquist "The Brave Marketer," calling him "part of a strong wind of change that is

I THINK MILWAUKEE IS A BEAUTIFUL PLACE TO RAISE A FAMILY.

There are lots of opportunities here if you prepare yourself to take advantage of them. As a community organizer, I want to help the city continue its commitment to diversify and make Milwaukee a good place for anyone who wishes to lead a productive life. Milwaukee is a very conservative, but progressive, city. I think it is very traditional in terms of people and their everyday life-style, but there is a very futuristic and progressive attitude when it comes to economic development. I think that by the year 2000, we are going to see Milwaukee as one of the best cities, if not the best, to raise a family in terms of services and opportunities.

MARIA FRANCO
Public information officer, United Migrant Opportunity Services

The City of Milwaukee has invested more than $3 million in decorative streetlights, landscaping, and a gazebo in the historic Third Ward to help transform it into a community of trendy shops and offices. Photo by Milwaukee DCD/ Dave La Haye

beginning to blow through American cities" and a "passionate supporter of free trade."

"We are very fortunate in the people we have as mayor and governor," says G. Edwin Howe, president of Aurora Health Care, a Milwaukee-based health care system. "Norquist is really interested in changing things to create a vibrant economy and Governor Tommy Thompson is a can-do governor. People aren't whining about the way things should be. They are spending their time and money getting things done."

Baird's Zempel agrees. "Ten years ago the business community's perception of government was that it regulated too much, taxed too heavily, and was generally insensitive to business needs," he says. "Since then, both Milwaukee and the state have turned their attitudes around. Now government is quite supportive of developing new business and fostering an environment that is conducive to creating new jobs."

Milwaukee's location, work force, and proactive government have helped nurture the business community. The local economy has seen a net increase in the number of new jobs in every year except one since 1983. In the late 1980s and early 1990s, when housing starts were falling nationally, Milwaukee was posting new construction records—and home values were increasing by 5 to 10 percent a year.

"Milwaukee provides a stable, solid environment in which to grow a business," says Tim Sheehy, president of the 2,300-member Metropolitan Milwaukee Association of Commerce (MMAC), which, along with its Council of Small Business Executives (COSBE), serves as an advocate for metro area businesses. "We have abundant natural resources and we have invested in our infrastructure. We have an outstanding telecommunications system, an efficient, well-run airport, good freeways, competitive energy costs, and a tremendously well-trained and dedicated work force."

The prospects for growth remain strong. In a 1995 survey of its members, MMAC discovered that more than half of the businesses surveyed believe Milwaukee's economy is performing above

average and that 42 percent of the businesses surveyed expect the economy to continue improving. In addition, close to a third of the smaller businesses surveyed said they planned to move to larger facilities within the next three to five years.

There are more than 40 office and industrial parks under development in the four-county area. More than one million square feet of downtown office space was added between 1988 and 1993, yet the area's office occupancy rate is among the best in the nation.

Manufacturing

Milwaukee has been a thriving manufacturing center since its founding 150 years ago. It remains home to some of the nation's most prominent manufacturers, including Allen-Bradley, Briggs & Stratton, Harnischfeger Industries, Harley-Davidson, Johnson Controls, Master Lock, and A.O. Smith.

Although there are more office workers than factory workers in the metropolitan area, manufacturing still plays a key role in the local

economy. Only two other cities—San Jose, California, and Detroit, Michigan—have a higher percentage of their work force in manufacturing jobs.

Manufacturing has changed substantially since the early 1980s, when high interest rates, a strong dollar, and a national recession shuttered the doors of many Milwaukee firms—most notably Allis-Chalmers, the worldwide farm implement dealer that had been the state's largest private-sector employer. Many smaller companies also closed their doors. In the five-year period from 1979 to 1983 more than 55,000 manufacturing jobs were lost in the Milwaukee area alone.

Milwaukee, however, didn't wither and die. Almost immediately, companies began retooling and restructuring their operations. Throughout the 1980s local corporations developed new ways to do business. Allen-Bradley created the Bud Whitney World Contactor Automated Assembly Facility, which utilizes computer-integrated manufacturing to assemble and package 600 custom-order contactors an hour. Briggs & Stratton developed a new line of overhead engines using work cells and a focused factory strategy to improve productivity and quality and to bring assembly line workers into the decision-making process. And A.O. Smith, the company that invented the automated assembly line in the early 1900s, invested more than $500 million in the 1980s to retool its operations so that it could enter new markets. The corporation now uses more than 300 welding and material-handling robots throughout its operations.

Since 1984 more than a half dozen new office buildings have been erected, including the 411 Building (above) and the newest addition to the Milwaukee skyline—1000 North Water (left). Top photo by Eric Oxendorf/Third Coast Stock Source; photo at left by Milwaukee DCD/Dave La Haye

The Pabst Mansion, built by legendary beer baron Captain Frederick Pabst, is a museum today. Photo by Milwaukee DCD/ Dave La Haye

Facing page: Once known as the Beer Capital of the World, Milwaukee still produces more than one-tenth of all the malted beverages brewed in the United States. Photo by Buck Miller/Third Coast Stock Source

Since the early 1980s smaller firms have created the bulk of the new manufacturing jobs. Between 1982 and 1992 the number of manufacturing establishments in metropolitan Milwaukee grew by 16 percent. More important, Milwaukee's manufacturing economy is much more diverse than it was in the early 1980s. Today no segment of the manufacturing sector employs more than 6 percent of the metropolitan work force.

Nationally, Milwaukee is probably best known for its breweries. At the turn of the century it produced more beer than any other locale, earning it the designation of "Beer Capital of the World." While brewing remains an important industry, it is no longer as dominant. Milwaukee still accounts for more than 10 percent of all malt beverage shipments in the United States, but less than one percent of the area work force is employed in brewing-related jobs. Miller Brewing Company is the city's largest brewer, employing more than 2,400 workers locally and producing between 6 million and 9.5 million barrels of beer a year at its Milwaukee facility.

Pabst Brewing Company is also headquartered in Milwaukee. Founded by Captain Frederick Pabst, the brewery has scaled down production in recent years, but still produces close to 750,000 barrels of beer annually.

In keeping with its heritage, Milwaukee is home to several microbreweries. The largest is Sprecher Brewing Co., which was founded in 1985 by Randal Sprecher, a former brewing supervisor at Pabst. Today Sprecher produces 10,000 barrels of beer and 12,000 barrels of root beer annually, and has just begun marketing a cream soda. Two of Sprecher Brewing's standard beers—Black Bavarian and Hefe Weiss—have been included on the "Top 24" list of brews worldwide, which was compiled by British beer expert Michael Jackson in 1995. In February 1995 Sprecher moved into expanded quarters that will allow it to produce up to 35,000 barrels of beer and 100,000 barrels of root beer annually.

Other Milwaukee microbreweries include Lakeside Brewery Inc., which was founded in 1987 and produces 1,700 barrels of beer annually on Milwaukee's east side, and the Water Street Brewery, a downtown brew pub that produces 1,500 barrels of beer each year, and Wauwatosa's Wisconsin Brewing Co., which opened in April 1996. Together these microbreweries create close to 30 distinct flavors of Milwaukee beer. These

Miller Brewing Company is the city's largest brewer, producing more than six million barrels of Miller, Miller Lite, Genuine Draft, Red Dog, and other brands each year. Photo by Scott Witte/Third Coast Stock Source

include year-round beers such as Special Amber, Dunkel Weizen, Cream City Pale Ale, and Klisch Pilsner, as well as Mai Bock, Pumpkin Beer, Oktoberfest, Holiday Spice, and other seasonal brews.

Milwaukee leads in the production of industrial controls and X-ray equipment. The metro area also produces more than 10 percent of the nation's internal combustion engines, iron and steel forgings, mining machinery, leather tanning and finishing, and speed changers, drives, and gears. More than half of the nation's X-ray equipment is produced in Milwaukee, thanks primarily to GE Medical Systems, the world's leading manufacturer of diagnostic imaging equipment, including X-ray, computed tomography (CT), magnetic resonance (MR), and ultrasound equipment. Marquette Electronics, another medical manufacturer, is a leading producer of cardiology equipment and patient-monitoring systems.

And although the tanning industry does not dominate the economy the way it once did, Milwaukee is still known as the Leather Capital of the Nation because of its many tanneries and leather-related businesses, including Pfister & Vogel Tanning Co. and U.S. Leather. In addition, the metropolitan area is home to two well-known leather goods companies—the Port Washington-based Allen-Edmonds Shoe Corporation, an international leader in the premium men's dress and casual shoe market; and Amity Leather Products

Co., which manufactures wallets and belts at its West Bend facility.

Several of the world's leading manufacturers call the city of Milwaukee home. Among them are:

Johnson Controls, which was founded in 1885 by Professor Warren Johnson who invented the thermostat to make his classroom more comfortable. Today Johnson Controls employs 63,000 people worldwide and generates $9 billion in revenues annually as a leading producer of building control systems, automotive batteries, and seating.

Allen-Bradley, a major business of Rockwell Automation, both with headquarters in Milwaukee. Employing more than 25,000 people worldwide and more than 4,600 people locally in Milwaukee and Mequon, Rockwell Automation has annual revenues of $4 billion and is a leading producer of automation control products, including control logic, sensors, machine interface, motors, power devices, and software.

A.O. Smith Corporation, a leading manufacturer of automotive structural components, electric motors, water heaters, and piping systems. It generates $1.5 billion in revenues annually and employs 13,000 people worldwide, including 2,750 people at its Milwaukee facilities.

Miller Brewing Company, the nation's second-largest brewery with $4.3 billion in revenues. It employs 6,900 people worldwide, including 2,300 people at its corporate headquarters and Milwaukee brewery.

Harley-Davidson Inc., which employs 5,000 people worldwide to produce the world-famous Harley-Davidson line of motorcycles, motorcycle parts, and accessories.

Master Lock Company, the world's largest manufacturer of padlocks and related security products. Founded in 1921 when Milwaukee locksmith Harry E. Soref patented a design using laminated layers of steel to create a virtually impenetrable lock, it now employs 2,500 people worldwide, including 1,500 people at its main manufacturing plant in Milwaukee.

W.H. Brady Co., which employs 2,400 people in 15 countries worldwide. It manufactures and markets signs, labels, splicing tapes, and adhesive parts for microfloppy disks, printing systems, and software.

The Falk Corporation, which produces components and systems for the power transmission industry. The company employs 1,300 people in Milwaukee and 1,500 people worldwide.

The surrounding metropolitan area is home to several other prominent corporations, including:

GE Medical Systems, the world's leading manufac-

Allen-Bradley worked with Automation Technologies to develop an in-line inverting device that allows Allen-Bradley to incorporate top and bottom surface-mount assembly on the same production line. Courtesy, Rockwell Automation/ Allen-Bradley

Milwaukee is home to a number of established companies that have developed nationwide reputations for excellence. Master Lock (opposite), started by Milwaukee locksmith Harry E. Soref, is the world's leading producer of padlocks. Harnischfeger Industries (left) is a leading manufacturer of earth-moving equipment. Courtesy, Master Lock and Harnischfeger Industries

turer of medical diagnostic imaging systems. The Waukesha-based corporation employs close to 3,600 people in the Milwaukee area and 14,000 people worldwide.

Harnischfeger Industries, which employs 17,000 people worldwide and 2,225 people in the Milwaukee area. Harnischfeger is a leading manufacturer of mining and material-handling equipment and papermaking machinery.

Briggs & Stratton Corp., a leading manufacturer of lawnmower and other small gasoline engines. The firm employs 7,400 people worldwide, including 4,500 people locally at its corporate headquarters in Wauwatosa and at its manufacturing facilities in Wauwatosa, West Allis, and Menomonee Falls.

Rexnord Corporation, which manufactures mechanical power transmission components. Rexnord employs 4,700 people worldwide, including 1,000 people at its corporate headquarters in West Milwaukee and at seven manufacturing facilities in the metropolitan area.

Ladish Co., which employs 1,600 people to produce closed-impression die forgings, rolled rings, and industrial pipe fittings for the aerospace, petrochemical, and automotive industries.

Founded by the inventor of the thermostat, Johnson Controls is a leading producer of building controls. It also manufactures automotive batteries and car seats. Photo by Dale Guldan/Third Coast Stock Source

Headquartered in West Milwaukee, Rexnord Corporation is a leading manufacturer of power transmission components and conveying systems. Courtesy, Rexnord Corporation

Two well-known consumer businesses are located in Washington County at the northwestern edge of the metropolitan area. Regal Ware Inc., which manufactures cookware and electrical appliances, employs 2,000 people and is headquartered in Kewaskum. The West Bend Co., a well-known brand of electric household appliances and direct-to-home cookware, is based in West Bend. It employs 1,310 people.

In addition to these corporate headquarters, several companies have large manufacturing presences in Milwaukee. Among them are Cooper Power Systems, which manufactures electrical distribution transformers and associated components; Delco Electronics Corp., which produces electronics for car radios and speakers, automotive instrumentation, air control electronics, digital control computers, inertial navigation systems, and avionics; Eaton Corporation, a leading manufacturer of industrial controls with facilities in both Milwaukee and Wauwatosa; the Delphi Automotive Systems Division of General Motors, which produces catalytic converters; and MagneTek, a leading manufacturer of electronic drives, medium-power transformers and substations, motors, generators, and lighting ballasts.

Milwaukee has a long heritage as a printing and publishing center. A half-dozen of the area's printing companies were founded more than a

century ago, several of them by lithographers who came from Germany to supply labels for the emerging breweries. Over the past two decades, commercial printers have been increasing their payroll at an average rate of 9 percent a year. Today metropolitan Milwaukee's printers, publishers, and allied industries generate $2 billion a year and employ more than 20,000 people.

"Pound for pound, Milwaukee has one of the highest concentration of graphics arts professionals in the country," says Jack Hayes, president of Printing Industries of Wisconsin. 'And as recently as six years ago, there were more offset web presses for color printing in Wisconsin than there were in all of Canada."

Much of the growth in the area's printing and publishing industry has been fueled by Quad/Graphics, which is based in Sussex. It is the

Only two other U.S. cities—San Jose, California, and Detroit, Michigan—have a higher percentage of their labor force working in manufacturing jobs. Photo by Bruce Buchanan

Although fewer people work in factory jobs today than 20 years ago, Milwaukee is still a manufacturing center known for its abundance of skilled workers. Courtesy, The Falk Corporation

largest privately held printer of magazines, catalogs, and commercial products in North America, with 13 facilities in six states and sales in excess of $900 million. Quad/Graphics created 800 jobs in 1995 alone and currently has 8,000 employees, including 4,000 in the metropolitan Milwaukee area.

The Service Economy

There's no question that white-collar jobs have been integral to the growth of Milwaukee's economy in recent years. Between 1982 and 1994 professional service firms created 85,000 jobs, retailers and wholesalers added 32,000 jobs, and financial services, insurance, and real estate firms put an additional 14,000 people on their payrolls. Together, these sectors of the economy accounted for 131,000 new jobs, or about 86 percent of the area's job growth, over the past 12 years.

The Milwaukee area is home to several companies that are well-known nationally and internationally:

Manpower International, the world's largest employer, providing more than 1.5 temporary workers to offices in 41 countries around the world.

Northwestern Mutual Life Insurance Co., also known as "The Quiet Company." Wisconsin's largest corporation, with $52 billion in assets, and the nation's sixth-largest life insurance company, it employs 3,300 people worldwide and its roots run deep in the Milwaukee business community. Local investments include significant holdings in several key financial institutions, including Robert W. Baird & Co., Mortgage Guaranty Investment Corporation, and Marshall & Ilsley Bank.

Foley & Lardner, the nation's 15th-largest law firm, with more than 550 attorneys at 13 offices in four states and Washington, D.C. The firm has the largest health practice in the nation, with more than 100 attorneys in that section of the firm alone.

The City of Milwaukee has gone to great lengths to ensure that modern buildings erected in the Third Ward match the turn-of-the-century warehouse district's unique charm and flavor. This structure artfully combines a parking and retail development that blends in well with the district's historic ambience. Photo by John Korom/Pohlman Studios, Inc.; courtesy, Eppstein Uhen Architects

Northwestern Mutual Life Insurance Co., one of the 10 largest life insurance companies in the nation, is based on Milwaukee's east side and is housed in some of the city's oldest and newest buildings. The main office (right) was built in 1914, while the NML tower (above, foreground) was completed in 1991. Top photo by Eric Oxendorf/Third Coast Stock Source; photo at right by David A. Jentz/Third Coast Stock Source

The Mortgage Guaranty Insurance Corporation (MGIC), a leading national private mortgage insurer. Since 1957 MGIC has facilitated 14 million American home loans by providing mortgage insurance for people. Today MGIC has more than $112 billion insurance in force covering some 1.2 million low-down-payment home loans.

Time Insurance Company, founded in 1892 and a Milwaukee institution since 1900. Time is part of Fortis Inc., a financial services company that is in turn part of Fortis, a worldwide group of companies active in insurance, banking, and investments. In recent years Milwaukee has become the headquarters for three Fortis units—Fortis Healthcare, which focuses on individual and small group products; Fortis Long Term Care; and Fortis Sales, which is the primary retail distribution network for the Fortis companies.

Strong Capital Management Inc., the state's largest mutual fund company and one of the nation's 20 largest no-load mutual fund companies. It manages $13 billion in mutual funds and $2 billion in private assets. It is one of more than a dozen mutual fund companies based in the Milwaukee area.

Two of the nation's largest bank-holding corporations—Firstar Corp. and Marshall & Ilsley

Fiserv, the nation's leading independent data-processing provider for major banks, savings institutions, and credit unions, has helped to make Milwaukee a center for financial services. Photo by Scott Witte/Third Coast Stock Source

Corporation—are based in Milwaukee. Firstar, which has in excess of $19 billion in assets, is a holding company for 39 banks in six states. Marshall & Ilsley Corporation, a holding company for 30 banks in two states, has more than $13.4 billion in assets.

Milwaukee is also home to all but one of the state's top 25 savings and loan institutions. The largest Milwaukee-area institution is Security Bank, S.S.B., which has more than $3.2 billion in assets and 20 locations in metro Milwaukee.

Fiserv, Inc., provides financial data-processing systems and related information management services to more than 5,000 banks, credit unions, mortgage firms, and savings institutions worldwide. It is the nation's leading independent data-processing provider for banks, savings institutions, and credit unions with assets over $25 million. A publicly held company based in Brookfield, Fiserv employs more than 7,000 people nationwide, including 450 locally.

M&I Data Services, a division of Marshall and Ilsley Corporation, is a leading provider of financial data-processing services and software. It employs close to 3,000 people and serves more than 1,000 customers, including 35 international institutions.

Health care is also a major employer. Milwaukee hospitals are well known throughout the Midwest and nationally: Froedtert Memorial Lutheran Hospital for its organ transplant and limb re-establishment program; St. Mary's Hospital for its burn center; St. Luke's Medical Center and Sinai Samaritan Medical Center for cardiac care; Children's Hospital, St. Joseph's Hospital, Sinai Samaritan Medical Center, St. Luke's Medical Center, and St. Francis Hospital for neonatal care; Columbia Hospital for its arthritis center; and West Allis Memorial Hospital for its industrial toxicology laboratory.

In recent years area hospitals, physicians, and other providers have banded together to create integrated delivery systems that are designed to reduce costs and improve the quality of care. Three of the area's largest private-sector employers—Aurora Health Care, Covenant Healthcare, and Horizon Healthcare—are integrated health care systems.

Aurora Health Care employs more than 10,000 people in the Greater Milwaukee area. Its network includes 10 hospitals and more than 100 clinics and other care sites, as well as several comprehensive home-health and family service agencies. Aurora is the largest health care network in the state, with facilities stretching along Wisconsin's eastern shore—from Michigan's Upper Peninsula to northern Illinois. Covenant Healthcare employs

Milwaukee is home to four integrated health care systems, which bring together hospitals, clinics, and home health care agencies to improve patient care. At St. Francis Hospital, which is affiliated with Covenant Healthcare, intensive physical rehabilitation services help patients recover more rapidly. Photo by Bruce Buchanan

close to 10,000 people in its network, which includes six hospitals and 21 clinics. Horizon Healthcare employs 8,400 people at eight hospitals and 28 clinics in the Milwaukee area.

There are eight hospitals in the Milwaukee area with more than 300 beds. They are St. Luke's Medical Center (711 beds), St. Joseph's Hospital (465), Sinai Samaritan Medical Center (379), St. Michael Hospital (346), Columbia Hospital (333), Clement J. Zablocki Veterans Affairs Medical Center (323), St. Mary's Hospital of Milwaukee (314), and Waukesha Memorial Hospital (301). The Milwaukee Regional Medical Center, one of the largest of its kind in the country, includes Children's Hospital of Wisconsin, the Medical College of Wisconsin, the Milwaukee County Mental Health Complex, the Blood Center of Southeastern Wisconsin, and the Curative Rehabilitation Center, the nation's largest outpatient rehabilitation center with 40 specialty clinics.

Telecommunications is one of the economy's fastest-growing areas. Ameritech Wisconsin, which employs more than 4,000 people and provides full-service communications and advanced

The Milwaukee Journal Sentinel *is the city's major daily newspaper. It is delivered to more than 285,000 homes each day and more than 462,000 homes on Sundays. Photo by Khris* Erickson/Journal Sentinel information services to more than 1.4 million Wisconsin customers, is investing $700 million to install digital switching and interoffice fiber and to bring fiber-optic cable to hundreds of secondary schools, colleges, universities, and public libraries. It is moving into video programming, and is slated to begin offering cable TV and interactive services in 1998.

Ameritech also has been working with health care providers to develop digital networks that can transmit data and images. It helped establish the Wisconsin Health Information Network (WHIN), a computer network that has been praised by President Bill Clinton as an effective private-sector approach to reducing paperwork and improving the flow of medical information. WHIN connects the proprietary information systems of more than 1,000 physicians, 100 pharmacies, 13 hospitals, 8 clinics, and 4 insurance companies in the Milwaukee area. Ameritech also is working with Covenant Healthcare to develop a $30-million communications network that will put all patient files on an electronic network. When completed, the network will include 32 miles of fiber-optic cable, 81 miles of copper wire, 6,300 telephones, 3,200 personal computers, and 432 miles of non-site phone and data cable to link Covenant's hospitals, nursing homes, labs, home health care agencies, and physician offices.

Warner Cable, which provides cable television service to 300,000 customers in 101 communities in southeastern Wisconsin, is investing $400 million to install 8,000 miles of fiber-optic cable so that its network can offer digital compression and interactive services. And by mid-1997 Warner will be offering local access telephone service to commercial customers.

Milwaukee also is home to the world's largest computer bulletin board system. Started in a closet-size bedroom on Milwaukee's east side, EXEC-PC now has 30,000 subscribers in 60 countries worldwide and is Wisconsin's largest Internet provider. Hundreds of telephone lines feed into EXEC-PC's 500 computers, allowing subscribers to access the Internet and EXEC-PC's 500,000 files.

Journal Communications, the state's largest communications company, is the owner of Milwaukee's major daily newspaper, the *Milwaukee Journal Sentinel*. In addition, it owns WTMJ-TV, WTMJ-AM, and WKTI-FM. It employs 3,000 people in the Milwaukee area.

Other major service-sector players include Kohl's, which employs 3,500 people at its family-oriented, specialty department stores; The Marcus Corp., which employs 3,500 people locally in its theater, hotel, and motel operations; JCPenney,

In 1994 WITI-TV (Channel 6) became a Fox network affiliate and expanded its commitment to news programming. It is now the largest broadcast news operation in the state, with more than 100 newsroom professionals. Courtesy, WITI-TV

Facing page: Wisconsin Gas, the state's largest natural gas utility, has been serving Milwaukee-area customers since 1852. The flame on top of the building forecasts the weather: Red means warmer weather ahead, gold means cold and blue means no change. Courtesy, Wisconsin Gas

The city is installing harp-shaped streetlights to accent the turn-of-the-century architecture of its downtown buildings. Photo by Eric Oxendorf/Third Coast Stock Source

which manages a catalog distribution center that employs more than 2,300 people; and Carson Pirie Scott, which employs 2,200 people at its P.A. Bergner's, Boston Store, and Carson Pirie Scott department stores.

In addition to Ameritech, there are two major utility companies that serve the Milwaukee area. Wisconsin Gas, a subsidiary of WICOR, is the state's oldest and largest natural gas utility, serving more than 365,000 homes and businesses in the metropolitan area. Its FieldTech unit, which has developed and installed automated meter-reading systems for gas meters, recently signed a $17-million contract with the City of Milwaukee to provide 137,500 automatic meter-reading units for water meters. Within five years all water meters in homes and small apartment buildings in Milwaukee will be read remotely by a specially equipped vehicle.

Wisconsin Energy Corporation is a holding company for Wisconsin Electric Power Company, Wisconsin Natural Gas Company, and several business development-oriented subsidiaries. Wisconsin Energy Corporation is awaiting regulatory approval for a merger with the Minneapolis-based Northern States Power Co. If approved, it will create the nation's 11th-largest energy holding company, based on market capitalization.

Tourism

Conventions and tourism are among the city's most important industries. Major attractions include the city's music festival, Summerfest, and the many ethnic festivals that are held on the lakefront. Other major draws include The Great Circus Parade, the Wisconsin State Fair, the Milwaukee County Zoological Gardens, the city's professional sports teams, and Potawatomi Bingo.

"Milwaukee is a major tourist destination because of our extraordinary festivals and our special events, such as The Great Circus Parade,"

THERE IS A CERTAIN FRIENDLINESS, OR A CERTAIN LACK OF PRETENSION, in Milwaukee that I feel is very healthy. It's definitely something you think about when you are on the road. One of the things I've seen change over the years is the economic base. An awful lot of jobs left this city in the 1970s and 1980s and I think we are still trying to pick up after that. I do see a number of neighborhoods undergoing a renaissance, but that is by no means a widespread phenomenon. And as much as I thought I would never say anything nice about a shopping mall, The Grand Avenue's Food Court at noon is a kind of crossroads for this town, a place where people meet. May there be more places like that.

PAUL CEBAR
Founder and leader of the musical group, Paul Cebar & the Milwaukeeans

says William Hanbury, president of the Greater Milwaukee Convention & Visitors Bureau. "Close to 20 major festivals are staged here every year. Many cities our size would be thankful for just two or three."

Over the past five years many new restaurants and bars have opened along Water Street, which straddles the eastern side of the Milwaukee River. A similar revival is occurring on Brady Street, where local merchants and the city are spending $1.4 million to install new curbs and gutters, decorative streetlights, landscaping, and decorative pavement. The fabled street, once home to waves of Polish and Italian immigrants, was the center of Milwaukee's counterculture in the 1960s and the 1970s and continues to be a popular destination for food and entertainment.

Tourism promises to play an even greater role in the area's economy with the completion of Miller Park, the Milwaukee Brewers' new baseball stadium, and the Wisconsin Center, both of which are slated to open within the next four years. Other draws to the city will be the growth of the downtown Riverwalk and related entertainment areas, and the expansion of the city's museums.

"Milwaukee has clearly been identified as an emerging national convention and tourism center," says Hanbury. "That means tourism will continue to be a very dynamic—and integral—part of the area economy."

Education

One of the keys to a vibrant and productive economy is a well-educated citizenry. The Milwaukee metropolitan area ranks above the national aver-

The Water Street Brewery serves several types of beer that are brewed on site. It is one of several popular bars and restaurants that have sprung up on the east side of the Milwaukee River, on the north side of downtown. Courtesy, Water Street Brewery

Recognizing that children are Milwaukee's most treasured asset, the Milwaukee community has invested in programs to help them grow, including the United Community Center (above) and the music programs offered by area schools (right). Top photo by Milwaukee DCD/Dave La Haye; photo at right by Bachmann/Third Coast Stock Source

age in its percentage of college graduates. In addition, the city's strong manufacturing heritage has made it nationally known for its skilled workers.

"Milwaukee would not have been able to recover from the early 1980s like it did without a skilled and flexible work force," says Robert W. Baird & Co.'s Clare Zempel.

This high level of educational achievement is attributable to a public commitment to quality education and the business community's active participation in making sure that its employees are skilled and well trained. The Metropolitan Milwaukee Association of Commerce has actively pushed for school reforms to improve learning in the schools. And in 1990 it established the MMAC Scholarship Fund with a $13-million endowment. The only one of its kind in the nation, the fund targets low-income graduates of Milwaukee public schools. Recipients are selected based on grade point average, financial need, and other criteria. The MMAC has already invested more than $2 million in 540 Milwaukee public school students attending

college or technical schools.

Milwaukee Mayor Norquist is a fervent believer in making educational excellence available to all citizens. He has been a vocal proponent of school reforms, including the use of vouchers that would allow low-income families to attend the schools of their choice. He also was instrumental in the city's decision to invest $1.3 million in the Milwaukee Public Library so that it could install 80 computers at 12 library branches and become the first public library in the state to provide Internet access to the public.

In any given year more than 84,000 people attend one of the area's nearly 20 colleges, universities, technical schools, and community colleges. Close to 47,000 people are enrolled in programs leading to undergraduate degrees, 24,000 students are enrolled in programs leading to associate degree and technical diplomas, and 13,000 people are participating in graduate and professional programs a year.

Of the more than 6,500 bachelor's degrees conferred on students each year, more than one-third are for business- or engineering-related programs. Another 11 percent are nursing or health related. Other major areas of study include communications and communications technologies, social sciences, and the visual and performing arts. Close to half of the more than 3,100 associate certificate degrees awarded annually are business or health related, and the majority of the 2,600 postgraduate degrees typically conferred are for education, engineering, business, and law.

The metropolitan area is home to two major

Milwaukee and the state of Wisconsin have a history of educational excellence. Wisconsin established the nation's first vocational, technical, and adult education system in 1911 and its current system is considered one of the best in the United States.

The University of Wisconsin-Milwaukee, the second-largest campus in the state's university system, offers degrees in a wide variety of study areas, including engineering and applied sciences. Courtesy, UWM/Alan Magayne-Roshak

universities, eight four-year colleges, and two specialty graduate institutions. The largest school in the area is the University of Wisconsin-Milwaukee, which has more than 23,000 undergraduate and graduate students. UWM is the second-largest campus in the state's nationally acclaimed University of Wisconsin system, which has 152,000 students at 26 campuses statewide. UWM offers degrees in liberal arts, engineering and applied sciences, architecture, urban planning, education, fine arts, nursing, business administration, social welfare, library science, and allied health professions. In 1993 the university moved the School of Architecture and Urban Planning to a four-story building that includes 140,000 square feet of classroom, office, and exhibit space. And in 1994 the university opened its $26-million facility housing the Business School, which includes 150,000 square feet of classroom and office space,

The Medical College of Wisconsin, which has an enrollment of 1,200, can trace its academic roots to two medical schools that began training physicians in the 1890s. Photo by Bruce Buchanan/Third Coast Stock Source

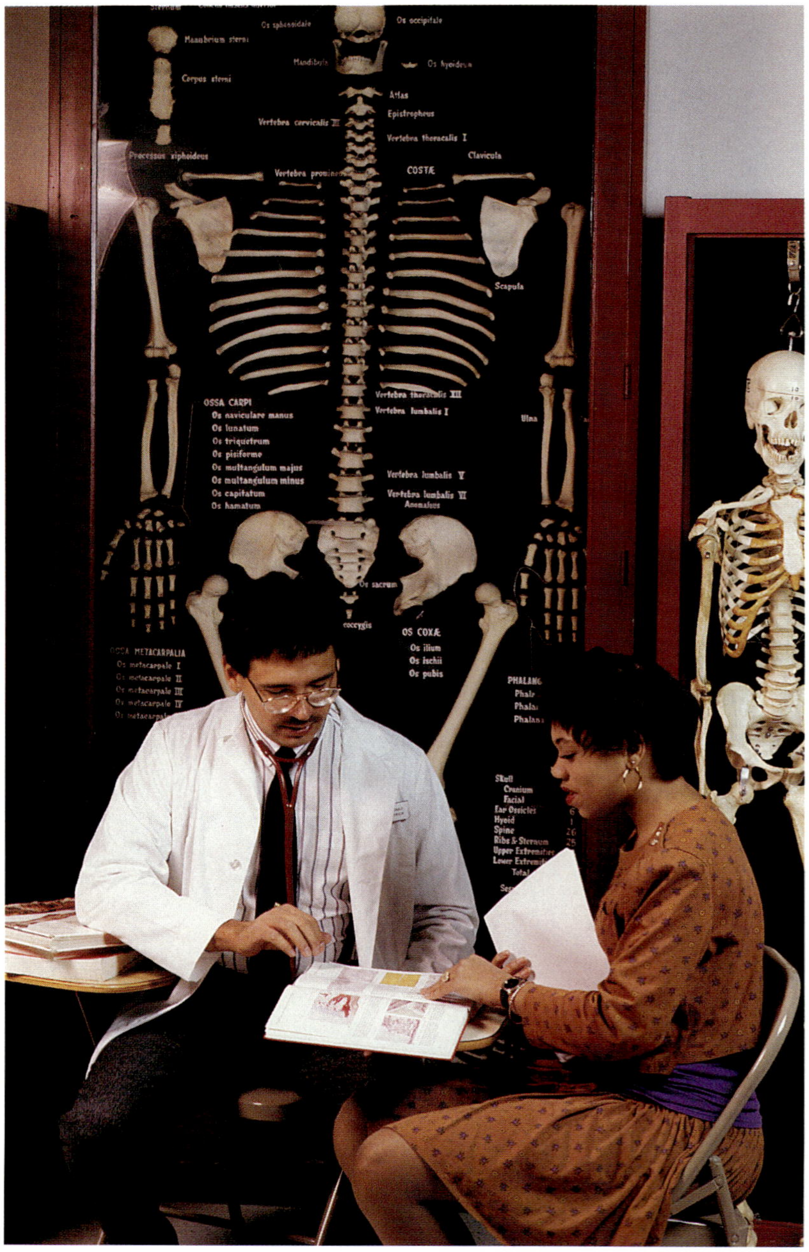

more than 400 computers, and three lecture halls.

Marquette University is a nationally acclaimed university known for both its basketball teams and its academics. *The New York Times* recently rated it as one of the "best buys" in college education.

Located on the western edge of downtown Milwaukee, the urban campus has more than 11,000 students pursuing undergraduate, graduate, and professional degrees in liberal arts, business, education, engineering, medicine, and law.

Cardinal Stritch College, a liberal arts school located just north of Milwaukee, has 5,200 students in undergraduate, graduate, and management programs. There are several smaller colleges

in the area as well. They include Alverno College, Carroll College, Concordia University, Mount Mary College, and Wisconsin Lutheran College. Together these schools enroll more than 10,000 students.

Milwaukee is home to several specialty institutions. The Milwaukee School of Engineering, which was founded in 1903 to meet the industrial community's engineering needs, has about 3,000 undergraduate and graduate students. The Medical College of Wisconsin provides graduate and professional degrees to more than 1,200 students. And the Milwaukee Institute of Art and Design offers degrees in drawing, painting, sculpture, photography, printmaking, graphic design, illustration, industrial design, and interior design at its new 245,000-square-foot facility in the city's Third Ward.

Milwaukee and the state of Wisconsin have a history of educational excellence. Wisconsin established the nation's first vocational, technical, and adult education system in 1911 and its current system is considered one of the best in the United States. The system's 15 technical colleges had vocational enrollments of 79,000 people in the 1994-1995 academic year.

The two largest technical schools in the area are the Milwaukee Area Technical College, which serves 22,000 students at four locations in Milwaukee and Ozaukee counties; and the Waukesha

UWM has a strong science program. Its chemistry department, which is located in the building above, combines internationally recognized lab facilities with exceptional research opportunities for undergraduate students. Courtesy, UWM/ Alan Magayne-Roshak

County Technical College, which serves 5,900 students at its Pewaukee Campus. Moraine Park Technical College serves students in Washington and Ozaukee counties. In addition to preparing students for vocational positions, the schools also offer specialized employee training and retraining. Together, they serve more than 10,000 employees from some 300 Milwaukee-area manufacturers each year.

Milwaukee's educational institutions have strong ties to the business community. The Milwaukee School of Engineering, for instance, is governed by a 53-member board of directors that includes area business and industry leaders, many of them company presidents and CEOs. In addition, there are several technology transfer facilities in the metropolitan area, which are designed to help industry transform concepts into products. The Milwaukee School of Engineering operates three centers—the Applied Technology Center, which conducts more than 100 industrially sponsored projects annually; the Fluid Power Institute, a nationally recognized center that has been researching and testing fluid power components and systems for more than 30 years; and the Rapid Prototyping Consortium, which helps companies reduce the product development cycle time for proven technologies.

The Biomedical Research Institute, which is affiliated with the Milwaukee School of Engineering, the Medical College of Wisconsin, and St. Luke's Medical Center, performs research and product development for medical instrumentation systems. The Medical College also operates the Medical College of Wisconsin Research Foundation, which helps transfer medical-related technology from academic settings to the marketplace.

Marquette University's Materials, Science and Technology Center addresses cross-disciplinary research challenges involving biomaterials, electronic ceramics, solid-state censors, and structural and electrical composites. The Milwaukee Area Technical College has a $2-million automated manufacturing center that allows businesses to test technology. And the University of Wisconsin-Milwaukee has created the Office of Industrial Research and Technology Transfer to serve as a one-stop information center for the university's research and development resources.

In addition, a consortium of Milwaukee-area business leaders have established the Riverworks Teaching Factory at the former Square D research and training facility. It is one of the nation's only shared manufacturing centers, where business can actually machine parts for production. Training at the center is provided by the German-based Fraunhofer Institute, a research and technology transfer organization that has contributed $600,000 worth of machine tools.

Milwaukee's strong business climate would

WHAT DO I LIKE MOST ABOUT MILWAUKEE? THE DOWNTOWN.

There is a richness in terms of the variety of shopping and restaurants. There are museums and art galleries. Downtown Milwaukee is a really neat place and I think that if you have lived here all of your life, you may not realize how neat it is. I also like the diversity of the business community. I came from Rochester, New York, which has a very monolithic economy with two or three very large companies employing almost everybody. Here you have a robust business community with lots of big, small, and medium-size companies. That makes it a much better place to work and to find employees. It also makes it a place where you can have a more robust discussion about what is going on in the business world because you have a variety of different businesses and opinions.

KATHERINE M. HUDSON
President and CEO, W.H. Brady Co.

not be possible without its solid infrastructure and supportive government. The city is fortunate in that it has been blessed with a history of successful partnerships between the public and private sectors. Two major business groups have helped foster this cooperative environment—the 2,300-member Metropolitan Milwaukee Association of Commerce and the 175-member Greater Milwaukee Committee.

Together these business groups have helped political leaders tackle challenges facing the community—from education and training to infrastructure improvements. In turn, they have helped transform Milwaukee from a Rustbelt casualty into an economic leader. One reason for the turnaround has been the public sector's commitment to improve the business climate. Thanks to a major overhaul of the state's tax system in the mid-1980s, Wisconsin's business taxes are now among the lowest in the nation. According to the Wisconsin Department of Revenue, the state's corporate tax is 20 percent lower than more than 15 other industrial and southern states.

Governor Tommy Thompson has been active in making state government more responsive to the business community's needs. He has expanded the state's Department of Development, which now has trade offices in Tokyo, Hong Kong, Seoul, Frankfurt, Mexico City, and Toronto. And he has implemented a major reorganization of state government that will reduce property taxes by $1.2 billion, eliminate 1,500 positions and dozens of agencies and programs, and begin a "sunset" process for 170 councils, boards, and commissions.

More important, the reorganization will realign government agencies to make them more responsive to the public they serve. The Department of Development, for instance, has been renamed the Department of Commerce. It will handle the vast majority of business-related programs, offering companies "one-stop shopping" at a central location. The new Cabinet-level Department of Financial Institutions will replace the four commissions that currently oversee banks, credit unions, and thrifts. And a new Cabinet-level

Milwaukee's strong ancestral ties to Germany was one of the main reasons German Chancellor Helmut Kohl and President Bill Clinton met here in May 1996 for a one-day summit. Photo by Milwaukee DCD/ Dave La Haye

Department of Tourism coordinates the activities of the state's fifth-largest industry.

Milwaukee Mayor Norquist, a fiscally conservative Democrat, has consistently lowered the city's portion of the property tax rate in each of the past eight years and has reduced city expenditures, when adjusted for inflation. He also has implemented quality-management programs in city departments to benchmark performance and improve service.

Norquist was instrumental in the establishment of the Capital Access Program, which eliminates bureaucratic paperwork and makes it easier for small businesses to secure bank loans. Since its inception, CAP has helped more than 100 businesses create 600 jobs. He has aggressively promoted the creation of manufacturing jobs in the central city. He was instrumental in the establishment of Steeltech Manufacturing, a minority-owned company that employs 220 people, and the development of the North Avenue Commerce Center, a 15-acre business park located in an economically disadvantaged area of the city.

"We're very concerned that the opportunities generated by the businesses in Milwaukee be made available to workers from all parts of the community," says Michael Morgan, commissioner of Milwaukee's Department of City Development. "In an era of demanding global competition, we need to make use of the talents of every individual. DCD helps match employers with the work force of the central city, using tools like the Development Zone tax credits and the Jobs Fund, which makes forgivable loans to companies that expand and hire the unemployed."

In addition to financial and technical assistance, local government leaders have worked hard to maintain and upgrade Milwaukee's physical infrastructure. General Mitchell International Airport, which is owned and operated by Milwaukee County, is located just 10 minutes south of downtown Milwaukee and handles 180 million pounds of air freight and 48 million pounds of mail a year. Eighteen air carriers serve more than 5 million passengers annually, providing nonstop or direct service to 51 destinations. In the past 10 years the airport has spent more than $80 million to expand the terminal and its parking structure. In addition to General Mitchell International Airport, there are seven general aviation airports in the Milwaukee area.

Milwaukee is also one of the few Great Lakes ports that is open to navigation year-round. It handles more than 3 million tons of cargo a year and is considered the premier heavy-lift port on the Great Lakes because of its 220-ton, stiff-leg crane.

Business development is no accident. Businesses are attracted to and thrive in regions that understand their importance. Milwaukee and the metropolitan area have many programs in place to help businesses start and grow. Milwaukee was the first major U.S. city to bank raw land for future industrial development. Since 1961 more than 650 acres have been sold and developed through the program. In 1995 the Land Bank contained approximately 100 acres, with lots ranging in size from two to 20 acres.

The Milwaukee Economic Development Corporation was founded in 1971 to help businesses achieve financing. A nonprofit corporation sponsored by the City of Milwaukee, MEDC operates in tandem with its affiliate, the Metropolitan Milwaukee Enterprise Corporation, using its own resources and those of the U.S. Small Business Administration to make financing available to create job opportunities and new investment. In 1995 the MEDC participated in 44 projects that resulted in $40 million worth of new investment in the city and created 500 jobs.

Wisconsin Energy has been a major player in the economic development of both the city of Milwaukee and the greater metropolitan area. Through its primary economic development components—Wispark Corp., its real estate development division, and Witech Corp., which provides funding for business expansions and relocations—Wisconsin Energy has invested in more than two dozen real estate projects and more than 20 companies since the late 1980s.

It has helped build more than 2,000 affordable housing units throughout metropolitan Milwaukee, and is a majority owner of East Pointe Commons, an upscale residential development, and East Pointe Place, a commercial development, on Milwaukee's lower east side. It partnered with the Northeast Milwaukee Industrial Development Corporation to convert an abandoned factory

complex on the city's northeast side into a 33-acre business park.

Wisconsin Energy's principal subsidiary, Wisconsin Electric Power Company, donated the former Wells Street power plant to the Milwaukee Center project to create the Powerhouse Theater, which is the new home of the Milwaukee Repertory Theater.

The parent corporation has also been active in the surrounding cities and counties. It has developed single-family subdivisions in Washington and Waukesha counties, as well as business parks in Waukesha, Racine, and Kenosha counties. And it has been one of the primary sources of funding for Forward Wisconsin, which promotes economic development throughout the state.

Wisconsin Energy is serious about its commitment to economic development. "A strong neighborhood leads to a strong community, which leads to a strong economy—and that is good for all of us," says Francis Brzezinski, president of Wispark Corp. and Witech Corp. and vice president of Wisconsin Energy and Wisconsin Electric.

Working together, the public and private sectors are enhancing a stable economy that is poised for growth. "Milwaukee has a superb combination of factors that make it an excellent place for business: excellent natural resources, strong financial institutions, a progressive government that works closely with business, a highly motivated work force, and fine educational institutions," says James D. Ericson, president and chief executive officer of Northwestern Mutual Life Insurance Co. "All of these bode well for exceptional economic growth."

General Mitchell International Airport, Wisconsin's primary terminal for commercial travel and freight shipments, serves more than 5 million passengers annually. Photo by Milwaukee DCD/ Dave La Haye

Epilogue

Even with a stable economy and a firm cultural foundation, change and uncertainty loom on Milwaukee's horizon as the city enters the twenty-first century.

Today Milwaukee and other medium-size cities are enjoying a renaissance. Millions of dollars are being invested in new downtown developments, upscale housing, and sports and entertainment facilities. Because of their size, they have become attractive places to live and to raise a family—large enough to offer entertainment, fine dining, and cultural activities, yet small enough to maintain a sense of community and security.

In addition, Milwaukee has benefited from a booming economy that has outperformed the national economy in recent years. Once written off as a casualty of "The Rustbelt," Milwaukee is now cited as a city to emulate in prestigious publications such as *Forbes*, *The Wall Street Journal*, and *The Economist*.

But every day starts anew, and the tomorrows that Milwaukee faces will be much different than the yesterdays in which the city triumphed. The digital revolution now sweeping the world promises to be as monumental as the Industrial Revolution that brought Milwaukee much of its wealth and power at the start of this century. And many of the attributes that made Milwaukee ideal as an industrial center—its location near the geographic center of the United States and its access to water and rail lines—will no longer be as important in the Information Age when products, services, and ideas will be transported across the Internet instead of the expressway.

So what does lie ahead for Milwaukee, and what are the challenges the city will face? Crystal balls prove murky over time and forecasting the future is even more troublesome than predicting the weather. But what is clear is that there are some issues that Milwaukee must address in order to ensure that it will remain vibrant in the twenty-first century.

As advances in computers and telecommunications allow more employees to work from

Milwaukee County's extensive park system, which includes the 640-acre Whitnall Park, is consistently ranked as one of the area's greatest assets by the people who live here. Photo by Dale Guldan/Third Coast Stock Source

their home or on the road, the need for a centralized work force—and a centralized office—will diminish. As both employees and employers become more mobile, issues such as quality of life will become more important than tax breaks on brick and mortar.

"One of the real problems facing every city is the mobility of businesses and their work forces," says Peter Beitzel, vice president of development for the Metropolitan Milwaukee Association of Commerce. "In the days when you had big factories and large office buildings you could count businesses as relatively permanent assets of the community. Today many businesses can pack up and move almost overnight, which means that political and civic leaders will have to work hard to make their cities a desirable place to stay."

A Growing Urban Area

Growth will be another key issue. By the time the city celebrates its 200th birthday, it is likely that Milwaukee, Racine, Kenosha, and Chicago will be connected by a seamless corridor of residential and urban development along I-94. The Milwaukee urban area, meanwhile, will also continue expanding farther west and north. The challenge for Milwaukee's leaders will be to make the city such an attractive place to live that suburban and rural communities won't lure away all of the affluent and educated residents.

"The question that cities like Milwaukee are going to have to ask is, 'Why would people want to live here?'" says David Zach, a futurist and president of Innovative Futures, a Milwaukee-based consulting firm. "Because of rural sprawl, they're going to have to focus in on a much stronger emphasis on quality of life. That means preserving green space and public areas, enhancing the city's cultural and entertainment activities, and maintaining the sense of community. Fortunately, Milwaukee already enjoys these advantages. We have a tremendous foundation to build on."

For Mayor Norquist, one of the primary challenges facing Milwaukee is getting politicians, civic leaders, and citizens to realize the importance of cities and how current state and federal policies are threatening to ruin them.

Norquist is among a handful of big-city mayors who have worked hard to slow urban sprawl and discourage the development of sterile

As computers change the way people work, quality-of-life issues will become increasingly important factors when people decide where to live. Top left photo by Milwaukee DCD/Dave La Haye; top photo by Bruce Buchanan/Third Coast Stock Source

Milwaukee is a "genuine" American city with strong family values and a rich religious heritage. Top photo by Ken Wardius/Third Coast Stock Source; photo at right by Alan Magayne-Roshak/Third Coast Stock Source

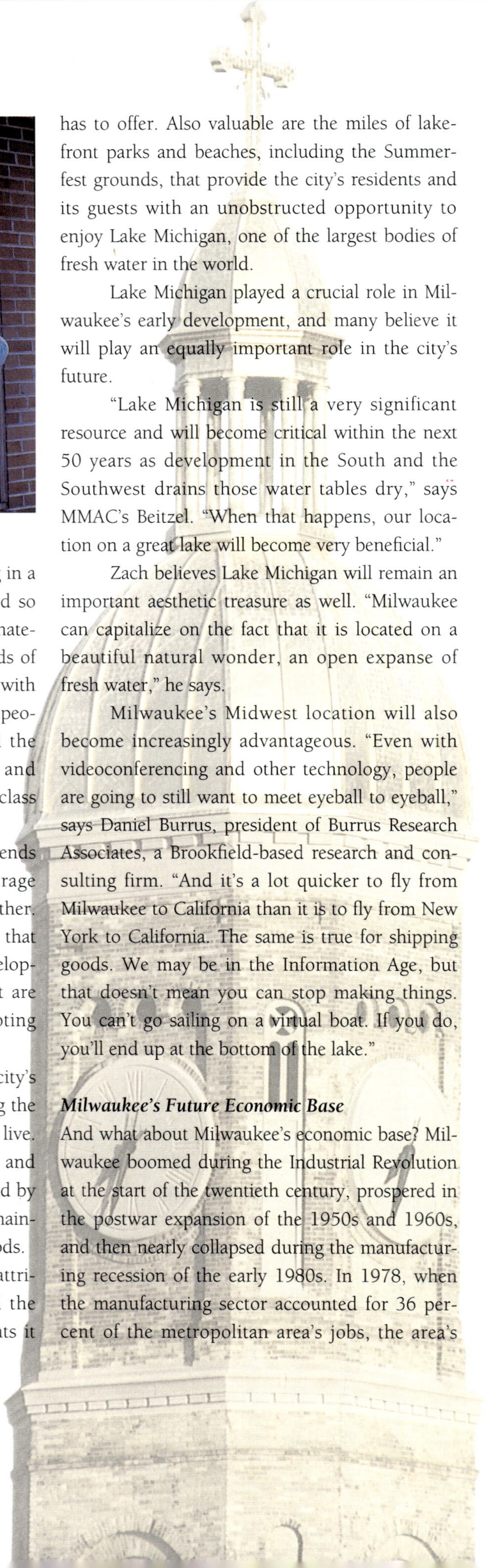

suburban subdivisions.

"One of the biggest advantages of living in a city is that people and businesses are located so close together," he says. "Since 1956, unfortunately, the federal government has spent hundreds of billions of dollars to gouge our urban centers with six- and eight-lane freeways, which separated people from markets. The freeways dispersed the economy, destroyed thousands of homes and businesses, and sucked millions of middle-class residents and businesses out to the suburbs."

For Norquist, the survival of cities depends on new transportation policies that encourage people to live in closer proximity to each other. "We need to develop and implement policies that enhance that concept instead of freeway development and other transportation policies that are devoted to decentralizing cities and promoting urban sprawl," he says.

At the same time, Norquist says the city's leaders must continually work toward making the city a place where people want to work and live. How? Through reductions in city spending and property taxes, by keeping crime in check, and by using zoning laws and political pressure to maintain the downtown and the city's neighborhoods.

Indeed, one of Milwaukee's greatest attributes may be its attractive downtown and the many sporting, shopping, and cultural events it has to offer. Also valuable are the miles of lakefront parks and beaches, including the Summerfest grounds, that provide the city's residents and its guests with an unobstructed opportunity to enjoy Lake Michigan, one of the largest bodies of fresh water in the world.

Lake Michigan played a crucial role in Milwaukee's early development, and many believe it will play an equally important role in the city's future.

"Lake Michigan is still a very significant resource and will become critical within the next 50 years as development in the South and the Southwest drains those water tables dry," says MMAC's Beitzel. "When that happens, our location on a great lake will become very beneficial."

Zach believes Lake Michigan will remain an important aesthetic treasure as well. "Milwaukee can capitalize on the fact that it is located on a beautiful natural wonder, an open expanse of fresh water," he says.

Milwaukee's Midwest location will also become increasingly advantageous. "Even with videoconferencing and other technology, people are going to still want to meet eyeball to eyeball," says Daniel Burrus, president of Burrus Research Associates, a Brookfield-based research and consulting firm. "And it's a lot quicker to fly from Milwaukee to California than it is to fly from New York to California. The same is true for shipping goods. We may be in the Information Age, but that doesn't mean you can stop making things. You can't go sailing on a virtual boat. If you do, you'll end up at the bottom of the lake."

Milwaukee's Future Economic Base

And what about Milwaukee's economic base? Milwaukee boomed during the Industrial Revolution at the start of the twentieth century, prospered in the postwar expansion of the 1950s and 1960s, and then nearly collapsed during the manufacturing recession of the early 1980s. In 1978, when the manufacturing sector accounted for 36 percent of the metropolitan area's jobs, the area's economy was dominated by several large factories that employed thousands of workers apiece. Today the manufacturing sector employs less than 22 percent of the work force and the vast majority of manufacturers are small shops with fewer than 100 employees.

"One of the great things about Milwaukee's economy today is that it is so diverse," says Beitzel. "We're not recession proof, but we're also not as vulnerable to a downturn in the auto industry or farming or in some other sector. We can withstand a national recession much better than we could in the early 1980s."

Burrus agrees. "One of the keys for economic success is not having all your eggs in one basket," he says. "Milwaukee learned that in the early 1980s. Today we're much more diversified. We are a center for banking, insurance, and service firms in addition to being a center for manufacturing."

Manufacturing will continue to be an important segment of the Milwaukee economy, but it is likely to employ fewer and fewer people. It will be increasingly difficult for local companies to compete on price with manufacturers based in China, Indonesia, Mexico, and other emerging countries. Advances in transportation and telecommunication will further encourage international commerce.

"Manufacturing could become much like farming, where you have a very small percentage of people producing all of the world's manufactured goods," says Beitzel. "For us, that means that some more manufacturers will probably close their doors and we will be left with the niche players who have focused on quality, high-end products."

Setting the Stage for Entrepreneurs

The city's industrial tradition, coupled with a new commitment to entrepreneurism, could set the stage for another golden era. "Milwaukee was

The Milwaukee skyline and the South Shore Yacht Club marina are viewed here from South Shore Park. Photo by Ralph Antczak/Crystal Studio

Among the city's new downtown developments are the River Houses condominiums, which are located on the east side of the Milwaukee River in the heart of downtown. Photo by Alan Magayne-Roshak/Third Coast Stock Source

once considered a center of innovation," Zach says. "We were the toolbox. The generation that was here at the turn of the century took the Industrial Revolution and ran with it, bringing a great deal of wealth to this city."

Zach believes small firms and startups will be the key to the city's economic future. They will have the flexibility and drive necessary to quickly adapt to and create the new technological trends that will reshape the economy and society. But in order for these companies to succeed, Zach warns, the public sector is going to have to relax its tendency to over-regulate. It must also enact policies that encourage risk-taking and innovation and change the way we educate our children.

"What we have to do in our schools, especially in our middle schools and high schools, is teach people to be entrepreneurial, to take risks, and to come up with multiple solutions to challenges," he says. "We assume that the future will be like the present but it's going to be dramatically different. If you free up the imagination you can have an extremely strong economy."

Today Milwaukee is one of only a handful of cities experimenting with school choice programs, which use vouchers to let low-income students attend the schools of their choice. Norquist, like other city leaders, believes school choice can create healthy competition among school systems, resulting in an educational system that does a better job of preparing students for the world. It is unknown whether school choice will survive the many court challenges it is sure to face, but few doubt that in the next 10 to 20 years there will be a major transformation in the way we educate our students. That's because in the Information Age, lines dividing society are likely to be based on a person's knowledge and education rather than race, gender, or ethnic heritage.

Milwaukee has succeeded in part because it has been able to maintain the skilled work force that employers need. In order to remain prosperous, the city must continue to develop educational models that address the needs of the economy.

"Probably the biggest challenge facing our community will be maintaining a quality work force," says Beitzel. "Companies will need highly skilled workers and they will go where they can find them." This bodes well for Milwaukee's educational institutions, especially those geared to developing specialized skills—such as the Milwaukee School of Engineering, Milwaukee Institute of Art and Design, Milwaukee Area Technical College, and Waukesha County Technical College.

In short, Milwaukee's future is inextricably linked to the people who call it home. Enhancing the qualities that have made the city a desirable place to live will ensure that future generations will want to live here as well. If these people have the skills and education that business needs, the Milwaukee economy will continue to flourish.

These issues are of concern to both the people who live and work in the city of Milwaukee and the 700,000 people who live in the suburbs and rural towns that comprise the four-county metropolitan area. Milwaukee is the region's heart, pumping economic energy to the surrounding communities. Without a vibrant Milwaukee, these cities, villages, and towns will become less desirable places to live.

The Excitement of City Living

Today many young professionals are rediscovering the excitement of city living. New upscale apartments and condominiums are springing up along the Milwaukee River and the Lake Michigan shoreline. There is a growing dissatisfaction with

In short, Milwaukee's future is inextricably linked to the people who call it home.

suburban subdivisions that are physically separated from stores and businesses. For the new breed of urban mayors like John Norquist, this renewed interest in city living is long overdue

"Cities have always been fundamental to civilization," Norquist says. "They are the source of wealth and culture. They will not lose their importance because of the telecommunications superhighway anymore than they did because of the invention of the telephone. Rebuilding cities is the way to restore civility and culture in America. Our cities should be rich; they should be admired as they are in most of the rest of the civilized world."

Landmark on the Lake, a 275-unit apartment property located on Prospect Avenue, offers concierge services and spectacular views of the lake from every unit. Photo by Dale Guldan/Third Coast Stock Source

Photo by Milwaukee DCD/Dave La Haye

PART THREE

Greater Milwaukee's Enterprises

BY DALE BUSS

with Linda Duczman

Courtesy, Wisconsin Electric

Chapter **SEVEN**

Networks

Milwaukee's transportation, communications, and energy firms provide vital connections, keeping people, information, and utilities circulating throughout the area.

Wisconsin Energy Corporation

To be a true pioneer in the business world, you must be a leader, set new standards of excellence, and develop cutting-edge products and services that benefit your customers. Wisconsin Energy Corporation truly meets those criteria. It has established an impressive record of service to its nearly one million customers, providing southeastern Wisconsin with reliable, low-cost electricity, natural gas, and steam services, fueling economic development through its diversified subsidiaries, and conducting a trail-blazing energy-conservation program.

Now, a century after its founding in 1896, Wisconsin Energy Corporation (WEC) is just as capably leading its customers—and the rest of its industry—through a time of dramatic changes in the utility business that will bring competition, sweeping deregulation, and swift technological progress.

Under the leadership of Richard Abdoo, WEC chairman, president, and chief executive officer, Wisconsin Energy's companies, including Wisconsin Electric Power Co., have carved out the leading edge of this new era. WEC has streamlined its corporate structure, reshaped its internal culture along the lines of more competitive industries, and—most important—arranged a merger that will make the combined entity the premier energy supplier in the Upper Midwest.

Employees of Wisconsin Energy Corporation companies address decision making and career consequences in programs to children in area schools.

Pending regulatory approvals, on January 1, 1997, Wisconsin Energy will merge with Northern States Power Company, based in Minneapolis, to create Primergy Corporation. The corporation will create the 10th-largest energy company in the United States and initially serve 2.3 million electric customers and 745,000 natural gas customers in portions of Wisconsin, Minnesota, North Dakota, South Dakota, and the Upper Peninsula of Michigan.

The merger-of-equals transaction will join two enterprises whose current combined market capitalization is more than $6 billion and create a combined enterprise that will be well positioned for an increasingly competitive energy industry. The merger is designed to achieve continued competitive energy rates over the long term for the companies' respective customers and to enhance value for the shareholders of both organizations.

"We've staked our future as a company on our conviction that individual consumers will soon make choices about power consumption in the same way that they now have unparalleled choices in every other sector of the American economy," says Abdoo, who will become chief executive officer of Primergy in 1998.

"And because we are reshaping the company to compete under this new paradigm, I also am confident that we will attain our ultimate goal: to be the energy provider of choice in our region."

Wisconsin Electric, WEC's principal subsidiary, headquartered at 231 West Michigan Street in Milwaukee, is primarily engaged in the generation, transmission, distribution, and sale of electric energy in a territory of about 12,100 square miles in southeastern Wisconsin, including the Milwaukee metropolitan area, the east-central and northern portions of the state, and the Upper Peninsula of Michigan.

The company has 955,000 customers, including 81,000 small commercial and industrial customers and 650 large commercial and industrial customers.

Wisconsin Electric employs about 4,500 people and Wisconsin Energy nonutility companies employ about 100 people.

Wisconsin Electric was a trailblazing concern even when it was born a century ago as The Milwaukee Electric Railway and Light Co. The company consolidated several electric and railway companies in the area into this new entity—and put an end to the freewheeling, sometimes economically destabilizing competition among a roster of smaller concerns that had characterized the early days of the electric utility industry. (The company changed its name to Wisconsin Electric Power Co. in 1938.)

Electric revenue for the first year of operation was slightly more than $250,000, a small operation compared to the railway business, and electricity sales were only about 5 million kilowatt-hours. By 1995, 100 years after the company's formation, electricity sales were nearly 27 billion kilowatt-hours, WE generated $1.77 billion in revenues, and the corporation's total assets exceeded $4.56 billion.

Wisconsin Electric acquired the predecessor company of Wisconsin Natural Gas Co. in 1950, and moved the headquarters of the subsidiary to Racine in 1962. Wisconsin Electric and Wisconsin Natural Gas merged in 1996. Serving about 380,000 customers in a 2,800-square-mile area that mostly overlaps the company's electric service territory, WE's gas operations are the second-largest natural gas concern in Wisconsin.

The company has been a constant innovator among its peers nationwide. For example, in 1970 Wisconsin Electric became a pioneer in providing efficient, safe nuclear power to its customers when it opened the first of two generating units at its Point Beach Nuclear Plant, located along Lake Michigan in Manitowoc County. The second generating unit came on-line in 1972.

Point Beach produces about one-third of the electricity generated by the company and has saved Wisconsin Electric customers more than one billion dollars in energy costs over its first 20 years of operation. According to the Utility Data Institute, Point Beach had the second-lowest production cost of any nuclear plant in the nation for the five-year period ending in 1992.

The Smart Money Energy Program, which began in 1987, was another innovative aspect of the company's efforts to keep its electricity affordable. Smart Money soon became one of the largest and most effective energy-efficiency incentive efforts ever undertaken by an energy company. The program provided industrial, commercial, institutional, and residential customers with rebates, interest-free loans, and other incentives to encourage investment in more efficient uses of electricity. Smart Money helped Wisconsin Electric reduce its peak electricity needs and, therefore, the need to construct more costly power plants. The program resulted in reduced energy bills for customers and encouraged responsible energy consumption.

These and other corporate initiatives allowed Wisconsin Electric to repeatedly cut its electricity rates in the mid-1980s. By 1990 its rates were seventh-low-

Above: A Wisconsin Energy Corporation line mechanic performs preventive maintenance.

Below left: A WEC gas operations employee works to expand natural gas pipelines in Wauzeka, Wisconsin.

est among 25 of the nation's largest metropolitan areas—and a full 40 percent lower than those of Commonwealth Edison, the utility whose service area in northern Illinois is adjacent to that of Wisconsin Electric's. WE also consistently was rated by outside evaluators as one of the best-managed, best-performing, and most consumer-oriented electric utilities in the entire country.

In 1987, under the direction of then-chairman and chief executive officer Charles McNeer, the company established its current holding company—Wisconsin Energy Corporation—diversifying its operations to stimulate business development in the firm's utility areas, create jobs, and generate additional returns on shareholders' investments.

Several nonutility subsidiaries were formed in this initiative, including Wispark Corporation, which has developed LakeView Corporate Park in Kenosha County, Racine's GrandView Business Park, and other dynamic business locations around southeastern Wisconsin, in part by capitalizing on Wisconsin Electric's tremendous cost advantage compared with Illinois utilities. Other nonutility subsidiaries include Witech Corporation, a venture-capital operation; Wisvest Corporation; Badger Service Company; and Wisconsin Michigan Investment Corporation.

An employee inspects the inside of the 202-foot-high boiler at WEC's Pleasant Prairie Power Plant.

The diversification drive proved to be a forward-looking first step in a process of girding Wisconsin Electric and its affiliates for a challenging future. Federal legislation passed in 1992 opened the door to unprecedented competition in the electric industry just as previously the government had deregulated banking, long-distance telecommunications, and airlines. The pressure to introduce competition to the electric market will continue because customers across the nation seek the benefits it brings.

But instead of resisting the inevitable, Wisconsin Electric has embraced the new era of competition and, in fact, has laid out a vision for it.

The company's vision calls for creating an independent energy marketplace that provides access to competitive power supplies for all customers. It would bring the benefits of competition in the power-generation and customer-service components of the industry but ensure that the transmission and distribution of power would be "re-regulated" and continue to be provided by the same electric company that serves customers today. This competitive energy market would force electric rates for all consumer groups to go down, so that only energy providers giving maximum value to the customer would succeed. The Public Service Commission of Wisconsin (PSCW) shares Wisconsin Electric's overall view of tomorrow's energy marketplace.

To prepare for a future that includes the merger and increased competition, Wisconsin Energy in 1995 began a revitalization of operations that included rebuilding its companies into business units that function as individual profit centers, and improving its work processes.

"This cultural change is going very well, and it will only be enhanced by the merger," Abdoo says. "We have a great work force that is closely involved in making the changes necessary for our continued success. And we have the beginnings of an entrepreneurial spirit that will serve us well as this new arena in our industry takes shape."

Working with the community will continue to be one of WE's major focal points in the future. In the

1980s Wisconsin Electric became one of the first utilities in the country to forge alliances with consumer groups and community-based organizations to achieve common goals, including the development of low-income housing. The company also has been involved in improvements such as backing a project to illuminate downtown Milwaukee landmarks and strengthening the education system through both private- and public-school initiatives.

In the 1990s, just as its competitive gaze has broadened, so has Wisconsin Electric's view of opportunities to make investments in the future. For example, Wisconsin Electric was one of about 30 U.S. electric companies that signed the Global Climate Challenge Participation Accord in 1994 with the U.S. Energy Department.

And to help protect air quality worldwide, Wisconsin Electric and several other energy companies purchased about 14,000 acres of rain forest—the flora that generates much of the oxygen in our planet's atmosphere—in the Central American nation of Belize.

"We're moving into more than one new paradigm at a time," Abdoo concedes. "But I know that this company and our people are up to the challenge."

Wisconsin Energy Corporation's Pleasant Prairie Power Plant in Kenosha, Wisconsin, is recognized as one of the lowest-cost generators of electricity in the United States.

Inset: A WEC electric operations employee works to meet customer needs in southeastern Wisconsin.

Wisconsin Gas

For more than 140 years—since 1852 to be precise—Wisconsin Gas has supplied thousands upon thousands of residential, commercial, and industrial customers across much of Wisconsin with dependable, inexpensive supplies of natural gas. For the past 65 years, there has been little change in the traditional public utility paradigm under which the industry operated here and nationwide.

Over the past 10 to 15 years, the federal government has deregulated the natural gas pipeline industry, laying the groundwork for opening local utility gas markets to competition. And in 1995 the Public Service Commission of Wisconsin established a set of principles for deregulating Wisconsin Gas and other gas utilities in the state.

The response by Wisconsin Gas to these sweeping changes has been typical of a company that has always challenged itself to meet the needs and demands of its customers, shareholders, communities, and all of its other constituencies: Bring on the new era of competition; we're ready.

"The new, deregulated environment has allowed us to focus on providing high-quality customer service as a gas distribution company, giving us a well-honed corporate mission that will encourage us to exceed even the high performance standards that we established when Wisconsin Gas was a traditional utility," says Tom Schrader, president and chief executive officer.

"Competition really is in the best interest of everyone," Schrader adds. "It is allowing Wisconsin Gas to create a more competitive environment in all markets, including the residential market, to sell new services to gas shippers and marketers and to earn its way based on the quality of its service rather than on a regulated rate of return."

Of course, competition is hardly new to Wisconsin Gas. In fact, the company had its origins in 1852 largely because of the specter of Milwaukee falling behind Chicago in the race for technological leadership in the Midwest. Chicago already had been lighting its streets with gas when a young engineer from Cincinnati convinced Milwaukee's city fathers to build its first municipal gas plant.

Soon, lights brightened all the major city streets. Commercial and then residential customers began signing up for gas service as well, including Byron Kilbourn, one of the leading businessmen of the city's early era. The distribution system and service reached out toward the suburbs, and new company outposts were added over the next several decades.

The company's major growth started in the early 1950s, when the Michigan

What's the weather today? The weather flame atop the Wisconsin Gas headquarters in downtown Milwaukee flashes colors to indicate the weather conditions. A poem explains the meaning of each color: "When the flame is red, it's warm weather ahead; when the flame is gold, watch out for cold; when the flame is blue, there's no change in view; when there's a flickering flame, expect snow or rain!" Photo by Michael F. Folker

Wisconsin Pipe Line Co. brought to Milwaukee natural gas service that transported the fuel from the newly developed fields of the southwestern United States. Its operations underwent radical changes because the new method of gas distribution varied so greatly from that for manufactured gas, which had been in use for almost a century.

In the 1950s the firm erected a weather flame atop its headquarters at 626 East Wisconsin Avenue. By indicating the next day's weather forecast via a three-color code and by uniquely punctuating the skyline, the artificial-gas flame became a leading landmark. It was extinguished during the energy shortage of the 1970s, but Wisconsin Gas reignited the flame due to public demand in 1985.

By 1995 Wisconsin Gas reached the half-million-customer mark, serving more than 500 communities around the state. It distributes about 40 percent of all the natural gas consumed in the state, and it serves more than 80 percent of the homes, and the majority of business and industry, in Milwaukee.

The company's modern-day markets encompass residential, commercial, and industrial space and water heating, manufacturing processes, dehumidifying, cooking, electric generation, and natural gas vehicles.

On the average, Wisconsin Gas moves about 125 billion cubic feet of natural gas each year through its vast 8,300-mile system of pipes.

Just as Wisconsin Gas has contributed to Milwaukee's growth and prosperity, today it is playing a new role in helping municipalities operate more efficiently.

Capitalizing on its years of experience in running a gas distribution system and managing customer accounts, the company in 1995 formed a business unit called FieldTech, which markets and implements meter-reading technology and systems to utilities and municipalities throughout the United States and Canada. In 1996 FieldTech became the prime contractor to supply an automatic meter-reading (AMR) system for the Milwaukee Water Works. Once installed, the city will be able to read 15,000 meters a day with a computerized van driving down a street, eliminating the need to enter a home or business.

In 1980 Wisconsin Gas formed WICOR, Inc., and became its primary subsidiary. The parent company founded WICOR Energy Services in 1995, an unregulated marketing subsidiary, to sell energy commodities and offer energy-related services.

The other arm of WICOR, about two-fifths of its business, manufactures pumps and fluid-processing and -filtration equipment for a variety of markets throughout the world. The manufacturing companies are Sta-Rite Industries Inc., SHURflo Pump Manufacturing Co., and Hypro Corp. The global strength of these manufacturing operations is an important part of the company's strategy for continued growth in the future.

Wisconsin Gas serves more than 80 percent of the homes and the vast majority of business and industry in Milwaukee. The company delivers natural gas throughout a network of 1,577 miles of underground piping within the city limits. Its total Wisconsin distribution system includes 8,300 miles of pipes.

Left: Thomas F. Schrader, president and chief executive officer of Wisconsin Gas.

WISCONSIN GAS
A WICOR COMPANY
Making Wisconsin's best energy value even better!

General Mitchell International Airport

General Mitchell International Airport has come into its own both as a fast-growing regional transportation hub and as one of the most convenient airports in the United States.

Passenger traffic at Mitchell jumped 15 percent in 1994, to a record 5.2 million, while it was also the first year that the number of passengers using the airport exceeded 5 million. That record was broken again in 1995.

Over the past 10 years, in fact, passenger traffic at Mitchell International has jumped to 5.2 million a year from just 3 million in 1985. And the vast majority of that long-term increase, airport officials say, is Wisconsin-based passengers although Mitchell is seeing an increasing number of Illinois-based passengers—hence its nickname, "Chicago's Third Airport."

"Travelers have positive experiences when they come here," says C. Barry Bateman, airport director for Mitchell International. "You certainly don't hear that about O'Hare and Midway. We know we're an airport of choice in this general regional market; when people have a choice, they do choose Mitchell."

The first air terminal at the site of the current airport was in a farmhouse. In 1940 a new terminal opened, and the next year the entire complex was named General Mitchell Field in honor of General William "Billy" Mitchell, Milwaukee's favorite son hero of World War I.

In 1955 another new terminal was put into service, followed by the addition of an eight-gate concourse in 1969, an international-arrivals terminal in 1975, an air-cargo center in 1983, and a major, $44-million expansion in 1985. In 1986 the name of the airport was officially changed to General Mitchell International Airport to reflect its increased international passenger and cargo traffic.

Nowadays, Mitchell employs about 4,000 Milwaukee-area residents in directly dependent jobs including airline and airport service, freight transportation, passenger ground transportation, and contract construction and consulting. Airport activities generate another several thousand jobs, and the airport pumps

A 16-gate addition to one of Mitchell International's three concourses opened in December 1990. The focal point of the addition is an atrium area with live ficus trees, a skylight, and a terrazzo floor. A moving walkway also was added to carry passengers from the concession mall to the new gates.

hundreds of millions of dollars in revenues into the state.

The reasons for Mitchell's current golden era are many. Perhaps most important is that the Wisconsin economy, source of most of Mitchell's travelers, has continued to be vibrant since the recession of the early 1980s. Another major factor, of course, is that air travel in general has continued to boom across the country.

But a number of reasons bespeak Mitchell's specific strengths, and many of those reasons say "convenience." The airport is just off Interstate 94 and only 15 minutes from downtown Milwaukee. Its parking facilities, expanded by 2,250 spaces in 1990 at a cost of $16 million, offer low fees. Passengers can trek from the parking garage to the farthest gate at Mitchell in 10 minutes. The recently redesigned concessions area in the main terminal offers more variety than ever, including a new self-serve food court, a big second-hand bookstore, an aviation-history museum, and meeting and even banquet facilities.

In fact, over the past decade Mitchell International has invested more than $100 million in improvements. But although it is operated by the Milwaukee County Executive and Board of Supervisors, these improvements have been financed by federal aviation funds and by the airlines themselves—not by property taxes. And user fees, including airline landing and space-rental fees, concession fees, and parking revenues, completely support Mitchell's operations.

Midwest Express has emerged over the past several years as the airport's flagship airline. The Milwaukee-based carrier accounts for about 27 percent of Mitchell's traffic. "They're something a lot of cities would give their eyeteeth for," Bateman says. "But fortunately, they aren't so dominant at this point that there isn't still a healthy level of competition."

Given the background growth trend at the airport, cutbacks or departures at Mitchell by any given airline no longer are economically traumatic events, except perhaps for their individual employees. New airlines emerge to fill in any voids in service, or existing airlines increase service on those routes.

Airlines continue to start up at Mitchell; American Trans Air began operations in 1992 with flights to Florida and Arizona and has grown quickly. It is now Mitchell's third-largest carrier.

General Mitchell International Airport features a spacious, airy concession mall with restaurants, shops, and services catering to the traveling public. More than 35,000 people a day visit the airport, including passengers and meeters-and-greeters.

Air cargo shipments also have increased enormously, largely due to the continued boom in overnight-delivery services, the growth of export shipments by Wisconsin businesses, and the increased implementation of just-in-time delivery techniques by local manufacturers. In 1995 Mitchell completed an expansion of the cargo area, which followed a previous expansion by only several years.

Mitchell International also serves as home base for the Wisconsin Air National Guard's 128th Air Refueling Group and the U.S. Air Force Reserve's 440th Tactical Airlift Wing. While things have been thankfully routine lately, Mitchell was a hotbed of activity while both units served key roles in supporting U.S. forces during the Persian Gulf War in 1991.

Because of anticipated economic growth and the continued rise in air travel, says Bateman, Mitchell's master plan foresees passenger growth of about 3 to 6 percent a year for the next several years. Two new concourses eventually will be required to accommodate it. After the turn of the century the master plan also foresees the need for a third parallel runway.

At the same time Mitchell also has voluntarily established a noise-abatement program, which began with a study of the generation of noise by aircraft using the airport. The airport offers to buy out homes in the areas closest to runways and provides sound insulation or home-sales assistance to people who live a little farther away. Bateman expects that the problem will be diminished also by federally mandated quieter engines on all airline jets after the year 2000.

USA Today reported early in 1995—using Federal Aviation Administration data—that Mitchell International will be the eighth-fastest-growing airport in the nation in terms of passenger use over the next decade.

Midwest Express Airlines

When Midwest Express Holdings, the parent company of Midwest Express Airlines, went public in September 1995, the listing of its shares on the New York Stock Exchange was not only another milestone in the airline's 11-year history—it was also an opportunity for some chest-thumping for the entire city of Milwaukee.

That's because the airline is based in Milwaukee, and General Mitchell International Airport remains its primary base of operations. It's also because, as much as any company these days, Midwest Express symbolizes the city's self-image: homey yet progressive, deliberate yet robust, stylish but not brassy. Better yet, its association with the city is something that is as important to people at the airline as it is to Milwaukeeans.

"We love being 'the hometown airline,'" says Brenda Skelton, senior vice president of marketing and customer service for Midwest Express. "The loyalty and support of the Milwaukee business community has been tremendous. And we have a high level of commitment to Milwaukee because we live and work here."

In 1995 Midwest Express' milestones included going public as part of a spinoff from its former parent company, Kimberly-Clark Corporation; celebrating one year of service at its second base of operations in Omaha, Nebraska; continuing its status as one of only two U.S. airlines to show a profit consistently over the past several years; and being named the best U.S. airline by a leading consumer report, the respected Zagat Airline Survey, and the readers of *Condé Nast Traveler*.

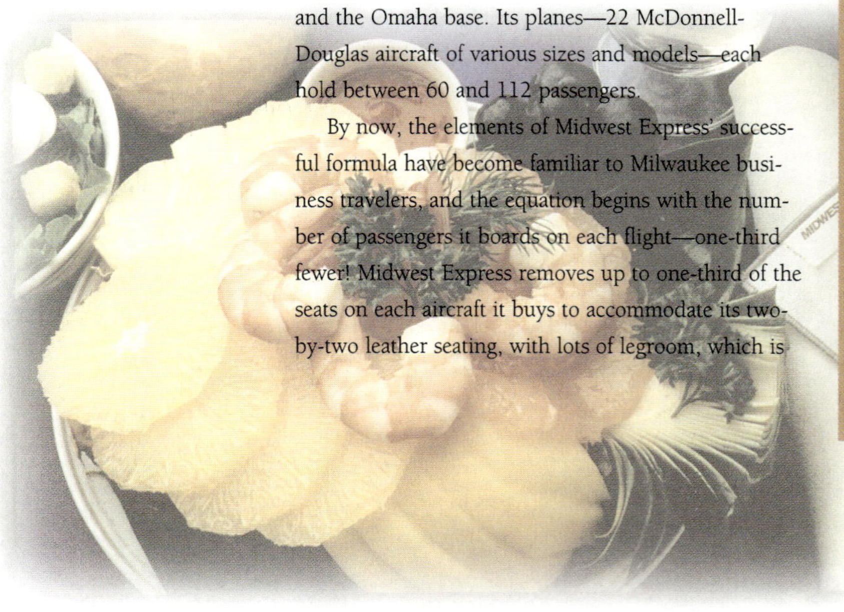

The delicious food served on-board is one of the airline's trademark amenities.

The airline now employs more than 1,000 people in Wisconsin and serves 23 destinations from Mitchell and the Omaha base. Its planes—22 McDonnell-Douglas aircraft of various sizes and models—each hold between 60 and 112 passengers.

By now, the elements of Midwest Express' successful formula have become familiar to Milwaukee business travelers, and the equation begins with the number of passengers it boards on each flight—one-third fewer! Midwest Express removes up to one-third of the seats on each aircraft it buys to accommodate its two-by-two leather seating, with lots of legroom, which is one of its trademark amenities.

Of course, so is the delicious food, which is served on real china with linen napkins and includes complimentary wine or champagne. And, on some flights, chocolate-chip cookies are baked right on-board. Midwest Express' meals cost more than twice the per-passenger amount spent by most airlines, making them much more memorable.

Midwest Express has been profitable while offering this premium service because it has found a successful formula and stuck with it. While its coach and discounted fares are competitive with those of other airlines on its routes, Midwest Express attracts a higher percentage of full-fare business travelers because of its comfortable on-board environment, convenient departure and arrival times, and a high number of nonstop flights.

One of the few airlines born out of deregulation that has survived, Midwest Express began service as an outgrowth of the Kimberly-Clark Corporation. The company, best known for its Kleenex product, was also familiar with the aviation industry. In 1969, with more than 20 years of corporate aviation experience, K-C Aviation was formed as a subsidiary to offer maintenance and refurbishing of corporate aircraft.

When airline deregulation in 1979 opened the door to the possibility of scheduled service, K-C executives

General Mitchell International Airport is the primary base of operations for Midwest Express Airlines.

decided to launch their own commercial carrier. In 1984 Midwest Express was born, and K-C Aviation's chief, Timothy Hoeksema, became the upstart's first and only president.

Success was small but steady at first. By late 1987, Midwest Express was launching a major, five-year, $120-million expansion. In 1989, through a marketing agreement with another carrier, Skyway Airlines was born to provide passengers with connections between smaller midwestern cities and Midwest Express jet service in Milwaukee, and point-to-point service between select markets. Now operated by a wholly owned subsidiary, Skyway currently operates 15 Beechcraft 1900D regional aircraft. By 1993, its biggest rival at Mitchell International, Northwest Airlines, had reduced its presence in the city, clearing the way for more growth by Midwest Express. And, in December 1994, the airline logged its one-millionth passenger in a single year.

During the past few years, as the airline continued to grow, questions arose about how transferable its formula might be to other markets. Hoeksema and his crew answered in 1994 by opening a second base of operations in Omaha, a city similar to Milwaukee: underserved by other airlines, with a dynamic and growing business community. Midwest Express has 115 employees based in Omaha and continues to gain market share on its Omaha routes.

"We're doing very well in Omaha," Skelton says. "We actually began making a profit in Omaha more quickly than when we started up in Milwaukee." An unexpected bonus: Internationally renowned investor Warren Buffett, an Omaha resident, saw the airline as so important to the area's business climate that he volunteered to do a print advertisement endorsing Midwest Express.

Midwest Express' comfortable on-board environment is enhanced by roomy two-by-two leather seating.

Skelton says that the airline would like to add another base of operations in the next three to five years but hasn't decided where yet. "The market is so dynamic, and competitive positions can change so much, that we can't make that decision yet," she explains. In the meantime, the airline continues to add on average about two planes a year to its jet fleet.

Its transition to public ownership has enabled employees to become stockholders in Midwest Express. Their direct stake and increased involvement has been very exciting. After all, Skelton says, "It's our people and their commitment that have been and will continue to be key to our success."

Harris Classical Broadcasting Inc.

WFMR Radio's colorful history includes ownership by some well-known Wisconsinites, a short-lived switch from its historical format, and the station's subsequent re-establishment as the beacon of classical music in metro Milwaukee, at 98.3 on the FM dial.

But for Harris Classical Broadcasting Inc., the family-owned operation that took over WFMR in 1992, the future remains the focus. And the company is adding the most promising chapters yet to the story of this business.

After 41 years on the air, WFMR remains one of the few independent, privately owned classical-format radio stations in the United States. The voice of culture in Milwaukee, it also enjoys one of the largest audience shares of its local market of any classical station.

Right: Partners David Bishop (seated) and Randall Harris own and operate the station.

"Milwaukee is proud of the fact that it has a stand-alone, commercial classical station," says Randall Harris, general manager and co-owner of WFMR. "And we are returning that intense commitment to the city. We took over a challenged radio station and have made it go on its own in this town, even while other classical stations all over the country are being bought up and, usually, switching formats."

Margaret Odya, on-air talent and news director for both WFMR and WFMI.

The most important factor in WFMR's continued popularity was its innovative change in 1995 from traditional concert programming to modern radio programming, tailored to today's more active listener.

It's the same great classical repertoire—just programmed to the rhythms of everyday life. During listeners' busy morning and afternoons, for example, WFMR's on-air selections are shorter and lighter. And during mid-days, evenings, and weekends, listeners hear longer performances that match life's more relaxing times. The station also broadcasts performances by the Milwaukee Symphony, Metropolitan Opera, Chicago Symphony, and San Francisco Symphony.

The Harris family's experience in the radio industry is another major reason for their success in guiding WFMR during the past few years. Harris has been involved in the industry at stations in Florida, Chicago, Detroit, and Dallas. Co-owner David Bishop, his brother-in-law, is the company's sales manager and also has an extensive background in the business. Both reside in the area.

Richard Harris, Randall's father and chairman of WFMR, is retired president and chairman of Group W Broadcasting's radio division, an operation that he built over several years from five AM stations to more than 25 AM and FM stations across the country. A resident of Florida, Richard Harris remains active in the radio business even beyond helping steer WFMR: He is chairman of the industry's music licensing committee, which negotiates with recording companies over royalties and other matters.

Right: Craig Heabler (left), WFMR morning show host, and Randall Harris, co-owner and operator of WFMR and WFMI.

Some of the station's staff.

Another prominent element in WFMR's success, of course, is the growing and loyal base of advertisers. These companies include many of metro Milwaukee's leading banks, furniture stores, bookstores, fine restaurants, and arts institutions.

"They keep coming back to us, because they know we're a good way to reach an audience of educated, influential adults," says Randall Harris—particularly those in the key 25-to-54-year-old demographic group, which includes baby boomers. More than four out of five members of WFMR's very attractive audience own their own home; about half have one or more college degree; more than two-fifths have a valid passport.

The adoption of state-of-the-art technology also has boosted WFMR in recent years. "We've upgraded our technology and our broadcast facility so that we're pure digital," says Randall Harris. "Everything is bits and bytes. You won't find a tape, a cassette, or anything like that in the building."

The company added another chapter to its success in 1995 by putting a second station on the air, WFMI, at a long-licensed but never-utilized FM frequency, 106.9 MHz. "Smooth FM" is devoted to the emerging jazz sound that is sweeping U.S. radio. Playing artists like David Sanborn and Anita Baker, WFMI took off upon its debut, posting Milwaukee's strongest ratings ever for a new adult format.

"As the population ages, they're a lot more interested in this kind of sound than, say, traditional rock and roll," Harris says. With its special emphasis on baby boomers, WFMI quickly has become the station of choice for advertisers seeking that market.

While WFMR broadcasts at 98.3 MHz, a translator system serving Whitefish Bay and Shorewood broadcasts at 104.9 MHz. The transmitter and business office are in Menomonee Falls.

FM broadcasting was in the midst of its turbulent infancy in 1955, when James G. Baker decided to start WFMR. He chose the call letters not only to incorporate the relatively new technology, "FM," but to stand for something else that has been the station's byword since: "Fine Music Radio."

Financial difficulties plagued ownership of the station from the start. Finally, in 1973, John Koss, founder of Koss Corporation, and Jerold Ross, of Industrial Towel and Uniform, purchased the station and pledged to keep alive its heritage of classical and jazz music. They built a new transmitter and antenna in Glendale.

In the fall of 1976 Douglass Cofrin, an arts patron and part of the founding family of Fort Howard Paper Co., purchased an interest in WFMR, and he became its sole owner in 1978.

In the early 1980s the station underwent a brief transformation from its historical classical-music format to formulized soft rock after it was sold by Cofrin to Cleveland-based radio mogul Tom Embrescia. The change threw WFMR's loyal listenership, and the arts community, into tumult.

Darrell Peters, the Chicago-based owner of WXJY, an easy-listening station in Menomonee Falls, realized the economic value of a full-time commercial classical station. He began to switch his station to a classical format, and even picked up the old call letters from Embrescia. In May 1983 the "new" WFMR, operating at 98.3, was sold to a concern primarily owned by H. Stewart Corbett, an investor based in Hilton Head, South Carolina.

Corbett rebuilt WFMR's studio and transmitter facilities at their current site in Menomonee Falls. After three years he sold WFMR to Milwaukeean Robert Caulfield, former director of the Milwaukee Symphony. The station doubled its power to 6,000 watts shortly before its purchase by Harris Classical Communications.

So the city's classical-music beacon now shines brighter than ever.

Community Newspapers Inc.

Each week, an invited guest arrives in more than 73,000 suburban Milwaukee homes with local news that families won't find anywhere else.

The guest is one of 23 award-winning newspapers published by Community Newspapers Inc., which celebrated its 40th anniversary on February 22, 1996. It is invited in that it is a paid-subscription newspaper, delivered by mail and designed especially for each of the individual suburbs.

"We have deep roots in our communities," says Thomas H. Krekel, publisher of CNI. "Our papers are unique in terms of local news and information."

Suburban readers find their community newspaper fits into their life-styles. It gives them information about what's happening with their taxes, local schools, community organizations, and prep sports, as well as articles about interesting neighbors and special events—all in one place and in one weekly edition. It covers people, all the way from births to weddings and obituaries.

Community Newspapers Inc. publishes 23 different editions throughout metro Milwaukee. Together, the publishing group delivers an upscale suburban audience.

"We've become part of the fabric of our communities," Krekel explains.

Most of the 23 newspapers also have been designated the official publication for their communities, meaning that local governments use them for legal notices, agendas, and the printing of minutes, and residents know this is where they will find this type of information.

"I think we cover the suburban communities better than any other publication," says Janet Raasch, CNI executive editor. "We print information people cannot get anywhere else—local news, news about people in their community, important things that are going on in their day-to-day lives."

Perhaps in recognition of that, CNI publications have received some of the top journalism awards in the state. In 1995 the company won all three general excellence awards from the Wisconsin Newspaper Association for the *Wauwatosa News-Times*, the *Germantown Banner-Press*, and the *Elm Leaves*. Each represented a different circulation category in the WNA competition.

"That's something we're really proud of," Raasch says. "That's the highest honor we can win in the state. And while these three papers received the awards, I feel confident that any of our newspapers we had chosen to submit would have won."

If news is the focus of the 23 publications, advertisers have also found the CNI newspapers to be an efficient way of spreading a particular message to a targeted audience. Businesses can zone their advertising, making it specific to a community, or choose certain areas where they want to focus their ads. CNI readers tend to be long-term subscribers and home owners with a higher-than-average disposable income, according to market research.

"In the final analysis, all business is local," Krekel says. "We help retailers and other marketers make a connection at that level. Advertisers can customize their ads for different locations, picking certain zones or target areas where they want to spend their money."

The newspapers also include local classified advertising sections, where readers can buy and sell items and services. The classified advertising is particularly popular as a source of information about local rummage or estate sales.

In addition to its 23 community newspapers, CNI also produces 12 free-circulation publications, advertising shoppers. More than 250,000 homes receive one of the 12 different *This Week* shoppers, which are also zoned for the greatest local impact.

CNI began in a small way, with the publication of just one community paper, the *Oak Creek Pictorial*, on February 22, 1956. The 10-page newspaper included much of the same type of information found in today's publications. It provided information on Oak Creek's first primary election, described the new $143,000 wing at Oak Creek Junior High School, and listed a schedule for church Lenten services in the community.

Published just after the city was incorporated, that first edition included an article titled "A New City on the March." In the same way, that edition marked the beginning of a community newspaper chain that would march throughout the Milwaukee area, bringing a sense of community to each suburb it entered.

In 1960 its founder, Duane Dunham, established a second publication called the *Greendale Village Life*; the *Greenfield Observer* followed in 1966. And as the Milwaukee suburbs continued to grow, so did the number of community newspapers. The company was expanding, but the focus stayed the same: to provide a link between readers and their community.

Dunham acquired the *Tri-Town News*, which is now the *Franklin-Hales Corners Hub*, in 1967, and three years later he spun off the *Muskego Sun* from the *Hub*, giving Muskego its own publication.

In 1972 Dunham purchased the *Cudahy/St. Francis Reminder-Enterprise*. The following year he established the *South Milwaukee News Graphic*. Then, in 1974, the direction veered to the north shore, where Dunham acquired five weekly *Herald* publications.

The largest acquisition of all came in 1979, when Dunham looked west and added Shinners Publications to the community newspaper chain. Through this purchase, the company now owned the *Brookfield News*, *Wauwatosa News-Times*, *Elm Leaves*, *Menomonee Falls News*, *Sussex-Lannon-Lisbon News*, *Germantown Banner-Press*, and *New Berlin Citizen*. In 1983 Dunham added the *West Allis Star* to the chain.

When Dunham retired in 1986 after 30 years of publishing the suburban newspapers, Community Newspapers Inc. was acquired by SunMedia Corp., which is headquartered in suburban Cleveland. Between the Sun Newspapers in Cleveland and CNI in metro Milwaukee, SunMedia now publishes more paid-subscription weeklies, by circulation, than any other company in the nation.

In 1987 CNI purchased the *South Milwaukee Voice Journal*, which was merged with the *News Graphic* and then renamed the *South Milwaukee Advice Graphic*. The *Bay Viewer* also was acquired at that time.

Now with 22 suburban newspapers in its fold, CNI decided it was time to have a new offspring—a local publication created just for the rapidly growing area to the north. Thus, in August 1993, the *Mequon-Thiensville Courant* was born, bringing this area the same kind of in-depth local news and neighborhood coverage that readers had come to expect in other communities.

Suburban areas are growing and changing; new families move in, put down roots, and grow with their communities. That's the same tradition CNI has established.

Suburban readers use CNI as a prime source of local shopping information, as well as for local news, community events, and prep sports.

Kalmbach Publishing Co.

Kalmbach Publishing Co. is recognized as one of the leading publishers of hobby and special-interest magazines and books worldwide.

Along with its flagship publication, *Model Railroader* magazine, which has since earned a reputation as the world's most popular model railroading magazine, Kalmbach is the proud publisher of a unique collection of hobby-related periodicals covering a wide range of interests.

Hands-on crafter's hobbies include fine-scale modeling, garden railroading, and miniatures. The firm also publishes magazines on toy collecting, classic toy trains, birdwatching, amateur astronomy, and the science of our planet.

Kalmbach publications are regarded by hobbyists as the finest high-quality magazines available, written by experts in their fields and noted for their helpful, reader-friendly approach ensuring hobby fans a lifetime of fun and discovery.

Kalmbach also publishes a full line of popular hobby books designed to complement several of the company's magazines. More than 200 titles are divided into two camps: how-to guides and railroad reference books, including a new Golden Years of Railroading series devoted to the trains of yesterday. Hobby fans also enjoy Kalmbach's annual publications featuring the year's best model railroad plans and layouts.

Most recently the company has added a line of award-winning videos, "Trains On Location," that take viewers trackside to the hottest railroading spots in North America. Kalmbach also offers a complete selection of beautiful hobby calendars.

The enterprise began in 1933, in the midst of the Great Depression, when a young Milwaukeean named Albert C. Kalmbach began a small printing and publishing business in a cinder block garage at 545 South 84th Street.

A victim of hard times, the ambitious college graduate had combined his favorite pastime, model railroading, with his enthusiasm for the printing industry in the hopes of creating a means of gainful employment.

On December 15 of that year, Kalmbach posed outside his new venture with all 272 copies of the first issue of *Model Railroader* magazine. Today, more than half a century later, the company remains committed to its founder's vision of publishing excellence and quality customer service. And that means playing an active role in the hobby community.

"We have a unique relationship with the customers we serve," says Walter Mundschau, president of Kalmbach. "We work together as partners to further the awareness of, and involvement in, our hobbies. It's a mutually rewarding experience."

Right: Kalmbach Publishing Co. is located in the suburb of Waukesha, just west of downtown Milwaukee and close to the famous Milwaukee Zoo.

Facing page, bottom: Kalmbach also offers a full line of informative collector's guides and how-to books that encourages readers to further explore their hobbies.

WITI has earned the distinction of being Milwaukee's journalistic award-winner. Over the past 10 years SIX IS NEWS has earned more news awards than its competitors combined. Year after year, The Wisconsin Broadcasters Association, Milwaukee Press Club, the Associated Press, and other organizations cite SIX IS NEWS for excellence in every facet of news coverage and community service.

Meet some of the award-winning SIX IS NEWS team: (clockwise from left) Bill Gaines, Tom Pipines, Janet Roach, Melodie Wilson, Jane Skinner, Vince Condella, Joyce Garbaciak, and Mike Bartley.

news and community-service awards, when research shows that Milwaukeeans see us as the station they most trust to help the community, I am honored and humbled. It seems like yesterday that this station gave a school teacher a chance to succeed; I hope I've helped the station do the same.

Don Roering, Chief Engineer
37 years with WITI

When I signed on with WITI, programs were in black and white. Commercials were often done live from the studio. Videotape was not yet in use. In 1960 we were the first station in the state to install tape machines. Back then, they filled the full wall of a room; today you could hold one in your hand.

In 1963 we completed construction of the station's tower in Estabrook Park; that was big news, because it was the tallest self-supporting tower in the United States. Even today as I make routine inspections of the tower, it's not uncommon for people to stop me to ask questions about its size, height, and design.

In 1978, when we moved into our new facility in Brown Deer, I was especially proud. I was responsible for designing the technical areas in a building that was nothing short of state-of-the-art.

Like everyone else at WITI, I believe we stand apart when it comes to giving people a hand. Our engineers speak at career days, take the news microwave trucks to schools for "show and tell," and while out on assignment often conduct impromptu truck tours for curious viewers.

Personally, I enjoy helping the viewers who call in with questions about their TV sets, their VCRs, or their reception. My favorite memory: a call from a woman who couldn't get good reception on our competitor's channel. I gave her some advice, but couldn't help asking why she didn't call that station. "I did," she said, "but they wouldn't talk with me, so I called Channel Six."

Tom Hooper, Contact Six
32 years with WITI

I joined WITI in the 1960s, when our newscasts were taking on their special people-oriented identity. It was clear to me that this was a station where we took the news seriously—but never took ourselves too seriously. Characters like sportscaster Earl Gillespie and Albert the Alleycat (Jack DuBlon) saw to that. Carl Zimmermann was the authority figure, Earl and Albert the rascals who put the fun in sports and weather.

People would ask us if we really were having as much fun on the air as it seemed. I would always tell them that it was—and still is—true. WITI is a family. It's a far bigger family than we ever dreamed it could be, but it remains a close one. Nothing reminded us more of that than the passing of our friend and colleague Vince Gibbens in 1995. The community

Left: WITI president and general manager Andy Potos joined WITI in 1961.

During the past 25 years WITI has helped raise more than $19 million to support the Muscular Dystrophy Association's fight against neuromuscular disease.

reached out to us, comforting us as a family experiencing a terrible loss.

I think people reached out to us because we've always reached out to them. When I was given the assignment of heading up Contact Six in 1972, I never dreamed what a gift it would be. Few stations were doing this kind of consumer/problem-solving style of reporting, where the concerns of the viewers are as important as the news conferences called by the well-knowns. It has been my privilege to come to work each day, knowing I can use the voice that television gives us to help people.

Maria Tully, Station Manager and Vice President of Sales and Marketing
22 years with WITI

In 1974 I worked in a clerical position at another Milwaukee TV station. I dreamed of moving into sales. There was only one other woman in TV sales in Milwaukee at that time, and no people of color. I interviewed at all three stations. Only one saw me as an opportunity instead of a risk—WITI.

Here I was told to just go out and get the job done. Like everyone else, I was judged on performance. Seven years later, in 1981, Andy Potos promoted me to sales manager. While it was a first for Milwaukee, it was business as usual here. Visitors to the station still are surprised to see so many women in managerial positions. We're so accustomed to it that we don't see it as anything but the normal working environment.

While working in sales at WITI I've raised a family, volunteered for community boards and projects—all with the encouragement of the station, especially president and general manager Andy Potos.

Today, as we work with businesses on advertising or their involvement in our station projects, our clients are the sons and daughters of the business people I first met with WITI. It is wonderful to share that sense of history and community. It is why, after 22 years, I still love coming to work each day.

Jill Geisler, News Director
23 years with WITI

I grew up watching Channel 6. We were a south-side blue-collar family, and Carl Zimmermann's newscasts were comfortable and down to earth. When Carl hired me as a reporter in 1973, I soon realized that the

Right: Contact Six reporter Tom Hooper, news director Jill Geisler, station manager and vice president of sales and marketing Maria Tully, and chief engineer Don Roering have a combined 114 years of experience working at WITI-TV.

newscasts reflected his personal philosophy: to look out for the little guy. Carl wanted us all to look out for the humanity in every story we did.

In 1978, when I was named news director, it was considered news: There were only a handful of women heading news departments in the entire country, but around here it was really nothing revolutionary. That's one of the reasons that WITI is so special: We don't just talk about fairness or balance or concern for the community; we live it. We don't just identify problems; we roll up our sleeves and volunteer to help.

It has been a joy to guide the growth of this newsroom and to applaud the staff for the awards we have earned. Our news expansion in 1994 made us Wisconsin's largest broadcast news operation. And even as we added staff and added newscasts, we kept our commitment to quality and to the simple mission that defined us from the start: helping people.

SIX IS NEWS
WITI • MILWAUKEE

Warner Cable

In Milwaukee and 111 other communities in southeastern Wisconsin, Warner Cable is known as the cable television provider, and the company is investing more resources to expand this role into Wisconsin.

But increasingly, thanks to a wide-ranging and ambitious program of civic involvement, Warner Cable also is becoming known in the communities it serves as one of the best corporate citizens around.

The Milwaukee Division of Warner Cable, part of Time Warner Inc., already provides cable TV service to more than 310,000 subscribers in southeastern Wisconsin.

And along with the variety of channel offerings and the other growing capabilities of cable TV, Warner's subscribership in the area is growing. In fact, during 1995 the Milwaukee Division experienced its largest subscriber growth in the past several years: more than 25,000.

"Our goal is to provide state-of-the-art technology and outstanding customer service that will bring a valuable product into the homes of our customers and enlighten their lives," says Tom Sharrard, the Milwaukee Division's president. "We think this growth is a strong indication that we're doing exactly that."

Warner Cable is planning to invest $400 million in Wisconsin by the turn of the century to deploy a 12,000-mile-long fiber-optic network that will deliver better TV picture quality to customers, provide for fewer outages, and greatly increase channel capacity.

The fiber-optic network also will allow Warner Cable to serve customers with telephone and interactive services for the first time. By providing local-access telephone service, interactive video capabilities, and high-speed data, Time Warner Communications will usher its customers into the new era of telecommunications.

Top: Wisconsin Senator Herb Kohl and the Milwaukee division of Warner Cable hosted Kohl's "Classroom Connection." In a teleconference, division president Tom Sharrard (center) looks on as student Dawn Nierode and teacher James Belland watch the senator.

Below: Tom Sharrard with the Milwaukee Bucks' Randolph Keys and the Milwaukee Admirals' Gino Cavallini along with the student hosts of the 1996 Warner Cable Hang Tough video contest.

"In the future, people are going to want their entertainment and news on an interactive basis and will want to have one provider be able to bring it all to them," says John Blount, vice president and general manager of Time Warner Communications' Milwaukee Division, a Warner Cable affiliate. "We're going to be the ones to do that for them."

That's far from all that Warner Cable is investing in Milwaukee, however. The Milwaukee Division has more than 550 employees at its headquarters in the Schlitz Park office development at 1610 North Second Street in Milwaukee and works with an additional 150 contractors in the area.

And Warner Cable has made a substantial commitment to the betterment of the communities it serves, ranging from the annual conference it hosts for minority- and women-owned businesses to support of the Make-A-Wish Foundation and the Boys & Girls Club.

Education is the company's special focus. Warner Cable has wired, installed, and equipped more than 860 schools free of charge, and has donated hundreds of TVs, VCRs, computers, and software packages. It provides 525 hours of free educational cable television programming to each of these schools each month, a service that has an annual commercial value of more than $350,000. Warner also sponsors a variety of other programs, including grants to teachers and scholarships for students interested in communications.

"This technology and our services really bring the world into the classroom," says Bev Greenberg, vice president of community and government relations. "We feel we're helping to make the world a much more accessible place, and the empowerment that that gives students, parents, and teachers is tremendous."

The Milwaukee Community Journal

Echoing the motto of the country's first Black newspaper (*Freedom's Journal*) in the 1830s—"We wish to plead our own cause"—*The Milwaukee Community Journal* offers readers an African-centered perspective on news, features, issues, and the arts.

Editor and associate publisher Mikel Holt describes the mission that the *MCJ* has chosen to follow as a course that will empower Black people and improve conditions for those living in the central city.

The year 1996 marked the *Community Journal*'s 20th anniversary of publication. The largest of Wisconsin's African-American newspapers, it reaches 62,000 readers with Wednesday (available by subscription) and Friday editions.

Winner of more than 20 national awards for journalistic excellence, in 1996 the newspaper received two awards from the National Newspaper Publishers Association—for best special edition (a magazine supplement discussing how to combat crime) and for best news story (an article on the Million Man March).

In 1994 the *MCJ* was the recepient of the A. Phillip Randolph Messenger Award for an article that examined the failure of school desegregation. That award, which was chosen by a distinguished panel of judges that included journalism deans representing several Black colleges, included a $5,000 donation in the *MCJ*'s name to the Thurgood Marshall scholarship fund and $2,000 to Harambee Community School.

According to Holt, the *Community Journal* pursues its mission taking the position that there are "no permanent friends, no permanent enemies, just permanent issues," and in the process challenges both the Black and the White status quo.

A recent example of this is the paper's strong advocacy for parental choice in education. *The Milwaukee Community Journal* has found itself at odds with many traditional allies over its support for what some describe as a conservative issue. (Holt dismisses that description, noting that surveys show 80 percent of Black Milwaukeeans support choice. Most view it as a way to empower Black parents.) A chapter in former presidential speechwriter Daniel McGroarty's recently published book about Milwaukee's education reform movement, *Break These Chains*, discusses the *MCJ*'s critical role as a supporter and lobbyist for parental choice.

Its position on this and other issues where it finds itself pitted against what Holt describes as the status quo has cost the newspaper financially. Because of its strong advocacy of Black concerns, the *Community Journal* is often at the vanguard of national campaigns. It is not unusual for the paper to refuse advertising from businesses with questionable policies or products.

But Holt vows that the *Community Journal* will continue to follow a course that will empower Black people. He reaffirms the paper's deep commitment to African-centered culture and the Black family, and says it will do everything possible to see that the Black family, Black institutions, and African-American culture survive.

The Milwaukee Community Journal was founded and is owned by publisher Patricia O'Flynn Pattillo. Mikel Holt also has a small ownership interest.

The *MCJ* employs a full-time staff of 15, two part-time photographers, and several free-lancers. Many premier Black journalists launched their careers at the paper, which also provides career opportunities for women.

Milwaukee Black Pages

When Katherine Bailey moved to Milwaukee from Kansas City in 1990, she brought with her a vision: Her "new hometown" would have a new directory of black-owned enterprises to augment the community's other available business references.

A former property manager and sales manager at an auto dealership, Bailey modeled the *Milwaukee Black Pages* after similar publications already found in some 70 cities across the United States. So her vision for Milwaukee was realistic.

And there was opportunity here: a well-established, vibrant community of black-owned businesses that didn't have the benefit of a comprehensive, self-referencing directory that covered the entire metro Milwaukee area.

Right: The most recent edition of the Milwaukee Black Pages *is a 96-page compendium of information about more than 200 black-owned businesses throughout the area.*

Six years later Bailey's *Milwaukee Black Pages* is an unqualified success. The latest edition is a 96-page compendium of information about more than 200 black-owned businesses throughout the area.

Katherine Bailey created the Milwaukee Black Pages *in 1990, and today the business directory is an unqualified success.*

"We know that lots of people use our *Black Pages* in their purchasing decisions, and they look forward to the new edition every year," says Bailey. "We get calls on a daily basis from people looking for a copy."

Bailey says that there's increasing awareness in the black community "of the need to support black-owned businesses. I find that people are actively going out of their way to do so, and the *Black Pages* is a good tool for them.

"I think it's more than just the information that our guide contains," she adds. "The *Milwaukee Black Pages* has become not only a point of reference but a point of pride in the minority business community. It's like a book attesting to our economic progress."

Upon her arrival in Milwaukee, Bailey began the creation of the *Black Pages* here by obtaining information about black-owned businesses from government sources and then informally canvassing many of them to see what they thought of the idea.

"Most people were pretty receptive," Bailey recalls. "But there were still some scary moments that first year, getting a new business off the ground, cash flow, that sort of thing." Nevertheless, the first directory ran about 80 pages, with about 180 business entries.

Nowadays, the *Black Pages* features a strong lineup of regular advertisers, including ACM Construction, BC Art Gallery, DWK Heating, Hubbard's Heating and Cooling, Sales & Marketing Communications Associates, and Satin Wave Barber Shop. Construction and home improvement is the largest category of lister, followed by attorneys and barber shops.

The directory also features "corporate partners"—some of the largest businesses in the city, non-black owned and many of them publicly held, who advertise seeking minority-owned vendors and minority job candidates. Miller Brewing, American Family Insurance, and many major Milwaukee banks are among the corporate partners.

Bailey says she enjoys giving small black-owned businesses a chance for the recognition the *Black Pages* provide because some of those operations can't afford a listing in the regular *Yellow Pages*. Many of them are just getting off the ground—a position with which Bailey herself can readily identify.

Photo by Garry Gay/The Image Bank

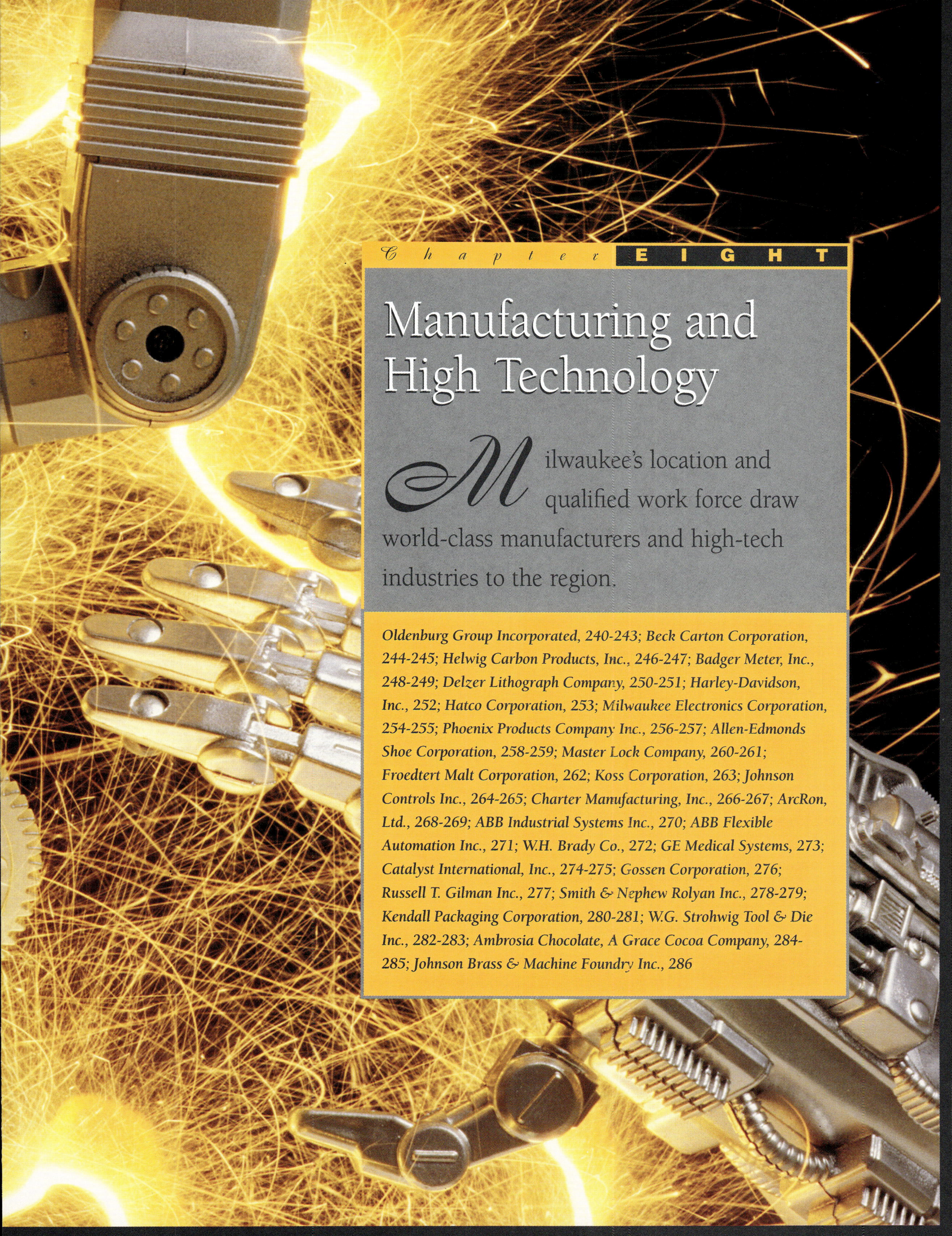

Chapter **EIGHT**

Manufacturing and High Technology

Milwaukee's location and qualified work force draw world-class manufacturers and high-tech industries to the region.

Oldenburg Group Incorporated

Oldenburg Group Incorporated is one of the largest and fastest-growing privately held businesses in Wisconsin. Headquartered in Milwaukee, and with four factories in Wisconsin, Oldenburg Group conducts its operations worldwide. In addition to 12 U.S. distribution and customer support facilities, the company has nine factories in the United States and one each in Australia, Mexico, and England. Its operations include the manufacture and distribution of architectural products, high-technology components, medical devices, heavy equipment for mining, forestry, construction, maritime, and military applications, plus various specialized industrial equipment.

The company focuses on products that require extensive and sophisticated design and engineering, and that demand complex manufacturing processes and critical quality standards. Many of the company's products are designed to work in difficult and unique environments: surface and underground mining equipment handling and moving the mined material in the exceptionally harsh environments encountered in mining. Timber harvesting equipment continually taking the abuse of cutting and processing large trees deep in the forests and on hills. Sophisticated cranes and material-handling equipment used on military ships at sea and on tanks and other ground combat vehicles, and even tiny bone fixation devices, pacemaker parts, and other medical products that must perform inside the human body. All of these applications, and many others for which the use of Oldenburg Group's products

Surface Mining Equipment

are intended, require absolute certainty of product integrity and operation. The product cannot fail, there cannot be downtime where the customer's operations are slowed or shut down, or the mission cannot be accomplished.

The importance of the performance of its products and the degree to which its customers depend on it is one of the driving factors behind Oldenburg Group's significant and ongoing investment in building and maintaining highly sophisticated manufacturing, assembly, and distribution facilities that use state-of-the-art manufacturing machinery and exceptionally well-trained and highly skilled welding, assembly, and machining personnel. This manufacturing base has proven to be not only exceptionally cost competitive, but able to create products of unquestioned world-class quality.

Above: Timber Processing Equipment

Left: Underground Mining Equipment

All of Oldenburg Group's major product lines are market share leaders in their respective businesses. Each of the group's subsidiaries focuses on high-value-added niche products that require intensive design and engineering, and an extreme commitment to quality in the manufacturing process. Its diverse subsidiaries share a precise focus of purpose that has earned each operation a unique position in its markets. This unwavering focus includes guaranteeing that customers are totally satisfied and receive exceptional product and service. It also includes providing employees the opportunity and the support to maximize their personal potential, as well as their value-added contribution to the customer and the company.

Oldenburg Group subsidiaries provide a wide range of products and services. Heavy equipment for surface and underground mining and civil tunneling is manufactured and distributed by several Oldenburg Group subsidiaries including Stamler Corporation, Lake Shore Mining Equipment, Inc., Lake Shore Mining Company, Inc., Oldenburg Group Mexico, S.A. DE C.V., and Oldenburg Australasia Pty Ltd. The mining products are sold and supported at virtually every area in the world where mining operations are conducted. The mining equipment includes feeder breakers, bunkers, surge cars, continuous haulage systems, battery- and diesel-powered haulage and utility vehicles, rock drills, crushers, shaft-hoisting systems, and conveyors.

Surface construction equipment, including cranes, excavators, trucks, and crushers, is the major focus of Contractor's Machinery Company.

Timberline Inc. specializes in computer-controlled, high-tech timber harvesting equipment.

Swiss-Tech, Inc., provides ultra-precision machined component parts for medical and high-technology, electronics, and aerospace customers.

Visa Lighting Corporation is the market leader in

Architectural Lighting Fixtures

surface-mounted architectural lighting fixtures.

Lake Shore, Inc., produces equipment for several industrial markets, as well as providing equipment to the armies and navies of the United States, Spain, Korea, Taiwan, and many other allies of the United States, including heavy cranes, deck equipment, material-handling equipment, underway replenishment systems, mine sweep equipment, barges, causeways, and other systems.

Wayne Oldenburg, the chief executive officer and sole shareholder of Oldenburg Group, describes the company's approach to its customer relationship by saying, "We simply, and emphatically, guarantee total customer satisfaction. We believe in working closely with our customers in a partnership that has the goal of reducing their costs, enhancing their productivity, and increasing safety for their workers. We don't just make a sale and walk away. Our company is committed to unequaled after-market customer support and ongoing service."

Many of the customers of Oldenburg Group attest to the fact that the company never just treats a transaction with them as a sale. Instead, it's a series of interactions in a long-term relationship that helps to build the integrity and reputation of Oldenburg Group and its individual subsidiaries. These customers seem far more confident trusting a vendor that has consistently proven it is dedicated to total customer satisfaction, and Oldenburg Group has repeatedly proven it deserves that trust. The management and employees of Oldenburg Group bring an attitude to the transactions with customers that focuses on each interaction being a win-win situation. It is a means of continuing to strengthen a long-term partnership alliance.

Virtually any employee of any Oldenburg Group subsidiary will echo the company's core belief that they must, and do, stay close to the customers so that they can design and manufacture what the customers want and need, rather than trying to convince the customers that they want and need what Oldenburg Group happens to manufacture. The company believes that its attitude of providing customers the products they want, completely guaranteeing their satisfaction and supporting those products with unparalleled after-market customer and product support, has so differentiated the business that it has provided Oldenburg a competitive advantage.

There is an intensity among Oldenburg employees interviewed that indicates they are committed to absolutely being there when customers need them and being there with the products, the service, and the attitude the customers need. Perhaps this somewhat unique philosophy is one of the reasons for the rapid growth of Oldenburg Group. For five years in a row, Oldenburg Group was listed on the Inc. 500, *Inc.* magazine's list of the most rapidly growing privately held companies in the United States. Oldenburg Group has also consistently made the *Milwaukee Journal Sentinel* list of the Wisconsin 100, the largest privately owned businesses in Wisconsin. Oldenburg says his companies are striving to continue that growth. "Through our continuing commitment to research and product development, our acquisition of businesses with related product lines, and geographic expansion to all areas in which our customers do business, we will not only continue our growth, but continue to apply our highly sophisticated design, engineering, and manufacturing technology to reducing our customers' costs and enhancing their productivity and safety in whatever areas of the world they conduct business."

Medical and High-Technology Components

Each of Oldenburg Group's wholly owned subsidiaries is operated with a commitment to total employee involvement. The philosophy that "the people who are closest to the work know best how to do it" permeates all activities in each of the group's subsidiaries. All employees in each subsidiary are on a bonus program tied to their company's performance and to their individual contribution. Sharing the value-added, providing each employee a piece of the action, is reflective of Wayne Oldenburg's belief that all employees should have the opportunity of being capitalists and to earn more personal value if they're able to provide more value to the company's operations and to their customers.

This total commitment to individual employees and the support for their continued training, development, and growth, while at the same time sharing a "piece of the action" with them through performance bonus plans, has been identified as a key factor in continuing to attract the highly motivated employees that have been necessary to staff the growth of Oldenburg Group subsidiaries. With manufacturing and customer support facilities in 10 states and three foreign countries, Oldenburg Group has been able to find and retain highly energetic and committed people—a key to achieving the firm's commitment to total customer satisfaction.

Military Equipment

Beck Carton Corporation

Beck Carton Corporation is becoming known for leadership on at least three fronts: as a fast-growing innovator in the packaging industry, as an exemplar of beneficent corporate culture, and as an industrial trailblazer in the architectural and economic rejuvenation of Milwaukee's Third Ward district.

Owner Tom Wamser wouldn't—or, rather, couldn't—have it any other way. "We never can do anything less than the best here," Wamser says. "We want to be the best company we can be, employing the best people, in the best building, in my favorite city, which also is my hometown. And we're making a pretty good stab at it."

Headquartered in a 250,000-square-foot facility that occupies three buildings at 311 East Chicago Street, Beck employs about 95 people in the design, development, and manufacture of folding cartons. In the past decade and a half, Beck's revenues have increased more than fivefold and its earnings several times over as well.

Beck's customers comprise a wide variety of top-quality manufacturers throughout North America. Its industrial clients include a number of leading Milwaukee-area manufacturers, while Beck's rapidly expanding base of high-end consumer products customers include many of the nation's leading pharmaceutical and cosmetics companies.

Beck Carton is headquartered in a 250,000-square-foot facility that spans three buildings at 311 East Chicago Street, Milwaukee.

The Chicago Street building's facade, highlighted by strong pillars and huge expanses of plate glass, is perfectly complementary to the architectural renovation of the historic Third Ward. What Beck Carton is doing behind the building front, however, is even more impressive: Wamser has been sumptuously rejuvenating the entire facility, beginning with the manufacturing areas where most of his employees work.

What the company has become has made its rather inauspicious beginnings dim by now. It began as a folding carton manufacturer in the same facility, as F.J. Schmidt Co., sharing warehouse space with the telephone company. By the late 1940s the original owner had arranged to sell the business to a partnership of B.J. "Ben" Beck and several associates from Chicago.

After being in partnership for a year or so in ownership of Beck Box & Label, Beck and his Illinois investors decided to part ways. According to Wamser's recollection of company lore, Beck and the Chicago financiers flipped a coin for rights to first choice of the manufacturing equipment. Beck continued to build the company and also nearby founded Transpak, a contract packaging concern that, naturally, used materials manufactured by Beck Box & Label.

When Beck's son, Don, graduated from college in the mid-1960s, he went to work for his father's firm. Then Ben sold Beck Box & Label to Don and, later, Transpak. Don gradually built the fortunes of both companies.

That's where Wamser came in. After a career in corporate sales and marketing, Wamser had established a steel-fabricating company in Menomonee Falls in 1980. In 1982 he bought Beck Box & Label from Don Beck. By 1989 Wamser had become so happy with his latest venture that he also bought Transpak from Beck, who retired, and Wamser sold his steel-fabricating company.

When Wamser acquired the company, Beck supplied the vast majority of its products to industrial customers. The cartons tended to be rather uncomplicated and didn't require tremendous graphic capabilities. In fact, the clients supplied most of the design work.

But since then, Wamser has moved Beck steadily further into consumer packaging, requiring the company to make huge investments in package design and graphics personnel and equipment. "We wanted to grow and nurture the business, and the question was what direction to go toward," Wamser says. "I believed that we had the right people, so we decided to put the right equipment in place for them to use."

Today Beck completes all of its own artwork on a computer-aided design (CAD) system that enables, among other things, efficient electronic transfer of proposed designs and revisions back and forth between Beck and customers. And to complete carton designs that are increasingly complicated, Beck utilizes plotting tables. The equipment "allows us to produce samples as if they were done by a machine, but without having the expense of producing dies to do it," Wamser says. Installation of a new eight-color press in the fall of 1996 is expected to make Beck state of the art in that area as well.

The firm's ongoing renovation of its historic complex complements its Third Ward location.

"The investment for us to be able to do this kind of work has been worth it because it has enabled us to move the company more and more into value-added work," he adds. "Packaging is what sells consumer products these days. Sometimes, it's worth more than what's inside!"

In a similar fashion, Wamser has gone about investing in the look and feel of Beck's Third Ward complex. He started by renovating production areas such as printing, die cutting, and folding and gluing, converting them into appealing, light-filled rooms that provide modern, attractive surroundings for production employees.

Wamser also has renovated Beck's executive offices, appointing them with rich cherry and marble accents and decorating offices and conference rooms with original paintings and other artwork from around the country, some of which he has personally commissioned. Because the project has been ongoing for several years, Beck even has retained its own staff of carpenters, electricians, and other construction workers.

Refurbishment of an area of the first floor of the Chicago Street building is the last major piece of renovation that remains. A public reception area and Beck's sales and marketing staff, who now are dispersed throughout the facilities, will occupy that area once it's completed.

More important than any of that, however, has been Beck's investment in its people. For one thing, the firm's employees have an unusual degree of autonomy to identify corporate needs and authorize actions to meet them. Also, Wamser has preferred to bring in employees at entry- or lower-level positions, develop their capabilities, and promote from within.

All of that means that when Beck hires, "we pay close attention not only to skills but to how a person is going to fit into our culture, which is very accessible and open all the way around," Wamser explains.

The company also invests in its hometown through major, continuing contributions to dozens of organizations including Boy Scouts, Junior Achievement, and the United Performing Arts Fund.

"We're here for the long haul," Wamser says. "We want everyone at Beck Carton to work hard, but we also want them—and everyone our company touches—to get some enjoyment out of the ride."

Helwig Carbon Products, Inc.

Even as times and technology change, commitment—to customers, employees, an industry, and a community—continues to foster business success. To see this for themselves, Milwaukeeans need look no further than to the Bradley Woods Industrial Park on the city's northwest side.

In its attractive 100,000-square-foot manufacturing and office complex, completed in 1989, Helwig Carbon Products thrives as the world's leading manufacturer of carbon brushes and brush holders.

Founded in 1928, Helwig manufactures and supplies the carbon brushes essential for the cost-effective operation of DC-driven motors and generators. The smooth movement that can be achieved with highly controllable, consistent DC current is critical for powering machinery in the paper- and steel-making industries, mining, transportation, as well as elevators and many other industry and commerce operations.

Helwig builds and sells the highest-quality OEM and replacement parts, internationally. It also leads the industry in innovative product development and its engineers are recognized experts in carbon technology.

Carbon brushes are electrical contacts that require frequent replacement due to mechanical wear and electrical erosion. Helwig research concentrates on improving carbon brush life through the use of design features and materials ideally suited to specific customer applications.

These efforts have resulted in innovations such as the RED TOP multiflex brush. The RED TOP's patented dual material top improves brush contact and reduces uneven wear, extending the life of the brush and the contact surface. Helwig Carbon also optimizes brush performance and wear life with its unique ability to coordinate brush and brush holder design as one cohesive unit.

The company has also brought other innovations to market, including bias multiflex, composite-grade

The company's attractive 100,000-square-foot manufacturing and office complex provides a comfortable and productive working environment.

brushes, constant pressure holders with wear indicators, and quick-disconnect terminals.

Walter O. Helwig founded the business in the family garage, back in the days when most industrial motors, electric streetcars, and carbon arc lights ran solely on DC power. The brushes needed to help generate that power were produced almost exclusively in the industrial regions of Pennsylvania and New York, and supplies in the Upper Midwest often ran short.

Helwig Carbon has steadily grown to supply an ever-increasing share of the carbon brush market.

When Walter O. Helwig died in 1985, his son-in-law John Koenitzer was elected president and chief executive officer. Today Koenitzer serves as chairman and chief executive officer and his son Jeff, a professional engineer nationally known for his expertise in carbon products, is president. Another son, Jay, is vice president of marketing. Many other families within the company are also dedicated to Helwig Carbon, which provides a unique family atmosphere.

Keeping pace with advances in manufacturing and servicing technology, Helwig Carbon today maintains an inventory of 2,000 different styles, types, and sizes of brushes, ready for shipment. The company takes pride in servicing both small and large orders with a strong sense of urgency. Turnover is low among the more than 300 dedicated Helwig employees, who include well-trained customer service representatives, regional sales and service representatives both in the United States and abroad, and one of the most respected technical staffs in the industry.

Helwig Carbon is committed to quality, from computerized order entry through shipment of the finished product. It works with over 100 grades of material and credits "knowing what to use where" for putting Helwig ahead of its competitors. The firm has earned the prestigious ISO 9001 certification, an internationally recognized standard for design and manufacturing excellence.

Under the leadership of Helwig's son-in-law and grandsons, the company reveals the same pride and professionalism that its founder always espoused. An elaborate ventilation system continuously disposes of the carbon dust created by precision cutting and shaping processes. On the outside, the facilities are carefully landscaped and the building itself is attractively finished with decorative stone. Inside, manufacturing areas and the cafeteria are air conditioned, as are the offices, guaranteeing manufacturing and office employees alike a safe, comfortable, and productive working environment.

Company leadership is quick to point out that not all aspects of quality are tangible, but its well-trained, dedicated work force makes it possible to service even the most demanding orders in a timely fashion, often exceeding customer expectations.

Solid-state electronics have been steadily replacing the carbon brush in AC to DC power conversion. Helwig Carbon has responded to this mature market by investing in new developments and applications of carbon graphite products, such as self-lubricating bearings, steam joints, and various seals and rings. It has also distinguished itself as a major player in the international marketplace, with its engineering and production expertise. Sales have increased from $14 million in 1985 to $26 million in 1995. The company is proud of the fact that it has never laid off employees due to lack of work.

Helwig Carbon's leadership believes its relationship to the community is as important as its business activities. Management and employees devote numerous volunteer hours to various community organizations and direct 4 percent of company profits back into local hospitals, colleges, community groups, and other charitable organizations.

Jeff Koenitzer, P.E., president; John Koenitzer, chairman and chief executive officer; and Jay Koenitzer, vice president of marketing (left to right), are at the helm of today's Helwig Carbon Products.

Badger Meter, Inc.

Over a decade ago Badger Meter, Inc., designed a long-term strategic plan that consisted of several basic elements: Make major investments in new technology; energize marketing; expand exports; and invest further in its employees.

As reliably as water streams forth when the tap is turned on, the Milwaukee-based manufacturer of flow-measurement systems has been fulfilling each of those goals—and then some. In fact, having marked its 90th anniversary in 1995, Badger Meter is pursuing its strategic direction even more aggressively than when it was originally set.

"Because of trends in the economy and society, each of these goals looms even larger than when we set them," says James Forbes, Badger Meter's chief executive officer. "They set us on the right path, and now we're making steady progress down that road."

Badger Meter Mfg. Co.'s first building was on Third Street in downtown Milwaukee, in a garage behind the old Republican Hotel. Photo circa 1905.

Badger Meter, now headquartered at 4545 West Brown Deer Road, was founded in a garage behind the old Republican Hotel on Third Street in downtown Milwaukee by four men who saw a market opportunity for a "frost-proof" water meter they had invented. The early meters that had been installed by the city's water department and by other northern cities were being damaged by freezing temperatures in unheated basements.

The innovative meter featured a bottom plate of soft cast iron, which would rupture in the event of a water line freeze-up, relieving pressure and preventing damage to the meter's working parts. The bottom plate was easily and inexpensively replaced. By 1918 Badger Meter was manufacturing more than 10,000 meters a year.

The company has steadily enhanced its meters, and meter-reading technology, since then. By the early 1970s Badger Meter had introduced a remote reading device known as the Read-o-Matic®, which registered usage so that meter readers no longer had to go into homes.

In 1991 the company introduced a radio-frequency device owned by American Meter Company and distributed by Badger called TRACE®. Meters are retrofitted with the device, which can be read either by a hand-held data collector as the meter reader walks by or by a specially equipped van that accumulates readings while driving by residences. The company also produces a telephone-based automatic meter-reading system known as ACCESSplus®.

Over the years the company diversified into industrial markets, including pharmaceuticals, petroleum, chemicals, and food and beverages. At first, Badger Meter simply adapted its basic water meters, but by the 1970s it was designing meters specifically for industrial markets. Its line of lubrication meters dominates the quick-lube market. Its miniature valve line, produced in Tulsa, Oklahoma, is known worldwide for its superior quality and is used in hundreds of different applications. Today the Industrial Division contributes about half the company's profits.

Badger Meter is making several major technological investments in the future. While it will continue to emphasize its own meter development, the company is entering partnerships with other concerns that will supply various components of what are expected to be highly reliable and efficient systems.

Right: During World War II Badger Meter—at the request of the federal government—switched 95 percent of its production from meters to bomb fuses. By the war's end the company had produced seven million fuses.

At the firm's Flexible Machining Center, multiple operations are performed on large bronze meter housings while remaining in one machining cell, virtually eliminating changeover time.

Inset: Badger Meter's Recordall® line of meters.

"Our strategy now is to supply the meter and interfacing—our core competency—with whatever information-delivery device the utility customer wants," says Forbes. "The technology is moving so fast, and it's so costly, that we think it's best for us to continue to specialize in what we do best and be prepared to work with any companion technology that proves itself." As an example, in one of the nation's biggest such municipal projects ever, in 1996 Badger Meter will begin supplying devices for automatic reading of all the water meters in the city of Milwaukee.

A second technological initiative for Badger Meter is ultrasonic measuring devices for waste water. Its progress in this area has made the company the only one in the market to supply technology for measuring both potable and waste water. With more and more municipal utilities seeking to manage water as a total, recyclable resource, and many old Eastern Seaboard cities trying to get a handle on leakage from their aging sewer systems, demand should rise significantly.

Finally, Badger Meter is attempting to develop alliances that will exploit the potential of its new device for measuring natural gas flows. It provides accurate data not just on gas volume itself but, using sophisticated measurements and software, on how much energy given flows actually will yield. "It's an excellent product, it's passed regulatory hurdles and standards committees, and now we need a good sales and marketing partner," Forbes says.

Exports are providing brighter horizons than Badger Meter had envisioned as well. Now less than 20 percent of revenues, international sales may account for as much as half of the company's revenues in the years ahead.

Badger Meter has enjoyed recent success, for instance, with a project in which the Mexican government awarded a contract for which Badger Meter is the exclusive water-meter supplier for one-fourth of Mexico City. A bit surprisingly, instead of having the company install less-sophisticated, automated technologies like the other suppliers, the government asked Badger Meter to provide TRACE devices. Forbes believes other cities in Mexico might follow suit if the country's recent, halting recovery from the peso devaluation of late 1994 improves.

Forbes also plans to invest the company's resources in further development of its human capital. One symptom of Badger Meter's longevity and success, the high seniority of many of its hourly workers, will contribute to a labor crunch over the next few years. Automation and other productivity improvements already have allowed the business to produce twice as many meters in its Milwaukee plant today, with just 225 workers, as it did 12 years ago with 600 workers, but the company will continue its productivity drive.

Badger Meter also is making a concerted effort to identify the issues that motivate—or discourage—its workers and to address them. Forbes and other corporate leaders encourage their employees, and the company itself, to become involved with high school-based initiatives and other programs that not only could supply the company with future workers but will also improve the community at large.

"We're going to spend the time on this because it's a major issue now," Forbes explains.

Delzer Lithograph Company

Milwaukee has always been a haven for printing and printers, and Delzer Lithograph Company has been proud to be part of that heritage for nearly 50 years.

But the Waukesha-based, family-owned operation has been even happier to stand out from the crowd of its local competitors by paying careful attention to customers, adapting new technologies as they become available, and capitalizing on the decades of printing-management experience that have been influenced and guided by Eric and Marc Delzer, the brothers who own the business.

Founded in 1949 as Delzer-Marlow Lithograph Company, the firm provides sheet- and web-fed offset lithography to 300 customers throughout metro Milwaukee, Wisconsin, and the United States in businesses ranging from professional sports teams—Delzer prints Brewers and Bucks programs—to manufacturers, advertising agencies, and other service companies. In 1995 it was ranked 459th in a list of the Top 500 printing companies in North America by *Printing Impressions* magazine.

The elements of the firm's success include the fact that printer's ink runs in the Delzers' blood because their father, Armand Delzer, founded and nurtured the business through its formative years. Having been a part of that growth has helped equip the brothers to run the company during its current expansionary mode.

"One of the key ingredients to making a printing company successful is to have grown up in the business, know the market, and be involved in production as well as sales," says Eric Delzer. "You have to have a feel for how to run the business, and to know your customers well, particularly in printing. It's usually a small business, and just because you have the largest and best equipment doesn't mean you're going to succeed. Some printers around here have failed even though this is a pretty friendly area for the industry."

Delzer also credits the perfectionist, customer-pleasing approach of the company's workers. "Our people here want to make sure that things are done absolutely correctly, and get them done exactly when and how they're supposed to," he says. "That's an attitude that always has been and always will be a big part of our corporate culture."

The company's willingness to invest heavily in new technology is another factor in its success. For example, in 1994 Delzer added a 20 x 26, six-color, sheet-fed waterless press, and a five-unit, double-web press. In 1995 a full-size five-unit web press was also added. Web-fed presses print materials from a continuously fed roll of paper, as compared with sheet-fed presses, which require insertion of individual sheets. Web-fed is four to five times as fast. Also, it saves paper in savings realized from buying paper in rolls, and in-line folding and finishing capabilities.

Delzer Lithograph Company operates in an 80,000-square-foot modern plant in Waukesha and employs about 130 people.

To make room for the latter press, Delzer had to make some major changes to its physical plant. The new press is housed in the space formerly occupied by the company's lead-management and distribution center, so Delzer built an 18,000-square-foot addition to house its growing distribution service. The expansion includes the addition of a new completely automated storage-and-retrieval system for over 6,000 printed-literature items, greatly enhancing the number of literature orders that Delzer can fulfill in a day.

The system, which processes over 3,000 outgoing orders each month, works like a dry cleaner's rotating rack, wheeling around shelves instead of garments. A computer inventories where things are stored, and when an operator calls for specified documents, the shelves rotate and deliver the order to him. The operator transfers the items to a conveyor, which transports them to a packaging area.

The presses were a logical extension of Delzer's sheet-fed capabilities and allow customers the opportunity to have more of their printing done under one roof. The addition of the three presses, in fact, has made Delzer one of the most flexible and versatile printers in the Milwaukee marketplace.

"It is another step in making sure that we're doing the right things to sensibly grow the business," Delzer says. "Before, we couldn't do runs of, say, a couple hundred thousand; now, we can. Also, having the web-fed capability has helped us generate more business for our sheet-fed presses."

Employment at Delzer has grown from about 70 before the installation of the two new presses to nearly 130 now. Delzer's revenues were about $14 million in 1995.

Delzer expects its solid growth to continue, in part because of how the firm is handling the march of technology in its business. Eric Delzer says that, whatever the technological change, the company is ready to embrace it after a period in which the new approach has proven itself.

That's what happened several years after Delzer was founded, when the invention of offset lithography eliminated the need for the traditional letterpress method of printing. Much the same tremendous change is occurring today, as well, as electronic digitization of images "has affected the industry totally in terms of how pre-press and production work is done," Delzer explains. "We're evolving into it."

Delzer's new automated literature fulfillment system is an example of the company's commitment to continuous investment in cost-reducing and service-providing equipment.

Harley-Davidson, Inc.

As chairman, president, and chief executive officer of Harley-Davidson, Inc., Richard Teerlink enjoys sharing the tale of the company's phenomenal success of the past decade with a wide variety of audiences across the country. And more often than not, a questioner will ask him something like, "How do you keep the success going?"

Teerlink's answer consistently is basically this: The employees of Harley-Davidson are committed to identifying and capitalizing on opportunities that will perpetuate the company's growth. What's more, they are determined to have fun while doing it!

Unique among Milwaukee companies, Harley-Davidson combines a breathtaking business success story with undisputed status as a major American cultural icon.

Its motorcycles have become revered for their style, power, and quality by riders ranging from *Fortune* 500 CEOs to traditional "bikers." Clothes and accessories carrying the Harley-Davidson brand have made their own mark on consumers worldwide. Since Harley-Davidson became a publicly held company in 1986, its revenue and net income have increased at compound annual growth rates of 18.5 percent and 44 percent, respectively. The company topped 100,000 in motorcycle sales in 1995 for the first time ever.

Today Harley employs about 5,000 people at its headquarters at 3700 West Juneau Avenue in Milwaukee, its plant on Capitol Drive in Milwaukee, its Tomahawk, Wisconsin, plant, its other major production facility in York, Pennsylvania, and a test facility in Talladega, Alabama. Harley-Davidson cycles are sold through more than 1,000 dealers worldwide, and the Harley Owners Group has 295,000 members around the globe.

"There are a lot of people who have become very dedicated to what we are," Teerlink says. "Our job is to not disappoint them."

Harley began in a shed in the Davidson family's Milwaukee backyard, where in their spare time the Davidson brothers—William A., Walter, and Arthur—and William S. Harley crafted their first motorcycle using mostly their hands and their ingenuity. In 1903 they built three motorcycles and began Harley-Davidson Co.

Successive decades saw Harley repeatedly jolt the motorcycle industry with technological and style innovations, the "motorcycle culture" take shape, one run of public ownership, a diversification into recreational vehicles, the company's purchase by a larger concern, a buyout of Harley-Davidson by senior management in 1981 that was led by then-chairman Vaughn Beals and then a revival of the company's public status.

More than any other element, Teerlink says, Harley's continued success depends on the company's ability to get its various stakeholders—from customers to dealers, from employees to members of riders' groups—to embrace common values and regard one another's input as significant to every issue the company faces.

Teerlink says that demand for H-D motorcycles and parts should continue to grow, especially in foreign markets including Europe and Asia, and so the company plans to double its annual output to more than 200,000 vehicles by 2003.

"Throughout the world, there's a significant excess demand for Harley-Davidson motorcycles," he says. "Our job is always to be ready to meet that demand."

Top: Harley-Davidson's first "factory," in 1903. The founders built three motorcycles that first year of operation.

Bottom right: Arthur and Walter Davidson, William S. Harley, and William A. Davidson (from left to right) inspect the first 61-cubic-inch V-twin to come off the firm's assembly line, in 1936.

Below: One of Harley-Davidson's 1996 models is the Road King. Photographs courtesy, Harley-Davidson Juneau Avenue Archives; all rights reserved

Hatco Corporation

Hatco Corporation still manufactures the basic type of sanitizing booster water heaters that its founder, Gordon Hatch, introduced in 1950. But today the company is also going in new directions, technologically and otherwise. Nearly a half-century after its originating product, Hatco continues to provide solutions to the current challenges facing the food-service industry.

Hatco boosters, which provide a 180-degree, bacteria-killing final rinse in commercial dishwashers, offer restaurants and institutional food-service operations an effective and efficient method of meeting U.S. health standards.

The booster heaters were the firm's mainstay product into the 1970s. Since then, by developing quality-engineered new products with a state-of-the-art design approach, Hatco has addressed customer needs and expanded its business in the restaurant, hotel, hospital, school, and other food-service markets in the United States and internationally.

Now the Hatco product mix includes an extensive line of infrared foodwarmers as well as heated drawer warmers and merchandising food-holding equipment, which keep foods hot, safe, palatable, and attractively displayed until serving time. The low-temp cook and hold ovens combine radiant and convection heat to prepare entries in advance of demand. Hatco conveyor toasters are also a feature item that can improve service in any operation, large or small.

David G. Hatch, who is chief executive officer and owner, directs the company from its headquarters at 635 South 28th Street in Milwaukee. Its production facilities are in Sturgeon Bay and Hatco employs over 250 people at its two locations.

A longtime advocate of food safeness and sanitation, Hatco management is active in numerous industry organizations that focus on a wide range of food-service issues—from environmental concerns to energy efficiency and labor education to government regulations. An emphasis on quality and customer service has always been a Hatco trademark.

As a leading manufacturer serving multinational markets, Hatco is dedicated to providing its customers with equipment that can meet the demands of tomorrow's food-service operations.

Right: The company's state-of-the-art production facilities are located in Sturgeon Bay.

Hatco Corporation is headquartered at 635 South 28th Street, Milwaukee.

Milwaukee Electronics Corporation

Just as the city of Milwaukee celebrates its economic growth and diversity, so does Milwaukee Electronics Corporation. P. Michael Stoehr believes that what you sow, you also reap—which is good. The owner and president of Milwaukee Electronics Corporation applies that philosophy to business in a number of ways.

For one thing, the company, which began in Milwaukee in 1953 as one of four affiliated corporations started by Hyman Smith, has grown significantly since being acquired by Stoehr in 1985. Now the vision to optimize Milwaukee Electronics' accomplishments is to control its size, separate some of its operations, and diversify into smaller affiliates—a structure similar to that under which it began. This will empower its work force for both personal growth and additional technology jobs.

P. Michael Stoehr, president of Milwaukee Electronics.

Milwaukee Electronics is primarily a contract manufacturer. It specializes in the design, development, and production of electronic products for commercial applications, ranging from microprocessors to power supplies, utilizing both analog and digital technologies.

Its customers are "blue chip" original-equipment manufacturers that choose to rely on external sources for their electronics capabilities. Included are Milwaukee-based mainstays Harley-Davidson and Harnischfeger Industries along with New Berlin-based ASEA Brown Boveri, a unit of the Swiss conglomerate, and Waukesha-based Waukesha Engine. Allen-Bradley, of Milwaukee, also is a customer although it is involved in electronics manufacturing itself. While this represents a significant local customer base, more than one-half of product sales are outside of Wisconsin.

Service and reliability are Milwaukee Electronics' hallmarks. To achieve this reputation, the company has evolved beyond the role of "circuit-board stuffer" for which many electronics manufacturers have settled. Today it functions as an integrated electronics specialist, providing all functions for complete product delivery, including in-house product engineering, software development, computer-aided design, prototype manufacturing, customized testing, and detailed quality assurance, with lot traceability and just-in-time delivery.

An accomplished engineering staff offers innovative solutions to design and product requirements.

At its headquarters, in Milwaukee's Northshore area, the company has a state-of-the-art SMD Technology Center and fully equipped assembly facility including a machine shop, and painting and silk screen departments. A multidisciplinary engineering staff includes specialists in electronics, electromechanical, and hydraulic engineering and pneumatic design.

At Milwaukee Electronics, a team approach to effective customer service brings its people and services toward one common goal—total customer satisfaction through production of "Perfect Product." Team members are treated as partners of "small companies" within Milwaukee Electronics and are empowered to take control and initiative with management as their support. All employees make a personal commitment to total customer satisfaction in the signing of the company's quality creed, which they incorporate into activities each day.

Stoehr also believes in operating Milwaukee Electronics according to the Christian principles that motivate his own life. These values are openly cultivated among employees, customers, and suppliers alike, as Stoehr believes that a forthright corporate reliance on these ethics most benefits his business and those it touches. These values can be seen in the company's outside activities as well. Support on a corporate basis through both funding and participation is given to the Fellowship of Christian Athletes, the Christian Businessmen's Committee, and the Milwaukee Public Schools Science Olympiad.

Ten years ago Stoehr wasn't able to visualize the Milwaukee Electronics of today, with seven times as many employees and its growth in multicultural diversity. Revenues have grown more than 14 times their level from when he acquired the company. Because this business had to pay off acquisition-related debt with proceeds from its own operations, Milwaukee Electronics was put on an aggressive growth track. The early years centered around military defense contracts whose fulfillment brought revenues as well as diversification of the company's capabilities. After this, Milwaukee Electronics embarked on the second phase of its business plan: the expansion of contract manufacturing for commercial customers, which was timed with the direction of the market. Beginning in the late 1980s many major manufacturers began "outsourcing" their own production of electronics and other devices at an unprecedented pace.

Now Milwaukee Electronics is entering its long-planned third phase: developing and introducing its own proprietary products. In 1988 it took the first step in that direction by acquiring Chicago-based Macromatic Corporation, which makes a diversified line of time-delay relays. This acquired division was later moved to Milwaukee.

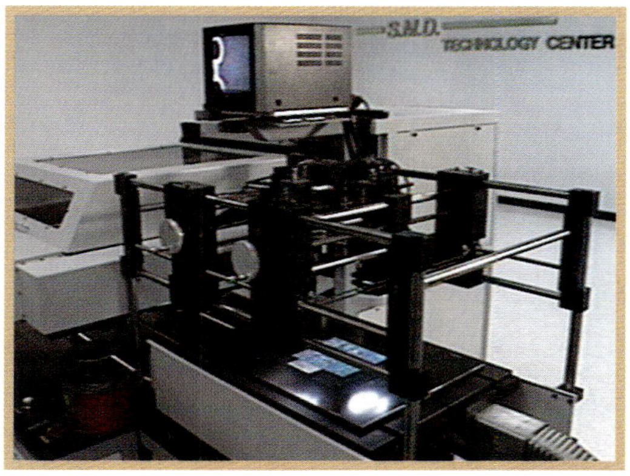

In various stages of market introduction are products in the food preparation, hydronic heating, commercial dryer, and material-handling industries. Some of these items are products that Milwaukee Electronics has developed, with the permission of its customers, as enhanced versions of contracted devices. Other items are proprietary applications developed for these industries. The series of controls for electronic conveyor systems will be marketed through Milwaukee Electronics' Automation Controls Group, located in Wilmington, North Carolina.

Above: Milwaukee Electronics is a contract manufacturer specializing in the custom design, development, and production of electronic products.

Left: Within its 63,000-square-foot facility, the company has a state-of-the-art SMD Technology Center and fully equipped assembly plant.

Key to making this strategy work is the philosophy that the company will remain small enough for everyone to feel a responsibility of empowerment. Each employee feels the importance of serving each customer to a level that sets a new standard for the industry.

In addition to the economic benefits of such an approach, its allows Milwaukee Electronics and its affiliates to build a working environment where relating and caring are crucial. The company's goals are to continuously provide "Perfect Product" to its customers and regularly introduce new products. It believes in being a leader in technological advances and providing the best minds in the business, as it partners with customers so they can benefit the most from new technology. This is all achieved in an environment that has employees who are eager to work with customers to explore the limits of technology and expand those limits whenever possible with a service level that is second to none.

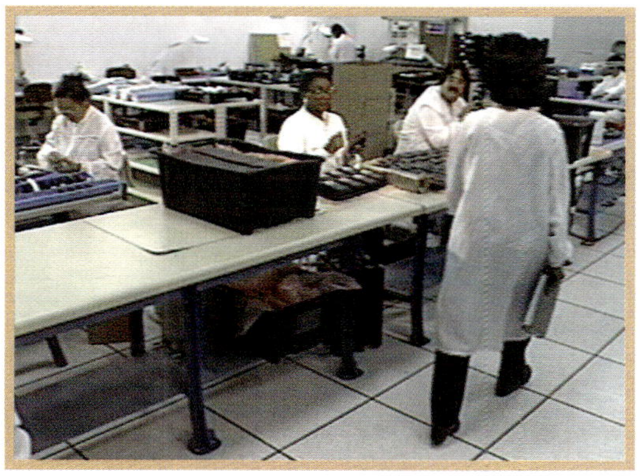

Each employee within the customer-focused divisions makes a personal commitment to total customer satisfaction through the creation of "Perfect Product."

Phoenix Products Company Inc.

Phoenix Products Company has a long and prosperous history in the city of Milwaukee.

Founded 104 years ago (in 1892) by George Wordingham, an English immigrant, the company has consistently and with purpose maintained its base of operations within the city. Ownership of the corporation has remained within the Wordingham family, which is now in partnership with Anthony L. Chirchirillo.

The product mix of Phoenix has changed dramatically over the years and, along with an outstanding work force from the Milwaukee area, this has been the cornerstone of the company's longevity. The last four generations of Milwaukeeans have seen the business change from a small basement print shop called Phoenix Printing Company into a sophisticated multi-division enterprise of the 1990s and beyond.

The first half of this century saw Phoenix evolve from that small print shop into one of this country's largest purveyors of flexible packaging materials for the laundry industry (which was significant in size before the invention of the automatic washer after World War II). Changes in the world and Phoenix's markets brought on by the Great Depression and World War II forced Phoenix to change its thinking and to diversify.

The war years brought the company to its first planned diversification outside of the flexible packaging industry with the acquisition of a small metal fabricating firm. As the small print shop of 1892 was the genesis of the company and its current flexible packaging business, this 1943 acquisition was the genesis of Phoenix's current Metal Products Division.

Today Phoenix is a progressive niche-oriented company operating in several different industries.

- Phoenix Lighting, with its roots in the Metal Products Division, produces specialty lighting for the marine, mining, industrial, and architectural fields.

Phoenix Health Care Products is a leader in sterile medical packaging.

Whether traveling the high seas, extracting worldwide mining resources, or illuminating Las Vegas Boulevard, Phoenix Lighting leads the way.

- Phoenix Health Care Products, with its roots in the early printing and flexible packaging operations, is a recognized leader in sterile medical packaging.

  Phoenix medical packaging can be found worldwide in hospitals (surgical gloves), physicians' offices (sutures and wound dressings), and home medicine cabinets (bandages).

- Phoenix DryRod® Ovens, also with its roots in the Metal Products Division, is the dominant supplier of welding rod ovens in the United States.
- P-H-X, an affiliate of Phoenix chartered in 1993, is a quality supplier of water-based adhesive and cohesives.

Although diverse, there is a common thread throughout Phoenix's history linking all of its businesses: deliver high-quality products to fulfill unmet customer needs while adhering to the highest standards of business ethics.

The company's products and markets may change, but its commitment to principles and values does not. Phoenix's 104 years of growth in Milwaukee, its five different locations within the city, and its outstanding work force have been built upon an atmosphere of uncompromising integrity, honesty, quality, respect, and the ability to change.

The future of Phoenix is bright and exciting. From its 220,000-square-foot headquarters located at 6161 North 64th Street, the company's progressive ownership, dedicated management, and outstanding work force are leading the hard charge into its second hundred years and into the twenty-first century.

Phoenix Products is headquartered at 6161 North 64th Street, Milwaukee.

Inset, left: Phoenix DryRod® Ovens is the dominant supplier of welding rod ovens in the country.

Inset, right: Phoenix Lighting produces specialty lighting for industry.

Allen-Edmonds Shoe Corporation

John Stollenwerk believes in change, but not change for its own sake. In a maxim, that describes how his company, Allen-Edmonds Shoe Corporation, has become the standard for excellence in a very traditional market—high-quality men's footwear—without standing still or even taking the predictable path.

While much of the rest of the American shoe industry was waving the white flag in the face of an invasion of imported footwear in the 1980s, for example, Stollenwerk and Allen-Edmonds successfully moved into the Japanese market. And when the company had established itself at the pinnacle of its luxury niche, Allen-Edmonds diversified into the highly competitive casual-footwear market a few years ago.

"To be a viable organization in business, you have to change," says Stollenwerk, president and owner of Port Washington-based Allen-Edmonds. "But it always has to be done within parameters that make sense for your organization. For us, that means high-quality, high-value men's footwear."

Elbert W. Allen, Sr., began defining that niche with his founding of Allen-Edmonds in 1922. That's when his idea of manufacturing a fine leather shoe without nails and without a stiff steel shank began to revolutionize the men's shoe industry. Allen's co-worker at a Milwaukee shoe company enthusiastically endorsed the idea, and the entrepreneurs joined forces to purchase the Belgium Shoe Co. in Belgium, Wisconsin. Before long, they were manufacturing a line of flexible footwear marketed under the name and slogan "Osteo-Path-Ik: The shoe that needs no breaking in."

Later, when Allen's eldest son, Bert, had taken over management, he pushed for national sales and promoted "Allen-Edmonds Footfitters" as the "shoe of tomorrow." Every pair carried a guarantee that if the wearer didn't find his shoes to be the most comfortable ever worn, the purchase price of the shoes would be refunded. There's no record of how many refunds—if any—were issued, but the company certainly prospered. Navy contracts during World War II introduced the shoes to thousands of sailors, many of whom became loyal postwar customers.

In 1980 the business was sold and reorganized by a new management team headed by John Stollenwerk. Seven years later Allen-Edmonds founded Woodlore, a manufacturer of aromatic cedar shoe trees and related cedar products. To thwart an out-of-state buyout in 1989 and to prevent off-shore production, Stollenwerk, along with several co-workers, purchased Allen-Edmonds. Sales more than quadrupled from the previous decade.

Today Allen-Edmonds' handcrafted footwear for men is sold in the most fashionable stores throughout the United States and in 33 other countries of the world, for prices ranging from about $170 to $1,600 a pair, with $250 for a pair of black cap-toes about typical. The company also has its own chain of retail stores. Sales in 1995 climbed to about $55 million.

Sole stitchers from the Allen-Edmonds Bottoming Department share a joke with John Stollenwerk. At the Port Washington plant are (left to right) Tim Goetsch, Dick Eder, Bob Rassel, John Stollenwerk, and Bernie Risch. The four craftsmen have a combined total of 56 years of service with the firm.

Much of Allen-Edmonds' success has been driven by Stollenwerk's conviction, arrived at in the mid-1980s, that marketing would be key. So the company has cultivated—and, yes, promoted the loyalties of—high-profile customers ranging from President Bill Clinton and former President George Bush to media celebrities Ted Koppel and Sam Donaldson, from pro basketball star Grant Hill to actors Danny DeVito and Clint Eastwood.

The company also has made a statement by not taking "no" for an answer when it came to penetrating the Japanese market. Those efforts included Stollenwerk's "crashing" of the 1987 Tokyo Shoe Fair, forcing Japanese officials to allow him to exhibit Allen-Edmonds shoes in the lobby of the trade show, which initially had refused him entrance even though it was allowing European shoe manufacturers to exhibit.

Though Allen-Edmonds today still sells only a few thousand pairs of shoes in Japan, Stollenwerk notes that sales have increased significantly in the past couple of years as that nation's growing affluent class acquires a taste for the company's quality product line. And, says the globe-trotting president, sales in quality-conscious European countries are strong too.

The company's flair for the unexpected also extended to its introduction in 1993 of *Lifestyles*, a collection of casual, after-work shoes. In 1995 the firm fanfared *Corporate Casuals,* softer-soled footwear designed to work in a relaxed atmosphere. "The consumer is looking for more casual footwear, and this has become a significant part of our business," Stollenwerk explains. "We did it because we need not only to respond to our customers' needs but to be proactive in anticipating them."

But while innovation has become the byword of Allen-Edmonds' approach to marketing, tradition still dominates how the company manufactures its shoes because each pair is handcrafted. The egalitarian ideal is promoted and respect for each associate's contribution to the company is stressed.

Allen-Edmonds' approach to corporate culture also ventures into the paternal. For example, when the company's main plant in Belgium, Wisconsin, burned to the ground during a sub-zero-temperature night in 1984, Stollenwerk gave most of the employees two weeks' paid vacation and the promise that they would be back at work soon. Everyone pitched in together and had Allen-Edmonds back on its feet, albeit at a new location in Port Washington, within several months.

Tradition still dominates how Allen-Edmonds manufactures its shoes because each pair is handcrafted.

Similarly, even though many companies headquartered 30 miles away from Milwaukee turn their backs on the big city that anchors the local economy, Stollenwerk and Allen-Edmonds have embraced Milwaukee wholeheartedly. Both the company and its president boost the city in major initiatives ranging from corporate sponsorship of the Great Circus Parade, the Greater Milwaukee Open, Ride for the Arts, UPAF, and other events to Stollenwerk's memberships on the boards of several companies and his activities on behalf of private-school choice, health care institutions, and the performing arts.

"We want to give back to the community some of the things that it has given to us," Stollenwerk says.

And the relationship between Allen-Edmonds and Milwaukee will grow even further. While about 10 percent of the company's workers now commute from Milwaukee, Stollenwerk plans to boost that proportion substantially in the next few years. Such an effort would make more workers available to Allen-Edmonds—and increase the ways in which it can give back to Milwaukee.

Master Lock Company

Master Lock Company has earned an outstanding reputation as the world's largest manufacturer of padlocks and other security products. Headquartered at 2600 North 32nd Street in Milwaukee, it began with one newly patented product in 1921—the laminated padlock. Since then, Master Lock has expanded its product line, facilities, and market share many times. Today the organization competes internationally in the broader security marketplace. It enjoys an unparalleled 97 percent brand name recognition among U.S. padlock purchasers.

The now widely accepted and frequently copied laminated padlock was invented by the company's founder, Harry Soref. An innovative inventor, Soref created a new lock design that initially met with a great deal of resistance because it was different from the locks in use at the time.

Trade engineers, patent attorneys, and lock manufacturers rejected Soref's invention as too radical. At a time when lock design was simple, he was proposing a complicated lock with about 50 parts and nearly 100 production steps. It was, however, superior to the solid-body locks of the day. Soref eventually earned the trust and financial backing of friends and launched production of the lock that would revolutionize security.

As Soref's lock design became accepted by consumers, the Master Lock laminated padlock quickly became the benchmark for security. During Prohibition, shortly after Soref launched his company, his padlocks gained national notoriety as federal agents used them to secure liquor supplies and drinking establishments.

By that time, Soref was recognized as one of the world's foremost lock authorities and was even sought out by the Great Houdini, another Wisconsin native, for advice on keys that would help him escape from handcuffs during his stage act.

Top: One-key, double-locking deadbolt security is available to homeowners with Master Lock's TwinBolt™ door lock and handle set.

Safety lock-outs as well as high-security industrial locks are made especially for commercial consumers.

The Master Lock line of products has grown to hundreds of padlocks and doorlocks, including combination locks and a wide assortment of specialty locks for bicycles, lockers, guns, outboard motors, trailers, machine controls, and heavy-duty industrial uses. Related products include chains, cables, hasps, padlock identification tags, magnetic key cases, and industrial-safety lock-out products.

Master Lock prides itself on its special order service for nonstandard padlock keying and shackle requirements that is unequaled in the industry for scope and time of delivery. Its line of door hardware is manufactured in Auburn, Alabama, and includes high-quality door locksets and hardware for residential, light commercial, and retail markets. Master Lock products are sold internationally in more than 75 countries.

Although the company has earned its reputation for quality, it continues to invest in processes that will enhance the quality and security of its products. Master

Lock is moving toward a total home security focus based on technological innovations.

Master Lock recently implemented a state-of-the-art order management system to enhance its commitment to total customer service. "We have invested in equipment, facilities, and employee training," explains Jim Beardsley, president and chief executive officer. "We will continue to question our methods, examine our markets, and look for new opportunities to compete smarter.

"But the underlying theme of our company will remain the same: to make the best product we can. Master Lock is committed to our business here in Milwaukee, to our employees, and to our customers."

As a major employer in central-city Milwaukee, Master Lock takes an active role in community service. It provides both financial and volunteer support for many educational and social service institutions, including the Next Door Foundation, Clarke Street School, the Mary Ryan Boys & Girls Club, and the United Way. The company primarily focuses its efforts on its neighborhood, including community and industrial revitalization, and family-oriented services.

The Master Lock brand name is internationally recognized for the quality products it represents. The company is most famous for its series of "Shot Lock" commercials that have gained prominence through their association with Super Bowl advertising.

Master Lock is part of MasterBrand Industries, Inc., a subsidiary of American Brands, Inc. This focused consumer products company markets powerhouse brands with leading market positions in distilled spirits, hardware and home improvement products, office products, international tobacco, and golf and leisure products. Besides Master Lock, its brands include Jim Beam, Moen, Aristokraft, Waterloo, ACCO, Swingline, Titleist, Foot-Joy, and Cobra.

Above: The "Shot Lock" has become Master Lock's symbol of security to the world.

Left: Master Lock's product line includes high-quality padlocks and door hardware.

Froedtert Malt Corporation

For more than a century Froedtert Malt Corporation's fortunes have paralleled those of the American brewing industry, traveling on an upward curve. During the past decade, however, Froedtert Malt has taken on the additional role of supplier of quality malt to international brewers, in markets such as Latin America and Asia. Today the Lesaffre Group of malting facilities, which includes Froedtert Malt, is the fourth-largest malting company in the world.

In addition to its headquarters and manufacturing facility at 3830 West Grant Street in Milwaukee, Froedtert Malt also has a facility in Winona, Minnesota. Processing barley selected by Froedtert's experienced barley buyers in Minneapolis, these two facilities produce enough malt annually to brew 10.5 billion bottles of beer and employ 200 people in the United States!

Froedtert began in 1866, when brothers William and Jacob Froedtert founded a small brewery with an adjoining malthouse in Milwaukee. After a fire destroyed the brewery, the malthouse was operated alone, incorporating the business as Froedtert Grain and Malting Company. The company grew along with Milwaukee's fledgling brewing industry and then really boomed when Kurtis R. Froedtert—son of William and founder of Milwaukee institutions such as Froedtert Hospital and Southgate Mall—took over and in 1919 acquired two malthouses in Minnesota. The company prospered through a diversification into and out of non-malting operations in the 1950s and 1960s. While Froedtert has preserved elements of Kurtis Froedtert's eclectic sense of 1950s style in the architecture and interior design of the company's Milwaukee headquarters, it has taken great strides in equipping its manufacturing facilities with the latest malting technology.

In 1986 Froedtert was purchased by International Malting Corporation, which is majority owned by Lesaffre et Compagnie, a privately held multinational agribusiness based in France.

It is Froedtert's mission to be the premier malting company in the Americas. In order to succeed, it has initiated a "customer-driven" culture among all its employees. And the company is continuing its highly successful plan to increase its export business. Froedtert's president, Gabriel Pujol, enjoys his role of fostering each of these areas of growth and improvement within the company. "I find Milwaukee to be a well-kept secret in many ways," says Pujol, who is relatively new to the city. "Especially surprising is the level of interest our employees have in learning about and developing our international accounts."

"Success in the malting business also rests on the ability to stay ahead of the changes that are continuously brewing with Froedtert's customers," comments Frederick A. Barney, Froedtert's executive vice president of domestic sales and marking. "As national brewers such as Miller, Pabst, Heileman, and Anheuser-Busch strive for greater variety in their products, Froedtert's experienced technical staff has been at the forefront of the company's drive to meet their needs."

"Due to the increasing range of our customer base and corresponding product development, we have done a lot of work over the past five years to modernize our technology and to broaden the technical capabilities of our people. A strong team of both technical and commercial people is essential in providing absolute quality," explains Susan E. Welch, vice president of international sales and marketing.

Froedtert's growth strategy of exporting to the fast-growing beer markets of Asia and Latin America has been pursued for the past 10 years. Froedtert is well suited to grow in these expanding markets in part because it has historically performed against rigorous competition in the relatively unregulated U.S. market while European and Canadian competitors have been blanketed by protectionist policies.

The future looks to be as bright as a glass of freshly brewed lager for Froedtert Malt—plans are now under way for a third manufacturing facility in Oregon.

Froedtert Malt Corporation's Milwaukee plant is located at 3830 West Grant Street.

Koss Corporation

For nearly 50 years Milwaukeeans have lent their ears—and frequently, their eyes, and even much of their hearts—to Koss Corporation, the world leader in stereophone technology.

Few companies know how to render sound as delightfully as Koss. It produces the highest-quality stereo headphones, computer speakers, and other electronic audio equipment at its headquarters at 4129 North Port Washington Avenue, and markets them across the United States and in many foreign countries as well.

"Being in a consumer-products business is always a constant challenge to our creativity," says Michael J. Koss, president and chief executive officer and the second generation of family leadership. "We always have to be doing something that's appropriate, timely, and responsive.

"Yet we began and grew very humbly, so we've forced ourselves to accomplish a lot with limited resources. That's been the key to our success."

In fact, Koss began as a hospital-TV rental company when Michael's father, John C. Koss, combined a $200 wedding gift from his folks with another borrowed $800 to begin his entrepreneurial career. Soon he brainstormed an idea for adapting a phonograph for earphone listening, and his lifetime business was born.

Today the firm produces a complete line of stereophones, ranging from cordless stereophones for home theater to studio-professional models costing $800. Koss also has established a strong presence in the growing computer-speaker business.

And Michael Koss says the company plans to conquer many emerging fields that continue to stem from its base expertise. For example, Koss is developing headsets for computers, cellular phones, and other communications devices. It is perfecting "active noise cancellation" headphones that actually quell outside noises before they reach the ear. Under an alliance with the Dutch trading company Hagemeyer, Koss is licensing its brand name and logo to Hagemeyer-designed and -built products in non-competing market segments such as tabletop stereos.

Potentially most important, Koss also plans to introduce in 1996 a cordless stereophone that utilizes a 900-megahertz transmission system to beam a stereo signal throughout an entire household. Five discrete channels will prevent interference with and from other frequencies.

The firm's most public face is its famous billboard on Interstate 43 just north of Capitol Drive, which displays clever, soft-sell advertising slogans that continually find new take-offs on the word "Koss."

But the Kosses and their employees also contribute to Milwaukee in countless other ways that out-proportion their size. For example, John C. Koss, chairman of the board, has been one of the city's biggest boosters of Junior Achievement, and Michael Koss has been instrumental in the development of Koss Classics recordings of the Milwaukee Symphony orchestra. The company was one of the first sponsors of the Milwaukee Children's Museum and has endowed a Koss Center for auditory research and treatment at the Medical College of Wisconsin.

"We live here, and so do 250 other people on our team," Michael Koss says. "So we want to make Milwaukee the best place we can make it."

Top: Koss' top-of-the-line stereophones, the ESP/950 Electrostatic Stereophone System.

Below: John C. Koss, founder and chairman of Koss Corporation; John Koss, Jr., vice president of sales; and Michael J. Koss, president and chief executive officer (from left to right).

Below right: John C. Koss, 1954.

Johnson Controls Inc.

Johnson Controls Inc. is the largest publicly held corporation based in Wisconsin and is more than a century old. But rather than being slowed by size and age, the company entered 1996 in the midst of one of its largest growth spurts ever—and as a vital, innovative, major force in each of its industries.

That's because Johnson Controls is diligently fulfilling its mission to continually exceed customers' increasing expectations. The company and its 64,000 employees, in more than 900 locations worldwide, believe that if they deliver even more than what their customers expect, those customers will return again and again, asking Johnson Controls to contribute even more to their success.

"We've always lived by this philosophy, but we've determined that it's more crucial than ever because our customers and potential customers are asking us to help in so many more areas nowadays," explains James H. Keyes, chairman and chief executive officer of the company, which is headquartered at 5757 North Green Bay Avenue. "And their needs today aren't the same as their needs of 10 years ago."

The reach—and responsiveness—of Johnson Controls has expanded remarkably since 1885, when Professor Warren Johnson founded the business to manufacture his invention, the electric room thermostat. From that single invention, Johnson Controls has grown into a multibillion-dollar corporation.

Even at that size, the company's sales advanced a remarkable 21 percent for fiscal 1995 (ending September 30), to $8.3 billion from $6.9 billion for fiscal 1994. Fiscal 1995 was the 49th consecutive year of sales increases and the 20th successive year of increases in stock dividends, which have been paid consecutively since 1885.

Top: Thousands of buildings around the world are more comfortable, safe, and productive because of the Metasys facility management system from Johnson Controls. The industry-leading system automatically monitors and controls mechanical and electrical systems in non-residential buildings.

Nearly half of Johnson Controls' revenues come from its automotive systems group, the largest independent supplier of seating for the worldwide automotive industry. At its 118 plants across the globe, the automotive group designs, engineers, and manufactures complete seating systems, seating foam pads, mechanisms, and metal frames, as well as interior components and systems, to nearly every major auto maker in the world.

Controls account for another third of the firm's sales. Johnson Controls is the world leader in the design, manufacture, installation, and service of systems to control energy use, heating, ventilating, air conditioning, lighting, security, and fire management for nonresidential buildings. Products range from simple room thermostats to complex computer-based systems. Services include complete mechanical and electrical maintenance as well as full-time, on-site management of customer facilities. This operation has 330 sales and service offices, 500 facility-management sites, and 10 manufacturing plants worldwide.

The plastics technology group is the world's largest

Below: Johnson Controls' corporate headquarters in suburban Glendale, Wisconsin, also serves as the headquarters of its battery group.

supplier of polyethylene terephthalate (PET) plastic bottles—the type commonly seen with soft drinks, water, and other beverages, foods, and personal-care items. The group also designs and assembles plastics blow-molding machinery. It has 33 manufacturing plants in the United States and Europe.

The company's battery group is one of the largest U.S. manufacturers of automotive batteries for cars, trucks, construction equipment, boats, and other vehicles. It sells batteries under private labels to both the replacement and original-equipment markets. The group has 12 North American manufacturing plants.

In all four of these businesses, Johnson Controls is doing more for its customers than it did just a few years ago. The vast majority of those opportunities are being created as customers "outsource" functions they used to perform themselves—and now find that Johnson Controls can handle them more capably and cost-effectively.

For example, automakers increasingly are outsourcing their seating requirements to Johnson Controls to improve quality and reduce costs. Today they also look to the firm to do more than just manufacture a complete seat or seat component: They look to Johnson Controls to design it, engineer it, integrate it with surrounding parts, and deliver it globally. Many battery retailers are asking the company to manage their battery inventories in addition to manufacturing batteries for them.

Meanwhile, building owners are asking Johnson Controls to take complete responsibility for operating and maintaining their buildings in addition to providing them with Metasys Facility Management Systems that automate their buildings' heating, ventilating, air conditioning, lighting, and security equipment. As a result, the firm's employees are in customer facilities every day, providing a comprehensive range of services to ensure a total quality building environment.

"We're performing functions that we had never been involved with before," Keyes says. "But our customers recognize that by applying our core skills to each function, we can perform it better than they can. Our partnerships just grow."

The company is one of the largest makers of automotive batteries for both the replacement and original equipment markets. At its Milwaukee battery plant, it manufactures specialty batteries for telecommunications and uninterruptible power supply applications.

Continuous improvement in quality, service, productivity, and time compression is a fundamental component of the Johnson Controls mission to exceed customer expectations. For example, in the automotive battery business, such efforts have resulted in increased battery life and reduced costs.

A major component of the company's growth is that as customers expand around the world, they take Johnson Controls with them. For instance, following successes in North America, the firm's customers are taking its high-heat-handling PET plastic bottles into their European markets for beverages such as iced tea, juices, and sports drinks.

Overall, about 30 percent of Johnson Controls' sales are now in foreign markets. In emerging markets like the Pacific Rim, sales are expected to total $500 million annually by 1998, up from just $50 million in 1992.

But while its facilities and employees are spread across the globe, Johnson Controls' loyalty to Milwaukee—where it employs more than 2,500 people—has endured. Charitable giving by the company, its employees, and the Johnson Controls Foundation to southeastern Wisconsin organizations in 1995 alone amounted to some $2 million.

"The climate for business here has become very friendly," Keyes says. "So while we may hang our hat in more and more places, Milwaukee has always been our home."

Left: The controls group headquarters in downtown Milwaukee was built by company founder Warren Johnson at the turn of the century.

Charter Manufacturing, Inc.

Charter Manufacturing Company has been prospering quietly for decades, establishing strong positions in several national specialty-steel markets as it grew into a major manufacturing force in metro Milwaukee.

In 1995 the firm was named a Supplier of the Year by General Motors Corporation, one of only 150 companies so recognized by the world's number one auto maker among its 10,000 or more suppliers worldwide, on the basis of product quality, engineering-design support, delivery performance, and prices.

Rather than boast of his organization's success, however, John A. Mellowes would rather talk about Charter Manufacturing's 850 employees and the company's relationship with them.

A billet caster in operation at Charter Steel's melt shop.

"If there's anything that's important to me beyond satisfying our customers, it's being a good employer and partner to our employees," says Mellowes, who is chairman, chief executive officer, and third-generation family owner of the company, which was founded in 1936 and now is a $200-million enterprise headquartered at 1212 West Glen Oaks Lane in Mequon.

Just after the turn of the century Mellowes' grandfather, Alfred Mellowes, had performed much of the pioneering engineering work on early electric refrigerators. GM actually bought out his first refrigerator company, and it later became Frigidaire. Briggs & Stratton hired him to start a refrigeration division in 1918 but then pulled the plug on it in 1922.

So Mellowes trained his engineering skills and entrepreneurial spirit on starting the Milwaukee Lock Washer Co. National Lock Washer Co. bought him out in 1927, and when his son, Charles, graduated from Cornell University, the 25-year-old scion urged his father to start yet a third new business: producing the wire that National's Milwaukee plant chopped into washers.

Charter thus began with a business that has been a core enterprise for it from the beginning: the highly specialized "cold rolling" of steel wire. By the late 1930s Charter also was producing flat wire for garden rakes, lampshades, and dipsticks as well as box stitching wire for cardboard containers. In the 1940s the company streamlined, refined, and expanded the process to meet practically any requirement a customer might present, including shaped steel used in everything from towel bars to sled runners.

Today, after several lateral expansions of new specialized markets, Charter consists of three separate but related operations: Charter Wire, Milwaukee Wire Products, and Charter Steel.

Charter Wire continues the firm's original focus on providing turnkey design and manufacturing services to produce precision, cold-rolled steel products for a wide range of industries, including horseshoes and grain augurs, rake tines and computer printer bars, valve locks and snowmobile skis.

Milwaukee Wire, originally an extension of Charter Wire, is a full-service engineering and manufacturing organization that creates high-volume products for the combustion-engine and power-train industries, including tens of millions of dipsticks a year and retainers and keys for U.S. and foreign automakers. Its engineers design for auto makers worldwide.

Charter Steel was founded in 1978 as a rolling mill for wire rod. Wire processing was added in 1985 and a steel-making shop was constructed in 1991. The mill has an output of 250,000 tons of specialty bar, rod, and wire a year. This will soon be raised to 400,000 tons. The mill is located in Saukville, Wisconsin, and supplies the other Charter plants as well as a large group of trade customers with raw material.

At the mill, Statistical Process Controls tests and audits ensure that the job is done right, allowing Charter Steel to compete on the most exacting quality applications. To accommodate customer demands, it produces many grades of steel in relatively small quantities. In turn, the mill's output is purchased by companies that use it in high-volume applications ranging from construction-equipment components to parts of Briggs lawn-mower engines.

Auto companies get by far the largest share of Charter Steel's output. "We've frequently considered diversification, but we keep coming back to the idea that the business we really want to be in is autos," Mellowes says. "There are ups and downs, but people eventually have to replace their cars, so it's not as cyclical as some other markets we could be in."

Gaining Supplier of the Year recognition by GM in 1995, Mellowes says, "has opened some additional doors for us," including the prospect of selling to GM of Europe versions of parts that Charter manufactures for the company's U.S. plants. Charter also is becoming in general a more significant part of the auto industry's dwindling number of suppliers.

"Their goal is to reduce their number of suppliers and concentrate their purchases with the best suppliers they've got," Mellowes explains.

Mellowes attributes much of Charter's good relationship with the auto industry to his employees, who continue to be in the vanguard of what has been called the employee empowerment movement in the American workplace. Back in the 1970s, Charter eliminated time clocks even for production workers and began dealing with their pay just as the company compensated white-collar workers (except for overtime).

Charter also organized workers in semi-autonomous teams that have "considerable latitude in managerial authority" compared with typical manufacturing workers, Mellowes says.

"Who knows better how to do a specific job than the people who actually are doing it?" he says. "It's better than having a wave of industrial engineers combing through the place with stopwatches and clipboards."

Mellowes says that Charter employees spend an average of 5 percent of their time just in job training. "And we cross-train people so they know how to do more than one job, then we pay them based on how many skills they have.

"They're really integral to what we do. The most exciting thing for me in recent years has been empowering our employees and getting them more involved in our business."

Charter Steel's rolling mill in Saukville, Wisconsin, was founded in 1978.

ArcRon, Ltd.

Welding and fabricating are what ArcRon, Ltd., does. But the company's business is satisfying customers, one at a time, time after time.

That's why the Menomonee Falls-based company, a one-source custom fabricator having full-cloth capabilities, has grown steadily for many years—and explosively over the past several. Sales jumped about 30 percent in 1995 and should grow in 1996 to nearly double 1993's sales.

Maintaining its focus has enabled ArcRon to cultivate a customer list that reads like a "Who's Who" of Wisconsin's major manufacturers. Among other relationships, ArcRon fabricates gas tanks for Harley-Davidson, motorcycle frames for Buell Motorcycle Co., hoist components for Harnischfeger Industries, Inc., and various other products for Oshkosh Truck Corp., Nordco, Alto-Shaam, Inc., M.G. Industries, Applied Power Inc., and Waukesha Engine.

"Many customers are turning to us because they don't want to invest in all of the capital equipment dedicated to handling particular product lines, but they can still retain ownership of the product," says Ron Wilfer, ArcRon's owner and president.

Wilfer founded the company in 1973 after working in his father's blacksmith and welding shop for 12 years. He saw a niche for a fabricating concern with a specialization in certified welding of items such as frames, tanks, and parts for a variety of industrial, transportation, and commercial applications. As the market's response confirmed his supposition, Wilfer acquired additional expertise and equipment to keep pace with soaring demand.

Today ArcRon provides American Society of Mechanical Engineers (ASME) and American Welding Society (AWS) qualified welding and fabrication of many types of metal, from light to heavy gauges of steel, aluminum, and stainless steel. Its capabilities also include shearing, punching, forming, flame-cutting, and machining. Finishing facilities include cleaning, phosphatizing, and painting to specification. In addition, the company performs final assembly, inspection and calibration, testing and qualifying, and packaging and crating.

In 1988 ArcRon established a sister company, Axtra Corporation, to manufacture and assemble Trashpacker waste-management systems for Chicago Trashpacker Corp. The stainless steel Trashpackers are sold to foodservice, health care, and commercial-industrial facilities that are faced with the challenge of efficient and economical waste disposal.

About 80 percent of ArcRon's business comes from repeat customers. One reason is that the firm has undergone the strenuous process of becoming a certified supplier for several of them. A major part of that effort is reducing production defects to almost none, as well as delivering on time.

For example, ArcRon receives performance ratings from its largest customer, Oshkosh Truck Corp. These reports have acknowledged a highest monthly quality rating of 99.7 percent on nearly 5,000 manufactured parts. And yet, Wilfer isn't completely satisfied even with that impressive number.

"We want to go for 100 percent," he explains. "Zero rejects is our goal. We're already there with the workmanship. Now it's just a matter of breaking down the other mistakes to their smallest detail and taking care of them."

To prepare ArcRon for the twenty-first century, Ron Wilfer continues to add to the company's capabilities in the form of equipment, systems, and personnel.

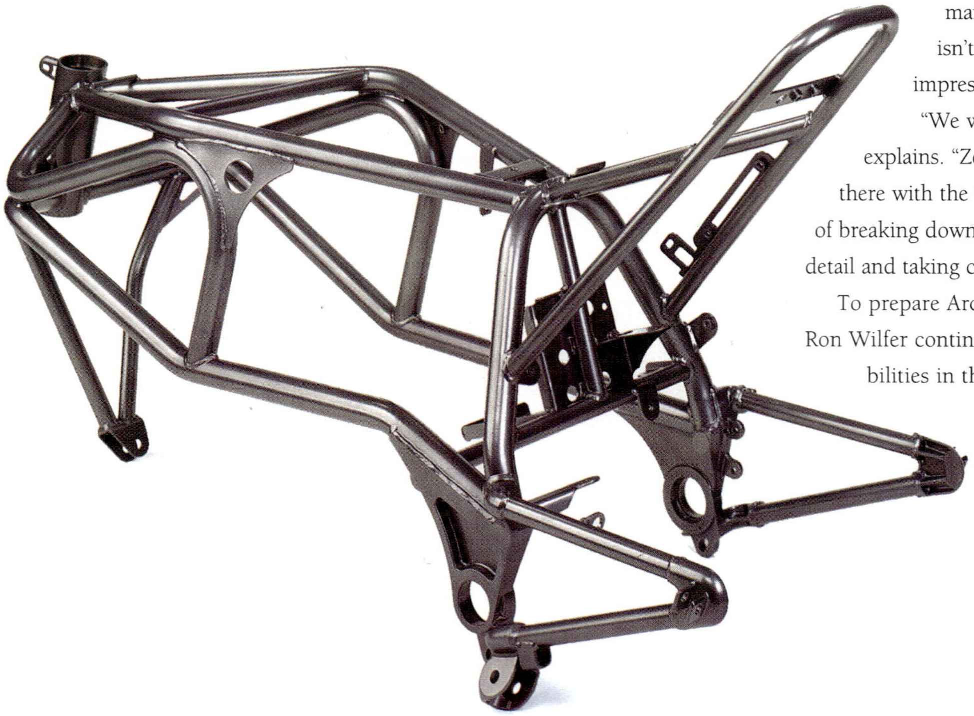

Complicated weldments like the Buell motorcycle frame reflect ArcRon's expertise in welding and fabricating.

For example, within the next several months ArcRon expects to have established "electronic commerce" with at least one of its customers that will allow completely paperless transmission of quotes, proposals, and other business documents. Wilfer eventually wants to expand that capability to service all of ArcRon's clients. The company also plans to implement a bar code labor entry system to effectively measure work order status and efficiency.

Continually satisfying the wide variety of customer needs means that ArcRon's 115-member work force must be extremely responsive. For example, a highly diversified Process Development department assists customers with feasibility studies, product designs, and prototype development, and a well-trained quality-assurance department is based on guidelines from the American Society for Quality Control.

"The key to our success is our team and their team getting together at our customers' facilities to work together," says James E. Wilfer, the company's director of operations, and Ron's cousin. "We get to understand our customers' systems, integrate our efforts with theirs, and become totally responsive."

The Wilfers and other top management are equally dedicated to partnership with their own employees. "We believe ArcRon's employees are our biggest and best assets, making the critical difference in how well ArcRon performs," reads the company's mission statement in part. "Their work effort separates ArcRon from all potential competitors."

Keys to ensuring that ArcRon employees can and want to execute that responsibility include constant communication about the company's activities, continuing education and training, distribution of responsibility, and widespread sharing of the rewards of success.

Ron Wilfer himself routinely walks the plant floor, and the management team conducts regular information meetings during which workers can broach any topic they wish. "There's a value in sharing," Wilfer explains. "It's our report card. The sooner you share information, the sooner you know how you've done and what you need to improve."

So that new employees can learn the company's culture as well as their specific jobs quickly and smoothly, ArcRon has created a "buddy system" under which each new worker is sponsored by a veteran who shows him or her around and answers questions. ArcRon also pays for employees to extend their education, to attend seminars, and to visit customers' facilities. For a passing grade in a company-financed course, workers can receive 120 percent reimbursement.

Full-time employees also are eligible for a bonus plan that Ron Wilfer established in 1993. A percentage of ArcRon's monthly profits is distributed in bonuses based on a three-month rolling average—and they're split evenly among all eligible workers.

The company also contributes to a wide variety of civic organizations and has made a priority of assisting Community Memorial Hospital in Menomonee Falls.

Although ArcRon will consider expanding outside metro Milwaukee and even Wisconsin if customers require such a step, Ron Wilfer foresees the company's home remaining basically where its heart is. "We're going to stick to our knitting," he says. "That's what's gotten us where we are today."

Trashpacker® units like these are an example of ArcRon's full-cloth capabilities.

ABB Industrial Systems Inc.

When the managers and employees of the Drives and Metals Systems division of ABB Industrial Systems in New Berlin think big, sometimes they outdo even themselves.

For example, they recently commissioned a mammoth motor and drive system for the National Aeronautics and Space Administration wind tunnel in Langley, Virginia, a 135,000-horsepower dynamo that is the largest such system ever assembled. No one has even attempted to design one so large before.

Increasingly, the 500 New Berlin employees of ABB Industrial Systems, including more than 150 involved in manufacturing, are making the phenomenal all but routine. Under the direction of Chuck Clark, senior vice president and general manager, they have doubled the sales value of the output of their facility in just the past three years.

Parent ABB Ltd., headquartered in Zurich, Switzerland, is the 38th-largest industrial company in the world with annual revenues exceeding $30 billion. Drives and Metals Systems is one of the primary operations for ABB's largest segment—Industrial and Building Systems. ABB is recognized as an international electrical engineering leader and the world's largest manufacturer of electric drives.

The New Berlin facility is responsible for the product development, applications design, manufacture, and servicing of AC and DC drives, engineered drives and control systems, and power converters for a wide range of industrial and commercial applications.

ABB offers the broadest range of adjustable-speed AC and DC drives and integrated drive systems of any manufacturer in the world. Ranging from 0.75 horsepower through the 135,000 horsepower provided to NASA, ABB's extensive portfolio includes LV and MV motors, power rectifier systems, AC machines and generators, and other electrical equipment, systems, and services.

Right: Operational excellence and teamwork are the cornerstones of ABB's industrial operations. Here, Chuck Clark, senior vice president and general manager, discusses customer specifications with drives manufacturing supervisor JoAnn Hall.

Major markets include metals producing, pulp and paper, web printing, paper, film and foil converting, power plants and utilities, textiles, chemicals, material handling, food processing, HVAC (heating, ventilating, and air conditioning), marine propulsion, cranes, hoists, and other applications.

The drives and controls produced by ABB Industrial Systems power everything from air-conditioning systems in Federated department stores to Birmingham Steel rolling mills, from airport shuttle trains to ski lifts, from fine paper machines to the presses that have added color to *The Wall Street Journal*. ABB also supplies high-quality control systems for the electric mining shovels produced by the P&H division of Harnischfeger Industries, a Milwaukee-based company. ABB's drives and control systems are also an integral part of the high-quality paper and paperboard products being manufactured at many of Wisconsin's Fox Valley pulp and paper mills.

At the 155,000-square-foot New Berlin facility (built in 1981), ABB Industrial Systems owns and operates one of ABB's most modern manufacturing facilities and has earned certification to industry's most stringent quality system standard—ISO 9001.

Below: ABB's modern New Berlin manufacturing facility employs some 500 people and is responsible for the design and production of electric motor drives and integrated control systems for a wide range of industrial and commercial applications.

ABB Flexible Automation Inc.

Manufacturers, whether automotive or general industry, are using the capabilities of ABB Flexible Automation to provide their manufacturing operations the strategic advantages that robotic systems offer—quality, reliability, and flexibility.

Headquartered in New Berlin since 1982, ABB Flexible Automation (formerly known as ABB Robotics) is one of the world's leading manufacturers of industrial robots and industrial robot systems.

In 1973 ASEA, one of ABB's predecessor companies, introduced the world's first all-electric robot, and in 1974 ASEA Robotics was established in Vasteras, Sweden. The company began U.S. operations in 1979 in White Plains, New York, and one year later opened the Automotive Division in Troy, Michigan.

The New Berlin facility houses one of ABB's Flexible Automation Centers (FACs), which assemble robot systems using robots that are manufactured in Sweden, Switzerland, and Norway. These centers, located in more than 24 countries, provide ABB's customers with a worldwide organization that has a strong local presence in individual markets. In North America, ABB's centers are located in Auburn Hills and Warren, Michigan; Fort Collins, Colorado; and Toronto, Canada. These centers represent a core of world-class technical expertise in design, engineering, process expertise, project management, system capabilities, and service support for robot systems. They facilitate the transfer of knowledge and expertise among countries and companies and assure customers the quickest and most cost-effective solutions for their manufacturing system requirements. The New Berlin Center provides robot systems for a wide range of industries that include appliance, automotive, food, glass, offroad, plastic, textile, consumer goods, and paper.

Widely used in industry, ABB's Flexpalletizer accommodates a wide range of case sizes, pallet patterns, and case rates and is easily modified for the changing nature of customers' packaging and warehousing needs.

ABB has more than 15,000 robots installed in U.S. plants, more than double the level of five years ago. In the past four years ABB's robotic business has increased more than 300 percent.

Automotive applications still dominate the robotic business. The Big Three American auto makers, of course, are major customers, including General Motors' utility-vehicle plant in Janesville, Wisconsin, which utilizes more than 240 robots—most of which are ABB robots. ABB Flexible Automation has won Quality awards from General Motors and Chrysler. Major automotive component suppliers also rely on ABB Flexible Automation, including Milwaukee's A.O. Smith Corporation as well as other Milwaukee and Wisconsin manufacturers such as Harley-Davidson, Falk, Bemis, and Penda.

Other industries, however, are the fastest-growing customers of ABB Flexible Automation. They have recognized—as automotive manufacturers did long ago—that ABB robotic systems ensure increased efficiency, enhanced productivity, and improved product quality. As time-based competition sweeps industry worldwide, customers are recognizing the benefits that ABB Flexible Automation provides in helping to shorten product-to-market cycles. With their high degree of flexibility, ABB's robotic systems provide ideal solutions for arc and spot welding, palletizing, painting, dispensing, machine tending, deburring, and grinding applications.

ABB robots and related equipment now have been a part of American industry long enough that some customers are upgrading to third- and fourth-generation products from ABB Flexible Automation. More also are turning their existing robotic equipment back to ABB for refurbishment and rebuilding. The New Berlin facility serves as ABB Flexible Automation's most extensive robot reconditioning operation and is the largest of any robot manufacturer.

Whether it's the handling of television tubes, the assembly of cylinder heads, the EMI shielding of portable phones, or inserting windshields into cars, ABB Flexible Automation provides North American industry with competitive manufacturing solutions.

W.H. Brady Co.

W.H. Brady Co. offers more than 30,000 different identification, safety, and specialty tape products for worldwide markets that manufacture products ranging from computers to airliners, videocassettes to medical equipment, and much more. Recently, the firm has expanded into a variety of related services as well.

Yet whatever its specific function, every sign, label, and marker produced by Brady ultimately is an expression of the core mission of the company, which is to be the global leader in unique identification solutions.

"We want to provide extra value in everything we do, making it easy for our customers to conduct business with us by supporting them and their needs—whatever business they're in," says Katherine M. Hudson, president and chief executive officer of W.H. Brady Co.

W.H. Brady Co. is headquartered in a sparkling reflective-glass complex at 6555 West Good Hope Road in Milwaukee. The facility also houses Brady's Industrial Products Division, a manufacturing operation that produces labels and markers to help other manufacturers identify and track their products.

That's how William H. Brady, Sr., started the enterprise in 1914 in Eau Claire, Wisconsin, turning out promotional materials for banks, feed mills, and ice cream parlors. The growing business soon became known for producing high-quality advertising specialties such as punch cards and personalized calendars.

In the 1940s Brady's youngest son, Bill, led the company in a new direction: making wire markers from pressure-sensitive tape. The product succeeded because it provided a way to permanently identify wires in the electrical control systems of military planes and ships.

Since then, Brady has created thousands of other high-performance identification products through its extensive experience and expertise in three core competencies: coating materials to adhere, resist chemicals and abrasion, and readily accept ink; converting these materials through laminating, color printing, and other processes; and engineering computer software, portable printers, lettering machines, and other electromechanical devices and electronic equipment to serve customers' increasingly diverse needs.

The company's main product lines include safety products like warning signs, valve tags, and lockout devices that prevent injuries and save lives in plants and offices; industrial labels, markers, and nameplates that help businesses identify wires, computer chips, and other components and ensure that critical information is in place, such as quality-monitoring data; and specialty tapes for shielding, masking, and other applications in data-storage, semiconductor, and audio-video markets.

Brady is always looking for ways to meet the many needs of its diverse customer base. For example, through the Automatic Identification and Data Collection operation it launched in 1994, the company is providing Boeing, Pepsico, and other major corporations with solutions that increase the speed and quality of product identification and distribution.

Selectively pursuing new markets like this has helped Brady to maintain steady double-digit annual growth in sales and profits and employment of more than 2,400 people at operations in Wisconsin, Minnesota, Florida, Connecticut, Canada, and 14 countries in Asia, South America, and Europe. More than 40 percent of the company's sales now occur outside of the United States.

Yet W.H. Brady Co. is highly committed to Milwaukee, particularly through various programs that boost education. For example, the firm began its Academic All-Stars program in 1990 to honor outstanding local high school students and, through 1995, had contributed more than $110,000 in grants and honored some 750 All-Stars.

Brady's customers demand quality and Brady employees deliver. Whether they're producing custom orders with special printing or stock products, Brady employees continually strive to create the best product at the best possible price.

GE Medical Systems

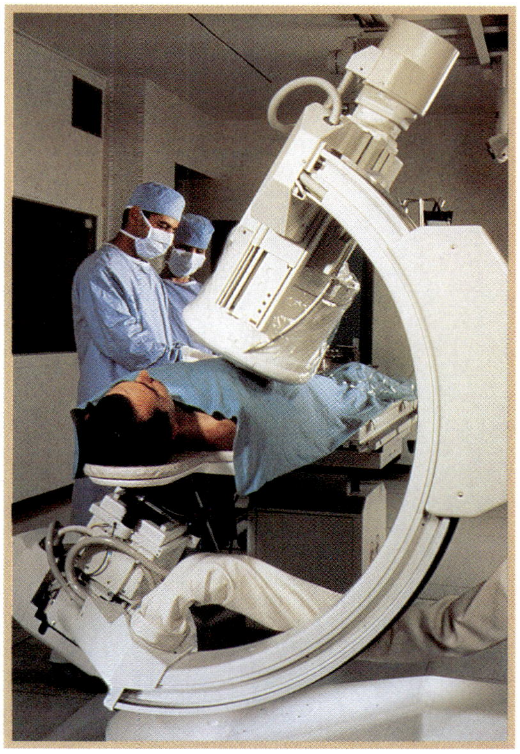

GE Medical Systems, a world leader in diagnostic imaging systems, truly brings good things to life.

While its parent company, General Electric Company, got its start in the medical industry with the advent of X-ray technology 100 years ago, GE Medical Systems today offers many products and services to help hospitals and clinics around the world provide high-quality health care to their patients.

GE Medical Systems provides X-ray, computed tomography, ultrasound, magnetic resonance, positron emission tomography, nuclear medicine systems, and radiation therapy systems to hospitals, clinics, and private health care providers for the diagnosis and treatment of patients. GE equipment is used in a range of medical areas, from pregnancy to musculoskeletal injuries to diseases such as cancer.

The firm provides additional value to the health care industry through a variety of services, including networking medical equipment and information management systems, maintaining biomedical and diagnostic imaging equipment, training medical professionals through its broadcast network, and providing asset-management services.

GE Medical Systems has blazed new trails in the area of service. Its InSite™ remote-diagnostic network enables GE equipment users around the world to get assistance, any time. For example, a user of GE imaging equipment in Brazil can immediately reach an InSite engineer in Paris should a problem or question occur in the middle of the night. The engineer accesses the equipment via a network and makes adjustments on-line or by guiding the operator. More than 11,000 GE imaging systems in 50 nations are on-line with InSite.

It also shares with its customers some of the techniques that have made GE such a productive enterprise; these include process mapping and cross-functional teams. The services are meant to help health care providers enhance productivity.

"We provide solutions to our customers," says John Trani, president and chief executive officer of GE Medical Systems. "This goes well beyond technological breakthroughs and high-quality equipment. It's the talent of our employees and the breadth of GE expertise that provide us and our customers an advantage."

In addition to manufacturing operations in countries including the United States, France, Belgium, Japan, China, Korea, India, Indonesia, and Taiwan, it has sales and service operations throughout the world—from Argentina to Russia, from Iceland to South Africa. Its world headquarters is in Milwaukee, Wisconsin.

Wherever it operates, GE Medical Systems prides itself on employing world-class talent—from its engineering organization to its highly trained field technicians. Through training programs, cross-functional teams, and the sharing of best practices throughout the business and with other GE businesses, GE Medical Systems' 14,000 associates are continually developing and driving the company to better service and performance—around the world.

Right: This state-of-the-art X-ray system designed by GE Medical Systems helps diagnose patients suffering from cardiovascular disease. Physicians use the Advantx system's cardiovascular images to examine a patient's heart and vascular anatomy.

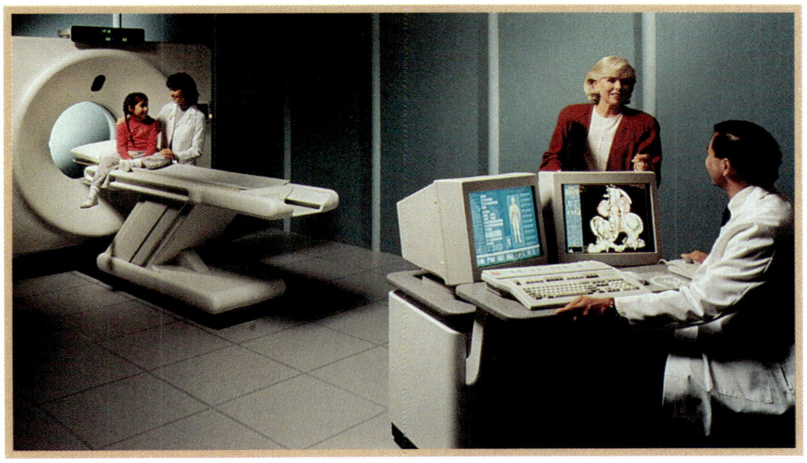

Below: GE Medical Systems designs and manufactures the highly advanced equipment used in performing CAT scans. This CT system is a diagnostic tool that helps doctors diagnose disease, view internal abnormalities, and assess trauma damage. Its highly precise technology enables doctors to view sections of anatomy as thin as 0.1 mm.

Catalyst International, Inc.

When Dennis Templar and Jim Stowers co-founded Catalyst in 1979, they were confident in their vision of a company that would supply the computerized logistic needs of the automated warehouse of the future.

What they didn't foresee is just how successful their venture would become. By developing and marketing warehouse software, first on a custom basis and more recently in standardized packages, Catalyst International, Inc., has grown to become a publicly traded, globally active industry leader with more than 280 employees at its headquarters in Milwaukee and at offices in Dallas, London, and Brazil.

"We're helping many companies around the world discover how aggressive technological management of their distribution operations can give them significant new leverage to improve everything from customer service to employee productivity to the company's bottom line," says Vaemond H. Crane, who joined Catalyst as chairman, president, and chief executive officer in 1992.

Vaemond Crane, chairman, president, and chief executive officer of Catalyst International.

Right: The firm's headquarters is located in Milwaukee.

Indeed, Catalyst is positioned at the cutting edge of a rapidly advancing movement to bring the benefits of automation to the warehouse industry. One after another, major corporations such as Glidden, Chrysler, Shopko, Abbott Laboratories, The Limited, and Pier One have grasped the benefits of automating their distribution operations, maximizing control over that crucial function and squeezing out wasted time and effort.

Catalyst's breathtaking recent growth has been a strong testament to its market-leading position in the warehouse management software business. Sales climbed to nearly $9 million in 1993, jumped to more than $16 million the next year, and reached nearly $21 million in 1995, when Catalyst made an initial public stock offering and became listed on the NASDAQ exchange.

And while employment was just 33 people as recently as four years ago, by 1995 Catalyst's work force had become 250 strong. And in 1996 alone, the company expected to add another 100 employees to that total.

Templar and Stowers founded Catalyst to meet industry's fledgling demand for software programs to run large warehouse operations. For the first several years of its existence, when it was headquartered in Grafton, Catalyst developed unique, customized solutions for each contracting company.

Its experience in designing and implementing custom systems led the business to develop and introduce the first configurable, standard solution for warehouses, in 1989. This product, the Catalyst Warehouse Management System (Catalyst WMS), provides complete control over every aspect of warehouse operations, from receiving and putaway to picking, shipping, and productivity management.

"We were the first in the industry to establish a successful standardized approach," says Crane. "A number of our competitors have tried to follow; the others are still trying to make the cumbersome customized approach work."

Catalyst WMS is a sophisticated software solution, operating in an open-system environment and providing a high degree of flexibility for the customer to utilize an extensive variety of hardware options and peripheral devices.

Enhancing the performance of Catalyst WMS, the company now also offers a Decision Support System (DSS), a management support tool that provides critical feedback on warehouse activities to allow the customer to make business decisions more confidently and accurately. Another offering, Flow-Through Support, helps move merchandise directly from incoming trailers to the shipping docks without storage in the warehouse—one of the rapidly growing trends in the efficiency-minded warehouse industry.

Catalyst also offers 24-hour, worldwide customer support, through a staff of more than 35 people—a larger number of employees devoted to this single function than comprise the total work force at all but four of its competitors.

The company provides support through its Catalyst Implementation Management Plan (CIMPL), which gives customers project management, rapid prototyping, training, and implementation support. A Conference Room Pilot at Catalyst headquarters, using the customer's own data and business strategies, demonstrates exactly how Catalyst WMS will work for the customer.

The company's evolution from a custom to a standard software product that can be configured to each customer's needs has introduced a number of major advantages. For Catalyst's customers, it has turned the dream of automation into a more economical, achievable reality, with faster installation, a proven system, and a quicker return on investment. For Catalyst itself, the "standard" strategy enables spreading costs over a broad sales base and greatly decreasing the software-development cycle.

Management has created what Crane calls an "employee-centered company" that values and implements continuing education and likes to foster ambition. At the same time, Catalyst helps ensure that its employees enjoy coming to work by operating an on-site cafeteria and offering a workout room that is open to staff and their families around the clock.

By fostering a dynamic corporate culture and by generating spectacular growth, Catalyst also has created a strong magnet for continuing to attract the quality software developers, customer service people, managers, and other employees who ensure future success. For entry-level people, Catalyst works closely with the University of Wisconsin campuses in Milwaukee and Madison.

A typical warehouse operation using Catalyst WMS.

"Because we're public, people can see the strength of our financial base and our growth," Crane explains. "And once they experience the environment we've created here, they feel at home. One way we know that is by the number of job candidates who are referred to us by our current employees."

Catalyst foresees an even brighter future for at least two reasons. One is that it continues to service major customers, such as Nestlé and General Motors, as those customers seek to automate operations abroad, in places like the United Kingdom and Brazil. About 30 percent of the company's revenues come from overseas.

"We saw early on the advantages of having global capabilities because our customers were demanding them," says Stowers, who now is Catalyst's senior vice president for corporate development and its chief international marketing officer.

Catalyst also is committed to ongoing research and development that will provide products to serve as the lifeblood of more growth. "The need for what we do is only going to grow," says Templar, now senior vice president of warehouse and systems technology. "And we're ready."

Catalyst®
Warehouse Management Systems

Gossen Corporation

A manufacturer of proprietary plastic and wood trim, accessory, and maintenance-free products for the home, Gossen Corporation has thrived in the modern era in which today's customers expect high-quality materials at affordable prices.

The business was established in 1928 when Martin Gossen invented the first spring-loaded window-sash balance, which eliminated the previous need for a counter-balancing weight for opening and closing a window.

By the 1960s his successor and son, John Gossen, had moved the firm into manufacture of what was then a new product that seemed to present limitless possibilities: polyvinyl chloride, or PVC. Specifically, Gossen developed a process for extrusion through the "free expansion" of PVC, in which the raw material expands when exposed to air.

The family sold Gossen to U.S. Gypsum, a major supplier of construction materials, in 1973. In 1985 U.S. Gypsum in turn sold Gossen to Coastal Mouldings, a Georgia corporation that manufactures wood trim products for construction. Today Gossen is a Wisconsin corporation with its headquarters located at 2030 West Bender Road in Milwaukee.

Since 1985 Gossen has nearly tripled in size and today is the 25th-largest profile extrusion manufacturer in North America, according to *Plastic News* publication, extruding in excess of 20 million pounds of polyvinyl chloride compound annually. Gossen employs about 150 people with manufacturing facilities in Milwaukee, Wisconsin, and Cartersville, Georgia. "Our continued success is attributed to the excitement our employees feel in working with every customer, as each customer is a new adventure. Because we don't have managers and supervisors, these adventures constantly challenge our employees to empower themselves to satisfying our customer needs. The result of this philosophy continues to drive improved technology and processes," says Jef Butterfield, president.

"Gossen manufactures products that compete with the look and some of the properties of wood. These products are sold to the new construction, do-it-yourself, and furniture industries, both nationally and internationally. They improve on previously available wood and vinyl products, because they cost less, they're more durable, and they're maintenance-free," explains Bob Simon, vice president of sales and marketing. Some examples are patented co-extruded weatherstripping, new exterior maintenance-free products, and new paintable/stainable mouldings.

Gossen employees exhibit excitement and show community pride by getting involved in various civic organizations including Al's Run, Appalachia Service Project, the Arts, Cleft Lip and Palate Helpline, Dinosaur Dash (Milwaukee Museum), Habitat For Humanity, Humane Society Walk, Mequon-Thiensville July Fourth Celebration, Milwaukee Aids Project, the Milwaukee Rescue Mission, Optimists Club, Polanki Inc. (Polish Women's Culture Club), and Summerfest, as well as various religious groups.

Gossen's future remains bright because of its unique culture and approach to identifying and satisfying customer needs. This approach keeps all Gossen employees enthusiastically involved in developing skills, new products, and process ideas, giving them a higher degree of job purpose and satisfaction.

Pictured from left to right are: Jef Butterfield, president; Bob Simon, vice president of sales and marketing; Jan Heyse, director of marketing and sales; Fred Ihlenfeld, director of PVC manufacturing; Dick Heller, Industrial Group manager; Erv Steffens, paint room operator; Imogene Burton, box maker; Karen Onan, chief financial officer; Byron Dedmon, skid builder; and Trena Wisniewski, marketing and sales assistant.

Russell T. Gilman Inc.

Russell T. Gilman Inc. wears fastidiousness like a badge. Its customers appreciate that. And so do its peers: The company received the 1995 Wisconsin Manufacturer of the Year "Spirit" Award from Wisconsin Manufacturers & Commerce, the state's largest business association.

The Grafton-based designer and manufacturer of precision components for machine-tool builders and users *must* be perfectionistic. Tight production tolerances are crucial to its success. Organization and cleanliness throughout its manufacturing facilities are a way of doing business.

And that approach has paid off. The company has grown steadily in more than four decades in the industry, and recorded an increase in sales of 60 percent during the past three years. It now has about 115 employees, occupies a nearly 90,000-square-foot headquarters, and, in any given year, services a list of more than 1,600 of its customers throughout North America.

"We're very quality oriented, and very perfectionistic, because those characteristics have gotten the company where it is today," says Paul Haas, president and chief executive officer of the family-owned concern. "We follow Russell T. Gilman, Sr.'s philosophy that the combination of manufacturing with the best equipment, employing the best people, and creating the best work environment produces the optimum outcome."

The company was founded in 1952 by Russell T. Gilman, Sr., who also established three other manufacturing companies in southeastern Wisconsin. Russell T. Gilman Inc. constructed its current plant in 1989, with additions in 1993 and 1994.

Gilman's total customer list exceeds 5,500, and most of them support the high-volume consumer products and automotive industry. Nearly all of the firm's production goes to customers in North America. However, Gilman is increasingly exporting components as well, particularly to international operations that are run by its U.S. customers.

Gilman's product line centers on machine tool slides, spindles, integral spindles, index tables, multi-axis modules, and other special components, predominantly for makers of metal-cutting machine tools.

Spindles built in Gilman's new spindle facility are manufactured under climate-controlled conditions. Workers assemble components in a Class 10,000 "clean room," meaning that the air is pristine enough for sensitive electronic and medical work. The company holds such extremely close tolerances of manufactured parts that it achieves tolerances of less than 1/10,000th of an inch in a measure that is often gauged in millionths of an inch.

Right: Russell T. Gilman Inc.'s 87,750-square-foot production facility is in Grafton, Wisconsin.

"I've gone into hundreds of machine shops, and this one is as precise and clean as they come," says Haas, a former vice president of a large machine tool manufacturer who joined Gilman in 1991, was named president in 1992, and chief executive officer after the death of Gilman Sr. in 1995.

Gilman also has become known for its devotion to its employees' own prosperity. The company's culture is based on strong in-house training, so that workers continually broaden their abilities, and on rotating employees to various production stations so their work includes variety.

And to ensure an ample supply of future employees, Gilman works hand in hand with local educational outlets to develop on-campus and in-house training programs and co-op and apprenticeship opportunities.

Haas says, "Our mission is to be the *premier* manufacturer of precision machine tool components to help our customers build machines for manufacturing."

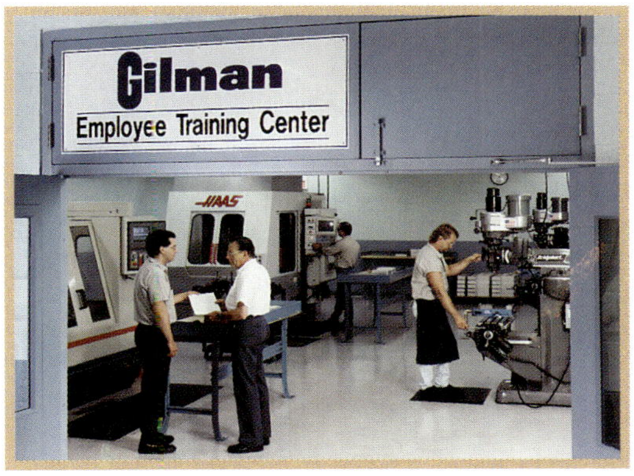

Gilman's award-winning employee training center offers MATC-accredited machinery classes.

Smith & Nephew Rolyan Inc.

The fast-growing employer of more than 300 people, Smith & Nephew Rolyan has become a local business legend. As its parent corporation's worldwide center of excellence for rehabilitative care, Smith & Nephew Rolyan is an international leader in its discipline.

Both are major facets of the personality of the 30-year-old company based in Germantown. And each plays an important role in allowing Smith & Nephew Rolyan to carry out its role as the world's leading provider of rehabilitative care goods in its product categories.

"Our job is to help people remain reasonably independent and maintain their self-image and dignity," says president John Clark, whose father founded the predecessor company. "We help them continue to enjoy their lives even if aging, or a traumatic event, has diminished their former capacities."

The major division of Smith & Nephew Rolyan designs, develops, manufactures, and markets products for the rehabilitation community, distributing them through health care providers, retailers, and a catalog direct to consumers. The merchandise it offers includes splinting materials, prefabricated splints for upper and lower extremities, clinic exercise products, and assistive-living aids for grooming, dressing, eating, and homemaking. They're used by occupational therapists, physical therapists, and consumers to help people who have been limited by acute injury, chronic disability, and the effects of aging.

Aids for Daily Living (ADLs) represent the fastest-growing area. These products enable people to retain as much independence as possible in everyday tasks. With people living longer and disabled people receiving care at home, the demand for ADLs should continue to grow indefinitely.

The company's other four divisions are the CPM division, which offers "continuous passive motion" machines to the rehabilitation community; the casting division, which serves as the company's cast room supplier; the thermoforming plastics division, which provides vacuum-formed parts and products to other divisions as well as custom-made thermoformed parts to outside businesses; and the buoy marine flotation division, which is the U.S. market leader in flotation devices.

When customers call to place an order, they talk to highly trained customer service representatives who help them order exactly the products they need. Commitment to fast delivery means that most U.S. orders are shipped the day they come in.

As part of the British-based company, Smith & Nephew, the Germantown concern also heads Smith & Nephew Rehabilitation and oversees the parent company's worldwide resources devoted to the rehabilitation market, including general management of and guidance of product development at plants in Great Britain and France.

"This company was the birthplace of the rehabilitation business within Smith & Nephew," says Jim McHargue, senior vice president. "All the expertise the corporation has worldwide starts here: We train others in the company in how to start rehabilitation businesses in new markets, and we produce all the education and training materials."

Unparalleled technical supports backs up Smith &

President John N. Clark (seated) and senior vice president Jim McHargue.

Smith & Nephew Rolyan Inc. is headquartered in Germantown, Wisconsin.

Nephew Rolyan's product line. The company employs nearly 50 therapists, and rehabilitation customers rely on the expert technical information they receive from these professionally trained consultants. A library of high-quality catalogs and promotional literature serves as informational aids. In addition, through training and workshop programs, Smith & Nephew Rolyan facilitates the exchange of ideas among therapists around the globe.

The enterprise was founded in 1966 as the Rolyan Manufacturing Co. by John Clark's parents in the family basement in Milwaukee, and they hired part-timers to help get it off the ground. The company started out making electrical assemblies, but soon turned to the manufacture of vacuum-formed plastic components and freshwater buoys.

Soon Rolyan moved out to Menomonee Falls. In 1983 Smith & Nephew acquired it, retaining existing management and employees. Clark and McHargue are proud of the fact that, more than a decade after the acquisition, the company retains a familial culture.

"There is a core of people here today who have been with us since we started," Clark explains. "They have built work teams around themselves and fashioned them in the image of a family company. We want to take good care of the people who work here."

At the same time, Smith & Nephew Rolyan contributes tremendously back to the communities in which it operates. It generously donates to causes ranging from the performing arts in Milwaukee to the Menomonee Falls Ranch, a facility for mildly mentally retarded adults, to the national Children's Arthritis Association.

Smith & Nephew Rolyan built and moved into a sparkling new headquarters in 1993. The company's fast-paced growth in part has been driven by the aging of the North American population and by the inexorable move of providers and of the health care financing system toward more post-acute care and home-based health care.

Smith & Nephew Rolyan's ability to capitalize on these trends will sustain its growth at a pace higher than the industry's average over the next few years, Clark expects. Boosting that effort will be the worldwide graying of the populations of most developed countries, global efforts to contain the rise in health care costs, and results of the company's current new initiatives to establish rehabilitative equipment markets among the fast-growing populations of China and India.

"We're going to see a lot more opportunities around the world, and we need to respond to those," says McHargue. "The challenge for us will be to respond and continue to grow the business while maintaining the family atmosphere of the company. We intend to do both."

Kendall Packaging Corporation

It doesn't have a high-tech image, but perhaps no industry has applied technology more intensively during the past couple of decades than that of food processing and food packaging.

Through it all, Kendall Packaging Corporation has been at the forefront of change—a reliable partner to an industry in continual transition. In fact, being mindful of its leadership role is part of what makes Kendall stand out in the food-packaging industry.

"Packaging is an important part of the continued development of the most efficient, productive, and cost-effective food-distribution system in the world—right here in America," says Eric G. Erickson, president of Kendall for more than 25 years. "And though we're a medium-size company, we remain committed to being a preeminent converter and supplier of flexible packaging materials for as long as we can foresee."

Kendall designs, prints, laminates, and converts flexible materials for a variety of packaging applications. Employing materials such as polypropylene, polyethylene, cellophane, and polyester, it converts these materials to its customers' demanding specifications.

"Our process printing capabilities are absolutely state of the art," explains Erickson, producing photographic reproduction of food vignettes that appear good enough to eat. It's this capability that produces packages that shout "Pick me up" to the shopper, who typically allows only seven seconds to look, in passing, at any item on the store shelf.

Kendall's primary packaging markets are cheese, pasta, snack foods, cookies, and candies. It also supplies nonfood markets such as textile, horticultural, and hardware. The company manufactures packaging at two plants: a three-year-old facility in Jefferson, Wisconsin, that covers 50,000 square feet and employs about 60 people, and a plant in Pittsburg, Kansas, that employs about 50 people. An administrative staff of 15 work at Kendall's headquarters at 633 West Wisconsin Avenue.

The company began operations in Milwaukee in 1948 (first on Erie Street and then at a plant on South Fifth Street) as a contract packager and fabricator of paper products such as nut cups, doilies, placemats, and similar items.

But soon the founder, Lowell Kendall, foresaw a new growth opportunity for his enterprise: printing on polyethylene. The technology developed at about the same time that bag-fabricating equipment was invented for both cellophane and polyethylene, and Kendall's transition from paper to a flexible-packaging converter was complete. Through the early to middle 1970s, poly bags accounted for about 70 percent of the company's business.

In 1970 Erickson acquired Kendall. He had been executive vice president for sales and marketing for industry giant Milprint Inc., a Milwaukee-based packaging division of Philip Morris, Inc. Over the next two and a half decades, Erickson—with the help of an outstanding group of employees—built Kendall from less than one million dollars in annual sales to a very substantial, medium-size business. Further help came in that effort when he was joined by his son, Eric III, about 10 years ago. Young Eric started in sales and marketing, moved to manufacturing and operations, and is currently executive vice president. Another younger family member, Jill, works in customer service and is a key player in Kendall's vaunted customer focus orientation.

Under the new ownership, Kendall's growth closely paralleled the expansion of the flexible-packaging industry as a whole. But several things began to set the company apart from the pack. For one thing, it

A dry bond adhesive laminator at Kendall's Kansas plant.

emerged as a specialist in fulfilling orders that were below the size range wanted by larger packaging manufacturers.

"The small regional companies need someone like us to produce their packaging," Erickson told the *Milwaukee Sentinel* when he bought Kendall. "Also, food companies specializing in private-label production usually order in smaller quantities. At the same time, we can supply the kind of quality that everyone needs."

Now, after a track record of success in making that prediction come true, Erickson explains how Kendall has stayed committed to that way of doing business. "Most large companies still can't adequately cope with smaller orders," he says. "We have a way of dealing with smaller companies, and responsiveness is crucial to that formula."

In fact, Kendall pioneered the development of a completely customer-oriented and -focused organization in the flexible-packaging industry. Its approach included rapid response to customer requests using teams built around specific customers, the capability of satisfying just-in-time inventory needs, and quick turnaround from order to shipment—all while maintaining world-class quality. For example, the rise of mass discounters like Sam's Club in the food business has put more of a premium on quick, responsive shipping because they specialize in rapid turnover of bulk-packaged foods.

The firm's state-of-the-art six-color printing press.

Another differentiating characteristic of Kendall has been its continuous growth and progress in innovative and creative implementation of emerging flexible film technologies, and bringing the advantages of those developments to its customers. Flexible packaging has come to serve a huge variety of purposes for food distribution and retailing, ranging from protection from oxygen, odors, light, and infestation to retaining flavor of the food within the package. Recent developments also have included the packaging of more and more forms of fresh produce with longer shelf life.

The combination of creativity and quality has won Kendall many awards for product innovation and performance and "supplier of the year" honors from several large national food producers and retailers. Most recently, for example, a retailer with more than $22 billion in annual sales and more than 750 suppliers selected Kendall as its top packaging supplier of the year.

"Source reduction" of the amount of material used in a single package also has become a top priority for Kendall, as it has for the entire packaging industry. And actually, it's an increasingly important part of the company's marketing strategy to point out the various ways that flexible packaging generates just a fraction of the waste resulting from cans, glass jars, or paperboard packaging.

As an engine of future growth, Kendall is investing heavily in the digitized technologies that are permitting completely digital communication and transmission of images that are to be printed.

"It's an exciting time to be in this business," Erickson says. "And it's an even more exciting time to be Kendall."

Left: Eric G. Erickson and his son, Eric G. Erickson III.

W.G. Strohwig Tool & Die Inc.

W.G. Strohwig Tool & Die Inc. has combined an entrepreneurial approach with canny business strategy, anticipation of customer needs, a mastery of industry technology, and a progressive management culture to accomplish in less than two decades what many other tool-and-die companies can't achieve in a century of trying.

The Richfield-based company has increased revenues at a double-digit annual pace for most of its history. In 1996 it expected to notch about $23 million in sales of its broad line of plastic-injection molds and die-cast dies, which the company produces for a wide variety of manufacturers across the United States, including such well-known brands as Briggs & Stratton, Kohler, Honda, Suncast, and Fellowes.

Strohwig employs more than 180 people at its 88,000-square-foot facility, which has already been expanded several times. Its total investment in plant, equipment, and offices has been nearly $20 million.

The company produces a broad line of plastic-injection molds and die-cast dies for a wide variety of manufacturers across the United States.

By no means is the firm finished growing, either. Its owners are ambitiously entering new domestic product categories, charting expansion of overseas sales, and aiming to make Strohwig a $35-million company by the turn of the century.

"We think we're a lot different than any other tool-and-die company that we know of," says Larry Glass, vice president in charge of sales and part owner of Strohwig. "And we're going to stay that way."

Wolfgang Strohwig, president and co-owner, founded the business with Glass in 1978 in a Richfield garage that they rented for $130 a month. They took out second mortgages to raise $15,000 to get them started. Using contacts they had established in manufacturing, and through cold calling, they forged ahead.

Early on, the two partners—who are brothers-in-law—determined that the company could grow quickly by adopting a can-do attitude that seemed lacking in their industry. They committed to invest in the equipment needed to make dies of ever-increasing size and complexity, and to help customers solve their problems.

One example: Several years ago Honda of America chose Strohwig over 161 other U.S. tool-and-die makers that it surveyed to design and build its first U.S. casting die for automobile-component manufacture.

"We find ways of getting things done rather than saying, 'no,'" Strohwig says. "We see change as a constant, so we might as well be proactive about it."

The approach helped Strohwig turn first-year sales of $200,000 into sales of $4 million by its 10th anniversary in 1987. In 1988 it was named one of the area's fastest-growing small companies by the Metropolitan Milwaukee Association of Commerce's Council of Small Business Executives; that year sales amounted to $7 million. By 1995 Strohwig's sales surpassed $20 million.

Its customers now include manufacturers of engines, lawn-and-garden equipment, automotive die-cast and plastic-injection parts, hardware, office equipment, plastic cutlery and utensils, shipping and recycling containers, and more.

Left: Strohwig's CAD terminals represent the company's commitment to provide state-of-the-art technological solutions to its customers.

Strohwig's facilities attest both to the company's attention to technology and to the raw capabilities of its manufacturing operation. Engineers and other employees work at dozens of computer-aided design (CAD) terminals scattered throughout the product development department, representing a commitment to provide state-of-the-art technological solutions for customers.

Through a door—and integrally connected to the design network—is the company's spacious manufacturing floor, where busy overhead cranes and hulking, computerized machine tools of many makes and varieties underscore Strohwig's investment in some of the most complex machine tools available.

"Everyone here can program and run computerized numerical controls," Glass says. "We've trained more than 160 of our employees ourselves." The company relies greatly on its location near the Moraine Park Technical Institute in West Bend, which turns out the best tool-and-die makers in the country. Strohwig also has been stepping up its participation in various local and regional programs that promote the labor-strapped industry to high school students and graduates.

Among the devices on the Strohwig factory floor are electric-discharge machines, which use an electrical current to cut metal, and three "gun-drilling" machines that Strohwig built from components; they quickly bore straight, true holes up to 60 inches long through practically any metal.

Also important to Strohwig's success is its responsiveness to customers who, in today's manufacturing environment, require minimum downtime and maximum cooperation from suppliers in meeting their tight production schedules. That approach helps Strohwig achieve its goal of becoming the number one vendor for nearly all of its customers, which is important in ensuring that its relationships remain strong in the event of a downturn in a given market or in the whole economy.

The company's participative culture is another major component of its growth. Strohwig has no traditional foremen, just one plant manager and several leaders of work teams. Each team is dedicated to particular customers, and its individual members manage one another and in a sense contract for services from other parts of the company.

W.G. Strohwig Tool & Die is located at 3285 Industrial Road, Richfield.

In the engineering department, for example, each four-man team includes a practitioner of each discipline, including a mold designer and a CAD modeler. "It's like several small shops within a large shop," Glass says. "And as we add business, we just add teams. It gives our customers a feeling that they're being taken care of."

The most recent new-market initiatives for Strohwig are automotive components and appliance parts. The company now is large enough to pursue such potentially large chunks of business "without worrying about how it might be feast or famine with them " Glass says. Strohwig's policy continues to be not relying on any one customer for more than 15 percent of revenues.

The company already exports about 15 percent of its products to customers in Mexico, Venezuela, Germany, and Japan. W.G. Strohwig plans to boost exports to about 25 percent, with a special effort focusing on markets in Mexico and South America.

Ambrosia Chocolate, A Grace Cocoa Company

Over more than a century in business, Ambrosia Chocolate/Grace Cocoa has carved a place as a genuine local manufacturing institution—wafting the sweet scent of cocoa processing into the Milwaukee air, and employing hundreds of area residents.

Yet for the past three decades, as a unit of Grace Cocoa, a subsidiary of giant W.R. Grace Co., Ambrosia—headquartered at 12500 West Carmen Avenue—also has been an integral part of a global chocolate and cocoa production network that stretches from Georgetown, Ontario, Canada, south to Guayaquil, Ecuador, from Singapore west to Berlin, Germany.

In fact, Grace Cocoa alone processes more than 10 percent of the world's cocoa crop each year, making it one of the world's largest cocoa processors. The company markets its pure chocolate, compound coatings, baking chips, cocoa powder, cocoa butter, and chocolate liquor (baking chocolate) to end customers in the industrial, foodservice, confectionery, and retail private-label markets worldwide.

"We work closely with the other members of the Grace Cocoa network around the world to provide one-stop shopping for our food-processing customers," says Ted Bertram, long-term site manager and vice president of operations for Grace's Chocolate Americas division.

"And for us, it's not just quantity that measures our competence. In fact, it's our commitment to quality and service that has earned us the reputation as one of the world's leading cocoa and chocolate suppliers."

Ambrosia Chocolate/ Grace Cocoa is an integral part of W.R. Grace's global chocolate and cocoa production network.

Ambrosia's role in the chocolate industry began in 1894, when Otto J. Schoenleber founded Ambrosia Chocolate Co. on Fifth Street, in the same small frame structure that he previously had used for manufacturing furniture. He and his partner agreed that the name "Ambrosia" would indicate that their products not only were delicious but of the highest quality.

By 1911 the business was going so well that Ambrosia constructed a five-story plant adjacent to its original building and added more personnel and products. Ambrosia's early line-up included favorite penny goods and solid-chocolate confectionery like angel food and non-pareils.

Soon the variety expanded to include rosettes, pecan rounds, milk chocolate cuts, and candy bars to fill some of the first vending machines. Ambrosia also did a good business in baking chocolate and breakfast cocoa, and began manufacturing such items for leading wholesale grocery chains under private labels. When World War I broke out, Ambrosia supplied carloads of cocoa to the U.S. Navy.

Gretchen B. Schoenleber, who had worked for her father's company since 1913, became its president upon his death in 1927. She guided Ambrosia through the Depression and World War II, actually expanding the company all the while. L. Russell Cook succeeded her as president in 1953 and expanded and modernized the firm's lab facilities as part of his emphasis on greater quality control.

W.R. Grace acquired Ambrosia in 1964, and Cook became head of Grace's chocolate and confectionery division. Under new ownership, Ambrosia continued to expand on and around its Fifth Street site. In 1982 it pursued a new market, private-label baking chips sold through supermarkets, and today Ambrosia is the largest such supplier in the nation.

The parent company formed Grace Cocoa in 1988, a combination of its worldwide cocoa businesses. It has three operating regions: Americas, Europe, and Asia/Pacific. The Americas region is comprised of additional plants in Mansfield, Massachusetts; Georgetown, Ontario, Canada; Guayaquil, Ecuador; Charlotte, North Carolina; and offices in Stamford, Connecticut. Sales are focused under the brands of Ambrosia, DeZaan, and Merckens.

In 1990 Ambrosia reconfirmed its commitment to Milwaukee by beginning construction of a state-of-the-art manufacturing facility on the city's far northwest fringe. Ambrosia executives wanted to keep the company's plant and nearly 400 associated jobs in Milwaukee, and they worked very closely with the mayor's office and other civic interests to do just that.

The solution: The City of Milwaukee annexed the land, part of Waukesha County, which was adjacent to its pre-existing borders.

Ambrosia completed the advanced, $90-million facility in 1992 and in the past few years has been updating manufacturing technology throughout the company to match what it has installed in the Milwaukee plant. Continual training of employees has been another crucial factor in enhancing and maintaining Ambrosia's product quality and responsiveness to customers.

Nowadays, Ambrosia and the rest of Grace Cocoa is gearing for the future by capitalizing on global food trends, such as demand for low-fat products, and by expanding into new areas to serve its growing customer base, such as Latin America. The company is focusing on the needs and tastes of specific markets and developing new products with its customers to grow their businesses.

"The way we're approaching our business today is very much like Otto Schoenleber did when he began Ambrosia: Serve the customers how and where they want to be served," Bertram says. "We'll be doing that from Milwaukee for a long time to come."

Continual training of employees has been a crucial factor in maintaining Ambrosia's exceptional product quality.

Ambrosia Chocolate is headquartered at 12500 West Carmen Avenue, Milwaukee.

Johnson Brass & Machine Foundry Inc.

From its origins in Milwaukee's Third Ward to its current home in Saukville, from exclusive involvement with nonferrous metals to its recent diversification into stainless steel castings, Johnson Brass & Machine Foundry Inc. has evolved steadily in its 91 years in business.

Today Johnson has become one of the world's leading centrifugal foundry and machining facilities, with a list of over 500 customers throughout North America, in industries ranging from automotive to mining, papermaking, marine, and defense. The product repertoire of the company and its 100 employees ranges from castings as small as two inches in diameter to as large as more than six feet, from those weighing only 10 pounds to some that register at six and one-half tons.

Yet several things have remained the same since the company was founded in 1905. First, the company's goal remains to provide castings of the highest possible quality, always meeting or exceeding customer requirements. Second, Johnson strives to improve its products constantly, through seeking out and using the most modern equipment and technology.

Finally, the company has always delivered customer orders in a reliable, expeditious way, eschewing the large order backlogs that many of its competitors rely on—but which often become an unnecessary roadblock to prompt deliveries and service.

"We remind ourselves every day where we came from, and how our customers got us here," says Lance Johnson, president. "And the only way we'll go further is to continue to listen closely to them and respond intelligently to their needs."

Another constant has been the company's family ownership. It has enabled Johnson "to maintain a continuity of purpose and a pride in craftsmanship even while traumatic events have been occurring elsewhere in the foundry industry," says Leland C. Johnson, the recently retired, third-generation president of Johnson. He was succeeded by Lance in 1994 and continues today as a consultant.

Lance Johnson has built upon the company's successful traditions to make it more diverse and more agile in today's more demanding marketplace. For instance, while the firm traditionally had been solely a manufacturer of castings from nonferrous metals such as copper and brass, he has moved it for the first time into the manufacture of stainless-steel castings because many customers were requesting them.

Similarly, Johnson has more often become involved in the complicated work of designing a unified casting to replace a fabricated component. "It's manufacturing for which other companies don't have the engineering capability or don't want to assume the risk that can be involved," he says. "But we can handle it, and there's good growth potential."

Johnson expresses its community spirit through its involvement in causes ranging from the local Boys & Girls Clubs to its pride in winning prizes in Saukville's annual Christmas-decorating contest. Even the company's tidily kept building and grounds reflect an attitude.

"It's basic pride in who we are and what we do," says Lance Johnson, "and it also comes through in our work."

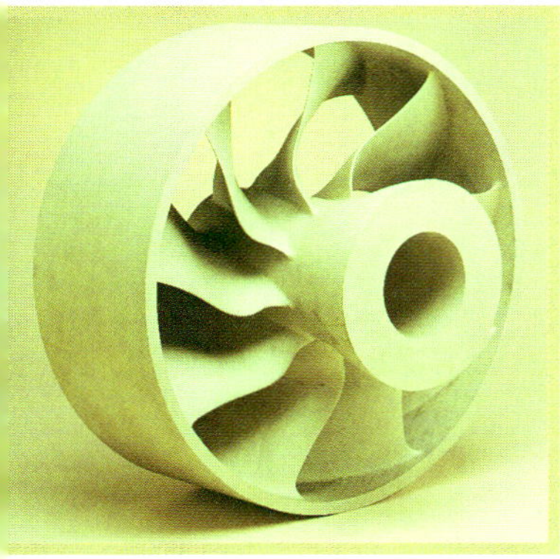

Near net shaping through centrifugal casting forms the outer cover for the marine propulsion system shown above.

Top: A Johnson Brass nickel aluminum bronze marine propeller.

Leland Johnson, chairman (seated), and Lance Johnson, president and chief operating officer.

Milwaukee has become a leading manufacturing center for high-tech components such as medical diagnostic equipment and automation controls. Photo by Steve Allen/The Image Bank

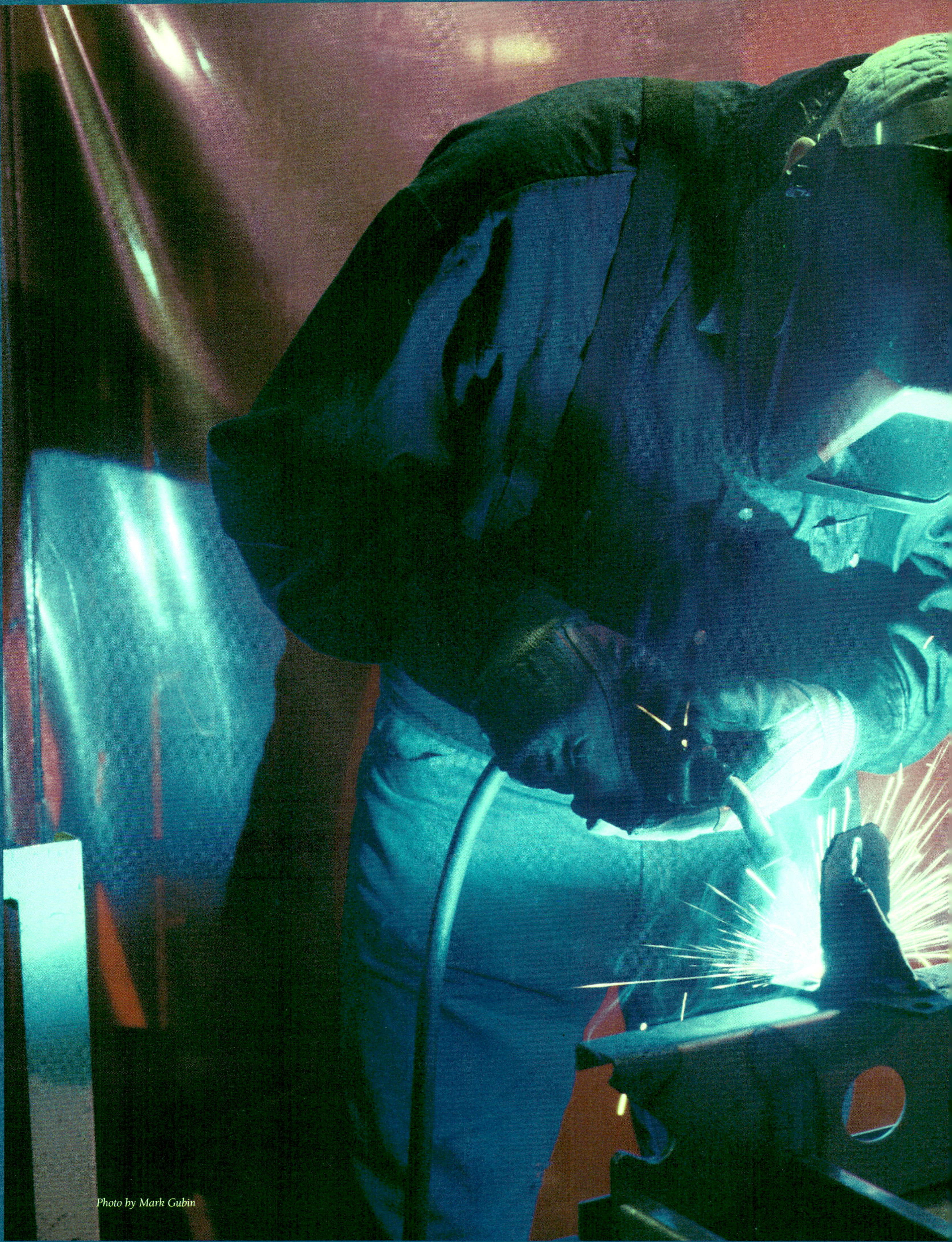

Photo by Mark Gubin

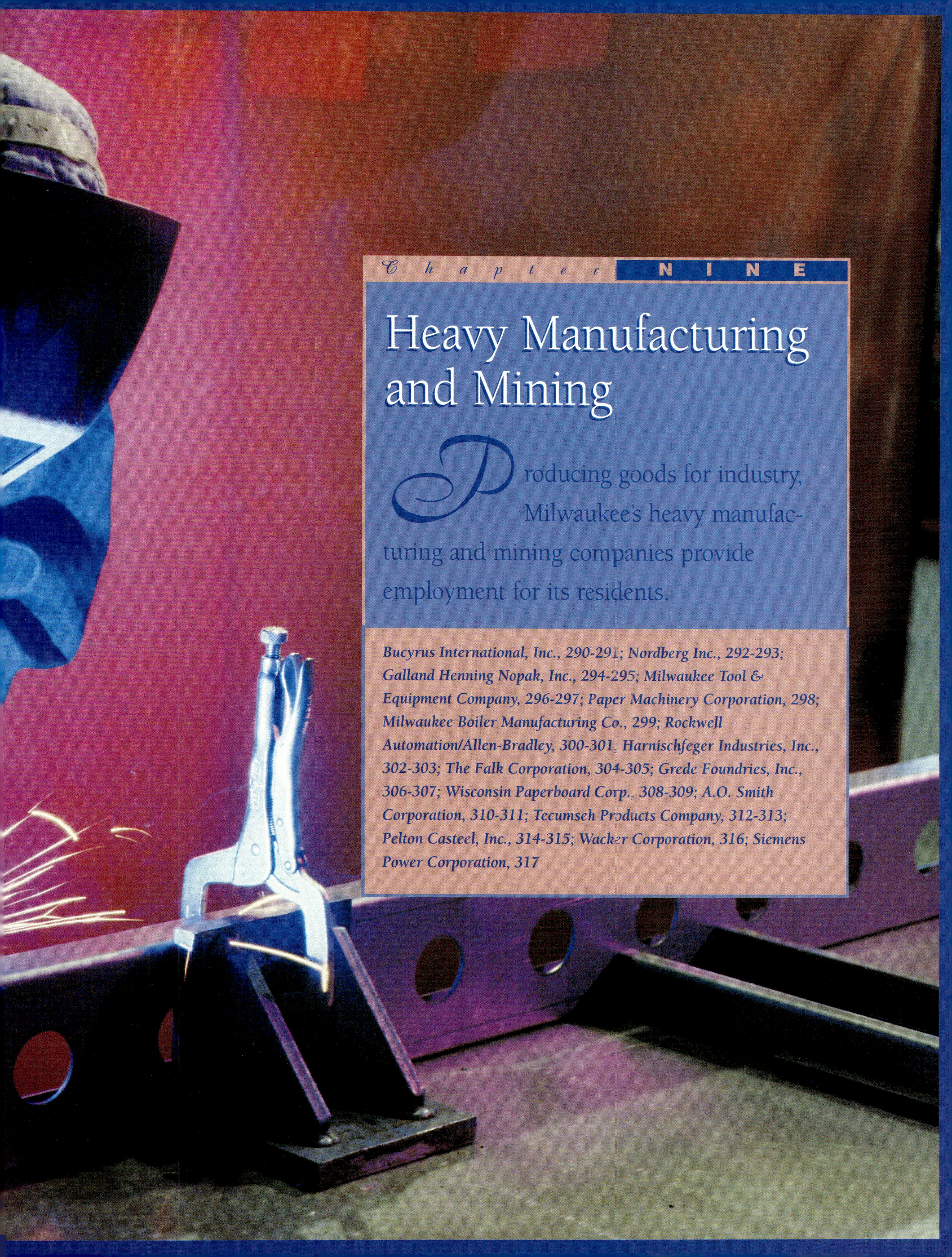

Chapter NINE

Heavy Manufacturing and Mining

Producing goods for industry, Milwaukee's heavy manufacturing and mining companies provide employment for its residents.

Bucyrus International, Inc.

The flagships of Bucyrus International, Inc.'s product line are giant excavating machines for surface mining. The mammoth scoops are difficult to maneuver, but once they acquire direction, they have a major impact on their target.

The 116-year-old company itself is much like its equipment. South Milwaukee-based Bucyrus has undergone a recent period of instability in its finances, ownership, management, and its approach to the mining equipment market, along with a recent name change from Bucyrus-Erie to Bucyrus International, Inc. But now that the company has regained its fiscal foundation, has new leadership, and has refined its marketing direction amid a strengthening sales environment, Bucyrus International has acquired momentum to take it and its 1,200 employees strongly toward the turn of the century.

"We're being drawn away from our comfort level in some respects these days by providing services that entail more risk," says Tim Sullivan, vice president of marketing and sales and a 20-year veteran of the company. "But there's an attitude of determination to go with it, and that gives us confidence that we're building a solid future."

The business was founded in 1880 as Bucyrus Co. in Bucyrus, Ohio, but moved to South Milwaukee in 1893 after the city lured it with the offer of $50,000 and 15 acres of land that included railroad access and two acres of dock area on Lake Michigan. The lake would connect the company to its southern Illinois coal-mining markets via the Chicago River. Its new home also gave Bucyrus a strong supply of engineering and manufacturing talent from the stock of European immigrants who were settling in Milwaukee.

Bucyrus merged with Erie Steam Shovel Co. in 1927 to become Bucyrus-Erie, and over subsequent decades the company built itself into one of the world's leading providers of major lines of mining and construction equipment, including shovels, draglines, and blast-hole drills. While 77 Bucyrus shovels excavated the Panama Canal, the company's primary markets became coal, copper, and iron-ore mining operations around the world, as well as some phosphate, bauxite, and diamond-mining sites.

Helping mining companies excavate mineral riches from the hard earth has required Bucyrus to execute

Bucyrus International is headquartered at 1100 Milwaukee Avenue, South Milwaukee.

President Teddy Roosevelt seated on a 90-ton shovel digging the Panama Canal.

some immense, world-renowned engineering feats. Taking them on in the first place hasn't always been an easy decision, recalls Tom Nelson, a 30-year employee of Bucyrus and now its marketing director.

"The customer is throwing all its dice toward you to do it right, and you're rolling all your dice at your engineering and manufacturing departments," Nelson says. "If it's not right, you both lose a lot of money."

Fortunately for Bucyrus and its customers, the company has always proved up to the task. In the late 1960s, for instance, it built the "Big Muskie dragline," the world's largest mobile land machine, which was constructed to work in the coal fields of Ohio. Its bucket capacity was 220 cubic yards, more than enough to hold the two school buses that were parked in it during the dedication ceremony for the $30-million machine.

Because of the price volatility of the commodities that Bucyrus equipment helps mine, the company rides an economic roller coaster. Sometimes the ride has been downright wild.

In the 1970s, for example, when the Arab oil embargo created a near-hysterical push to accelerate development of America's coal resources, Bucyrus-Erie's backlog grew from $50 million to $650 million in just six months. Emboldened by the surge of new business and motivated by the belief that the coal boom would last well into the twenty-first century, the company bought a foundry in Pittsburgh and a huge manufacturing plant in Idaho to meet production requirements.

But by the early 1980s the U.S. coal market came back down to earth as quickly as it had risen, and while Bucyrus had geared up for what proved to be an elusive era of unprecedented prosperity, it ultimately sold most of the extra facilities purchased in the several years before.

A brief foray was made into the defense-contracting business by purchasing Western Gear Corporation in 1982 and reorganizing into a holding company named Becor Western Inc. Two years later, among other moves, the new corporation sold its construction-equipment line of machines.

In 1987 Becor sold Western Gear and Goldman, Sachs & Co., and Becor managers bought the company in a leveraged buyout. In 1994 the enterprise filed for Chapter 11 bankruptcy protection and emerged as a new public company, once again known as Bucyrus-Erie Company, in December of that year.

Bucyrus-Erie managers and workers spent 1995 reorienting the firm toward its future. They were led through that process by an interim chief executive officer, Frank W. Miller. A new president and CEO, W.R. Hildebrand, was brought on board in March 1996. He and veteran executives will continue to streamline the company, taking steps to empower workers and managers in a decentralization of decision-making. Several million dollars are being invested in physical improvements including a reconfiguration of the bays where mining shovels and drills are manufactured, which is intended to speed production while cutting costs.

Traditionally, the company's customer base did not consider after-sales service as critical since the mines were fairly self sufficient. The consolidation and restructuring of domestic mining companies coupled with increased international sales to remote mine locations has put a new demand on Bucyrus. A different market approach was required.

So Bucyrus International is applying "a whole new mentality and a new skill set" toward its business these days, as Sullivan puts it, in boosting its provision of services. "More and more mining companies around the world want us to provide a full complement of product support," he explains. "Consequently, we must learn to service our customers to their satisfaction, while continuing to introduce technologically complex products."

A recently healthy world economy has helped the recovery. Bucyrus has long been a major exporter—for example, during the 1970s it became the first company in its industry to sell equipment in China—and in the past several years foreign purchases have become a majority of revenues.

Also crucial, says Nelson, has been the fact that Bucyrus has managed to retain most of its historical depth of manufacturing and engineering talent and, with it, the company's reputation for building well-designed, reliable products. "That part of our tradition continues and provides a strong base for the future," he says.

Top: The firm's 49R II in a Utah copper mine.

Below: A 495B in a West Virginia coal mine.

Nordberg Inc.

There have been many sterling days in the proud, 110-year history of Nordberg in Milwaukee, but surely one of the best was July 1, 1988. That's when the company's new ownership gladly hoisted the "Nordberg" sign back atop the headquarters building at 3073 South Chase Avenue, replacing the company's intermittent designation.

The letters of the new Nordberg logo were stylized unlike before. But once again, drivers heading east on Oklahoma Avenue toward Lake Michigan could look up and see the Nordberg name looming above them at the end of the street. And it had been 15 years since the company's dedicated employees had worked under the Nordberg banner.

It was a very happy day for everyone. Some people are second- and third-generation employees of Nordberg, and they probably welcomed it more than anyone.

Indeed, Nordberg has always been one of the backbones of industrial Milwaukee and an employment institution on the city's south side. It currently employs about 320 people in Milwaukee, manufacturing goods mainly for the company's traditional mining, aggregate, and construction markets. The operation produces large-scale rock-crushing equipment and systems, and related equipment such as mine hoists, and provides aftermarket support services. A 90-person Nordberg plant in Clintonville, Wisconsin, produces conveyors and other fabrications.

Top: The company is headquartered at 3073 South Chase Avenue.

Below: The company manufactures goods for the mining, aggregate, and construction markets.

Nordberg's main customers are quarries and other aggregate producers, civil engineering companies, mines and cement plants, and the rapidly growing recycle-crushing industry. Applications for Nordberg equipment and systems include mining uses such as reducing ore into workable pieces, and construction uses such as producing aggregate materials for the underlayer of highways.

Nordberg began in 1886 as the brainchild of a Finnish immigrant engineer named Bruno V. Nordberg, who with five other men opened a manufacturing business on the second floor of a building on Clinton Street. Their first product was a cutoff governor that increased the efficiency of steam engines.

After establishing a market in the steam engine business, the company moved to larger quarters and began building larger machinery, including steam engines, compressors, mine hoists, and steam stamps for crushing the solid copper imbedded in the rock of northern Michigan mines.

By 1900 employment already had grown to more than 300 people, and Nordberg and J.E. Friend—an attorney and early backer who had become president in 1895—moved to larger quarters by purchasing 20 acres at what is still the site of the company's headquarters on Oklahoma Avenue.

Around World War I the firm entered the diesel engine business after having made some early associations with the German inventor of the machine. By

1922 Nordberg had produced 27 engines for Phelps-Dodge alone, the most powerful diesels built in the United States up to that time.

By 1927, continuing its diversification, Nordberg had moved strongly into the manufacture of several devices designed to speed maintenance of the railroads by mechanizing the costly hand labor on track work. In 1929 the firm began to manufacture huge high-pressure gas decompressors.

A diversification move in 1928 shaped the Nordberg of today: It acquired the copyright to the Symons Cone Crusher, which employed an entirely new principle in crushing—one that would revolutionize the crushing practice of the mining and quarrying industries.

Always a pioneer, Nordberg even struck out abroad relatively early in its history. It established a London office in 1928. In 1912 it had become one of the first firms in Wisconsin to participate in a trades apprenticeship program.

During World War II Nordberg served its country by increasing production capacity and employment to produce half of the total U.S. Navy requirements for quintuple torpedo-tube mounts and all the triple torpedo-tube mounts for destroyer escorts, as well as 412 large diesel marine-propulsion engines. The company even manufactured 100 five-cylinder, 5,500-horsepower steam engines under direct emergency orders from the White House.

In the decades after the war, employment in Milwaukee peaked at about 3,000 as Nordberg's growth and diversification assumed even greater proportions. The company developed machinery for processing cement, ores, and industrial minerals including primary gyratory crushers, grinding mills, rotary kilns, and dryers, and acquired a conveyor manufacturer. It also began phasing out the manufacture of engines.

In 1970 Nordberg announced a merger with Rex Chainbelt, in what was one of the largest between two Wisconsin industrial giants. The combined entity changed its name to Rexnord in 1973, and by 1979 it had reached sales of one billion dollars, in part through continued acquisitions.

Recessions and the reshaping of the U.S. industrial economy took their toll on Rexnord, but it was still a vital concern when investor Jeffrey Steiner acquired the company in 1987 with the intention of selling it as separate operations.

Bringing Nordberg full circle in a sense, a large, diversified Finnish manufacturing company, Rauma Corp., acquired the operation in 1988.

Today Nordberg is the mainstay of one of Rauma's four business divisions, the Nordberg Group, which has 20 subsidiaries worldwide and strong sales in markets across the globe, including affiliated offices in Denver, Colorado; Charlotte, South Carolina; Allentown, Pennsylvania/the Caribbean; and Canada. More than one-quarter of the output of Nordberg Inc. in Milwaukee is exported.

Nordberg has been one of the backbones of industrial Milwaukee for more than a century.

Nordberg crushers set the standard for the industry, from workmanship to service to support—everything its customers need. And just like the company always has, Nordberg continues to innovate to serve its customers' needs. Nordberg offers "over 100 years of new technology."

Nordberg remains a pillar of its community as well, providing not only employment but also significant support for the arts, education, and local community causes.

The essence of Nordberg has remained through all the changes—a top-shelf heavy manufacturer that is widely admired by its customers, and appreciated by its employees.

Nordberg's machine shop.

Galland Henning Nopak, Inc.

What is so unusual about Galland Henning Nopak, Inc., which from "day one" has produced large, heavy capital equipment, and will celebrate in October 1996 its 107th birthday? Well, several things:

- It has always been owned and managed by the original founding family.
- It has had only one brief labor stoppage during its 106-plus years.
- It has had no capital debt nor external financing since the late 1930s.
- It has made a profit every year since those "Thirties"—which it generously shares with *all* its employees.
- It has had no significant layoffs during the past 40 years! (Rare indeed for a manufacturer of heavy capital equipment.)

Hermann Nunnemacher, chief executive officer of the company.

The Galland Henning story actually goes back more than a century and a half to 1843, when great-grandfather Jakob Nunnenmacher immigrated to America from his parents' home at Burg, Canton Bern, Switzerland. Previously, for five tedious years, he had hired out as a journeyman to master butchers in cities and towns of Switzerland, Austria, Bavaria, Württemberg, Baden, Alsace, and Burgundy. Because the guild associations prohibited apprentices from establishing their own shops, unless/until the master's exam had been successfully passed, these young, ambitious, pitifully underpaid artisans *walked* from temporary employment by a master in one town to the next—hence the term "journeyman." Little wonder that as soon as meager savings could buy passage, these journeymen escaped to "Amerika—The land of unlimited opportunity." Upon arrival, they were limited only by their skills and willingness to work in the rapid expanse of industry in the heartland (the valleys of the lower Missouri, the Ohio and upper Mississippi Rivers, and the lower Great Lakes). We are indebted to these tens of thousands of craftsmen who rapidly developed our "Inland Empire."

Jakob first landed in New York, where he quickly found work. He did not speak any English but his boyhood knowledge of German and French (Burg being only 2 kilometers from the French border) stood him well. Jakob arrived in primitive Milwaukee in 1844. Soon the flood into Milwaukee of European immigrants called for industrious skilled artisans. Jakob's butchering skills in preparation of meats and sausages met with instant success. He opened a meat stall in the City Market where the City Hall now stands. Later he purchased the land westerly to the Milwaukee River and erected a slaughterhouse on the present site of the Powerhouse Theater.

As his market prospered, Nunnemacher (he had dropped the fourth "n" to aid pronunciation) bought 1,000 acres of land and built cattle barns and a distillery. His country residence still stands near the intersection of Loomis Road and South 27th Street; it's now the Wildenburg Hotel and Tavern. A patron of the arts, he built the Nunnemacher Opera House, managed by his third son Jacob, which burned in 1882 after being sold to Captain Pabst, of the brewery, and was rebuilt as the present-day magnificent Pabst Theater.

Nunnemacher's youngest son, Robert, was established by father Jakob as a grain broker. At that time Milwaukee's harbor facilities made it a major shipping center for midwestern grain to the mills in Pennsylvania, Ohio, and New York that supplied the eastern bread market. In 1887 Robert Nunnemacher and his associates were approached by a German patent broker, desiring to license the American manufacture of malting drums and kiln turning machines to convert barley into malt. The associates began manufacturing Galland Henning machinery in Milwaukee in 1887 and incorporated in 1889 as sales of that ponderous machinery increased. Of the nation's 3,600 breweries—including Schlitz, Pabst, Blatz, and Miller in Milwaukee, Anheuser-Busch in St. Louis, and Jacob Ruppert in New York—many bought their malting equipment from the Galland Henning Pneumatic Malting Drum Manufacturing Co.

Galland Henning Nopak is located at 1025 South 40th Street, West Milwaukee.

Later, Galland Henning also equipped the commercial maltsters such as Zinn, Kurth, Froedtert, and Riebs in Milwaukee; Red Star, Columbia, Rickel, and Bauer Schweitzer elsewhere in the United States; as well as maltsters in Canada, Mexico, and South America. Robert Nunnemacher died in 1912 and was succeeded in the company by his widow, Louise, and their one son, Henry J. Nunnemacher.

In the lore of Galland Henning Nopak, the Prohibition years of 1920 to 1933 are known as the company's "dismal days of desperate diversification." With the breweries and commercial maltsters practically out of business, the company turned to other products: rock crushers, cider presses, pomace dryers, rotary gravel screens, vibrator screens, concrete mixers, structural steel rollers, hydraulic pipe benders, vacuum dryers, and scrap-metal balers. Of these, only the metal balers eventually became successful products. By 1930 the company, $300,000 in debt, almost succumbed to the ravages of the Depression. The repeal of the 18th Amendment in 1933 came none too soon.

Soon Galland Henning Manufacturing Co. was back in full swing, refurbishing long-idled malting machinery and building new machinery for the many plant expansions. But the firm had learned its diversification lessons well. It continued to improve the design of its scrap-metal balers and, after paying off its debt in 1939, never again borrowed working capital! The balers became the company's major post-World War II product, revolutionizing scrap-metal reclamation by "swallowing" junked automobile bodies and compressing them into dense bales necessary for blast furnace smelting.

As the balers grew in size to accommodate even larger cars, their *manually* actuated directional hydraulic valves had to be replaced with pneumatic pilot circuitry. This was the origin of the Nopak air directional control valves and double-acting cylinders that are now the company's mainstay. "Nopak" aptly describes the packless construction of these valves, the heart of which is a metal rotating disc, precision lapped against a complementary metal valve seat, sealed by line pressure. The name was copyrighted, and the company became Galland Henning Nopak, Inc., in the late 1950s.

Family shareholders Heath, mother Heidi, Heidi, and Hermann Nunnemacher. (Harry Nunnemacher, Hermann's son by a previous marriage, was unavailable for the family photo.)

In 1931 Henry Nunnemacher's son, Hermann, began work during school vacations helping to refurbish the long-idled malting machinery. He was named manager of Nopak products in 1942 and succeeded his father as president in 1960. In 1979 Hermann became board chairman and was succeeded as president by general manager Peter Weil, Jr. (now deceased).

Hermann is quick to credit his loyal employees for the success of Galland Henning Nopak. A centennial anniversary celebration, in October 1989, was held for all employees, suppliers, distributors, and customers.

In a history published to commemorate this event, Hermann cited three principles that have guided Galland Henning Nopak, Inc., through the years:

- The customer is always the ultimate boss.
- Never sacrifice principle for profit.
- The owners have a solemn responsibility to their loyal employees whose intelligence, dedication, and hard work have been essential to the company's continued success.

In 1996 Hermann, associated with GHN for 65 years, is still active in guiding its affairs. He is counting on his children to continue the family tradition. Today Milwaukee has only a handful of companies that are well beyond 100 years and still owned and managed by their founding families.

Hermann Nunnemacher (center) discusses the details of the shop's day-to-day operations with Dennis Urbaniak and James Grede.

Milwaukee Tool & Equipment Company

From its founding 119 years ago as a hay tool concern, to its role as a supplier of the U.S. railroad industry, to its more recent emphasis on forging the components of powerful construction and agricultural machinery, Milwaukee Tool & Equipment has been a reliable gauge of the progress of American manufacturing.

Today, operating as they have for generations at 2773 South 29th Street, Milwaukee Tool & Equipment Company and its foundry operation, Milwaukee Malleable & Grey Iron Works, continue to meet the ever-changing needs of their manufacturing customers.

"Our business is all about matching our unique manufacturing capabilities with the right producers of heavy capital goods, demonstrating the flexibility that they require, and then finding ways to further leverage how we have enhanced Milwaukee Tool & Equipment Company in the process," says Richard Gutenkunst, chairman, who leads the company along with his cousin, Tom, president of the third-generation, family-owned organization.

"That's what continues to make our company a growing and changing enterprise that will continue this basic approach into the fourth generation."

Founded in 1877 as Milwaukee Hay Tool Mfg. Co. to produce hay tools and dairy barn equipment, the company started pouring high-quality ferrous castings by 1899. Soon it was supplying castings and other components to growing construction and agricultural-equipment concerns like Caterpillar Tractor, International Harvester, and J.I. Case. By the middle of this century the firm also was supplying the railroad, auto, and truck industries.

In the early 1940s a hardware and workshop-vise line was introduced. The mid-1950s brought on a line of trench braces, roof supports, screw jacks, and supporting products, as the company sold the farm and dairy barn equipment lines. In November 1954 the name was changed to Milwaukee Tool & Equipment Company, reflecting its expanded product lines. A full line of heavy-duty industrial vises and related products was introduced during the early 1970s.

The company began to refine its approach to the marketplace and to its customers during the 1980s. This process has become continual as Milwaukee Tool and Milwaukee Malleable have woven their way through rapidly changing markets.

Beginning in 1979, Milwaukee Tool & Equipment committed to a major modernization program that helped repel foreign competition, combat recession, and meet the increasingly stringent quali-

Co-founders Charles A. Gutenkunst (second from left) and William Gutenkunst (third from left) pose with employees in front of the old factory, circa 1880.

Right: Melting and pouring iron in the firm's foundry division.

The machining area of Milwaukee Tool & Equipment's tool division, where heavy-duty machinist vises are manufactured.

ty demands of its customers. Over the next several years both companies helped reorient workers toward continuous manufacturing improvement. They added metallurgical and quality-control technicians, hired more skilled machine and maintenance workers, and installed spectrographs and other high-technology quality-monitoring tools. As a result, Milwaukee Tool and Milwaukee Malleable won quality certifications from their larger customers.

Both foundry and tool divisions began to emphasize value-added services, such as heat-treating, plating, specialty machining, and assembly of casting components for other manufacturers. This drastically cut production-cycle times for those processes.

The foundry began offering ductile castings in 1990, and more recently has begun making available to its customers "austempered" ductile iron, which undergoes a heat-treating process that gives it extra strength.

Milwaukee Tool & Equipment has aggressively strengthened its sales efforts as well as adding to its marketing force. With a resurgence in the railroad business in the past several years, the company is supplying more components for railroad-tiedown devices, handbrake assemblies, switching gears, and other equipment.

For one particular customer, a division of a New York Stock Exchange company, Milwaukee Tool has expanded offerings to include not only manufacturing of certain castings but also specialty machining, assembling, warehousing, and distribution of some parts with the just-in-time delivery that has become so crucial to American manufacturers. This customer eliminated other suppliers that couldn't match Milwaukee Tool's capabilities and consolidated its business with Milwaukee Tool. "They liked the way we were treating them and servicing their needs and the needs of their customers. When they decided to consolidate, there was no doubt they were coming with us," Dick Gutenkunst explains.

Milwaukee Tool & Equipment and Milwaukee Malleable & Grey Iron Works have emerged as one of just a handful of remaining operations in the entire country that can offer their customers the full range of malleable, ductile, and grey-iron castings and the machining and assembly capabilities to complement the foundry products.

Milwaukee Tool & Equipment Company

Paper Machinery Corporation

Paper Machinery Corporation has a palpable Wisconsin feel: a heavy industrial company founded in Milwaukee, designing and manufacturing machinery that converts one of the state's favorite commodities—paper—into cups, ice cream containers, and other food packaging.

Yet this home-grown company gazes far beyond the state's borders for its business, selling machinery throughout the United States and the world to small start-up companies and major brand names like Dixie and Sweetheart that use it for making cups and containers. Increasingly, Paper Machinery also ships abroad and now is garnering about 40 percent of its overall revenues from exports to 34 countries around the world.

"We pretty much dominate the key markets of Western Europe, North America, and Japan for state-of-the-art, high-speed automatic machinery," says John Baumgartner, executive vice president and member of the second generation of family ownership of Paper Machinery.

In 1990 Paper Machinery moved into a newly constructed, 110,000-square-foot headquarters at 8900 West Bradley Road in the Bradley Woods Industrial Park. Direct employment reached about 140 people in 1995, when Paper Machinery posted record sales and profits.

Baumgartner says that the company's emphases include keeping a tight rein on costs and quality levels by designing and manufacturing its own line of machinery. Steady investment in new technology, such as Computer Networked machining centers, keeps Paper Machinery at the forefront of its field. "We want to lead our industry in innovation and technology, with the design of state-of-the-art equipment," Baumgartner says.

Paper Machinery's push into international markets illustrates the persistence that is one of its hallmarks. The company's founder, Donald Baumgartner, began that effort in the 1970s, selling equipment even into the cloistered Japanese market.

Cracking—and now setting the pace in—the Japanese market may have been one of the firm's most satisfying victories. It demanded accommodation of different specifications and standards with tighter tolerances than are required for the U.S. market.

"Meeting Japanese quality standards helped put us well ahead of our competition everywhere else in the world," Baumgartner explains. "As a result, we now have an expanding export business."

The flexibility learned in dealing with Japanese customers, for example, helped Paper Machinery adapt its strategy successfully in the late 1980s, when it became evident that the company's best technology was too expensive and complicated for developing countries. Paper Machinery reintroduced machines based on 1970s technology—at greatly reduced prices. And now the company dominates the cup-making markets in developing countries like China, Baumgartner says.

"It takes time and energy to get into export markets, and many publicly owned companies don't have the luxury of being able to invest without showing immediate results," says Baumgartner. "Being privately owned has given us the ability to make quick decisions, reinvest our capital, and have the patience that allows us to succeed."

Donald Baumgartner (left) and John Baumgartner of Paper Machinery Corporation. Photo by Pat Goetzinger, Photographic Enterprises, Inc.

Milwaukee Boiler Manufacturing Co.

Your grandfathers and great-grandfathers called Milwaukee Boiler for boilers, smokestacks, foundry ladles, and the like. Today you call the firm for weldments and pressure vessels that evolved from those early manufactures, but were neither contemplated nor even possible then.

On Thursday, May 15, 1890, Milwaukee's daily, *The Sentinel: Milwaukee,* announced "yesterday's incorporation" of Milwaukee Boiler, organized for the purpose of manufacturing steam boilers by Edwin Reynolds, W.W. Allis, James E. Church, and James D. Miller. These individuals were better known through the E.P. Allis Company, the forerunner of Allis Chalmers, which produced steam engines and mining equipment. Not included in a part of the 1901 merger that created Allis Chalmers, Milwaukee Boiler continued instead as an independent manufacturing entity.

Above: Today's technology for precise control enables this hot rolling to extend Milwaukee Boiler's reach into heavier gauges of metals.

Right: Riveting with this elegant equipment, rare but necessary for productivity leadership then, would not be an economic method today.

Ownership of the firm passed along to subsequent generations. In 1929 Charles N. Stevens acquired a majority interest, which was transferred upon his death in 1951 to his widow, June C. Stevens. Along with other stockholders, she sold her interest to Richard W. Stevens in 1961. Stevens, an engineering graduate and professionally registered, serves as president of Milwaukee Boiler today.

As welding replaced riveting, technology and equipment changed accordingly. Milwaukee Boiler now has a complete heavy-gauge plate fabrication facility with one of the largest plate-bending rolls in the Midwest; computer-controlled water-quenched shape cutting of steels, stainless steels, aluminum, and aluminum bronzes up to four inches thick; upgrading craneways from 10 to 100 tons; and capabilities that provide the fabrication of heavy-gauge materials to radiographic examination acceptance criteria. A 5,200-ton press brake capable of forming 10-foot-long cylinders from six-inch plate, presently under construction, will be the largest in North America when completed.

An outgrowth of pressure vessel expertise led to the origination of machinery concepts now adopted and copied worldwide for constructing tunnels in soft ground. Milwaukee Boiler furnished the equipment utilized for the Mt. Baker Ridge tunnel, the world's largest-diameter soft ground opening. With the 1965 acquisition of Farrel Manufacturing for truck tank expertise, its demonstrated ingenuity led AMOCO's Amobar division to choose Milwaukee Boiler to design and manufacture the equipment for its ground-water control membrane concept utilized in the United States, Israel, and Egypt. Recently construction equipment components have been shipped to China's Three Gorges Dam project, the world's largest construction project.

The company's credentials include ASME authorization for the manufacture of both fired and unfired pressure vessels, and representation on various committees of professional societies such as the ASME, AWS, ASTM, and the Wisconsin Pressure Vessel Code Advisory Committee.

Milwaukee Boiler has thrived because of its ability to solve a wide variety of manufacturing problems. The city has provided an abundance of highly skilled workers over the years, and its central location is conveniently accessible to rail, truck, and water shipments.

Milwaukee Boiler has earned a reputation for innovating workable solutions for a wide variety of engineering and manufacturing assignments, proving its ability to make ideas take shape. To meet this need is its reason to exist today—and tomorrow as well.

Rockwell Automation /Allen-Bradley

With its celebrated four-face clock tower dominating the near south-side skyline, the plant on Second Street looks like a well-preserved relic of the days when heavy industry ruled America's economy. But behind the traditional trappings of Rockwell Automation's headquarters beats the heart of a global leader in advanced industrial automation—and the soul of a philanthropic organization that has had an indelible impact on the city of Milwaukee.

"We are proud of the leadership role that Rockwell Automation, and its predecessor company, Allen-Bradley, have played over the past 90 years in supporting the growth of Milwaukee as a major industrial city," says Donald R. Beall, Rockwell chairman and chief executive officer.

Lynde Bradley, along with his brother Harry and financial backer Dr. Stanton Allen, launched Allen-Bradley Company in the early 1900s to market a revolutionary crane controller. As the years unfolded, they introduced a wide range of additional labor-saving devices, all designed to help their customers improve both productivity and product quality. "Their innovations ultimately established Allen-Bradley as the nation's leading producer of top-quality motor controls," emphasizes Don H. Davis, Rockwell president and chief operating officer.

By World War II growth had become the primary constant for Allen-Bradley—a constant that continued to propel the company forward as Lynde Bradley's successors acquired and established new enterprises across the Americas, Asia, and Europe.

In 1985 Allen-Bradley's market leadership position in industrial automation was a key factor in Rockwell International's decision to acquire the firm. Allen-Bradley significantly strengthened Rockwell's commercial business base, which includes automotive components, avionics, and semiconductor systems.

Since then, the company had grown beyond even its founders' dreams. With Rockwell's support, it acquired such major businesses as Switzerland's Sprecher + Schuh and Cleveland's Reliance Electric. To unify their collective efforts, the enterprise was banded under the Rockwell Automation umbrella in 1995, and given the ambitious goal of becoming *the* world leader in industrial automation.

Rockwell Automation is well on its way to achieving that goal. Today the business employs more than 25,000 worldwide, providing 500,000 products to customers in fields from mining to metals, water treatment to pharmaceuticals, food processing to material handling. It boasts 70 manufacturing facilities around the world, as well as nearly 6,000 sales offices, distributors, agents,

Top: Lynde Bradley, co-founder of the Allen-Bradley Company.

Above: Harry Bradley, Lynde's younger brother.

Right: The firm's first office and drafting room, about 1904, located on the second story of a grocery store, at what is now the northeast corner of South First and East Madison streets.

The dual role of the company's Milwaukee facility is reflected in its building signage. The facility houses Rockwell Automation world headquarters and several major business units of Allen-Bradley.

and system integrators in more than 80 nations.

But numbers like these have not changed the character of this uniquely midwestern enterprise. Its headquarters remains in Milwaukee, and its history and presence continue to dominate the city's economic and cultural landscape.

That's due in part, of course, to the number of local employees. As of this writing, Rockwell Automation employs nearly 4,600 engineers, skilled workers, and professional staff members in the Milwaukee area alone—more than 21 percent of its total work force.

In fact, the Bradley brothers' spirit of giving has left an indelible mark on Milwaukee. Their belief in local philanthropy has been felt almost everywhere, from the Milwaukee School of Engineering and Milwaukee Institute of Art and Design to Marquette University and the Medical College of Wisconsin. Their belief in giving something back to their community has had a major impact on agencies from Goodwill Industries to the United Way.

"Their spirit has also had a tremendous effect on the city's civic and cultural life," comments Jodie K. Glore, Rockwell Automation president and chief operating officer. "It was the Bradley heirs who brought Milwaukee such monuments as the Bradley Wing of the Milwaukee Art Center, which transformed the museum into one of the best in the nation."

Lynde and Harry Bradley's legacy lives on for the employees of Rockwell Automation/Allen Bradley, for the citizens of Milwaukee, and for the hundreds of thousands of people around the world whose lives they have touched.

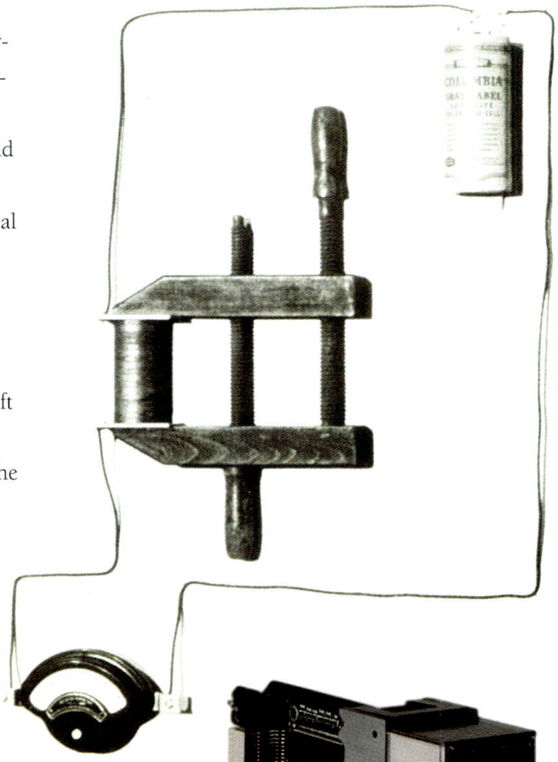

A rheostat that controlled electricity by carbon pile resistance was built in 1893 by Lynde Bradley, then a 15-year-old high school student. It was the basis for the company's first product, a carbon compression crane controller.

The PC-based Open Controller, a cutting-edge product introduced by Rockwell Automation in 1996, combines the reliability of a programmable controller with the flexibility of personal computer technology.

Harnischfeger Industries, Inc.

Since well before the turn of the century Harnischfeger has been a name synonymous with the industrial might of Milwaukee and Wisconsin. From a machine shop origin in 1884, the company today is known as Harnischfeger Industries, with global operations in the mining, paper, and industrial material handling machinery businesses.

Harnischfeger Industries, with its local manufacturing facilities, P&H Mining Equipment, P&H Material Handling, and the Beloit Corporation, employs 3,500 people in southeastern Wisconsin, contributing some $300 million to the state each year through payroll and purchased goods and services. Elsewhere in the United States and throughout the world, 16,250 employees work to manufacture high-quality products under the famous "P&H," "Morris," "Joy," and "Beloit" trade names.

While Harnischfeger's Wisconsin presence has always been substantial, its commitment to Milwaukee was reemphasized in 1995 with the decision to build its new world headquarters on a Lake Michigan frontage site in St. Francis, once home to the vast rolling mills that made Wisconsin a famous industrial city with its wonderfully diverse population.

Following some "tough years" in the early 1980s, the Harnischfeger Industries of the 1990s is a newly focused corporation with a clear vision. According to its chairman and chief executive officer Jeffery T. Grade, "The company's focus and growth is driven by five key characteristics for each of our core businesses: international scope, market leadership, strong aftermarket position, technological leadership in its field, and a positive potential for Economic Value Added (EVA), a way of approaching business that influences everything the company does. EVA involves all Harnischfeger people uniting together to maximize shareholder value."

The Mining Group has become the company's largest business segment, offering unparalleled products and service support for both surface and underground mining applications. Harnischfeger's acquisition of Dobson Park, a U.K. enterprise, in 1995 was its latest move to expand this business.

The group combines its long history in surface mining equipment, represented by P&H Mining Equipment, and its recently acquired underground mining equipment business, Joy Mining Machinery, to create a powerful presence in the industry. Dobson Park is being integrated into JOY to provide the most comprehensive underground mining equipment offered by a single manufacturer, enabling Harnischfeger to become a one-source supplier of integrated systems at the mine face.

P&H Mining Equipment serves customers around the world with a broad line of electric and hydraulic surface-mining shovels, draglines, rotary blasthole drills, and extensive replacement parts and service support. It has the world's largest installed equipment base, with more than 1,600 shovels, and facilities in Australia, Brazil, Canada, Chile, Germany, Great Britain, Mexico, Peru, Singapore, South Africa, and Venezuela, as well as the United States.

JOY, acquired in 1994, has more than 75 years of experience as a global leader in the development, manufacture, distribution, and service of underground mining machinery for the extraction of coal and other bedded materials. JOY manufactures continuous miners, longwall shearers, face conveyors and roof supports, and other equipment. The company has strategically placed its warehouses throughout the world to facilitate 24-hour delivery in nearly all global markets.

Through P&H Mining and JOY, Harnischfeger is strategically positioned with a global network to supply its customers with a full line of productive and reliable mining equipment, backed by around-the-clock service and parts availability. These capabilities are essential to meet the needs of mining companies worldwide, which are seeking greater productivity, reduced costs, and enhanced safety by dealing with just a few suppliers selling integrated equipment systems.

The papermaking machinery division of Harnischfeger Industries is Beloit Corporation, an international concern devoted to the development, manufacture, and servicing of pulp and papermaking

machines and systems.

One of three major paper-machine builders serving the industry worldwide, Beloit is the sole U.S. manufacturer of complete papermaking machinery and systems and is recognized as a technology leader. Beloit has built more than 1,500 paper and board machines for customers' mills in 50 countries, producing over 70 percent of the world's newsprint, writing, and printing-grade paper and about half of its tissue, towels, and napkins.

Service and sales of replacement parts have become as important to Beloit as the development and sales of new paper machines. Since papermaking equipment typically runs 24 hours a day, aftermarket parts and service represent a crucial component of productivity and product quality.

The papermaking machinery business is moving forward to the rhythm of a different and more beneficial demand cycle that favors rebuilding and upgrading of existing equipment over new machinery purchases. As a result of its focused efforts, Beloit is well known for its technological leadership in the industry.

P&H Material Handling is a world leader in the manufacture and servicing of overhead cranes, hoists, portal cranes, and container cranes. Equipment modernization and rebuilding, new and remanufactured parts, maintenance and repair service, and equipment installation are other important offerings of this group.

P&H Material Handling has the largest domestic installed equipment base augmented by a series of acquisitions that has expanded this business internationally. For example, the 1994 acquisition of Morris Mechanical Handling Ltd., headquartered in Great Britain, doubled Harnischfeger's material-handling business and provided a strong market position in the container and dockside crane and hoist markets. Recent acquisitions in Mexico, Canada, the United Kingdom, South Africa, Singapore, and Malaysia also have expanded P&H Material Handling's geographic base and solidified its position as a single-source provider to industry.

As Harnischfeger Industries continues to grow and succeed in the international marketplace, the company looks forward to a continued strong relationship with the Milwaukee community.

Harnischfeger Industries' new world headquarters is being built on a Lake Michigan frontage site in St. Francis.

The Falk Corporation

From traditional workshop to exemplary corporate culture, from domestic preoccupation to global leadership, from acceptable performance to its first steps along a planned explosive growth curve, The Falk Corporation has progressed rapidly in the 1990s.

Such transformations have become the norm at this mainstay of heavy-duty manufacturing in Milwaukee, a history-rich company that was founded in 1892 and became a subsidiary of industrial giant Sundstrand Corp. in 1968—but whose best years seem still ahead.

Headquartered at its imposing manufacturing facility at 3001 West Canal Street in the Menomonee River Valley, Falk manufactures the world's widest variety of mechanical power transmissions, marine drives, coupling and ring gears, and marine products for medium- and heavy-duty applications in industries that include mining, paper and pulp, cement, material handling, marine, and power generation.

About half of the product applications are related to bulk conveying operations. Falk's hundreds of specific products range from small steel castings up to 50 tons, from 50-horsepower drives to 25,000-horsepower marine drives, from small standard gears to 43-foot-diameter ring gears for mining equipment. Yet each is a carefully engineered, precision-manufactured solution to a challenge faced by one of Falk's customers.

"Quality and reliability are basic core values of our company and key contributors to our success so far," says Thomas Misiak, president of Falk, which earned the 1994 Wisconsin Manufacturer of the Year Special Award for High Dedication to Quality.

"Going forward, we see those principles, as well as our complete dedication to pleasing each customer, combining to build a position of global leadership for us."

Herman Wahl Falk founded The Falk Corporation as a machine building and repair business but hit it big in 1893 when he developed a revolutionary process to cast-weld streetcar rails. By 1910 Falk was pioneering the development and manufacture of helical-reduction gears and built such gears for nearly every destroyer commissioned during World War I. The company had an even greater role in supporting the World War II manufacturing effort.

By 1954 Falk had established a sterling reputation shared widely enough that customers heartily endorsed its decision to adopt "A Good Name in Industry" as its legal trademark. In 1968 the business became a subsidiary of Rockford, Illinois-based Sundstrand.

The 1980s hit Falk hard, just as the deep recession affected thousands of American manufacturers. But the company persevered. One byproduct of the difficult times was that Falk management and employees agreed to overhaul their traditional approach in favor of a new corporate culture based on shared decision-

This is the largest horsepower-driven ring gear in the world, and it's big enough to hold 64 of The Falk Corporation's employees who helped to make it. In 1996 the gear began work in a primary ore grinding mill at the Escondida Copper Mine in Chile's Atacama Desert. Custom made of cast steel, it is 43.27 feet in diameter and weighs 190,000 pounds.

In 1995 The Falk Corporation shipped its first marine propulsion gear drive for the U.S. Navy's new "Bob Hope" class of military landing ships, 950-foot-long craft designed to deliver equipment and troops to shore. This drive and a companion will be installed on the USNS Bob Hope, *being built at Avondale Shipyards in New Orleans. The two gear drives on each ship will drive two 22-foot-diameter propellers.*

making as well as accountability—which would, in turn, boost product quality and responsiveness to customers.

Falk encourages employees to achieve their maximum potential, providing continuous enrichment opportunities through work, academic, and social settings. Many employees have advanced from early apprenticeship programs into top leadership roles. The company covers 100 percent of the costs of continued education and offers a wide range of social and recreation opportunities for Falk workers and their families.

Over the past decade Falk has invested more than $120 million into capital improvements, which have yielded state-of-the-art flexible manufacturing facilities utilizing statistical process control and continuous process improvements that have resulted in a Total Quality Environment.

Today Falk's nameplate on power-transmission equipment is recognized worldwide as a symbol of product integrity and as the hallmark of superiority. Falk's process of design, manufacture, sales, and service also has been awarded with certification by Lloyds Register Quality Assurance of an ISO 9001 approval, one of the most demanding of international quality standards.

Falk sales have increased over 40 percent to record levels in 1995. In the past two years alone the company has hired about 400 new employees—most of them at its operations in Milwaukee and Wauwatosa—as its total work force has reached the 1,500-person level.

Falk's evolution into a truly global manufacturer has been another major factor in such growth. It established an international presence early in its history, and by 1955 the company had started its first international subsidiary, in São Paulo, Brazil. A joint venture in Mexico and a license agreement with a Japanese corporation followed within the next several years.

In the late 1980s Falk accelerated its international drive, opening new sales offices in Chile, Belgium, Singapore, the Philippines, and Australia within a four-year period. And since 1994 Falk has opened offices in Shanghai, Beijing, Taiwan, Germany, England, and Indonesia and added two new sites in Australia.

Today a global orientation pervades Falk. More than 30 percent of its sales were outside the United States in 1995, including cement plants in Thailand and Oman, paper and pulp applications in Southeast Asia, and significant mining activity in Chile.

Shipments of new products—such as Falk's new alignment-free drives that were initially put into service in Australia—can now go overseas just as easily as they can be sent to the traditional first user in the United States. And sales, promotional, and technical materials now are written in several languages as a matter of course.

Falk looks ahead to a continued focus on international opportunities, including delivering globally competitive products, achieving world-class customer satisfaction, capitalizing on growth opportunities in emerging markets, and taking advantage of strategic alliances.

Grede Foundries, Inc.

The U.S. casting industry has been dwindling for nearly 20 years, with only about half the foundries still running that were in operation at the end of the 1970s. Of any American foundry that demonstrated the wherewithal to make it through, Grede Foundries, Inc. can lay claim to being the biggest success story.

Now the largest privately held foundry company in the United States, Grede not only plowed through the 1980s and survived the recession of the early 1990s, but also doubled its sales, capacity, and work force in the past five years alone.

With a solid reputation for quality manufacturing and responsiveness to customers, plus the expected

outsourcing of more and more foundry work by auto makers, farm-equipment companies, and other major manufacturers, Grede expects to keep growing robustly well into the next century.

William J. Grede, founder of Grede Foundries, Inc.

Top: The Liberty Foundry, circa 1920.

Right: Burleigh E. Jacobs, chairman, and Bruce E. Jacobs, president.

Loyal Customer Base

To the leaders of the family-owned enterprise, Grede's longevity in some ways has become its own reward. "Our tenure with customers really counts for a lot," says Bruce Jacobs, third-generation president of Grede Foundries since 1989. "In an industry as volatile as ours, there is a need for customers to develop suppliers they know will always be here. That's us."

Adds Burleigh Jacobs, Grede's chairman and Bruce's father: "We really don't lose customers."

Grede's work force of about 4,500 people is employed at 11 foundries in eight states, mostly in the Midwest, and at the company's headquarters at 9898 West Bluemound Road. Grede pours gray iron, ductile iron, and steel to manufacture items such as compressor housings, valves, suspension parts, engine parts, axles, turbochargers, brake calipers, water pumps, and crankshafts.

The firm's markets now include farm, construction, and mechanical power equipment makers as well as large diesel engine makers and hydraulic valve manufacturers. And while Grede's automotive business has grown to about half of its revenues these days, even within that market the company supplies a diverse base of manufacturers, not depending on any one customer for more than 15 percent of sales.

Grede Becomes a Large National Player

Annual revenues have climbed from less than $30 million in 1970 to $100 million in 1980 and $400 million in 1995. In that time Grede has become not only the largest privately held foundry but the second-largest independent foundry in America.

William J. Grede purchased the Liberty Foundry, a gray iron facility in Wauwatosa, in 1920. By 1940 he had purchased a Waukesha gray iron foundry and a Milwaukee steel foundry, merging them together to form Grede Foundries, Inc. World War II represented the first boom era for the company, when demand for castings for tanks, tractors, and engines soared.

Grede continued to grow for the next several decades, expanding geographically into outstate Wisconsin, upper Michigan, and Kansas. The next boom era for the business was the 1970s, when sales doubled. The 1980s brought two recessions, but by the

end of the decade Grede was on the acquisition path again. It added a former White Consolidated foundry in Greenwood, South Carolina, in 1984; two former Eaton Corporation foundries in Vassar, Michigan, and Cynthiana, Kentucky, in 1986; and a former Dana Corporation foundry in New Castle, Indiana, in 1989.

During the 1990s Grede's growth has been aided by the outsourcing to its facilities of foundry work previously performed by the high-cost, captive plants operated by major original equipment manufacturers. Acquisitions have continued, too, including a former J.I. Case foundry in Pryor, Oklahoma, in 1994 and a former ME International foundry in St. Cloud, Minnesota, in 1995.

Training and Generous Benefits Make a Strong Work Force

The Jacobses believe that several factors have been crucial to the company's success. Perhaps most important is the interest Grede has in its work force. An early leader in offering generous benefits to employees, more recently Grede also has provided training programs for its workers, in everything from basic math and language skills to computer and supervisory training.

And when the recession of late 1989 and early 1990 hit, Grede kept everyone on the payroll. In turn, the company's loyalty to workers has paid off in remarkably low turnover and an ability to keep nearly everyone in its highly trained work force. There are several third- and even fourth-generation Grede employees.

Improved manufacturing processes have been another key to Grede's success, ranging from a thoroughgoing approach to reducing the cost of producing specific castings to close attention to production quality. While in 1960 the typical Grede foundry would produce about 100 molds a day, today many Grede plants are operating at rates of 200 to 300 molds an hour.

A Promising Future

The Grede family believes that another key to the firm's steady navigation of some turbulent times in U.S. manufacturing has been that it has remained conservatively financed and privately held.

For example, during the deep recession of 1982, Grede's sales fell off by 50 percent. But because it had little debt exposure, Grede was able to weather that period with its employment basically intact.

Pouring iron at the Liberty Foundry today.

The firm's devotion to private ownership runs deep. It gives Grede the advantage of not having to reveal its competitive strategy or to justify its short-term performance to outside owners. "Bill Grede never intended this company to be public, and the two generations after him don't either," says Burleigh Jacobs.

An ability to focus on upholding long-term principles also has allowed Grede to emphasize very successfully its commitment to the safety of its employees. The company's incidents per 200,000 hours of work are a phenomenally low 3.7, compared with the foundry industry average of more than 29.0.

"Safety is the most important thing that happens at Grede," says Bruce Jacobs. Underscoring that commitment, for example, is the firm's payment of a bonus of up to 8 percent of pay to all workers at plants with excellent safety records.

W. Stewart Davis, a cousin of Bruce Jacobs and a Grede vice president, sums up the company's approach by calling it a "philosophy of doing business that transcends the fact that we're a foundry." Its uniqueness often becomes evident when Grede acquires another operation. "It usually takes them several years to become 'Grede-ized,'" Davis adds.

The Grede approach to manufacturing didn't develop overnight, and its staying power is likely to take the company strongly past the turn of the century.

Wisconsin Paperboard Corp.

Hugging the east bank of the Milwaukee River as it courses through the central city, Wisconsin Paperboard Corp.'s hard-working mill is succeeding where many others in the paper industry have failed: cost-effectively manufacturing a wide array of recovered-fiber paperboards that display the highest standards of quality.

This operation is a vital part of The Newark Group Inc., a New Jersey-based venture that has become the nation's second-largest producer of recycled paperboard. Its many customers in turn convert Newark's products into a wide variety of end uses, ranging from shirt boxes to panels for ready-to-assemble furniture. American consumers' growing demand for recycled products has helped fuel that growth.

At Wisconsin Paperboard, the manufacturing process is both gritty and high-tech, capital-intensive yet dependent upon a dedicated and flexible work force, painstakingly efficient yet variable enough to produce hundreds of different paperboard varieties that emerge from essentially identical raw materials and basic production procedures.

Wisconsin Paperboard utilizes a wide array of recovered fiber.

The company also provides what amounts to a public service by energetically sustaining a market for the increasing amounts and types of recovered fiber that otherwise would have to find space in landfills.

"We strive to be the low-cost producer in the industry, and yet we must create an ever-more-uniform product because that's what our customers are demanding," says Converse Smith, a vice president and regional manager for the Newark Group and general manager of Wisconsin Paperboard.

Smith explains that the new standard in the industry is for converting companies to be "capable of 15,000 impressions an hour, up from only 6,000 not too long ago. That means our product has to have zero variation.

"We excel at something that is pretty basic but not necessarily easy: squeezing maximum value out of a raw material that is widely available to anyone who wants to try to compete with us," he adds. "It would be tough to duplicate our approach and much tougher to match our success with it."

For example, steam produced by its small on-site power house not only provides Wisconsin Paperboard with about 40 percent of its own electricity but also is used another seven times in various in-plant processes before it is spent.

The company's facilities at 1514 East Thomas Avenue began operation as an industry trailblazer. Founded in 1911 as Hummel & Downing Co., the enterprise became one of the first in the nation to produce and create a market for paper cartons as a shipping medium to compete with wooden containers. By 1920 Hummel & Downing helped convince American businesses that paper cartons not only were less expensive than wooden crates and barrels but adequately sturdy as well.

Subsequent owners expanded and reconfigured the facility frequently to keep pace with changes in papermaking technologies and markets. In 1959 the former St. Regis Paper Co. purchased the facility, devoting much of it to converting paperboard into various types of containers in addition to pure manufacturing. But in 1974, plagued in part by poor labor-management rela-

Quality assurance is an outstanding feature of the company.

tions, St. Regis closed and mothballed the plant.

In 1976 the Newark Group took over the facility, just as it was beginning to expand to its current total of 13 mills nationwide. The new owners rehired many of the facility's former workers and restarted one of the facility's two machines immediately; demand became such that Wisconsin Paperboard could put back into commission the other paper mill by 1981. While St. Regis' maximum output at the plant was 150 tons a day, Wisconsin Paperboard has been able to boost its output to about 450 tons a day.

While essentially the same as when the mill began in 1911, the manufacturing process at Wisconsin Paperboard remains a remarkable slice of industry.

The front-end substitution of recovered fibers as the raw material, instead of the traditional virgin pulp, is one of the major benefits. Federally mandated municipal government recycling programs in the Milwaukee area have come to rely on Wisconsin Paperboard as a major market for their scrap newspapers, magazines, cardboard boxes, and other paper materials.

The company also has deployed on-site bailers at 2,000 supermarkets and other stores, and its trucks daily pick up raw materials from those locations. In its pursuit of the lowest-cost recoverable paper fibers, Wisconsin Paperboard goes to every source possible, including corrugated scrap and fiber cake from nearby mills that produce bond papers.

All of that paper, several hundred tons a day, is dumped in the yard outside the plant and then sorted into various grades. Then, according to recipes aimed at producing the desired paperboard type in the end, the various types and amounts of fiber are dumped into vast "hydrapulpers."

Using water and agitation, the huge whirlpools begin to break the materials down into their building-block fibers. Screening processes take out contaminants like metals and plastics, then "refiners" transform the paper fibrils into uniform tiny lengths and give them a combinable texture.

Eight forming vats for each paper mill then slowly form new paper out of the fiber slurry as layer after layer of fibers build up on a synthetic felt. Once the wet paperboard takes form, vacuum, pressure, and heat reduce its water content to the right level. The product is customized by color, thickness, and other variables, and rolled or cut in sheets.

A sophisticated computerized distribution-control system orchestrates the entire enterprise. One of its most outstanding features is that the software has made the process understandable to—and, therefore, controllable by—most production workers.

That's because, in addition to technology, Wisconsin Paperboard's force of 200 employees is key to its success in a highly competitive business. Above-standard wages and benefits, and opportunities to stretch and grow on the job, help make the company employee-friendly.

From gameboards and puzzles to the covers of children's books, from toilet paper cores to tiny jewelry boxes, Wisconsin Paperboard and its employees supply the raw materials that help make paperboard one of the staples of the American economy.

A roll of the finished product is seen at the end of the rewinder.

The firm's fleet of trucks delivers its products to customers across the country.

A.O. Smith Corporation

Throughout its 122-year history, A.O. Smith Corporation has been dedicated to engineering excellence, innovation, and a never-ending quest for improved products. To paraphrase one of the company's early slogans, its history has been a continuing search for "a better way."

In large part because of those principles, A.O. Smith ended 1995 with record revenues of $1.54 billion and record earnings of more than $61 million. That marked the third consecutive year of record-setting financial performance. In addition, the corporation enjoys leadership positions in each of its major markets: automotive structural components, electric motors, residential and commercial water heaters, fiberglass pipe and fittings, and glass-lined storage structures.

A.O. Smith is considered among the leading practitioners of robotic arc welding methods in the world and has earned international recognition for its achievements in robotics.

Now the corporation is applying its time-tested values to its top priority for the 1990s: a renewed emphasis on growth that will help propel A.O. Smith into the twenty-first century.

"We're pleased by what we have accomplished over the long history of this corporation, and even more excited by our prospects for long-term, profitable growth," says Robert J. O'Toole, chairman, president, and chief executive officer of A.O. Smith, which is headquartered in the Park Place office complex in northwest Milwaukee.

"The corporation is in excellent competitive shape. We have the management infrastructure in place, the financial capabilities, and—most important—dedicated, enthusiastic employees."

The enterprise began in 1874 when Charles J. Smith, a 54-year-old machinist, grew dissatisfied with working for someone else and hung out his own shingle on Humboldt Avenue in Milwaukee. Soon he and his sons were specializing in forming metal parts for baby carriages, bicycles, and other products.

The Smith family undertaking soon turned its engineering talents to an ever-wider variety of pursuits, in many cases following customer needs into new applications. Over the decades this commitment to using technology to find a better way to serve its customers paid off in a number of engineering achievements.

One of the first significant breakthroughs by the firm came in 1906 with the first mass-produced automobile frames in North America. A.O. Smith also pioneered the use of automation in the United States—its automated frame assembly plant opened in 1921 and operated continuously for more than 35 years. Other innovations included the development of welding as the preferred method of joining steel, the invention of the first glass-lined water heater in 1939, and the development of some of the earliest industrial applications of fiberglass in the 1950s.

Today the corporation has five operating units. Automotive Products Company, the largest operation, is one of the leading suppliers of structural components to the North American automotive industry. Its products include full-frame assemblies for light trucks and sport utility vehicles, engine cradles for passenger cars and light trucks, trailing axles, and suspension modules.

Water Products Company is North America's leading manufacturer of standard and specialty commercial water heaters and one of the largest makers of residential water heaters. The Electrical Products Company is one of the leading domestic manufacturers of fractional horsepower and hermetic electric motors for applications including heating, ventilating, and air conditioning, as well as pumps, garage door openers, and air compressors.

Smith Fiberglass Products Inc. is a leading supplier of fiberglass pipe and fittings for various markets, including underground piping systems for service stations, downhole tubing and line pipe for the world petroleum production industry, and process piping for chemicals and industrial applications.

A.O. Smith Harvestore Products Inc. introduced the glass-lined Harvestore® structure in 1947, the towering blue "silos" seen on farms throughout America. Today Harvestore Products and Peabody TecTank—which was acquired in December 1995—serve the growing world market for liquid and dry bulk storage. Typical applications include storing water, wastewater, minerals, plastics, foodstuffs, and a wide range of other materials.

During the 1980s A.O. Smith made significant changes in response to rapidly evolving markets and growing global competition. The corporation invested extensively in automation, including robotics, to enhance product quality, improve cycle times, and reduce cost. Employees received in-depth training in such areas as statistical process control, advanced quality planning, and problem solving.

While the corporation remains committed to continuously improving its existing business, it is placing a renewed emphasis on growing new markets, both domestically and globally. The emphasis on growth can be summarized in four initiatives. The first is to capture the global value of today's business. A.O. Smith's exports totaled 12 percent of sales in 1995; the corporation's goal is to double that total by the year 2000. One example of that strategy in action is the three joint ventures established in China during 1995.

O'Toole has challenged A.O. Smith's operations to set "heroic goals" aimed at stimulating new ways of doing business. Heroic goals—doubling or tripling the size of a business—require managers to look for dramatic changes in products or markets served.

The third initiative is to use "out-of-the-box" thinking to look at existing markets from a fresh perspective. Such a view may lead to new products or services for traditional customers or markets.

Finally, the corporation is committed to developing and upgrading the talents and skills of its employees. This company-wide initiative, called "Management Excellence," focuses in particular on building effective, productive business relationships and on enhanced human resource systems.

With its emphasis on engineering and on maximizing the talents of its employees, assisting with educational efforts in metro Milwaukee has become a natural outreach of A.O. Smith. For example, in a partnership with Washington High School, the firm's employees mentor students and provide technical training.

"We know what role education must play in sustaining technology-driven companies like ours, and in fact the whole U.S. economy, in the future," O'Toole says. "And we want to play a big part in helping out."

Automotive Products brings extensive engineering and testing capabilities to new vehicle development programs. Research programs in Milwaukee include work with alternative materials, such as aluminum (above), material joining studies, and the development of new process technologies.

Left: A.O. Smith's Corporate Technology Center in Milwaukee supports the product and process development activities of all the corporation's units. Research in new coating materials and processing represents one of the center's core technologies.

Tecumseh Products Company

Tecumseh Products Company has been synonymous with efficient small-engine power for over 100 years, and for over 50 years of that time a big part of its reputation has been made by a major facility and dedicated employees in metro Milwaukee.

Tecumseh's Engine and Transmission Group worldwide is headquartered in Grafton, where more than 400 people are involved in the group's engine transmission and power systems for a wide variety of lawn and garden equipment and other power equipment.

Tecumseh focuses on innovation, technology, manufacturing efficiencies—and meeting customer needs. That is the heritage of this operation in Grafton, and it's the way Tecumseh Products has stayed successful in very competitive businesses.

Tecumseh was founded by Ray W. Herrick in 1930 as a maker of auto and refrigerator parts and small tools. By 1939 it became a major manufacturer of refrigeration compressors, and in 1947 Tecumseh diversified into compressors for window air conditioners.

The company came to Wisconsin in the 1950s in its drive to broaden its product base. In 1956 Tecumseh acquired the former Lauson Manufacturing Co., a New Holstein-based manufacturer of four-cycle, air-cooled engines for power equipment.

Tecumseh Products Company's Enduro 5.5-horsepower OHV horizontal engine.

The following year Tecumseh acquired Grafton's Power Products Corp. Originally established in 1946 by former executives of the West Bend Engine Co., Power Products initially manufactured engines for chain saws. By the time it caught Tecumseh's eye, Power Products was nationally known as a manufacturer of two-cycle engines and its products were also being used for rotary lawn mower applications.

These acquistions gave Tecumseh an ever-greater variety of products to sell to the swelling suburban market for lawn mowers and power equipment. Diversification continued in 1963, when Tecumseh bought Peerless Gear & Machine Co., a maker of transmissions, transaxles, and right-angle drives for the industry.

The former Lauson, Power Products, and Peerless formed the base for what is now known as Tecumseh's Engine and Transmission Group.

Today, in its Wisconsin plants, Tecumseh produces two-cycle engines from 1.6 to 5 horsepower and four-cycle engine products from 3.5 to 17 horsepower, which are sold under the Tecumseh brand name to major power equipment manufacturers including MTD, Murray, American Yard Products, Snapper, and Gardenway/Bolens.

Additionally, Tecumseh manufactures many of these same products as private-label engines for a number of the industry's best-known brand-name manufacturers, including Toro/Lawnboy, Ariens, and Craftsman. The company's relationship with Sears' Craftsman brand has been continuous since the 1950s.

The company also manufactures a line of "horizontal" engines for products including snowblowers, edgers, tillers, generators, pressure washers, log splitters, and chipper/shredders. The Grafton facility also manufactures components for its engines as well as a line of refrigerator compressors, and it houses the worldwide international parts, service, and distribution operations.

The company's other operations include an aluminum die cast and reclamation facility in Sheboygan

Falls. Engine and Transmission Group plants in Tennessee, Georgia, Indiana, and Italy also are part of the Grafton-based Engine and Transmission Group.

Tecumseh has succeeded in beating back the challenge posed during the 1980s by Japanese manufacturers of competing power equipment by providing continuous improvement in the technology and value of its products.

More recently, another major factor in the outdoor equipment market has emerged: the growing portion of sales that come from the big discount and home improvement chains. While they help sell more lawn mowers and snowblowers, their economic demands have created major financial pressures on Tecumseh and its rivals.

Again, Tecumseh and its workers have responded in part by making their manufacturing even more efficient and quality-conscious. In fact, the Grafton operations as well as all other engine operations have been certified for several years under the ISO 9000 series of international standards for quality.

For the forseeable future, the greatest technology and manufacturing challenge for Tecumseh will be meeting substantially stronger federal emissions standards, which went into effect in California in 1995 and are to sweep the rest of the country in 1996-1997.

"Every engine we build must be different from before in order to comply," states Tecumseh. About 50 percent of the company's research and development time in the first half of the 1990s was spent on this issue alone.

An alternative response by Tecumseh to tightening emissions regulations has been to develop a new line of electric motors for outdoor power equipment. The new mower motor system includes a rechargeable 24-volt battery, the motor itself, a control system, and a recharging system. One charge will be enough to mow an average lawn.

This is a new product line for Tecumseh, and a recognition of the fact that electric motors are zero-emissions products—a category it must be in as a major power components supplier to the industry. The first customer for Tecumseh's new electric-motor system: none other than Sears, its longtime partner.

In addition to being one of Grafton's largest employers, Tecumseh also takes pride in being a major corporate citizen, contributing significantly to a range of civic development efforts in the community.

Above: Tecumseh Engine and Transmission Group Worldwide is headquartered in Grafton, Wisconsin.

Left: The firm's Enduro 13-horsepower four-cycle vertical engine.

Pelton Casteel, Inc.

On the strength of proprietary advanced technology and decisive strategic management, Pelton Casteel, Inc., has transformed itself into an industry leader in the development and manufacture of steel castings for niche markets in transportation and other major industries.

Long one of the engines of Milwaukee's industrial south side, Pelton has redefined its approach to primary markets and invested heavily in new production equipment, work force expansion, and training.

"We have a long heritage of providing steel castings for an impressive list of satisfied customers," says Larry Krueger, chairman of the board and president. "Still, there's never been a more exciting time at our company than right now. We are working with customer engineers on a new breed of lighter, more aggressively designed steel castings that are penetrating rapidly in new applications."

Pelton employs about 210 people at its two plants. The foundry and headquarters are located at 2929 South Chase Avenue, and the finishing plant is located in Oak Creek. The company produces shell and green sand molded steel castings in carbon and low-alloy grades, serving customers in transportation, farm machinery, construction equipment, mining, electrical machinery, and general industrial equipment.

Top right: Frank Sobiecki "coins" a thin-walled steel casting in a 500-ton press to improve dimensional tolerances.

Below: Hal Birkey and Mike Gwyn examine a rapid prototype made from a solid-model steel casting design.

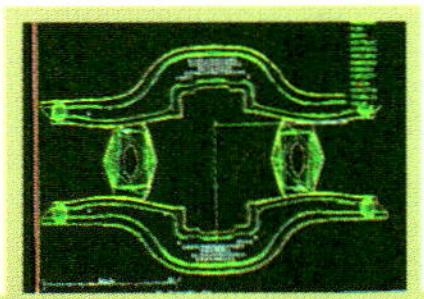

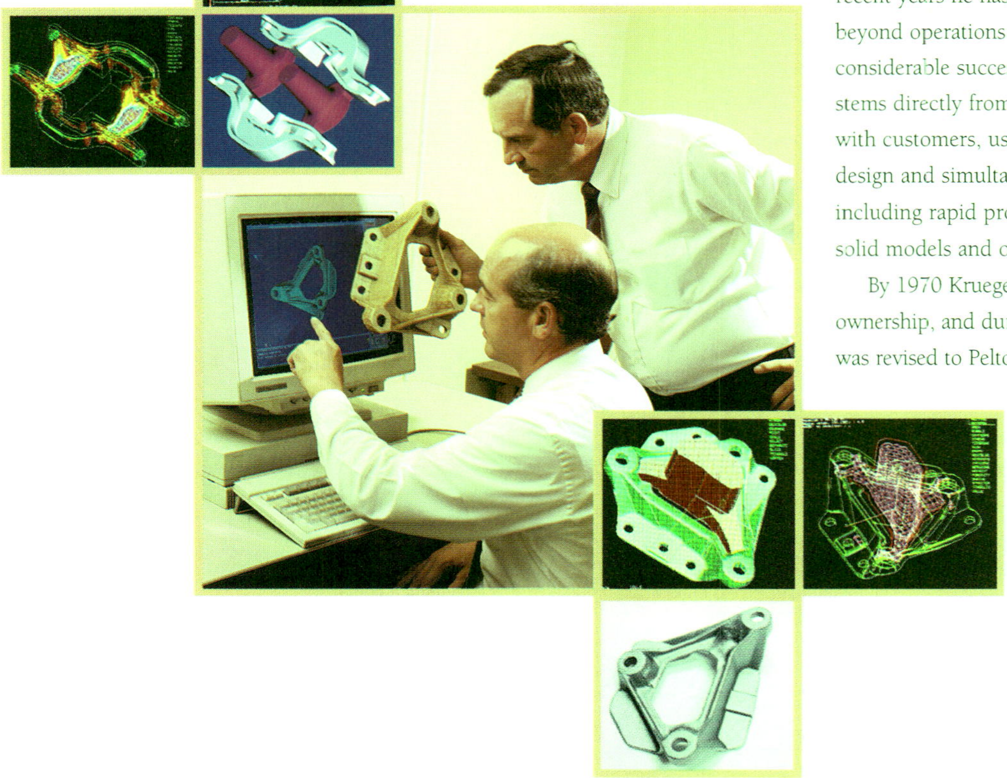

The company began in 1906 when three men incorporated Prime Steel Co., which operated a steel foundry at the site of the current Chase Avenue headquarters. Financial difficulties closed the business, but it reopened under new ownership in 1916 with Ed Pelton as general manager. In 1925 two employees bought the company and renamed it Pelton Steel Castings Company.

World War II brought peak demand for Pelton's castings. It also brought to the company Krueger, who joined as an hourly coreroom laborer in 1942. After serving in the Pacific theater during the war, he obtained bachelor's and master's degrees in mechanical engineering from the University of Wisconsin-Madison. Krueger resumed his Pelton career in 1948.

Krueger had maintained an engineering influence in the company's operating strategies for many years. In recent years he has guided the engineering influence beyond operations and into the marketing effort with considerable success. Much of Pelton's new business stems directly from close engineering relationships with customers, using advanced concepts in casting design and simultaneous engineering techniques, including rapid prototyping of castings designed via solid models and other CAD technologies.

By 1970 Krueger and two partners had acquired ownership, and during the 1970s the company name was revised to Pelton Casteel, Inc.

The following two decades brought the best of times and the worst of times. The mid-1970s were very strong for steel castings producers, with Pelton averaging 900 tons a month. Upon retirement of his partners in 1984, Krueger became sole owner. An unprecedented depression hit the steel foundry industry in 1980, worsened until 1983, and lingered on until the mild recovery of 1986. Steel castings markets had structurally and permanently changed, and survival was the priority for nearly all steel foundries.

In a bold gambit, Krueger leveraged Pelton to buy nearby Crucible Steel Castings Co., whose assets, order backlog, and similar customer base gave Pelton enough mass to survive the decade.

After that searing experience, the company made a crucial course change to lessen its dependence on the still-flat, and always-cyclical, construction equipment market. The course was based on two technologies:

1) Existing and unique Pelton know-how to produce unusually thin-walled steel castings, and 2) Leadership in a University of Wisconsin research consortium that was developing computer tools to predict liquid steel flow and solidification. Beginning in 1986, Pelton focused these two technologies on the transportation market's emerging desire for lighter-weight vehicles that could carry greater payloads. Pelton's shell molding capabilities have complemented these technologies with increased dimensional accuracy and sharper casting cosmetics.

Krueger explains, "The combination of these technologies has meant that we've developed a niche where we're competing with other manufacturing processes that make lightweight structural parts. Our advantages have been found in the toughness and long fatigue life of our lightweight steel castings compared to weld zone problems in stamped steel structures. Compared to aluminum, our steel casting stiffness and unlimited fatigue life capability enable us to excel in strength and

compete pound for pound."

Pelton's first major success was with Paccar, Inc., the parent company of Kenworth and Peterbilt trucks. Recent success has come in the light truck and utility vehicle segments of the automotive market. Not unrelated is new business in farm tractors and implements that are becoming bigger, more powerful, and in need of steel casting toughness without excessive weight.

Sales growth in these types of castings has Pelton straining its existing foundry facility and equipment, which was designed decades ago for the old breed of steel castings. The company has a $2-million equipment modernization and expansion coming on stream in early 1997 that is focused on shell mold production and pouring.

More sophisticated casting applications, simultaneous engineering/rapid prototyping, Total Quality Management, and new production processes have put a premium on the capabilities of Pelton's work force, which has expanded considerably since 1992. The company has been busy training and developing both the old and new "Peltonites."

"These are the people who are going to carry us to the next phase of our growth," Krueger says, "and they're getting prepared."

Gary Guzinski touches up a riser contact surface on a thin-walled casting.

Left: Debra Reschlein and Todd Stolpa report dimensions on a "first article" casting.

Wacker Corporation

One of the Milwaukee area's top 10 foreign-owned companies, Wacker Corporation is a leading force in the worldwide light construction equipment industry. A household name to contractors around the world who utilize hand-held products with names like vibratory rammer, flex-shaft vibrator, and roto hammer, this Menomonee Falls concern is a major international corporate citizen. A company with deep roots and ownership in Germany has become a significant presence in its adopted American home.

Today, in its 310,000-square-foot headquarters here, Wacker designs and manufactures more than 50 different models of construction equipment. The list includes rammers, plates, rollers, pumps, internal concrete vibrators, generators, and concrete trowels.

The firm employs more than 500 people in Menomonee Falls and at eight regional sales offices and two distribution centers strategically located throughout the United States. The international Wacker organization consists of 30 affiliate companies with more than 2,100 employees worldwide. Wacker construction equipment manufactured here is shipped to 80 different countries with 40 percent of the total product slated for export.

The Wacker family business started in 1848 as a blacksmith shop in Dresden, Germany. In 1930 the firm introduced mechanical soil compaction to the world with its first electric-powered rammer, commonly called a jumping jack. This new machine saved contractors a great deal of time and labor on the job site. After it was devastated by World War II, two Wacker brothers, Hermann and Peter, rebuilt the company from scratch, to levels that quickly exceeded its prewar size.

Top: Wacker Corporation's headquarters and manufacturing facility is located in Menomonee Falls.

Right: The vibratory rammer is one of Wacker's top-selling products.

Below: The firm's vibratory trench roller is sold around the world.

Peter Wacker came to America and established Wacker Corporation, originally in suburban Hartford, Wisconsin, in 1957. One major departure in the United States from the company's approach in Germany was to build sales through a network of independent distributors rather than through direct sales to contractors. With the help of key engineering and production people from Germany, the new American enterprise got off to a fast start. In fact, it became a major contributor to the parent company's technological innovations and product development.

Klaus Wacker, a member of the family's fifth generation of ownership, led the firm's U.S. operations for most of the past three decades, until his death in 1993. Today an executive team manages the company affairs—the first time since its founding that anyone other than a Wacker family member has led the business.

Capitalizing on Klaus Wacker's foundation for building a strong independent entity, the new executive team has focused on taking advantage of Wacker's international affiliations in the new era of global competition. At the same time, the company has been raising its profile locally; one example is its contribution toward a new cancer wing at Menomonee Falls Community Memorial Hospital. As a result, the Klaus Wacker Memorial Conference Room was established.

Wacker has been diversifying into new markets in its effort to continue its phenomenal growth. For example, do-it-yourselfers and homeowners can now rent this professional equipment from many different sources. The equipment is also finding unique applications, such as pumps for environmental cleanup and generators and light towers for emergency and movie set power and other locations with intensive, short-term needs for high-powered portable equipment.

And with the international spotlight on Wacker equipment, the future is brighter than ever for continued growth and prosperity.

Siemens Power Corporation

When it comes to Milwaukee and its German roots and traditions, it's only fitting that one of Germany's largest companies would have a presence here that connects it to the city's great industrial past—and assures Milwaukee's business community of technical leadership well into the future.

Siemens Power Corporation and its Fossil Division are located at what formerly was the Allis-Chalmers works in West Allis. Headquartered at 1040 South 70th Street, Siemens manufactures advanced, clean, natural gas-fired combustion turbines for the U.S. and global markets.

At Siemens, cost-effectiveness, fuel conservation, and pollution control have long been the fundamental goals of its power plant engineering. Siemens is a leader in providing high-quality products that generate power cleanly and efficiently.

In 1992 Governor Tommy Thompson and staff arrived at Siemens' manufacturing facility to commemorate the export shipment of the first U.S.-assembled Siemens gas turbine.

Right: Final assembly of a Siemens gas turbine in the firm's Milwaukee manufacturing facility.

The Fossil Division supplies power-generation products for fossil-fueled plants, including gas and steam turbine generators, hydrogenerators and generator motors, and power plant instrumentation and control systems. Today the facility spans some 500,000 square feet with manufacturing and component-assembly areas for nearly every part of the main turbine engine and auxiliary systems.

The plant here also is the largest turbine generator service facility in the country, encompassing more than 250,000 square feet of space. There is equipment to handle any type of repair on the largest components of all turbine manufacturers' products and the personnel to provide complete mechanical and electrical service capabilities.

Siemens AG's decision to situate a manufacturing facility here was no fluke: It was based on solid economic realities and a need to have a center for technical competence for the production of 60-hertz gas turbines.

An existing manufacturing infrastructure was one reason the Milwaukee site was selected. Allis-Chalmers received its first steam turbine generator orders in 1904 and became an industry power. But by 1962 a combination of economic, technological, and competitive forces moved the company to discontinue steam turbine production.

In 1968 Allis-Chalmers and Siemens AG organized a new joint venture, Allis-Chalmers Power Systems Inc., to manufacture Siemens steam turbines in Milwaukee. Several years later that production moved to Florida, and by 1986 Allis-Chalmers had begun liquidating.

But faced with manufacturing-capacity constraints in Berlin, Siemens announced in 1990 that it had reached an agreement with AC Equipment Services—a company salvaged from the remains of Allis-Chalmers and partially owned by Siemens Power Corporation—to manufacture certain components and to assemble gas turbines in Milwaukee.

In October 1992 Siemens purchased the remaining shares of AC Equipment Services and announced a major investment program to upgrade the Milwaukee facility and establish it as the center of 60-hertz gas turbine manufacturing for Siemens worldwide.

Renovating the Allis-Chalmers works to today's standards involved substantial effort—including the expenditure of more than $15 million on machine tools alone—and is ongoing. But for Siemens Power and Milwaukee, the investment has been well worthwhile.

Photo by John Nienhuis/Third Coast Stock Source

Chapter **TEN**

Finance and the Professions

An integral part of the city's infrastructure, the financial and professional community provides a wealth of service, expertise, and insight.

City of Milwaukee Department of City Development

The City of Milwaukee responds to the needs of local businesses by offering a climate of lower taxes and reduced crime, plus specific business-related services. With programs from full-service industrial parks to small business loans, Milwaukee's innovations have been nationally recognized.

Under the leadership of John O. Norquist, Milwaukee's mayor since 1988, the city has assumed its rightful place as a midwestern growth center, positioned for even more impressive economic accomplishments in the years ahead.

"We have spent the past several years laying groundwork that has put Milwaukee back on the national map in terms of economic development," says Michael L. Morgan, commissioner of the Department of City Development. "We'll spend the next several years happily building on that foundation."

Our Happy Home Day Care Center received a small business loan from the Milwaukee Economic Development Corporation. Courtesy, Dave La Haye, Department of City Development

The Department of City Development works directly with businesses to solve problems. The department's full menu of business development efforts includes working with the private sector to encourage creation of land ready for industrial development. The city also operates full-service industrial parks, which have proved popular sites for Milwaukee's many growing manufacturing and service businesses over the past several years. Bradley Woods, on the city's northwest side, has filled in particularly quickly and the newest parks, in the central city, position tenant businesses especially close to available labor.

An economic development corporation operated by the department makes loans to businesses of all sizes and operates some highly innovative programs. For example, by establishing a loan-loss reserve, the department's Capital Access Program provides banks with a way to loan funds to borrowers who are considered too risky for conventional lending. This has been a very popular program, and Mayor Norquist has pledged to expand the number of banks participating in it.

The city's Job Opportunity Bond Fund, through the Redevelopment Authority, has provided another method of financing economic development in Milwaukee. The fund gives local businesses access to national capital markets for long-term, fixed-rate expansion financing.

Mayor Norquist in 1993 created the Milwaukee Jobs Fund, which is administered by the Milwaukee County Private Industry Council. It makes forgivable loans to help central-city companies buy equipment to expand production and employment. The mayor recently approved the infusion of an additional one million dollars of Community Development Block Grant funds for the program.

The North Avenue Commerce Center is another innovation. It was developed with a private partner to provide new light-industrial space in the heart of Milwaukee's central city, where employment is most needed. Tenants began moving in early in 1996. Meanwhile, numerous service and technology startups have made the historic Third Ward area their home.

The department also has worked to ensure that minority contractors have full access to city contracts, despite the recent demise of race- and gender-based contracting programs. And the department has shaped its State of Wisconsin-sponsored development zone programs to bring new and expanded employment opportunities to central-city neighborhoods where unemployment is above average.

The Department of City Development is concerned that existing businesses in the city stay happy where they are. Downtown has been a major focus of corporate retention efforts by the city, which have included working with businesses to sponsor a downtown work force survey, developing partnerships to reduce graffiti and supporting parking enhancements including the ramp in the historic Third Ward, and a creative solution to downtown parking challenges faced by Johnson Controls.

In large part as a result, new skyscrapers have appeared on the Milwaukee skyline in the past few years, and several major firms and institutions have made long-term new commitments to downtown, including Northwestern Mutual Life Co., Firstar Corporation, Associated Bank, Sinai Samaritan Medical Center, and Marquette University.

While each of these strategic initiatives has been taking place, Mayor Norquist and the Common Council have reduced the city's portion of residents' property-tax levy each year for eight straight years. He has held the city's tax levy flat and the increase in municipal spending below the inflation rate. And Milwaukee business taxes—measured as a percentage of all state and local taxes—are far lower than the average for U.S. municipalities.

Equally important to business confidence in the city has been the fact that, since 1990, crime rates in Milwaukee have fallen in virtually every major category. Since 1990 Mayor Norquist has added nearly 300 new officers to the Milwaukee Police Department. Other anti-crime initiatives have included creation and expansion of the Drug Abatement Program, creation of a Robbery Task Force and a Gang Crimes and Intelligence Division, expansion of the Auto Theft Investigation Unit, and installation of a computer-driven dispatching system.

Milwaukee City Hall and downtown Milwaukee. Courtesy, Dave La Haye, Department of City Development

Combined with the city's long-standing advantages and major new projects, these efforts have positioned Milwaukee very competitively for future economic development. That competitive edge also includes the city's accessibility to more than 25 percent of the U.S. population and more than one-third of its manufacturing volume within 600 miles; a strong transportation infrastructure; a positive business-tax climate; an abundant supply of Lake Michigan water for "wet" industries; strong educational and technical institutions; and a well-educated and highly motivated work force. In fact, hardy Milwaukeeans boast an extremely low rate of absenteeism caused by illness and bad weather.

There's also the fact that the city has completed its major required sewage-system improvements, while many U.S. cities of similar age and size haven't addressed their looming and expensive problems.

The construction of the new Wisconsin Center convention complex downtown will add to the department's development arsenal. "As productive as the past several years have been," says Morgan, "we're even more excited about Milwaukee's economic future."

Great Lakes Friction Products is another small business that received assistance from MEDC. Courtesy, Dave La Haye, Department of City Development

Metropolitan Milwaukee Association of Commerce

The Metropolitan Milwaukee Association of Commerce (MMAC), representing 2,500 metro area businesses, is helping to build a future rooted in a strong economy for employers and employees.

With that focus, the MMAC, during its 135 years of operation, has emphasized different issues, befitting the phases of Milwaukee's growth and maturation as an economic force. For decades after the chamber's founding in 1861, it promoted industrialization. After World War II it was refitting the city to a postwar economy. Today initiatives such as streamlining taxes, facilitating exports, encouraging entrepreneurship, and retaining and expanding business in metro Milwaukee have become leading objectives. MMAC works to bring together those elements that define Milwaukee's character and envision possibilities for its future. "We believe our role is to review the community balance sheet, strengthen our assets, and minimize our liabilities," says Timothy R. Sheehy, president of MMAC.

Most recently, the MMAC has become instrumental in two of metro Milwaukee's most significant developments for the future: ensuring construction of the new Miller Park baseball stadium for the Milwaukee Brewers, and reforming the area's education system.

MMAC's members believe that to continue the promising economic environment Milwaukee always has had, the metro area must provide tomorrow's workers with a solid education.

"The success and survival of our members—and the entire economy—depends on hiring qualified, capable people, but it is difficult to find applicants with basic skills and solid work habits to fill their jobs," says James H. Keyes, current chairman of the association, who is chairman and chief executive officer of Johnson Controls Inc.

To address that problem, MMAC leadership has invested heavily in education reform during the past few years. Its campaign has included working with Milwaukee Public Schools administration on mutually agreed-upon initiatives, establishing a lobbying team acting at various levels of government and actively supporting pro-reform school board candidates.

The centerpiece of MMAC's efforts has been joining forces with Parents for School Choice, a lobbying group of 3,500 central-city parents who want to make expansion of school choice a reality for their children. While in 1996 the Supreme Court was holding up implementation of Governor Thompson's school-choice expansion initiative, MMAC's members continue to believe that the most effective way to improve all schools would be to help parents create competition by enabling them to choose the best system for their children's education.

To give students a better understanding of career options, MMAC co-sponsors a World of Business program for MPS teachers, which instructs them about general economics and the specific jobs available in Milwaukee. "Teachers spend time on-site in plants and offices, learning about jobs so they can relay to their students what the world of work outside the classroom is like," Sheehy says.

The association also has invested heavily in higher education, by founding the largest private scholarship program in the region and one of the largest of its kind in the nation. In 1991 MMAC sold its credit bureau operations and used the proceeds to establish a $13-million scholarship trust.

Income from this fund helps MPS graduates from six target high schools who have at least 90 percent attendance and a 2.5 grade point average attend area colleges. Since its inception the program has provided more than $5 million in financial aid, helping more than 800 students attend college. In the spring of 1995, when 63 MMAC scholars were among those receiving degrees from area colleges and technical schools, metro Milwaukee got its first returns from the chamber's investment in higher education.

Of course, MMAC's community leadership extends well beyond education. For example, in the fall of 1995 its newly established Workforce Diversity Institute began offering members help, through a series of seminars, in promoting hiring and retention of minority employees. MMAC consistently advocates public policy that improves the community, finds ways

to better use resources, and creates opportunities for business growth. During the next few years issues at the top of MMAC's legislative agenda will include the transporation budget and welfare reform. MMAC lobbyists have been at the forefront in recent years of a variety of efforts to enhance the business-friendliness of Milwaukee, from initiatives to hold the line on taxes to efforts to promote a reasonable approach to making the city's environment even cleaner.

MMAC's Council of Small Business Executives (COSBE) has become a major community force for members with fewer than 300 employees. COSBE, which celebrated 10 years of dedication to small business in 1996, offers a number of programs designed specifically for smaller companies. The CEO Roundtable program allows small business owners to share ideas and concerns in a unique peer setting. Low-cost seminars are provided on a variety of topics such as sales and marketing, business planning, hiring and firing employees, and cash-flow management. COSBE also sponsors the annual "Future 50" list, which spotlights young, fast-growing small businesses in metro Milwaukee.

The MMAC also staffs and supports the 1,400-member Milwaukee World Trade Association, which offers seminars and information to help members conduct business overseas. MMAC also sponsors Milwaukee: First in Quality, a network of employers working to increase the competitiveness of area companies through continuous improvement.

Many members say they join the aasociation for the chance to meet fellow members and market their goods and services. MMAC provides literally hundreds of opportunities each year for members to network and develop valuable business relationships. Other member benefits include group health, life, and disability insurance; a long-distance telephone discount plan; economic reports and other information; and access to staff experts in various areas.

"Everyone who cares about Milwaukee economically is in this together. It's our job to translate that passion into direction—and impact," says Sheehy.

Above: MMAC is helping to build a future rooted in a strong economy for Milwaukee employers and employees. Photo by Jeff J. Voelz

Left: Providing leadership for MMAC are (from left to right) president Timothy R. Sheehy, immediate past chairman Robert J. O'Toole (chairman, CEO, and president of A.O. Smith Corporation), Council of Small Business Executives chairman John R. Howman (president of Allied Computer Group Companies, Inc.), and current MMAC chairman James H. Keyes (chairman and CEO of Johnson Controls Inc.). Photo by Doug Edmonds

Northwestern Mutual Life Insurance Co.

Northwestern Mutual Life Insurance Co. is the largest company in Wisconsin, with assets of $55 billion and annual revenues exceeding $10 billion. It is also the sixth-largest life insurer in the United States with insurance in force of $380 billion at year-end 1995.

For a firm known as "The Quiet Company," Northwestern Mutual Life certainly receives a great deal of attention. The company is held in high esteem nationwide by competitors, policyowners, the news media, and others.

There are other reasons for cheer as well. The firm is as financially robust as it ever has been. Its diverse investments in other financial services sectors continue to prove prescient. And Northwestern Mutual Life has put its stamp on its adopted hometown, Milwaukee, in ways unequaled by perhaps any of its corporate neighbors.

James D. Ericson, president and chief executive officer.

Top right: Northwestern Mutual Life has consistently ranked among the top 15 companies in the book, The 100 Best Companies to Work for in America.

Yet of all the duties that fall to Jim Ericson, president since 1990 and chief executive officer since 1993, one of the most important is not to allow the company to rest on its considerable laurels.

"I think one of the worst things that can happen to a company sometimes is to win too many awards," says Ericson. "It's important to keep moving forward, to keep improving, and to keep looking for problems that need solving."

As Northwestern looks to the twenty-first century, it is recognized today as perhaps the preeminent U.S. life insurer. For the 13th time in as many years, in 1995 the firm was the "most admired" of the nation's 10 largest insurance companies included in *Fortune* magazine's survey of corporate reputations. In a 1995 survey conducted among 290 life insurance company chiefs, a division of the Towers Perrin consulting firm found that Northwestern was regarded as "best positioned to deal with the issues facing the industry."

The company repeatedly has been included in the book, *The 100 Best Companies to Work for in America.* And in a Gallup survey commissioned by *Sales & Marketing Management* magazine, a notable trade publication, Northwestern Mutual agents were named the nation's best sales force of any kind. Northwestern's exclusive sales force consists of more than 7,300 agents, associated with 101 general agencies and 246 district agencies. Exclusive means just that: They are the sole outlets for Northwestern Mutual products.

Because it is a "mutual" and not a stock company, Northwestern is owned by its 2.5 million policyowners. In 1996 the firm will pay more than $2 billion in dividends to policyowners.

During 1995 the company's total financial surplus increased $753 million, reaching a record level of $4.2 billion. Total assets rose by 14 percent, to $55 billion, and investment earnings were up 19 percent, to $3.7 billion.

Perhaps the company's most impressive number, however, is its "persistency rate" (the measure of policyowners who keep their policies in force from year to year). For all life policies, persistency reached 95.9 during 1995, versus the most recent industry average of 91.1 percent.

"This persistency rate is the lifeblood of our company and a major benefit to policyowners," Ericson

The home office of Northwestern Mutual Life has been located at 720 East Wisconsin Avenue since 1914.

explains. "It is an important factor in keeping costs down and both dividends and surplus up. It gives us a consistent cash flow, so we can invest differently—far more long-term than our competitors." Perhaps most important of all, the extent to which Northwestern policyowners stick with their company is a sound indicator of their underlying confidence and satisfaction with Northwestern Mutual Life.

The strength of relationships with policyowners is increasingly important to the company as it bucks the tide in the life insurance industry. While more and more life insurers are de-emphasizing life policies and stressing diverse moves into mutual funds, annuities, and other financial products, Northwestern sticks with its three tried-and-true product lines: individual life insurance, disability insurance, and a variety of fixed-dollar and variable annuities. Today life insurance amounts to only 35 percent of the entire industry's total premium. By contrast, life policies still account for 81 percent of Northwestern Mutual Life's total premium. Ericson sees an opportunity for Northwestern Mutual Life to grab an increased share of a market in turmoil.

Ericson credits Northwestern Mutual's sales force, in addition to its products, for much of the company's strength. Agents work on a commission basis, so they tend to be highly entrepreneurial. The firm provides extensive training for agents throughout the year. For example, five two-week-long "career schools" for newer agents are conducted at the home office each year.

Northwestern Mutual has managed to tap into opportunities in other financial services sectors by holding major stakes in the Robert W. Baird & Co. securities firm, the MGIC Investment Corp., and Marshall & Ilsley Corp. And while each has proved a worthy investment, it's characteristic of Northwestern Mutual that each of these entities also is headquartered in Milwaukee.

The company has been a pillar of the Milwaukee community since it moved to the city in 1859 from Janesville, Wisconsin. Northwestern Mutual occupies a multi-block complex downtown called Northwestern Mutual Place, with the latest building having been completed in 1990. Ericson and other top executives have been prominent in leadership of many civic ventures ranging from the new Brewers Stadium to the United Way, and Northwestern Mutual Life strongly encourages its 3,300 employees at all levels to become involved in their communities. Its annual meeting of several thousand agents downtown is one of Milwaukee's highlight gatherings.

While Northwestern Mutual Life has gradually increased its attention overseas and looks to possible joint ventures there—about 5 percent of its assets now are invested outside North America—Ericson foresees the company's devotion to Milwaukee only growing. That's while some other major corporations in the city have been dwindling or pulling back on their civic profiles.

"We've always played a major role in this city," says Ericson, "and we'll be doing that for a long time to come."

The "Roots and Wings" run kicks off the annual meeting of Northwestern Mutual agents, which brings thousands of agents, family members, and staff from around the country to downtown Milwaukee every July.

Milliman & Robertson, Inc.

Imagine operating a company at the center of not one but four businesses that are changing as fast as whirlwinds. And your job is to remain calm, keep informed, and give your clients surefooted advice about how to negotiate these storms.

That's a picture of the challenge that faces the more than 100 professionals and staffers at Milliman & Robertson every day. As the largest consulting actuarial operation in Wisconsin, the Milwaukee office of the Seattle-based firm is helping clients around the region cope with the monumental changes that have been reshaping health care, retirement benefit programs, property and casualty insurance, and life insurance.

The Milwaukee office of M&R is among the nationwide firm's five largest outposts, outsizing those in big insurance centers like Chicago. It opened in 1961 as the company's first eastward expansion. Bill Halvorson, a Wisconsin native who had successfully managed the firm's San Francisco office, returned to the Midwest and established an office in downtown Milwaukee. The firm relocated to Brookfield in 1975.

About half the business conducted by the Milwaukee office involves health care, about 25 percent relates to property and casualty work, about 15 percent is pension and benefit work, and the remainder is life insurance. While many actuarial firms specialize, Milliman & Robertson prides itself on being able to help clients in each of these major market segments.

As actuaries, what the firm does for clients in all four areas is use complex mathematics to reduce the uncertainty in a client's financial-security programs. M&R analysts help calculate appropriate insurance premiums, pension-benefit contributions, and related questions. Each project is carefully tailored to meet the client's needs.

"Our firm doesn't take strong positions," says Thomas K. Custis, one of M&R's Milwaukee partners. "Our role is to help people understand the implications of certain programs and provide tools and information—not to establish policy."

Nevertheless, the pressures are great on M&R to correctly diagnose market factors and conduct well-founded analysis for its clients. And these days, that can be the rub: Each of its market segments is changing at an accelerating rate.

During the past three years, for instance, legislative reform efforts, the continuing cost spiral, expanding technology, diversification of provider systems, and other factors have made health care insurance a dizzying blur. "What seem to be simple solutions are not so in this kind of environment," Custis explains.

But in the midst of the turmoil, among the initiatives M&R has undertaken are producing and publishing health care management guidelines and financial projections. It also offers strategic consulting, risk projection, general financial analysis, product development, rate structure analysis, and other services to its clients, which range from health insurers to health maintenance organizations to governmental agencies.

"One area we've always emphasized in health care is research," Custis says. "Solutions in this arena rest in having the best knowledge and the best analytical tools avail-

Milliman & Robertson is the largest consulting actuarial operation in Wisconsin.

able to assess the implications of certain changes."

In the property and casualty area, M&R offers loss and expense reserve calculation, pricing and funding, and merger and acquisition valuations. In addition to insurance companies, this unit also consults with self-funded workers' compensation programs and with insurance pools such as for medical malpractice. This segment is fast-changing as well due to continual changes in legal, regulatory, economic, and social conditions.

Some of the biggest sources of instability have been recent acts of God ranging from the 1989 San Francisco earthquake to 1995's horrific hurricane season, the sum total of which put many insurers in financial trouble. M&R has been helping clients analyze and react to all of these external pressures.

Retirement and related employee benefits are a third quickly changing market in which M&R stands watch. Its consultants advise on plan design, plan services, government and regulatory compliance, benefit projection and forecasting systems, cost monitoring, and other components of the specialty.

And in this area as well, the fast-shifting backdrop has taken aback many M&R clients. The biggest change, Custis says, is that overregulation of pension benefits, and the concomitant higher administration costs, has pushed more and more companies away from offering traditional pensions to their employees and into providing 401Ks—or no pension at all.

"The net effect of all these changes has been devastating and dramatic," Custis says. "It has affected the nation's cumulative savings pattern, and the number of individuals who now will be covered by pensions when they retire has been dwindling."

M&R tries "to help our customers understand the phenomena involved in this" and also designs programs for client companies to communicate to their employees the "implications of today's decisions on future retirements."

By comparison to the other three market segments, life insurance—which underwent convulsive changes in the 1980s—is relatively more stable nowadays. M&R offers advice in strategic planning, product development and analysis, and other areas including mergers and acquisitions and demutualizations (converting a mutual company into a stock company). Advancing computer technology allows this group to tackle increasingly complex asset/liability matching applications.

Given the routine dynamism of the businesses in which it is expert, perhaps it's not surprising that M&R exhibits flexibility with its own strategy, when changing circumstances dictate. For example, its M&R Services data-processing and computer-software affiliate, a point of pride just a few years ago for this data-intensive company, no longer exists. The need for it was eliminated by the decentralization of computing power into PCs on each analyst's desk.

Part of M&R's future vision includes membership in Woodrow Milliman, a global affiliation of 22 actuarial and consulting firms that was formed to offer comprehensive international services to their respective clients. While integration of the firms has been slower than expected, Milliman & Robertson principals still share a strong belief that Woodrow Milliman needs to strengthen and grow. "To be competitive in the markets we serve, we have to be global," Custis says.

The firm prides itself on being able to help clients in its four major market segments—health care, life insurance, property and casualty work, and pension and benefit work.

Top left: M&R professionals help their clients understand the implications of certain programs and provide tools and equipment.

As actuaries, the firm uses complex mathematics to reduce the uncertainty in a client's financial-security programs.

Time Insurance Company

Time Insurance Company is looking ahead to the twenty-first century with the same tradition of innovation, service, financial stability, and integrity that have helped it grow and succeed since 1892. The company has been located in downtown Milwaukee since 1900, and its current headquarters is at 501 West Michigan.

Time is part of Fortis, Inc., a financial services company that is part of Fortis, a worldwide group of companies active in the fields of insurance, banking, and investments.

In 1993 Fortis, Inc., consolidated all U.S. individual and small group health insurance operations under the Milwaukee-based management team; this organization currently uses Fortis Healthcare as its informal operating name. Fortis has offered long-term care coverage through its health care division since 1988. In 1994 Fortis Long Term Care became a separate division. Formed in 1990, Fortis Sales is the primary retail distribution network for the Fortis companies.

All of these business units draw on a history of successfully adapting to changes and challenges in the business environment with customer-focused products and services.

Time Insurance began as the La Crosse Mutual Aid Association in La Crosse, Wisconsin, in 1892. It was the first insurance company in the United States to provide disability income benefits for illness as well as accident. In 1900 the company moved to the state's population and transportation center, Milwaukee.

When Time Insurance celebrated its centennial year in 1992, its headquarters at 501 West Michigan was decorated with a centennial banner. The firm has made its home in downtown Milwaukee since 1900.

In 1910 La Crosse switched from a being a mutual firm, an organization owned by a group of policyholders, to a stockholder-owned company and changed its name to Time Insurance. Over the next several decades the company expanded geographically, outside its Wisconsin territory, as well as in its product diversity, adding individual and group health insurance and life insurance.

In 1978 Time became part of N.V. AMEV, a holding company based in The Netherlands. In 1990 N.V. AMEV joined forces with a Belgian company, A.G. Groupe. These combined operations adopted the name Fortis, from the Latin word for strength, in 1991. In the years since the acquisition, employment and earned premiums of the Fortis business units in Milwaukee increased substantially. In 1991 the Mutual Benefit Life Insurance Company's group health operations, based in Kansas City, Missouri, became part of the Fortis, Inc., operations. The Kansas City health care operations, along with benefit centers in Atlanta and Dallas, and health operations in Woodbury, Minnesota, began reporting to senior management in Milwaukee in 1993.

The 1990s brought quick and dramatic change to the health care marketplace as states enacted significant legislative reforms, managed-care concepts flourished, and new forms of competition emerged. These changes had a particularly strong impact on individual and small group health insurance. However, Time and the Fortis health care operations continue to focus on developing a broad portfolio of products and services to meet the needs of health care customers in this new environment. Time is one of the top providers of individual and small-group health insurance in the country. The company's innovative Short Term product, designed to fill gaps in insurance coverage, is an industry leader. Examples of new products include Student Select, which offers enhanced medical coverage for college students; Medicare Supplement; and Provider Excess insurance. Provider Excess, a new product developed by Fortis Healthcare's operations in

Woodbury, Minnesota, is designed to help doctors, hospitals, and other providers manage their financial risks in new types of managed-care arrangements.

Fortis Long Term Care is committed to filling a different type of customer need, but one that is rapidly increasing in importance. As the U.S. population ages, there is a growing need to finance long-term care services. Fortis Long Term Care is dedicated to working in partnership with the government to fill this void. This division offers high-value products and services to assist individuals and families in preserving their financial and emotional independence. Fortis Long Term Care policyholders can choose from a variety of coverages for at-home care, assisted living, and traditional nursing home care.

Time's sales force was the core of another new operation formed in the 1990s—Fortis Sales. As the primary retail distribution network for the Fortis companies, Fortis Sales delivers the strength and opportunity of Fortis products to its 15,000 independent agencies across the United States. Fortis Sales furnishes these agents with the tools and services they need to provide their clients with Fortis products. Fortis regional sales managers are assigned to territories throughout the country, offering agents one-on-one assistance with their businesses. These Fortis employees not only provide expert knowledge about Fortis products and marketing insight, they also are informed about their territory's local economy and legislative environment. They are the strong link between the independent agent and the home office. In addition, Fortis Sales offers other advantages to its independent agents such as continuing education courses at no cost, marketing and advertising support, incentives and recognition to reward superior achievements, computer software support, and much more.

Fortis Sales regional sales managers are the critical link between the home office in Milwaukee and the agents who sell Fortis insurance products.

Fortis Sales agents approach their business on a high, professional level. Ranging in size from large brokerage operations to one-person businesses, these agents focus on their clients' needs rather than "making the sale." Fortis Sales agents are also committed to ethical business practices and gathering knowledge about their changing industry through long-term continuing education initiatives.

Through all the years of change, Time and Fortis have continued a long tradition of care for the community. The Time Insurance Foundation, established in 1973, provides grants to a variety of health and human service organizations in southeastern Wisconsin, with a focus on epidemic health issues, substance abuse, and economic revitalization. The foundation also matches employee and retiree contributions.

The Fortis business units in Milwaukee also have an active volunteer program, and offer employees paid time to donate to community organizations. The company established an award-winning education partnership with Sholes Middle School in 1989. Employees tutor students at the company offices, and serve as mentors. Company volunteers are active in a wide range of other community activities and support both the United Way and the United Performing Arts Fund.

Left: Fortis Long Term Care offers products and services to assist individuals and families in preserving their financial and emotional independence. Policyholders can choose from a variety of coverages for at-home care, assisted living, and traditional nursing home care.

Marshall & Ilsley Corporation

Marshall & Ilsley Corporation, one of the nation's top-performing bank holding companies, has a long and significant history in Wisconsin.

The company was founded in 1847 by Samuel Marshall, a 27-year-old Pennsylvanian who arrived in Milwaukee in a two-horse stagecoach. With several thousand dollars in inherited funds and many years of experience in the hardware business, he began a bank in a rented half of a shoe repair shop. In 1849 Charles F. Ilsley, an insurance executive, partnered with Marshall, resulting in the now-familiar name Marshall & Ilsley, or "M&I." M&I Marshall & Ilsley Bank is the oldest Wisconsin bank in continuous operation and is the foundation of Marshall & Ilsley Corporation.

Samuel Marshall (top) and Charles F. Ilsley (bottom), founders of Wisconsin's oldest bank in continuous operation.

Over the years M&I has grown steadily into a diversified bank holding company with more than $13 billion in assets and industry-wide regard as one of the best-managed financial institutions in the country. Today the company has 29 affiliate banks serving Wisconsin through more than 225 offices and one bank in Arizona with 12 offices.

M&I's most recent major addition was its 1994 acquisition of Valley Bancorporation. The merger helped M&I expand into attractive new markets in the Fox River Valley and increased its market share in the state. The merger also afforded M&I an entry into supermarket banking.

Besides its banking sector, M&I also serves midwestern and national markets through separate subsidiaries in brokerage, leasing, merchant banking, investment management, and mortgage banking. In addition, the company provides trust and custodial services to corporate, institutional, and individual clients through three trust subsidiaries: Marshall & Ilsley Trust Company in Milwaukee, M&I Marshall & Ilsley Trust Company of Arizona, and Marshall & Ilsley Trust Company of Florida.

Despite the importance of these businesses, M&I is perhaps best known for its data-processing services. What began in the 1960s as an in-house processing center has grown to become one of the most advanced suppliers of financial data processing and software in the country. M&I Data Services not only satisfies M&I's own data-processing needs, it also sells data processing, outsourcing, systems integration, and a range of software products to more than 600 banks throughout North America, Europe, and the Pacific Rim. M&I Data Services remains the only major data-processing provider that is owned by a financial institution.

The scale and expertise of M&I Data Services has permitted Marshall & Ilsley to become a pioneer in the rapidly growing world of electronic banking. In addition to banking by ATM and phone, customers can access information about M&I's products and services through the Internet's World Wide Web.

While the banking industry has changed dramatically since Samuel Marshall first opened his bank nearly a century and a half ago, the success of M&I has been fueled by a constant ingredient: its people. Their leadership and commitment to serving customers and the communities in which they live and work has been the company's hallmark throughout its proud history.

Right: M&I's main office building at 770 North Water Street, Milwaukee.

Fleet Mortgage Group

One of the country's largest mortgage lenders has made Milwaukee the home of one of its major operations centers, and Fleet Mortgage Group plans to grow its presence here for years to come.

Fleet Mortgage Group, whose headquarters is in Columbia, South Carolina, services more than $100 billion in loans for 1.4 million customers nationwide and in 1995 alone, originated mortgages of nearly $16 billion. That makes Fleet the nation's number three mortgage lender, according to *Inside Mortgage Finance*.

In Milwaukee, Fleet employs more than 900 people who operate at a 250,000-square-foot headquarters building at 11200 West Parkland Avenue; the facility also includes a retail loan-origination office and regional sales and servicing center. The location has companywide responsibilities for a range of functions, including asset management, customer service, loan accounting, payment processing, payoff-release, and mortgage-assumption processing.

"Our company has found a good home in Milwaukee," says Richard J. Franas, senior vice president of Fleet, and the site manager here. "The community has the kind of work force we need, it's a central location geographically, and we also have a good-size retail base in the area."

The Milwaukee base of Fleet has deep roots both in the community and the industry. It was an outgrowth of a firm originally called Amortized Mortgages Inc., founded in Milwaukee in 1936 by William Bunge. Amortized reportedly was one of the first firms in the nation to make a business of buying and selling Federal Housing Administration (FHA) mortgages.

In 1957 several small mortgage banking firms merged to form Mortgage Associates Inc. In 1973 Mortgage Associates joined with Industrial National Corp., a bank-holding company headquartered in Providence, Rhode Island; Industrial changed its name to Fleet Financial Group Inc. in 1982. Later that year Mortgage Associates changed its name to Fleet Mortgage Corp.

Thus the 23-year relationship between a Milwaukee-based mortgage banking operation and a Providence-based bank holding company is the foundation of Fleet Mortgage's good relationship with its parent, Fleet Financial Group. The South Carolina arm of Fleet Mortgage grew up on a separate but similar track, and the Milwaukee and Florence operations were fully merged, then their functions reorganized, in 1995.

Franas says that technology continues to transform the mortgage industry. For example, it will soon slash the wait for processing a mortgage application because Fleet loan-origination officers will be able to visit a customer, enter information on his laptop computer on-site, and then immediately transmit it from that remote location via modem to an 800 number at the company.

But while the sophistication of a computerized information network means that Fleet could be located just about anywhere geographically, the company likes having a home in Milwaukee. Fleet supports a number of local causes with major contributions, including the United Way, Junior Achievement, and even the Serengeti Circle at the Milwaukee County Zoo.

"We also encourage our employees to participate in the community in any way possible," he says. "It's just the way we do business."

Fleet Mortgage Group employs more than 900 people at its 250,000-square-foot facility at 11200 West Parkland Avenue in Milwaukee.

Firstar Corporation

The financial services sector of the American economy experienced a profound change in the late twentieth century. New technology transformed the industry, much as it did agriculture a century ago. New competition from nonbank rivals raised standards for efficiency and quality, much as overseas challengers had forced improvement in American manufacturers.

Firstar Corporation's response to these fundamental changes was to meet them confidently and aggressively, reinforcing its historical role as one of the strongest financial services providers in the Upper Midwest. In so doing, it began forging an identity as one of the most innovative and competitive banking institutions in the nation.

"The banking industry has evolved dramatically in recent years, to the point where even the word 'bank' has become somewhat outdated," says Roger L. Fitzsimonds, chairman of Firstar. "A more accurate description of Firstar today is 'financial service provider.' To remain competitive, we must deliver a wide range of financial services when, where, and how our customers desire them."

Firstar already has moved a great distance toward that goal. While bank after bank has been acquired across the United States over the past decade or so, Firstar has grown bigger and stronger, reaching nearly $20 billion in assets at the end of 1995—even as its relatively conservative approach toward lending has helped keep it exceptionally sound.

Nowadays, from its headquarters in the Firstar Center, Wisconsin's tallest building, Firstar serves its primary market, the Upper Midwest, through 240 Firstar banking offices and 1,100 correspondent financial institutions. Its customer base comprises more than 1.2 million businesses, institutions, families, and individuals.

The scope and availability of its products and services are impressive and growing. For example, through its Mastercard and VISA credit cards sold under the Elan brand, Firstar has become the 40th-largest credit-card issuer in the country. Its cash-management services process more than $7 billion each day. Its check-collection operations, among the largest in the Midwest, clear three million items each day. And its nationally respected investment management business has more than $18 billion in assets under management.

It was to satisfy a broad, if somewhat more modest, range of daily financial needs that a group of businessmen pooled their resources in 1853 to establish Farmers & Millers Bank, as Firstar was known then. The new bank grew along with Milwaukee, reaching $100 million in assets by 1919.

Renamed First Wisconsin National Bank, the institution continued to grow through merger and acquisition, surviving the Great Depression as well as a decades-long branch-banking freeze in the state. That restriction made expansion difficult, but by purchasing smaller banks and operating them as affiliates, First Wisconsin grew throughout the state.

Following enactment of Wisconsin's interstate banking law in 1987, the company began making out-of-state acquisitions. It currently operates in Illinois, Iowa, Minnesota, Wisconsin, Florida, and Arizona. In keeping with its multistate franchise, First Wisconsin became Firstar Corporation in 1988.

Firstar continues to expand throughout the Upper Midwest. By 1996 it was the largest bank holding company headquartered in Wisconsin, the second-largest in Iowa, the third-largest in Minnesota, and the sixth-largest in the Chicago area.

In 1995 Firstar took a bold step to help ensure its continued independence. The company launched a top-to-bottom examination of the corporation, eliminating redundancies, streamlining processes, and investing millions in new technology. The goal: to give both customers and shareholders more value by making Firstar one of the most efficient financial institutions in the nation.

While technology has become increasingly important, it's still a "people business," Firstar's leaders say. The main reason Firstar has survived while so many of the city's other banks have disappeared over the years is that "we have a long tradition of employing outstanding people," says president John A. Becker.

The Firstar Fireworks, shot off each July 3 at the lakefront, are one of the many ways in which Firstar contributes to the community's quality of life. The Firstar Center, shown left of center, is Wisconsin's tallest building.

"Our most basic business strategy is to develop long-term, multifaceted customer relationships. You do that by delivering value and building trust. And you do *that* through dedicated, talented employees."

At the same time, Firstar believes that it can only be as successful as the people it serves. That's why it also has a long tradition of involvement in its communities. "Since 1853 Firstar has channeled billions of dollars in financing, charitable contributions, and volunteer time to the people and institutions of Greater Milwaukee," explains Fitzsimonds. "Throughout those years the citizens and businesses of this community have, in turn, been largely responsible for this company's success."

Firstar's commitment to Milwaukee includes, for example, the company's 12 bank offices in or immediately adjacent to Milwaukee's lower-income neighborhoods as well as the Firstar Community Investment Corporation, which give Firstar a prominent role in the redevelopment of the heart of its hometown.

Firstar also has left its imprint on Milwaukee through efforts ranging from its support of the annual nesting by endangered peregrine falcons atop the Firstar Center to its sponsorship of Firstar Fireworks on July 3. The family-oriented Firstar Eve celebrations have transformed New Year's Eve in many of its Upper Midwest markets.

"The city and the bank were founded within a few years of each other," Fitzsimonds notes. "We grew and prospered together. Today both Milwaukee and Firstar are widely recognized for the success each has achieved. The link between the city and the bank is mutually supportive and very strong. It always will be."

Fiserv, Inc.

In just 12 years in existence, Fiserv has helped create an industry—third-party financial data processing—and has quickly vaulted to the forefront of it nationwide. The company has become a nearly billion-dollar concern and one of the area's leading corporate success stories.

The combination of the Fiserv vision, its ability to execute a sound strategy, the capabilities of its 8,000 managers and employees, and favorable trends in the economy portend well for the future, too, of the company headquartered at 255 Fiserv Drive in Brookfield.

The core business of Fiserv is providing data processing services to the financial services industry, helping to improve efficiencies within an institution's automated record keeping and transaction processing. The firm offers a broad array of information management products and related services, ranging from full-service processing to software system development, item processing to check imaging, mortgage banking and plastic card products to electronic banking and retirement plan services.

Fiserv brings advanced technology, deep industry experience, and extremely productive research and development to its efforts. Yet the company prospers because it maintains an ever-present focus on the end customers of its financial services clients.

"Ultimately, our success is measured by them," explains George D. Dalton, Fiserv chairman and chief executive officer. "While our direct clients are financial institutions, the end users of our services are the institutions' customers—and we believe no one wins if they aren't satisfied with the service they receive."

Former data processing executives at banks in Milwaukee and Tampa, respectively, Dalton and Les Muma launched Fiserv in 1984 on the strength of the increasing willingness of financial institutions to rely on outside companies to handle their data processing. As Fiserv proved its capabilities and efficiency, the company grew quickly. More than 50 acquisitions also fueled its growth.

Fiserv continues to acquire complementary companies, just as the spread of the outsourcing trend to larger and larger banks also benefits the company. And the proliferating number of new financial products and services that are available to Americans today, most of which are transaction oriented and fee based, help ensure the growth of Fiserv even as the consolidation of the U.S. banking industry eliminates some client institutions.

The firm's principal focus on the American market will continue indefinitely. Yet Fiserv has a growing international presence as well, with business support centers in London and Singapore, and ongoing client relationships with more than 5,000 financial institutions in over 50 countries.

And the company always keeps an eye out for the interests of its hometown, including involvement with a wide variety of general charities plus specific sponsorships such as the Hat & Mitten Fund Drive for Stueben Middle School in Milwaukee.

Fiserv touches Milwaukee through its support of the community, and through its leadership position within the financial industry.

Fiserv corporate headquarters, Brookfield, Wisconsin.

IDI Corporation

The technological demands faced by its customers have exploded, but IDI Corporation's capabilities have grown right along with them.

Once largely a resource offering short-term engineering personnel, IDI now provides the computers and software they work on as well, in an approach that is aimed at providing complete solutions to the technological challenges faced by its customers.

Founded in 1967 by Charles R. Burke as Industrial Design Incorporated, IDI provides specialized technical support on a contract basis, from all branches of engineering, to industries ranging from automotive to metalworking, electronics, gas and oil, papermaking, architecture, and construction. It places hundreds of engineers and technicians throughout the mid-section of the country, from three offices.

Faced with customers' needs to expand and contract their engineering capabilities quickly, IDI became one of the first contract-personnel companies to provide temporary engineering and technical help. It also has developed a corps of computer-aided design (CAD) experts who are unmatched by nearly any company of IDI's size.

The dramatic expansion of the role computers play in industry has spawned a broad range of computer-assisted design platforms.

IDI has built up its capability to provide CAD hardware and software as well as operators at a single hourly rate. That has proven very popular with customers that don't care to invest the extra thousands, or tens of thousands, of dollars to purchase equipment when their need to use the machines—and CAD operators—may be short term.

When American-based operations of foreign companies require it, IDI's employees also travel abroad, for clients including many of the world's largest companies.

"Everything we do is in response to our customers' needs," says Robert Agnew, current IDI president. "What we really do is provide scarce technological resources in ways that make it very cost effective and productive for companies to use our capabilities."

Some clients do require permanent expansions of technical personnel. To fill this need, IDI pioneered a contract-to-direct-hire plan that gives clients the option to hire specialists after a six-month trial. IDI also has an affiliate, Techni-Search Inc., that recruits people for permanent technical positions. The combination of these two extra capabilities "is a major differentiating factor" for the company, Agnew says.

Despite the fact that there's a tighter supply of some engineering specialists than ever before, Agnew says that the rising importance of—and respect granted to—personnel contracting has made IDI a more and more attractive place to work. "Twenty years ago personnel contracting was a small activity," he says. "Now there's a large pool of people we can draw from for whom the kind of flexibility we offer is a preferred way of life."

Agnew says it's a good way. "With industry undergoing significant changes in organization and staffing, our ability to supply engineers and designers along with computer hardware and software makes IDI a valuable partner with industry," Agnew says. "Business has gotten more and more complex—but more and more fun, too."

IDI Corporation is headquartered at 20875 Crossroads Circle, Brookfield.

EBI Companies

EBI Companies describes itself as a human service organization that happens to offer insurance. This approach, bolstering a belief that all workplace accidents are preventable, not inevitable, is making a dramatic difference for policyholders, agents, and workers in the communities it serves.

Wisconsin's third-largest workers' compensation insurer, EBI believes it only makes business sense to protect valuable employees from accidents and injuries, and they're proving it.

EBI's senior management team (from left)—Ralph Herrmann, senior vice president; Ray Jacobsen, chief executive officer; and Jon Gice, president—is dedicated to bringing the best service to independent agents and policyholders.

EBI is successfully driving down the cost of workers' compensation by making accidents far less frequent and severe. When injuries do occur, they make sure the finest medical and rehabilitative care is available to workers. This is critical to getting people back to work and productive again as soon as possible, which serves the best interests of workers and their families.

EBI considers all accidents—work-related injuries, including medical only and lost-time injuries and illnesses—unacceptable. They call this their "ZAC^{SM}," Zero Accident Culture^{SM}. Zero Accident Culture^{SM} is not a program, but a corporate cultural evolution. ZAC^{SM} treats every accident in a way that it will never happen again. It takes root and develops as EBI works with policyholders and their agents, encouraging the idea that everyone is responsible, and ultimately accountable, for safety.

EBI takes an aggressive approach to risk reduction that is as straightforward as it is effective. First, eliminate the hazard. If elimination is not possible, modify or control it. Finally, conduct safety training as the situation demands.

The approach is completely hands-on in terms of both loss prevention and claims handling. The company recognizes that customer satisfaction and insurance renewal decisions hinge on these factors.

Early in a working relationship, it's not unusual for EBI people servicing a policyholder to make weekly visits. The firm distinguishes itself from other insurers and builds long-term relationships due to high levels of service from a dedicated team of professionals.

EBI is well aware that the impact of a workers' compensation claim goes far beyond the insured costs. The impact includes lost production; the recruiting, hiring, and training of replacement workers; and possibly even equipment replacement.

The company is proud that its Zero Accident Culture^{SM} is helping policyholders gain control over all these costs and rechannel these resources into the growth of their own businesses.

EBI Companies is owned by the publicly traded Orion Capitol Companies of New York. Its corporate structure is as unconventional as its business philosophy. In place of a headquarters, EBI supports its work

Bottom right: EBI's policyholders include St. John's Home of Milwaukee, which is celebrating 128 years of service. Pictured are Rob Fronk, EBI branch manager; Pattie Millot, EBI underwriter; Dennis Gralinski, St. John's president; Christine Patnode, St. John's director of human resources; and Susan Digaudio, EBI claims examiner.

force nationally from field services centers, including one in metro Milwaukee, in the Brookfield Lakes Corporate Center.

While conventional business wisdom touts consolidation and centralization, EBI is committed to the small branch office as its primary operating unit.

The firm believes small branches are most conducive to the atmosphere of teamwork and relationship building so important to service delivery. EBI is committed to opening multiple branches in a single city before allowing any given location to grow beyond its ideal size.

Another sign of deep commitment to this structure is creation of its SDS, or Service Development Specialist, position. SDS provides training at the branch level to improve services to customers, including policyholders, agents, and EBI's internal teams.

The company operates without any procedures manual. Its business philosophy remains consistent and is guided by 24 principles that evolved in the late 1980s.

While competitors attempt to emulate their initiatives, EBI's approach is resulting in impressive growth. In 1987 the firm employed 57 people statewide. By 1995, of just under 1,100 "team members" nationwide, over 160 were working in five Wisconsin offices. EBI's teams include loss prevention, claims, underwriters, rehabilitation nurses, house counsel, industrial hygienists, in-house surveillance, human resource consultants, and medical quality assurers.

The company historically has served health care and manufacturing employers and selected organizations in other industries, including hospitality. Founded in 1969, EBI was purchased by Orion in 1981. That same year its base in Oregon and California was expanded to the Midwest. In 1995 Oklahoma, Tennessee, and Minnesota joined the roster of 20 states in which EBI's 40 branches now operate.

While continually seeking new territories, the company remains committed to its primary product, the prevention of workplace injuries and rehabilitation services. EBI also actively pursues development of new services.

One of EBI's most recent service offerings is IEB, Integrated Employee Benefits, which combines group health coverage and long- and short-term disability with workers' compensation.

Jerry Kozik, vice president of operations at Gardetto's, and Cynthia Byrne, EBI accident prevention specialist, observe Gardetto's conveyor system which has helped reduce repetitive motion injuries.

Facing page, top: Pictured are Diane Wilhite, EBI claims representative; Rob Fronk, EBI branch manager; Allen Siebel, vice president of finance, C&H Distributors Inc.; Chris Krier, independent insurance agent with Schueller-Owen & Associates; and Karen Wagner, C&H Distributors Inc. personnel administrator. This team focuses on reducing workplace accidents.

The company's Management Development Services began as a pilot project in Wisconsin. This consulting service helps customers assess their own organizations' strengths. EBI has packaged the communications, training, empowerment, and teamwork expertise it has developed in creating its own effective corporate culture and is now making that available to customers.

EBI Companies is also exploring excess insurance coverage for self-insured employers. EBI does not plan to unbundle their services, however.

One EBI manager described the firm's typical policyholder as a company that sincerely cares about its employees, whether it is having safety problems today or not. EBI looks to partner with people who want a workplace that is safe, productive, and satisfying.

EBI services are available only through independent insurance agents. The company maintains a low profile and relies on word of mouth as marketing. It has been referred to by some as the "very quiet company."

EBI is working to make the workplace in Milwaukee, and throughout Wisconsin, a better place for everyone.

Zigman Joseph Stephenson

Zigman Joseph Stephenson helps interpret Milwaukee, its companies, and institutions to the rest of the world. No one else does it as much—or as well.

The firm, headquartered at 100 East Wisconsin Avenue, is a major, marketing-oriented public-relations consulting firm serving corporations, professional service firms, nonprofit organizations, medical and educational institutions, and individuals. It is one of the largest independent PR firms in the Midwest.

In this metro area and region-wide, ZJS has been at the forefront of the evolution of public relations over the past few decades from simple boosterism to a sophisticated, information-intensive, strategically oriented approach to marketing clients and helping them achieve their broad communications objectives.

"We've always worked to transform ourselves continually so that we represent the state of the art in this market," says Linda Stephenson, who became president of ZJS in 1988. "Whoever heard of satellite media tours 10 years ago? The whole dynamics of the profession are changing, and we are on top of it.

"But these days, we're hired above all to play a counseling role, for our brains and not just gimmicks. And that's what we're best suited to do."

Linda Stephenson has been president of ZJS since 1988.

For many years after the company's founding by Robert Zigman and Jules Joseph in 1959, that meant the development of specialties in marketing consumer products, issues management, promotions, and media relations.

Under Stephenson, ZJS has added a distinctive focus on the growing need for PR for professional services clients, who face greater competition in their businesses and therefore must market themselves more aggressively.

Says Stephenson: "Our focus today is far more on marketing, using qualitative market research and a comprehensive array of other services that I call 'tactics.' What we do for our clients is much more strategic now, more planned, more structured to reflect key methodologies that address specific audiences and stakeholders."

Among specific areas of the firm's expertise are corporate and employee communications, investor relations, government relations, issues management, lobbying, media relations and publicity, meeting planning and coordination, newsletter and brochure development, opinion and market research, retail marketing, speech writing, spokesperson training, sports marketing, and representation of U.S. subsidiaries of foreign companies. ZJS is affiliated with major PR firms throughout the nation and abroad via the International Public Relations Exchange.

The firm's 22 staff members have backgrounds in areas as diverse as journalism, media, business, law, government, public affairs, education, and retailing.

Another important factor in the firm's success has been its steadfast dedication to the community, through major events, organizations, and causes such as the American Heart Association and the YMCA. ZJS was instrumental in the founding of the Milwaukee Symphony Orchestra and the United Performing Arts Fund.

"We don't only want to put Milwaukee in the best light," explains Stephenson. "We want to help make it the best."

Kahn has represented purchasers, sellers, investment bankers, lenders, and investors in both private and public transactions. The firm's corporate attorneys have participated in a wide variety of mergers and acquisitions, including leveraged and non-leveraged buyouts, tax-free exchanges, and contested acquisitions. Their experience with mergers and acquisitions also includes working with publicly traded clients on methods to maximize stockholder value and takeover defense planning.

Godfrey & Kahn's securities team represents public and private companies, startup ventures, underwriters, investors, and others in a broad range of transactions, while also participating in ongoing strategic planning and counsel regarding regulatory compliance matters. In the public finance area, Godfrey & Kahn, S.C., is a nationally recognized bond counsel firm.

The firm's proactive approach helps to resolve issues in challenging areas such as public- and private-sector labor law. Godfrey & Kahn counsels employers who face difficult personnel issues, union organizational issues, unfair labor practice proceedings, discrimination suits, workers' and unemployment compensation matters, as well as wage and hour and employee safety issues. The firm also advises counties, municipalities, and school districts in labor, school, and public law as well as municipal financing issues.

In the burgeoning area of health care, the firm's health care practice group represents health care professionals, managed-care organizations, and the entities they create. In response to sweeping reforms in the health care industry, the firm has actively represented medical and dental groups involved in the purchase, sale, and merger of professional practices and the organization of integrated delivery systems.

The law firm's broad-based practice facilitates the mutual and effective integration of a wide variety of legal disciplines. For example, the real estate practice group (assisting clients in all aspects of real estate transactions, including municipalities, developers, investors, lenders, contractors, real estate brokers, architects, and property managers) works with the firm's environmental, estate planning, securities, and tax groups to address the broad range of issues facing participants in today's diverse and complicated real estate market.

Godfrey & Kahn attorneys practice law with the philosophy that the most successful attorney-client relationship requires a thorough understanding of the client's business and goals and the belief that the client comes first. Although some law firms make a clear distinction between "business" and "legal" issues, Godfrey & Kahn does not. It is not unusual for the firm's attorneys to spend non-billable hours touring a new client's facility in an effort to better understand that company's motivation and goals. The firm has earned a reputation for helping clients identify and seize growth opportunities while developing considerable expertise in structuring and facilitating complex transactions.

The firm strongly supports and encourages its members to contribute their time and talents by assuming leadership positions in professional, civic, and charitable organizations. Through the years Godfrey & Kahn attorneys have served as president of the State Bar of Wisconsin and as chairs of its various committees, president of the Milwaukee Bar Association, and chairman of the United Way of Greater Milwaukee, as well as in a variety of other key leadership roles. Godfrey & Kahn's professional and community practices reflect its ongoing efforts to effectively serve its clients' needs and its commitment to the businesses and governmental agencies located or doing business within the state of Wisconsin.

Godfrey & Kahn attorneys provide comprehensive advice to clients ranging from small businesses to international corporations.

New England Financial Services/ The Marris Group, Inc.

New England Financial Services is one of the very, very few companies that have been part of the Milwaukee scene since the city's origins. But if William C. Marris hadn't become manager and then owner of the local agency in 1984, The New England Wisconsin would have become just another local business casualty.

Headquartered in Brookfield, Milwaukee's New England agency—known as The Marris Group—now is a thriving player in the metro Milwaukee and Wisconsin insurance markets. With about 100 associates in Brookfield, at another primary office in Madison, and at satellite offices around the state, The Marris Group also includes a diversified array of other insurance-oriented operations.

William C. Marris, CLU, president and chief executive officer of the firm.

"I'm proud of the fact that we were able to restore life to The New England franchise here in Milwaukee," says Marris. "But I also am happy with how the overall company has grown into a very entrepreneurial enterprise that can offer our clients a number of other specialized concentrations where our expertise and service are second to none."

Founded in Boston in 1835, The New England is the oldest chartered mutual life insurance company in the United States. Its first Wisconsin policy was written in 1844, and the Wisconsin agency, which dates back to 1846, is the company's 28th in order of creation.

Josiah Noonan, the prominent Democratic Party activist and newspaper publisher, was appointed the first agent. Another very early Milwaukee agent was Philetus C. Hale, who established the city's first bookstore and circulating library. Agent Matthew Hale Carpenter became a U.S. senator and a noted orator.

The Marris Group's professional associates serve the firm's more than 30,000 Wisconsin clients.

Despite that pedigree, however, The New England—trying to do business in the shadow of Northwestern Mutual Life Insurance Co., which is headquartered in Milwaukee—nearly shut down its poorly performing office here. That's when Marris left a local job with another insurer to become general agent of The New England here, the youngest so appointed in the country. Now he's 100 percent owner of the agency.

Marris set about capitalizing on New England Financial Services' extensive menu of services by selecting a few in addition to traditional life insurance—such as group sales and pension sales—in which to specialize. With this strategy, the Milwaukee agency has climbed from near the bottom into a position where its annual performance generally ranks among the top 25 percent among all offices of The New England nationwide.

Marris also expanded The Marris Group's product portfolio by establishing additional areas of expertise in the form of affiliated companies including Compass Benefits Specialties, Inc.; Maritime Financial Advisors Ltd.; New England Securities; and Letteney/Marris, Ltd., a national franchise, including a copyrighted training program, that The Marris Group is offering through a large Milwaukee-based insurance company.

Besides this savvy product and marketing strategy, Marris attributes his company's culture with a big share of its success. "We emphasize interpersonal relationships in a horizontal sort of management structure," he explains. "And that includes a great deal of concern about our associates' families as well. With an agency 'family' population of some 400 individuals, I view my job as being similar to that of mayor of a small town."

The Marris Group

Serving Wisconsin Since 1846

Firstar Center, the tallest structure in Wisconsin, towers above the venerable Mitchell Building with its elaborate ornamental figures. Photo by Alan Magayne Roshak/Third Coast Stock Source

Chapter ELEVEN

Building Greater Milwaukee

From concept through completion, Milwaukee's architects, engineers, developers, and real estate professionals shape tomorrow's skyline.

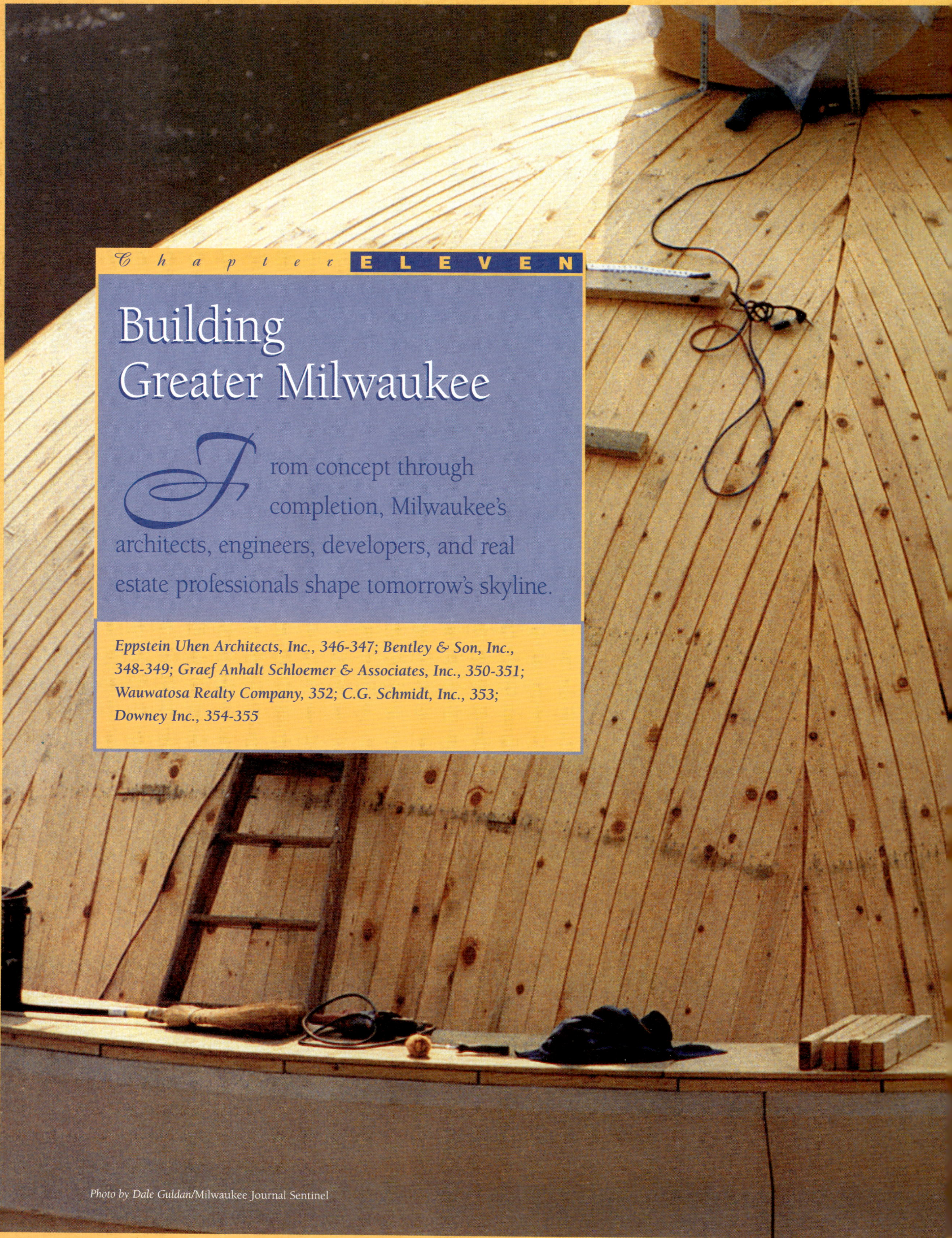

Photo by Dale Guldan/Milwaukee Journal Sentinel

Eppstein Uhen Architects, Inc.

"We have evolved as a firm throughout the twentieth century, sometimes in response to changes in Milwaukee's economic base, but more often in anticipation of where this city is headed," says Greg Uhen, president of Eppstein Uhen Architects. As one of the largest architectural firms in the city, Eppstein Uhen's design legacy reaches back to 1907 and is deeply imbedded in the urban landscape.

Firm founder William Herbst came from the lofty design environment of Frank Lloyd Wright's studio. An early focus on public and institutional buildings produced monumental structures like the stately Shorewood High School campus and the Gothic Revival buildings of Mt. Mary College. Commercial buildings like the Kunzelman Esser store on Milwaukee's south side also made a strong architectural statement and reflected an era when cost was secondary to design.

According to Uhen, "When Sam Eppstein took the reins in the early 1980s, he brought a business perspective that was unique to architecture. The egos were tucked away on the shelf and we got serious about high-value services." As Milwaukee's economy shifted away from a largely manufacturing base to one with growing service and financial sectors, the firm became increasingly adept at understanding each client's business environment while focusing on deadlines, budgets, and innovative modes of project delivery.

The spectrum of high-profile projects completed since then is far reaching. They include the Iron Block Building restoration, Marcus Amphitheater, the renaissance of Schlitz Park, Marquette Campus Circle, Discovery World Museum, the Milwaukee Riverwalk, East Pointe Marketplace, the comforting and nostalgic Osthoff Resort in Elkhart Lake, and the elegant Strong Funds corporate headquarters in Menomonee Falls. At present, Eppstein Uhen is the local anchor for the team designing Milwaukee's new icon Miller Park.

Eppstein Uhen Architects offers true market expertise in several key areas including office, industrial, residential, commercial, and educational/public buildings. Organized via a "studio" system, each specialized team has developed an intimate understanding of specific project types, individual clients, and building users. As a result, over 95 percent of the firm's business comes from satisfied former clients. According to Sam Eppstein, "Our mission is to give our clients the best service they will ever have. That 'service' is dictated to us by our clients at the outset of every job. It becomes our challenge—to deliver what they want, the way they want it, each and every day."

922

Bentley & Son, Inc.

The legacy of Bentley & Son, Inc., goes deeper than the foundation of any of the buildings the company has constructed in southeastern Wisconsin.

Founded in 1848, Bentley has spanned five generations of family leadership and has survived twice when the vagaries of lineage produced an only child. As a general contractor and construction manager, the company has erected hundreds of structures, many of them landmark edifices, spreading from the banks of Lake Michigan to the Pacific Ocean, though primarily in southeastern Wisconsin. The firm has prevailed as a single, continuous economic entity through history-shaping events stretching from the Civil War to the recession in the early 1980s.

No wonder, then, that in the lobby of its headquarters in Brown Deer, Bentley has prominently posted memorabilia ranging from founder John Bentley's citizenship papers to a 1974 citation from the Milwaukee County Board congratulating Bentley Construction for 125 years of operation.

The legacy also has engaged Thomas Bentley III, the current president and owner, in a relentless effort to document that his firm is one of the oldest—if not the oldest—continually operated, family-owned construction companies in the entire United States. He's already certain that Bentley & Son is the oldest in Wisconsin and considers it likely that it is one of the most historically significant firms in the entire Midwest.

The Rite Hite Corporation chose Brown Deer, Wisconsin (in Milwaukee's northern suburbs), as the site for its extraordinary corporate office headquarters. Bentley & Son was the general contractor for this building. Thomas Bentley III (left) and Thomas Bentley, Jr., are pictured in the firm's luxurious atrium lobby.

"Our heritage has created a solid reputation for integrity, service, and quality construction at a competitive price for our company, and I believe we're only enhancing that over time," Bentley says. "It's exciting to try to determine just how unique that staying power has enabled us to be!"

John Bentley established the first predecessor company, Bentley Construction, as a carpentry concern; by the turn of the century the firm had developed a full general contractor capability. Bentley craftsmen built historic Milwaukee landmarks including the North Point Water Tower (near St. Mary's Hospital), the original Lincoln Memorial Bridge, Immanuel Presbyterian and St. John's Episcopal churches, and the ornate Tripoli Temple on West Wisconsin Avenue.

The Bentley family also built the north and south wings of the state capitol in Madison and the San Francisco post office/courthouse at the turn of the century—a stout structure that withstood the devastating 1906 earthquake.

More recently, Bentley & Son has overseen projects including the Johnson Foundation's Wingspread Conference Facility designed by Frank Lloyd Wright, the remodeled and expanded Weyenberg Library in Mequon, M&I's Data Center expansion in Brown Deer, and multiple locations for major chain operations including McDonald's. Under Thomas Bentley III, in the past decade annual sales have climbed from $4 million to over $20 million.

Bentley attributes his company's longevity and success not only to bloodlines and family tradition but also to an extraordinary attention to quality, a devotion to continuous improvement, and the development of a cooperative spirit among employees as well as with architects and other project partners.

Lately, Bentley has added an aggressive implemen-

The firm is known for providing quality construction and construction management services. Featured at left is Weyenberg Library, a project that involved a 15,000-square-foot addition and a complete remodel of the existing facility.

tation of new technology to the firm's success formula. Extensive computer networks link most employees to one another as well as to many suppliers and even customers. Sophisticated work-scheduling software enables Bentley to bid projects with unprecedented accuracy and to execute them within budget and on time.

"We've just become much more professional in the past 10 years," says the amiable executive. "That's helped us grow from a small, reputable firm to a larger, highly capable and professional organization now. We pursue excellence in every area."

And despite the robust growth of the past decade, Bentley is careful not to become intoxicated by the smell of success. While satisfied customers, like national chains, are tending to pull Bentley farther and farther afield from its southeastern Wisconsin base with new projects, Bentley has chosen to limit the company's geographic expansion.

"That's one of the things that can cause firms to fail," he explains. "If we want to be the best mid-size construction company in southeastern Wisconsin, we'd better stick with that. We have plenty to do in Wisconsin in the next three to five years."

And who's going to be in charge of ensuring Bentley & Son's prosperity into the next generation? Bentley has three children who already can appreciate a fine building.

Bentley World Packaging, Ltd.

With highly skilled carpenters as a resource, Bentley Brothers received many requests for special packing and crating services for overseas military shipments in World War II. That began the company's incursion into export packaging.

Above and left: Bentley & Son has built many interesting and unique structures for well-recognized Milwaukee area businesses. The law office of Cannon & Dunphy is a remarkable building, from the concrete block exterior to the impressive interior finishes of marble, architectural-grade columns, mahogany doors, and architectural moldings.

Increasing customer requests for export-packaging services in the 1970s prompted Thomas Bentley III to spin off that operation into a separate corporate entity. The boom in exports by Wisconsin companies has kept Bentley World Packaging, Ltd. prospering into the 1990s.

In 1996 Bentley World Packaging's sales approached $10 million—the largest export packager in the state. In 1989 it received the Governor's Export Achievement Award; in 1990 the firm was honored with the prestigious Presidential "E" Award for contributions to U.S. export efforts.

"To better serve its customers, the company expanded into a 300,000-square-foot facility in Milwaukee," Bentley says. "With the continued growth of exports, this should be a growing business for a long time to come."

Bentley & Son has provided construction services for many retail clients throughout the Milwaukee area, including McDonald's restaurants, Osco Drug, Haasch Appliance, and Flanner's Audio and Video.

Graef Anhalt Schloemer & Associates, Inc.

Graef Anhalt Schloemer & Associates, Inc. (GAS), has successfully handled some of the most impressive engineering tasks in the modern history of the Milwaukee metropolitan area, providing engineering services for the Milwaukee County Criminal Justice facility, the downtown Grand Avenue mall, the Marcus Amphitheater at Henry Maier Festival Park, the "deep tunnel" sewage system beneath the city, the parking structure and the Concourse D expansion at Mitchell International Airport, and the Pettit National Ice Center at Wisconsin State Fair Park.

GAS' first generation began when Luther Graef, Leonard Anhalt, and Robert Schloemer founded the firm in 1961. Today it has 22 principals and employs more than 230 people in offices in Milwaukee, Green Bay, and Madison, Wisconsin, and in Chicago, Illinois. The firm installed a second-generation president, Richard M. Bub, P.E., in January 1995.

GAS' goal is to provide quality professional engineering services to solve clients' needs in the most cost-effective way through technical competence, innovation, creativity, and high motivation. The firm supplies six major markets: structural, public works, industrial/architectural, environmental, transportation, and field services.

Structural services include bridge designs for the Santa Monica Boulevard Bridge in Fox Point; building design for the Wisconsin Center, Marcus Amphitheater, and Pettit National Ice Center; and parking structure design for Mitchell International Airport.

The Wisconsin Center, downtown Milwaukee's state-of-the-art convention facility, will highlight the firm's expertise in innovative structural design.

Public-works services include wastewater-treatment facilities for the City of South Milwaukee, the City of Waupaca, the Town of Bristol, the Village of Sussex, and the Milwaukee Water Pollution Abatement Program, which was the largest public-works project in U.S. history to have been completed on time and within budget.

The firm's site-selection, regulatory audits, and other industrial and architectural services have assisted Quad/Graphics, Inc., Briggs & Stratton Corp., Allen-Bradley Company, Phoenix Products, Aldrich Chemical Company, and Harnischfeger Industries. GAS also offers industrial architecture services, including manufacturing plant layouts and expansions.

GAS' environmental services include groundwater remediation, storage-tank management, landfills, wetlands, and industrial-pollution issues.

Transportation services include traffic management, highway design, and site development. Projects include the I-90-94 reconstruction near Wisconsin Dells, Wisconsin, the Main Street Bridge in Green Bay, Wisconsin, and the FTMS (Freeway Traffic Management System).

GAS supports clients with all phases of a project, from design through final construction. "We envision the state of the art for that project five to 10 years from now and build that sort of flexibility into the project," says Harold Farchmin, vice president.

One way the firm accomplishes this goal is by incorporating the most sophisticated technology at every stage, including computer-aided design and computerized surveying instruments. It also supports continual career education for its professionals, with a tuition-reimbursement plan and encouragement of attendance at professional and educational seminars.

GAS has become a player in the design-build industry. Teams of architects, engineers, builders, and others present an integrated proposal in design-build programs.

Graef Anhalt Schloemer & Associates' environmental services include wetlands issues.

The Pettit National Ice Center, training home of the U.S. Olympic Speedskating Team, was one design-build project in which the firm participated. With the grand opening of the facility scheduled to take place within a year from the date GAS' team was awarded the contract, it was an extremely fast-track project.

To beat the deadline, GAS worked with its partner architects and contractors to design elements of the project on which construction could begin even before the rest of the Pettit National Ice Center was actually designed. They provided a team that worked well together and was flexible.

The Wisconsin Center, downtown Milwaukee's state-of-the-art convention facility, is another design-build project that will highlight GAS' expertise in innovative structural design. Phase I of this fast-track project is scheduled for completion by late 1997. Cream City Associates, the design-build team working on the Wisconsin Center, is comprised of GAS and the country's most prominent construction firms, general contractors, subcontractors, design firms, and consultants.

The firm plans to continue its balance between private- and public-sector projects. While remaining a fixture in metro Milwaukee, GAS also has committed to expanding its business in Wisconsin and Illinois. Currently operating with 29 employees there, the firm would like to expand its Chicago office to equal its Milwaukee-based operation.

One of the firm's major projects in Chicago was the reconstruction of the Deerfield Toll Plaza, which will relieve congestion on the Illinois Tollway's busiest checkpoint. The plaza will use new "flyby" lanes, which charge tolls to individual drivers using a transponder system.

Recently, GAS determined that it could best maintain the firm's long-term growth by focusing on selected market groups. It will continue to service all of the markets it does now, but will intensify on certain areas.

As it reshapes itself for the changing marketplace, another constant will remain for GAS, as it has for 35 years: its reputation as Milwaukee's premier engineering firm.

Bottom left: The Pettit National Ice Center was a fast-track design-build project in which GAS participated. ©HNK Architectural Photography, Inc.

Below: Quad/Graphics' Sussex facility benefited from GAS' industrial and architectural services.

Wauwatosa Realty Company

Innovation. Integrity. Service. These are the elements that comprised the vision of John A. Horning when he founded Wauwatosa Realty Company in 1946. And these principles have helped the company reach and retain its leadership position through the years.

"We know Wisconsin home-selling markets better than anyone," says Donald E. Horning, president of the company. He and his cousin, John E. Horning, chief executive officer and son of the company founder, have run Wauwatosa Realty since 1970.

"Independent management has been crucial for us," adds Don. "Making the decisions here—whereas in the chains we compete with, decisions are made in New York and California."

Wauwatosa Realty always has used the flexibility and quick decision-making benefits of independent management to continually meet the demands and needs of its home-buying and -selling customers.

For instance, in the early 1980s, when a deep recession wracked southeastern Wisconsin and interest rates spiraled into the double digits, Wauwatosa Realty helped its customers by buying mortgage money and then offering it to gratified home buyers at substantially reduced rates.

And since the company's beginning, it has been an industry leader in innovative marketing strategies to sell its customers' homes. Wauwatosa Realty pioneered the use of full-page newspaper ads, radio, billboards, and television to market homes.

More recently, the firm has stayed at the forefront of an increasingly dynamic local housing market with new technologies. In the 1990s Wauwatosa Realty was the first to computerize all of its listings so that all of its local offices had access to the company's entire data base of properties.

In 1993 Wauwatosa Realty established its well-known Real Estate Hotline, which logged more than one million calls in its first year. And in 1995 the company continued to push the envelope of technology by opening its own home page on the Internet, expanding its market worldwide.

In addition to such marketing innovations, Wauwatosa Realty has been aggressive in other areas. In 1969 the company established Wauwatosa Real Estate Institute, which trains hundreds of new agents each year and ensures a steady stream of professional, highly qualified Realtors. The company also started a relocation division in the 1970s, Heritage Title Services, Inc., and Wisconsin Mortgage Corporation in the 1980s, and entered the commercial real estate industry in 1995 as Birdsall-Horning & Associates.

Such gambits, executed with confidence and competence, have enabled Wauwatosa Realty to expand to a total of 11 company-owned and four franchise sales offices, in addition to its headquarters at 17450 West North Avenue in Brookfield. All told, 650 people are associated with Wauwatosa Realty's family of companies.

Yet, as Wisconsin's largest, most successful real estate company celebrates its 50th anniversary in 1996, the elements of that success remain firmly and safely planted in its corporate philosophy.

"The quality of our people and our management has enabled us to put together this kind of track record," says John E. Horning. "It's important to us to remain a family-owned business, and we plan to continue being that. We have a reputation for integrity and for being part of the community. Wauwatosa Realty is something special in Milwaukee."

Top right: This 1946 advertisement in the Wauwatosa News Times *introduced Wauwatosa Realty to the community.*

Donald E. Horning (left), president, and John E. Horning, chief executive officer.

C.G. Schmidt, Inc.

Satisfying clients is the primary goal of C.G. Schmidt, Inc., and the main reason the Milwaukee-based construction company has remained a leader in its industry for more than 75 years. Seventy percent of its business comes from repeat customers, as exemplified by C.G. Schmidt's 50-year business relationship with Waukesha Memorial Hospital.

C.G. Schmidt, Inc., has grown through building Greater Milwaukee: commercial edifices with personality including Mutual Savings Bank's new headquarters, welcome civic treasures such as the Italian Community Center, health care landmarks such as the Blood Center of Southeastern Wisconsin, and infrastructures including the new parking facilities at General Mitchell International Airport, the Bradley Center, and the Historic Third Ward.

Since 1920 three generations of the Charles Schmidt family have guided C.G. Schmidt, Inc., nurturing the company into one of the largest construction firms in Wisconsin and one of the top 400 general contractors in the country.

Richard Schmidt, grandson of Charles and the current chief executive officer, recently celebrated the firm's 75th anniversary. The company employs about 50 people in its offices at 4199 North Richards Street and 150 in the field. "I take personal pride in our people and our reputation," Schmidt says. "Integrity, performance, professionalism—and community involvement—are what we're all about."

C.G. Schmidt leads its industry through its cutting-edge approach to industry trends and technologies. The firm pioneered the first major environmentally and historically friendly construction project at the century-old School Sisters of Notre Dame facility in Elm Grove. It has also expanded its services in response to the rising market for design/build construction, a trend in providing single-source responsibility for the design and construction of a project.

Strong growth in revenues—more than 70 percent over the past four years—and in market share produced the largest backlog in company history in 1995. To help maintain such expansion, Schmidt has diversified geographically with an office in Racine and project management throughout the Midwest. Of course, there is no substitute for the hard work and commitment C.G. Schmidt employees devote to each project.

C.G. Schmidt has given to and gained much from Milwaukee. The company is committed to giving back to the community, says Schmidt, in ways ranging from employment of inner-city residents, to financial contributions to institutions, from sponsorship of scholarships, to encouraging employee community service. And, just as in the past 75 years, C.G. Schmidt's main business will always be to build Greater Milwaukee.

Recent C.G. Schmidt projects include the Milwaukee School of Engineering's Student Life and Campus Center (below), completed in 1991, and the Blood Center of Southeastern Wisconsin headquarters facility (right), completed in 1995.

CGSCHMIDT INC

Downey Inc.

Downey Inc.'s business always reflects Milwaukee's economic challenges of the times. For more than 130 years the company's story has been that of people applying state-of-the-art technology and good business sense to meet those challenges.

From Milwaukee's famous City Hall built in 1893, to the landmark Bradley Center completed in 1988, to the current expansion of several major medical facilities, as a leading mechanical-contracting and engineering firm Downey has helped construct many of the area's landmark buildings—and much of its economic infrastructure.

Located at 2207 West Wisconsin Avenue, Downey is a diversified, full-service company engaged in piping, plumbing, sprinkler systems, heating, ventilation and air conditioning, water and sewage treatment plant construction, sheet metal and pipe fabrication, application engineering, and mechanical systems service. In the past two decades, Downey has helped complete more than $200 million worth of industrial, commercial, and institutional projects in southeastern Wisconsin.

Downey has always undertaken its work with a dedication to quality that stands as prominently as some of the structures it has helped build. "Our core values really are built around dedication to quality," says Gregory Coffman, president and a member of the third family that has directed Downey, which today is owned by its key employees. "Sometimes, with today's competitive forces, that's been difficult, but our persistence about quality has been a key to our success."

Hazen Mooers, who was a boilermaker at the old E.P. Allis Co. in Milwaukee, founded the predecessor of Downey in 1863 to manufacture steam heating boilers. In 1880 William K. Downey was employed and became a partner in 1888. Two years later the compa-

The Metropolitan Milwaukee Sewerage District 4500kv methane gas co-generation facility was a Downey project.

ny installed Wisconsin's first mechanical ventilation system in a new Milwaukee school.

Building from this, over the next several decades the firm and its affiliates grew with added mechanical-contracting capabilities including plumbing and fire protection. Downey became a major environmental systems supplier for many signature building projects including City Hall, Milwaukee's Pfister Hotel, the state prison in Waupun, the Badger Ordnance Works at Baraboo, Wisconsin, and the Milwaukee Arena.

The Downey family sold the business in 1970 to AZCO Inc., a mechanical contractor headquartered in Appleton. Kenneth Coffman, Gregory's father, had joined Downey as general manager and, after the sale, stayed on to direct the company for AZCO. In 1983 the Coffmans led a buyout of the firm.

Under employee ownership, Downey has continued

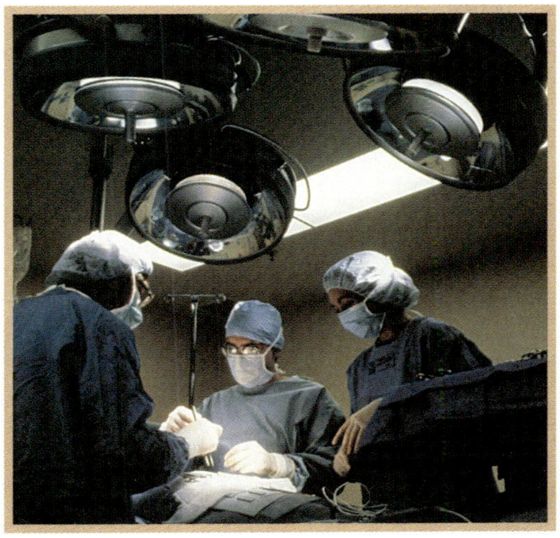

to diversify to meet changing market needs; for example, it became a major participant in Metropolitan Milwaukee Sewerage District facilities expansion including both mechanical and prime construction. While Downey provided total environmental system design and construction for the Reuss Federal Plaza, it also served as joint venture partner and associate contract manager for the design and construction of this innovative blend of government and private office space.

Today health care construction is an area of emphasis, including additions to Children's Hospital, Froedtert Hospital, the Veterans' Administration Hospital, and St. Luke's Hospital. Downey remains diverse enough also to be the lead mechanical contractor for the new Frank Lloyd Wright-designed Monona Terrace Convention Center in Madison and to be mechanical systems contractor at several high-tech industrial facilities including new plant development as far away as Mexico.

Helping to continue the quality of Milwaukee's work force, the company has become a leading sponsor of educational innovation. Coffman is currently co-chairman of Milwaukee Public Schools' School-to-Work Business Community Committee.

"MPS School-to-Work is the public education reform that has the highest potential to do the most long-term good for Milwaukee," Coffman says. "As dedicated as we are to this city, we want to always be involved in it."

Above: Downey provided the Northwestern Mutual Life Insurance Co. headquarters data facility with energy recovery heating and air conditioning systems. Courtesy, Northwestern Mutual Life Insurance Co.

Above left: Downey provided critical mechanical systems for Froedtert Memorial Lutheran Hospital's surgical suites.

SQUID
ANATOMY
Loligo sp.
SPONGE
COLLECTION
Grantia
Leucosolenia
Spongilla
salt

Chapter TWELVE

Quality of Life

Medical and educational institutions contribute to the exceptional quality of life enjoyed by residents and visitors.

Photo by Bachmann/Third Coast Stock Source

Family Health Plan

When Family Health Plan Cooperative began in 1979, its rather modest goal was to address the acute shortage of primary-care physicians on Milwaukee's south side. Thanks to community leadership and the availability of some federal funds, the first Family health center opened on West Edgerton Avenue and did just that.

But other interesting things began to happen. As the cost of and access to health care became more important questions throughout metro Milwaukee and the rest of the nation in the 1980s, Family found that its not-for-profit, community-based, comprehensive, family-oriented approach to solving those problems worked well.

Today Family Health Plan remains the only staff-model health maintenance organization in Milwaukee. Unlike other HMOs, Family provides its own services to its consumer-members, for a fixed fee, through its network of seven health care centers, 103 employed physicians, 200 affiliated providers, and more than 1,200 employees overall. Family has a facility within a 20-minute drive of everyone in Milwaukee and Waukesha counties, and each center is affiliated with a major hospital in the area.

Financially the healthiest HMO in Wisconsin, with annual revenues of about $180 million and assets of more than $60 million, Family Health Plan now serves roughly 105,000 members. And its enrollment is broad based, including 1,500 Medicaid members and 7,726 Medicare enrollees.

Family is especially proud of its emphases on being responsive to its members, on offering most of its own services, and on effective practice of preventive medicine. Its success begins, says executive director Conrad Sobczak, with Family's organization as a cooperative. "We have a strong consumer orientation because we are organized and managed on the part of our underly-

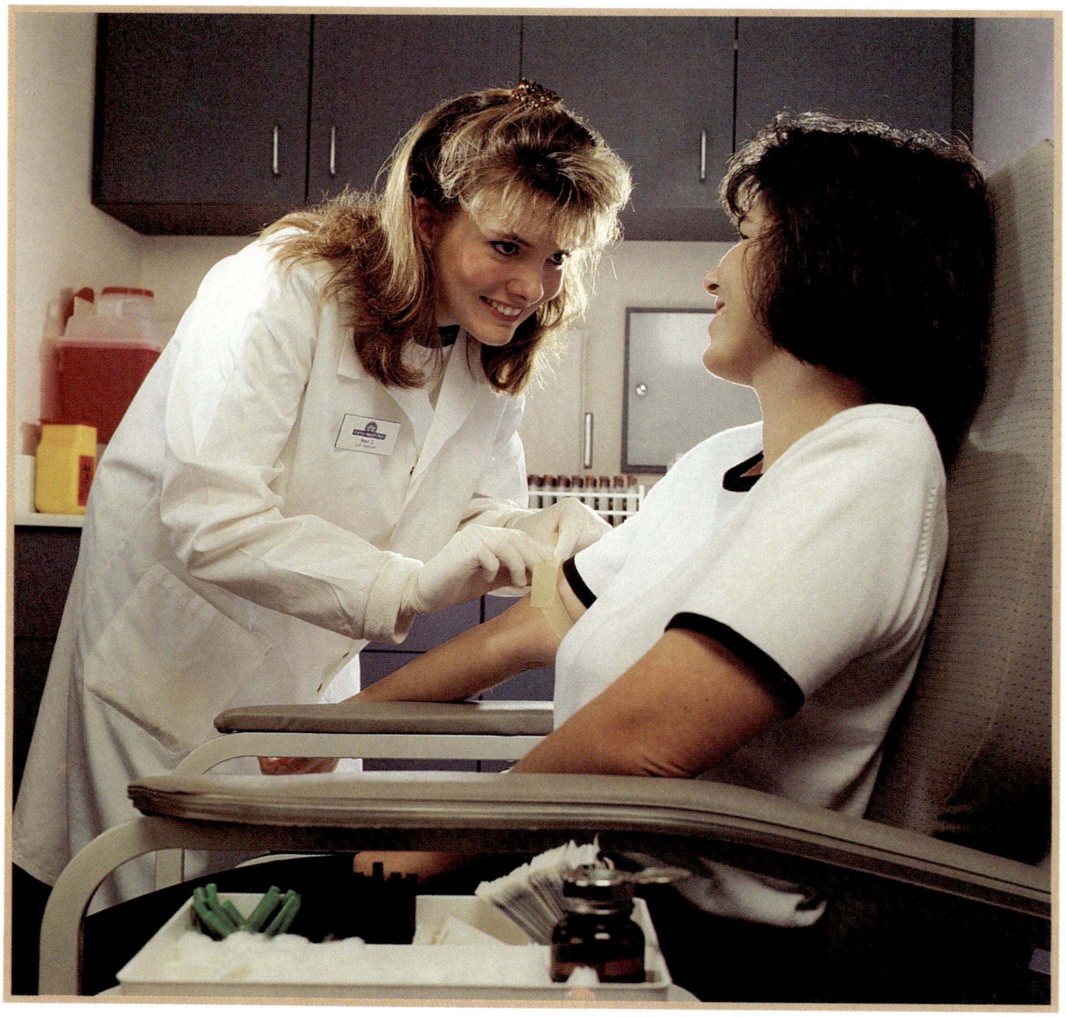

Each of Family Health Plan's seven health centers features a lab, pharmacy, X-ray, dietician, and health education services in addition to primary care. Chiropractic, optometry, mental health, maternity care, pediatrics, and other specialty services are also provided at many Family health centers.

ing membership." Recent member surveys reveal strong member satisfaction associated with Family Health Plan's convenience, broadness of benefits, the appearance of the centers themselves, and Family's doctors and hospitals.

Primary care is the core of Family's services, but the co-op has added a cadre of some 17 specialists in obstetrics, radiology, and general surgery and its own corps of nurses, nurse practitioners, physician assistants, and certified nurse midwives. "In-house, we can provide 85 percent of the care that people will require," Sobczak explains.

Perhaps most important, he says, is that Family has built an extremely effective preventive-medicine program because it is such a highly integrated health care source for its members. "Our health centers have become the focal point for our membership so that using an HMO is not only simple, but we can also organize and promote our prevention programs very effectively."

For example, Family's staff-model structure makes it easy to promote awareness among women of the need for mammograms—and to provide the exams as well. "We've got mammogram machines running six days a week now," he says. On similar bases, Family promotes prenatal care, immunizations to members of all ages, blood-pressure screening, eye and ear exams, and other procedures meant to improve life for patients—and keep costs down for everyone.

"Americans have had this love of high tech and they view health care as a fix-up product, like, 'I can live my life the way I wish, and then it's up to you to do the overhaul,'" Sobczak says. "But we're finding that there's a cultural transformation where there is more of an emphasis on health and wellness, and in our area, we're doing a lot to promote that."

That point is proven in part by statistics generated by Family for an "HMO report card" project recently sponsored by the National Committee for Quality Assurance. Family's scores surpassed many local, state, and national results, including the fact that 81 percent of member children had all of the recommended immunizations by the age of two and the fact that 95 percent of pregnant women had prenatal care during the first trimester, as compared with the national average of 76 percent.

Controlling other costs has enabled Family Health Plan to invest effectively in technology, usually a costly category. For example, Family has special telecommunications equipment at its switchboard that helps hearing-impaired members, and nurses carry laptop computers that they fill with data about patients and their progress as they visit each contracting hospital every day.

Family Health Plan's Waukesha Health Center is one of its seven Milwaukee-area centers.

All of this has made Family Health Plan attractive to physicians even though the traditional dream of medical doctors has been to build their own practices. Those who join Family often want to forego the business side of their practices because they don't enjoy it, and many want to work collegially with other physicians. Also, because many of them are family practice physicians, they often have access to a higher level of technological resources by being part of Family than they could have expected to enjoy on their own.

Sobczak says it's gratifying to see the rest of the local health care system follow Family's lead in terms of its structure and orientation. "Hospital systems now are trying to recruit and hire physicians," he cites as an example. "And you're seeing the consolidation of hospital systems and a greater emphasis everywhere on integration for cost-effectiveness."

Family intends to continue to progress so that it can stay at the forefront. For example, the co-op now finds itself closely aligned with Covenant Healthcare, a regional, integrated health care system featuring several local hospitals and other facilities.

"We have the benefit of having been engaged in this approach to our industry for more than a decade while other health care systems haven't," he says. "But I don't expect them to be slow learners."

Aurora Health Care

More than a decade ago, in its formative years, Aurora Health Care forged a strategic vision that successfully anticipated the dramatic change that has marked the health care industry since then, including an emphasis on reduced cost and the redefinition of how care is provided.

Aurora's foresight has allowed it to rapidly move toward its goal of becoming the leading health care provider in eastern Wisconsin, offering an Aurora care site within 15 minutes of just about anyone in the region. Aurora is a highly integrated, quality-conscious, cost-effective organization that encompasses the entire continuum of care from obstetrics to geriatrics, from primary prevention to organ transplants.

So it's interesting to hear G. Edwin Howe, president of the not-for-profit organization, tell what he sees unfolding in the decade ahead for health care. And for Aurora, Howe's current vision doesn't involve resting on its laurels.

"There's no breathing time available at all—in fact, we have to move a lot faster," Howe says. "By implementing a patient-centered philosophy that is committed to total quality improvement, Aurora is bringing together physicians, therapists, nurses, psychologists, social workers, and other health care providers to create a team whose purpose is to maintain and improve patients' health. It's an exciting time."

The beginnings of the Aurora system occurred in 1984, with the affiliation between St. Luke's Medical Center on Milwaukee's south side and Good Samaritan Medical Center, which in 1987 merged with Mount Sinai to create a new downtown medical center combining three hospitals with long and diverse histories of health care service. Aurora's expansion and integration as a much larger organization was driven by the same forces that are at work today across Wisconsin and the nation—business and civic leaders and hospital trustees urging providers to pool their efforts to reduce costs and better match the delivery system to the community's changing needs.

Aurora spent the next several years consolidating its management services and creating the information systems that would enable the organization to operate as an integrated system—not just a collection of hospitals and clinics. By 1992, with health care reform looming and market pressures mounting, Aurora was poised for growth. Four years later the system, based at 3000 West Montana Street in Milwaukee, had stretched its service boundaries along eastern Wisconsin from the Illinois state line to Marinette County, welcoming as partners clinics, hospitals, and a visiting nurse association intent on preserving quality, improving services for patients, and reducing costs.

Strategic alliances formed in 1993 with the United Health providers in the Fox Valley region, and in 1995

An Aurora affiliate, The Visiting Nurse Association of Wisconsin (VNA) is the leading provider of home health services in Milwaukee and is dedicated to providing personalized, high-quality, cost-effective home care. VNA services allow patients and their families to achieve the maximum level of independence in the community.

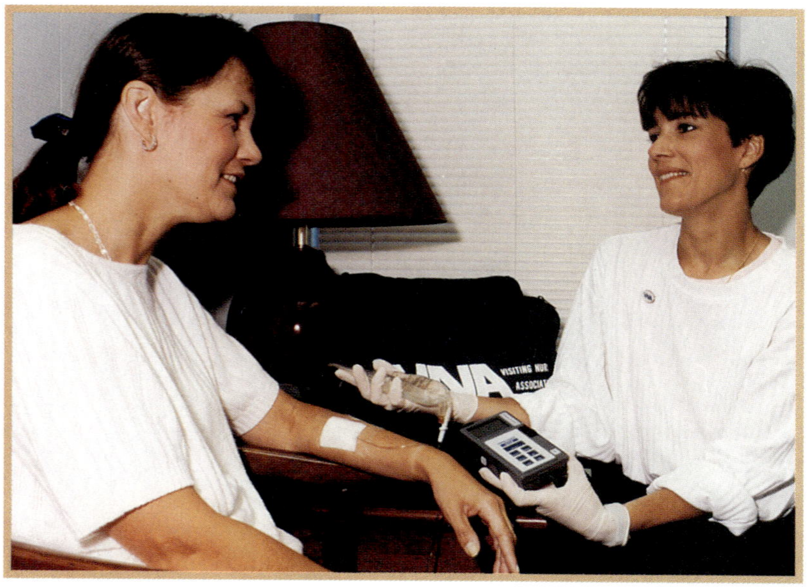

As one of the nation's leading cardiac care centers, St. Luke's Medical Center offers a cardiac rehabilitation program that provides patients with personalized counseling and therapy, resulting in significantly improved patient outcomes.

Aurora Health Care's Heil Center, on Milwaukee's near south side, houses a wide variety of corporate departments including accounting, linen services, purchasing, creative services, marketing, public affairs, and information services. These departments provide support to Aurora affiliates in Milwaukee and throughout the regional system.

with Bellin Health System in Green Bay, brought Aurora into other partnerships designed to improve the efficiency of health care delivery in Wisconsin.

Today Aurora serves the region through 15,000 employees working in 100 facilities located in 15 counties, including nine general hospitals and medical centers, a psychiatric hospital with nine psychiatric outpatient centers, 75 community clinics, more than a dozen rehabilitation centers, a family service agency, two skilled-nursing facilities, two home-care agencies, and several other health care delivery sites. It's governed by a board of trustees selected to represent the communities it serves, including not only business and community leaders, but nurses and physicians, among them University of Wisconsin Medical School faculty.

Aurora has grown and succeeded because its basic approach made sense. Geographic expansion has enabled large territorial employers and insurance companies to receive a full range of services regardless of location. Adding new members has allowed economies of scale in purchasing, clinical lab work, billing, and other back-office functions that help Aurora remain cost-effective.

An emphasis on providing outpatient and in-home care—and moving patients out of expensive hospital beds to the extent possible—also has been a major factor in Aurora's success. In 1995, for the first time, Aurora cared for more patients in its clinics and in patients' own homes than in hospitals. Hospital care now accounts for less than half of Aurora's business.

"In downtown Milwaukee alone, there used to be 1,700 beds in seven hospitals," says Howe. "Now there's just Sinai Samaritan. We've helped eliminate the cost burden of 1,500 excess beds in that area, while being absolutely committed to supporting the only remaining downtown hospital."

The creation of "an environment that lets people be successful at what they do," Howe says, also has contributed. For example, because Aurora believes it is essential for physicians to play a leading role in shaping the health care delivery system as well as coordinating patients' care, the organization developed the Aurora Medical Group as a distinct physician services corporation focused on the delivery of primary and ambulatory care.

Aurora is also developing state-of-the-art communications systems so that, across its system, the same patient record is shared. This "seamless" system cuts costs by avoiding duplication of services and improves quality because the provider of each type and increment of patient care will have access to necessary information from the complete medical history.

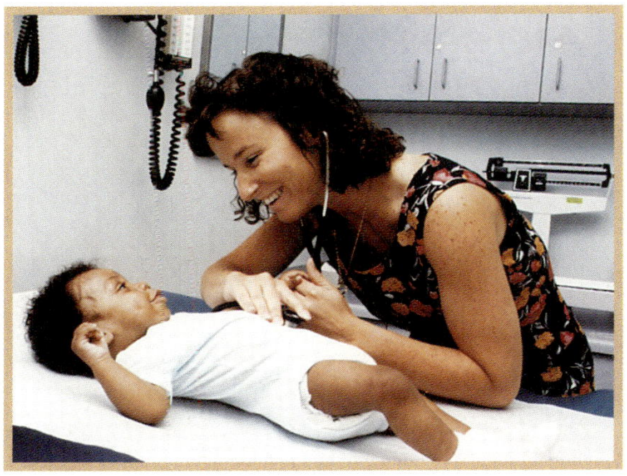

The new Outpatient Health Center at Sinai Samaritan Medical Center, which opened in 1995, has allowed the hospital to consolidate many of its clinic services, including pediatrics, in a convenient, accessible, single site.

Another key to Aurora's approach is to address social problems as interlocked with health care needs. For example, Family Service of Milwaukee, which joined the Aurora system in 1995, helps build and repair families and neighborhoods by offering prevention programs for high-risk families, counseling for families in crisis, and special services for the elderly and their families.

And, as Howe suggests, Aurora won't stop innovating. Recent fresh approaches include the Wisconsin Health Information Network, which links even competing health care providers electronically to cut administrative costs, and the Executive Fitness Program at the Milwaukee Heart Institute, which provides 10 weeks of supervised activity and customized guidance from an exercise physiologist and a registered dietitian.

"While many people are waiting to see what the government will do, we're aggressively seeking new solutions," Howe explains.

St. Mary's Hospital of Milwaukee

From their humble beginnings in Milwaukee in 1848, caring for the typhus-stricken passengers of an immigrant ship, to the opening of a state-of-the-art outpatient medical facility in Ozaukee County in 1994, St. Mary's Hospital and the Daughters of Charity have always worked to provide for the health care needs of individuals and families throughout southeastern Wisconsin.

Grateful that the Daughters helped prevent the spread of disease in the small Milwaukee community, the city fathers gave them three and a third acres of land for a hospital on the present northeast location overlooking Lake Michigan. The Sisters built the first St. Mary's Hospital in 1909, and constructed a 100-bed addition in 1959. In 1976 St. Mary's opened a new 314-bed patient tower.

Nine years later St. Mary's purchased a hospital in Port Washington that became its first Ozaukee County facility. In 1994 St. Mary's opened a replacement facility in Ozaukee County, an 80-bed hospital near I-43 in Mequon. The visually striking, well-appointed facility provides cost-effective health care with an emphasis on outpatient care.

In the fall of 1995 the Daughters of Charity accepted a transfer of sponsorship from the School Sisters of St. Francis for Sacred Heart Rehabilitation Hospital, a Catholic health care institution with over 100 years of service dedicated solely to the needs of the physically challenged. Now located on the St. Mary's Hospital campus, Sacred Heart continues to offer a full continuum of inpatient and outpatient programs throughout the community ranging from general rehabilitation and sports medicine to brain-injury and coma recovery.

Several of St. Mary's other specialty programs include a full-service Cardiac Care Center, with cardiology and electrophysiology services, surgery, and rehabilitation for both routine and high-risk patients; a broad range of services for women and children, including infertility treatment, a Neonatal Intensive Care Unit and transport team, and a Center for Women's Health; oncology services including radiation oncology and an inpatient Hospice; a Regional Parkinson's Disease Center; a Regional Burn Center; and a Long Term Respiratory Unit.

St. Mary's also has numerous satellite medical clinics, an important example of the Daughters' commitment to providing preventive medicine, behavioral medicine, health education, and wellness services in local neighborhoods.

St. Mary's continues to demonstrate the vision and mission of the Daughters of Charity by placing a strong emphasis on family practice medicine. A Family Practice Residency Program and Clinic promote the "art" as well as the "science" of medicine, while providing care for families in underserved indigent urban communities surrounding Milwaukee's east side.

As a member of the community-based network, Horizon Healthcare, Inc., St. Mary's Hospital is working with other member hospitals to create a stronger community health care network recognized for value and cost-effective services. In addition, a joint operating agreement between St. Mary's Hospital and its Horizon partner, Columbia Hospital, will further promote, restore, and maintain the health of individuals and families in Milwaukee and Ozaukee counties.

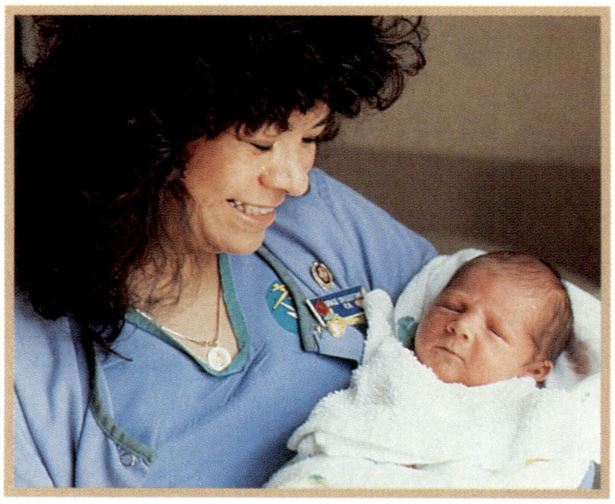

Sinai Samaritan Medical Center

When Sinai Samaritan Medical Center consolidates its operations at a single campus in downtown Milwaukee about two years from now, the move will represent yet another bold step in the evolution of an organization that has adapted to the sweeping changes in health care at the same time that it has stuck by its philosophy of health care.

At its future headquarters on 12th Street between Kilbourn and State streets, Sinai Samaritan plans to construct a five-story patient tower and a physicians' office building. The organization also will add facilities that stress special areas of care, such as women's medicine and physical rehabilitation services, to a complex that already houses Sinai Samaritan's renowned Milwaukee Heart Center and the new Outpatient Health Center.

"To maintain and even improve the high quality of care that we have provided historically, our facilities must be as highly integrated as possible," says William I. Jenkins, president of Sinai Samaritan, which plans to phase out its other current campus, at 21st Street and Kilbourn. "This move will help us continue to position ourselves at the center of health care in metro Milwaukee."

The Milwaukee Heart Institute of Sinai Samaritan Medical Center provides a full range of cardiac care services emphasizing prevention and wellness.

Even as change has been a constant for Sinai Samaritan, the values of the founders of its various member entities have endured: excellence in caring, devotion to service, and strength from diversity. Sinai Samaritan's origins were in 1863 when Lutherans founded Milwaukee Hospital, the first Protestant hospital west of Pittsburgh, which later became Lutheran Hospital. Jewish leaders opened Mount Sinai Hospital in 1903. And in 1910 the precursors of today's United Church of Christ founded Evangelical Deaconess Hospital.

As consolidation pressures began to reshape health care in the modern era, the three institutions responded. In 1980 Lutheran and Deaconess hospitals merged as Good Samaritan Medical Center, and in 1984 Good Samaritan affiliated with St. Luke's Medical Center. The joining of forces came to a head in 1987, when Mount Sinai merged with Good Samaritan to form what is now Sinai Samaritan Medical Center.

By 1993 Sinai Samaritan had formulated strategic goals that included continuing to provide excellent medical facilities downtown, ensuring top-notch care for the city's urban population, and maintaining affiliations with the University of Wisconsin Medical School, the Medical College of Wisconsin, and other educational entities, supporting excellent training for the state's physicians, nurses, and other providers.

The opening of the Milwaukee Heart Institute in the fall of 1993 was another manifestation of Sinai Samaritan's vision. The institute represented "more than just a repackaging of services," Jenkins says. "It was the enhancement of a center of excellence for a crucial segment of medicine with a commitment to a way of delivering heart care that is noninvasive and preventive—stressing diet and exercise, for instance—as well as therapeutic, which is very much the direction that the managed care of health services has been heading."

Similarly, Sinai Samaritan has moved to facilitate the trend toward more efficient outpatient care, as its average length of stay has declined to fewer than five days now from about seven days at the beginning of the decade. "We're showing that our patients can receive the same quality of care they're used to receiving from Sinai Samaritan even as we find more cost-effective ways of delivering our services to them," Jenkins says.

Right: The Outpatient Health Center of Sinai Samaritan Medical Center opened in 1995 to serve the medical center's patients.

The Blood Center of Southeastern Wisconsin

By extending its diligence and attention to quality of related blood services, clinical laboratory work, and research such as its pathfinding work in marrow donation, The Blood Center of Southeastern Wisconsin has become known as an international leader, an institution that truly has made "world class" and "Milwaukee" synonymous in its field.

The Blood Center's determination to provide leadership well into the future was underscored in 1994 when it moved into a spacious, bright new headquarters building on the site of its longtime headquarters at 638 North 18th Street.

Blood Services

The seeds of that move had been sown in 1946 by the foresight of the Junior League of Milwaukee. The Medical Society of Milwaukee County told the league that a blood bank was needed in the community to centralize the blood supply and provide immediate access to all blood types to nearby hospitals. In 1947, after it had contributed $38,000 to the center finances, the Junior League Blood Center opened on Wells Street.

Just as important: Unlike most other blood centers opening around the country, the Junior League determined from the start that research would be a part of the basic mission of the Milwaukee Blood Center—a decision that continues to benefit the region.

With the regional efficiencies of blood collection providing the driving rationale, what became known as the Milwaukee Blood Center grew steadily over the decades. Today, working with tens of thousands of volunteer donors, The Blood Center of Southeastern Wisconsin annually provides the gift of life through 200,000 transfusions of blood and blood components to nearly 20,000 patients at 32 hospitals throughout the region.

Through its innovative telerecruiting methods and state-of-the-art testing systems, The Blood Center has become a self-sufficient provider of safe supplies of blood, even providing assistance to patients in other parts of the country where not enough blood is available. In some ways, The Blood Center is the largest volunteer organization in the region, with more than 100,000 donors always on file, drawn from the ranks of businesses, churches, schools, labor unions, and the metro area at large.

The Blood Center also has gained a sterling reputation for quality work in areas such as platelet disorders and treatment and a myriad of organ and tissue transplantation fields. In fact, it has provided more donors for lifesaving unrelated bone-marrow transplants—more than 250—than any other donor center in the world.

Clinical Laboratories

The Blood Center's Clinical Laboratories provide some blood-testing services that aren't available anywhere else in the country, such as DNA-based diagnosis of diseases and testing of certain bleeding, clotting, and immune disorders. And they continually search for new and better ways to diagnose and treat illnesses.

For example, a new laboratory was created in 1993 that helps doctors fight the most frequently seen form of adult leukemia with a test that is less expensive and more effective than anything previously available. And much faster: The work that formerly took up to six weeks now can be completed in two days.

Research

An early commitment to research has kept The Blood Center unraveling mysteries of blood disease and developing medicines from blood components. Researchers operate in a separate Blood Research Institute facility on the grounds of the Milwaukee Regional Medical Center. The Blood Center Research Foundation also owns the Genetic Testing Institute in Brookfield, which markets health care products such as blood-testing kits and generates dividend income for the foundation.

The Blood Center of Southeastern Wisconsin saves lives by ensuring the reliable, safe collection, storage, and transportation of blood and blood components to hospitals throughout this region of the state and beyond.

Waukesha County Technical College

Waukesha County Technical College nears the turn of the century having accomplished a big task: satisfying the varying educational needs of its diverse student body at the same time that it is fulfilling the lofty expectations of local employers.

Yet WCTC isn't resting on its widespread recognition as one of Wisconsin's finest centers of technical education. Instead, it is in the midst of a process of soul searching that is likely to be transformational for WCTC, which offers more than 50 programs and 2,000 different classes on its 130-acre campus in Pewaukee to more than 33,000 students.

"We're saying that probably the old answers aren't good anymore even though we've done some wonderful things," says Dr. Richard Anderson, a former guidance counselor at the school who has been WCTC's president since 1973.

Above: A WCTC instructor discusses career path options with a student.

Twenty years ago WCTC determined to seek to meet the emerging needs of two "customer bases": students in search of a career, and local companies in search of qualified employees. WCTC focused on offering depth in fewer programs than it might have, the most cost-effective, highest-quality approach, instead of risking shallowness over a greater number of disciplines.

So while the school's programs today range from architectural drafting to child care and development, from emergency medical technician to machine-tool operation, from nursing to retail management, its most important criterion is that each program present the highest quality in practical instruction.

WCTC also developed "workplace learning centers" at employers' office and factory sites, giving it "the ability to provide a traditional education anywhere," as Anderson puts it. Overall, WCTC's contracts for employee training grew from just a few thousand dollars in the late 1980s to $1.4 million in 1994.

Nowadays, says Anderson, with the rise of computer literacy and a growing shortage of qualified workers in Waukesha County, WCTC is trying to leverage its resources by "thinking more in terms of brokering educational programs rather than offering all of them ourselves."

So, for example, WCTC has struck up a partnership with Blackhawk Technical College in Janesville to offer a dental-hygienist program that neither institution could justify previously because of its cost-ineffectiveness, even though dentists in both locales had been pleading for just such an initiative. New compressed-video technology helps instructors teach interactively, as one class, two groups of students who are physically separated by 100 miles.

WCTC has also tapped into the Internet. The technology is used in the traditional mode, giving students access to research from around the world. The college also uses the Internet as a means of delivering instruction in selected courses.

And now the college is forming "occupational transfer" alliances with Marquette University, Marian College, and other institutions under which certain two-year WCTC degrees qualify recipients for junior status at the four-year schools.

"Everything we're doing is aimed at making us more customer-oriented than institution-oriented," Anderson says.

The Pewaukee campus of Waukesha County Technical College offers more than 50 programs and 2,000 classes to some 33,000 students.

Milwaukee Area Technical College

Local employers and employees have offered Milwaukee Area Technical College a major challenge: Help us succeed in the fast-changing, ever-more-demanding business markets of tomorrow.

If MATC's recent performance is any indication, the college will be more than up to its charge. The comprehensive, two-year technical institution, with major campuses in downtown Milwaukee and three area suburbs, has more than 35,000 students studying in more than 120 occupational programs.

In May 1995 more than 2,400 individuals graduated from MATC with a diploma or associate degree, and as of mid-1995, 93 percent of them were employed—and 95 percent were satisfied with their MATC training. And in recent surveys of Milwaukee-area residents, MATC has consistently finished as one of the top 10 factors that contribute to the quality of life.

Yet the demands for even greater performance in the years ahead are many. Thousands of employers throughout metro Milwaukee and beyond are depending on MATC to help supply them with a sufficient stream of qualified workers in a setting where a basic shortage of candidates has intensified—and in which the pace of technological change is making it harder than ever to keep current.

At the same time, the needs of MATC's student constituency are growing as well. More and more of them are retooling their skills as job demands and technologies change and grow or as careers change and grow. And many of the new jobs that will be created in the next decade will require training beyond high school but less than a baccalaureate degree—in other words, they'll require exactly the kind of education MATC is prepared to provide.

MATC has risen to the challenge by continually recasting the institution for an even more dynamic future. Local business owners and executives serve on college advisory committees to inform MATC about their needs. One result is an increased number of cooperative arrangements with businesses to assist the school with the capital equipment it requires to adequately train people. For example, the hardware for MATC's new Pre-Press Technology Center was mostly funded by the printing industry.

The college also is offering a greater number of shorter courses so that it can more immediately alleviate the urgent skill needs of local employers. For example, in the fall of 1996 MATC debuts a new 15-credit phlebotomy certification course. Not only is the phlebotomy (drawing blood) program filling local health care providers' needs for technicians, it is also launching students enrolled in the program onto a career track that often leads to advancement in the health field.

An integral part of Milwaukee for 85 years, MATC looks forward to helping the city and its residents prepare for the challenges of the next century.

Right: MATC's Milwaukee Campus is located in the bustling Westown area of the city's vibrant downtown.

Below: Hands-on instruction and one-on-one attention from knowledgeable faculty members are among the hallmarks of an MATC education.

St. Luke's Medical Center

A Seattle woman flew all the way to Milwaukee to have metal mesh tubes, called stents, placed in her arteries to brace them after a heart attack. That's because she determined that St. Luke's Medical Center was the best hospital, with the most experienced doctors in the country for the type of surgery she required.

People from 45 states and 20 foreign countries have come to St. Luke's for treatment in just the past three years. While it's on the cutting edge of research and treatment in many areas, St. Luke's has achieved a special reputation in two fields: heart and cancer care.

Located at 2900 West Oklahoma Avenue and part of Aurora Health Care, St. Luke's has focused on these specialty areas as part of its approach to the major consolidation of health care providers in southeastern Wisconsin and nationwide. Having established a reputation as a pioneer and a top-shelf practitioner in these two key areas has helped ensure the future of all that St. Luke's does to serve the community.

Wisconsin's Leading Heart Care Center

More heart surgeries, heart transplants, cardiac catheterizations, and angioplasties are performed at St. Luke's than at any other hospital in Wisconsin. Innovation and dedication to excellence have continued to place St. Luke's on the leading edge of cardiac care for decades.

Among other firsts, St. Luke's had the first heart catheterization program in the state and performed the first heart transplant in the Midwest, in 1968. By 1993 St. Luke's had performed more than 200 heart transplants. The next year St. Luke's became the first hospital in the Midwest to implant the vented electric Heartmate ventricular-assist device. In 1996 St. Luke's was the first facility in the nation to implant an atrial defibrillator, a state-of-the-art device used to correct rapid heartbeats.

St. Luke's offers the very latest cancer-treatment techniques, from surgery and chemotherapy to radiation therapy, autologous bone marrow transplantation, and immunotherapy. In 1994 the hospital treated the highest volume of cancer patients of any hospital in southeastern Wisconsin.

Its approach includes advanced technology, treatments, and rehabilitation; the Vince Lombardi Cancer Clinic for outpatient services; comprehensive prevention, screening, and education; and understanding and knowledgeable support groups. St. Luke's opened its first Vince Lombardi Cancer Clinic affiliate site in Sheboygan in 1994 and its second affiliate site in Slinger in 1996. St. Luke's established a comprehensive breast care program, and expanded its Musculoskeletal Tumor Service as well as programs in lung, prostate, and gynecologic cancers.

St. Luke's also is responding to the growing demand for women's health care services and offers a full range of diagnostic, medical, surgical, therapeutic, and education health services specifically for women throughout the different phases of their lives.

Yet St. Luke's doesn't focus on its core specialties to the exclusion of its important role in the community at large. In 1994 alone, it opened a health care center in New Berlin, the Madison Street Outreach Clinic on Milwaukee's south side, and the Mitchell Point Family Health Center, a community-based family practice clinic co-sponsored by Sinai Samaritan Medical Center and staffed by University of Wisconsin physicians.

St. Luke's is committed to working closely with the communities it serves to improve the health of all residents.

Top: Clinic coordinator Steve Ohly, RN, MS, examines a young patient at St. Luke's Medical Center's Madison Street Outreach Clinic. St. Luke's is committed to working closely with the communities it serves to improve the health of all residents.

Below: More heart surgeries, heart transplants, cardiac catheterizations, and angioplasties are performed at St. Luke's Medical Center than at any other hospital in Wisconsin.

Penfield Children's Center

Nothing hurts a community more than an inability to care for its disadvantaged children. And in the past few years, more and more such kids have been coming for help to Penfield Children's Center.

Fortunately, the center and its programs have managed to keep pace with demand, and Milwaukee's continuing interest and support promise to make Penfield Children's Center the focus of children's assistance efforts in the county for years to come.

"We've been getting tremendous support from the organizations that fund us, from our volunteers and staff, during a challenging time of transition," says James R. Ryan, president of the center. "That gives me confidence that we—and especially the children we serve—can look forward to an even brighter future."

Photo by Troy Withington Photography

Headquartered at 833 North 26th Street, Penfield Children's Center was founded in 1967 as a Montessori school. But within a couple of years, local neurologist Dr. Wilder Penfield helped create an institution that was much, much more. To carry out his notion that early intervention into the lives of physically or emotionally imperiled children was crucial to their complete and proper development, Penfield transformed the school into a comprehensive center to help such youngsters.

Because Penfield generally serves Milwaukee's most vulnerable population—infants from birth to age three, living in the most disadvantaged central-city environment—demand for its services has been rising steadily over the past several years as conditions have worsened for many of those kids.

In 1992 Penfield served 364 children. The following year the number rose to 616; in 1994, to 720 children; and in 1995, to 867. In large part to adequately service its quickly growing clientele, in 1995 Penfield doubled the size of its building, to its current area of 40,000 square feet.

Today more than 90 full-time professionals and staff and hundreds of volunteers serve Penfield's children over the course of a year. Invention and creativity rule as staff mix traditional and nontraditional approaches to learning.

Trained in disciplines ranging from child development and social work to physical therapy and speech pathology, Penfield's staff responds to social problems and conditions by implementing new programs, positioning the center at the leading edge of social and medical issues.

Programs at Penfield are multifaceted. Specific components offered through full-day treatment and individual outpatient programs provide a full range of services.

They include child development, in which individualized programs stimulate children's curiosity, abilities, and self-confidence; educational services to help youngsters reach their fullest learning potential; children's care services such as specialized day care for infants and young children with disabilities; special care for medically fragile babies; rehabilitative services; nursing services; family support such as home visits and family-development sessions; dietary services; and transportation.

Even better than the range of Penfield's services, however, is that hundreds of volunteers—complemented by a growing number of central-city residents—annually come from all sectors of metro Milwaukee to help.

Penfield Children's Center is a non-profit organization whose sole purpose is to rehabilitate infants and young children with disabilities through education, therapy and family programs so that they can attain their fullest potential.

Courtesy of WITI-TV SIX IS NEWS

Goodwill Industries of Southeastern Wisconsin

Goodwill Industries of Southeastern Wisconsin is happy to be renowned for its retail store operations. But behind the racks of bargain-priced clothing is an organization arrayed in the finery of human dignity.

Headquartered at 6055 North 91st Street, Goodwill in fact is a highly diversified, not-for-profit, community service organization whose purpose for the past 76 years has been to achieve the full participation in society of all individuals, especially through the provision of vocational opportunities to people with special needs. The majority of these individuals—almost 10,000 received services in 1995—are welfare recipients.

Goodwill's vision is to be the recognized leader in helping people who want to work—but who face barriers to employment—develop work skills, find work, and successfully perform that work. This vision is accomplished by unifying human services and business operations, innovations in resource utilization, and effective collaborations with others.

Goodwill's various business enterprises—retail, industrial, environmental, and laundry—work toward a common goal of offering employment and training opportunities, thereby assisting men and women in gaining the experience necessary for successful community employment.

Daily, almost 300 Goodwill program participants complete industrial, laundry, material-handling, and in-store processing tasks through the Work Services program. A starting point for many program participants is the Work Adjustment Training Program, where men and women are exposed to the meaning, value, and demands of work and learn or reestablish work skills and behaviors.

Goodwill Industries has collaborated with multiple public and private organizations to establish successful job centers in Kenosha and Milwaukee. Strong results have been achieved through leadership, innovative programming, and interagency cooperation. Photo by Maria Huebner

Goodwill programs promote independence for all participants. From the Community Support program in Racine, which assists persons with mental illness, to the community programs in Milwaukee and Waukesha counties, programs are created to successfully integrate adults with multiple disabilities into the community.

Goodwill firmly believes that collaborating with other community-based organizations effectively utilizes resources while offering greater opportunities for the individuals who need services. This is certainly true in Kenosha County, where late in 1989 Goodwill helped in the development of the Kenosha County Job Center. This was the first one-stop job center in Wisconsin and one of the first in the nation. From this successful beginning grew a second job center initiative—the Milwaukee Job Center North.

Right: Goodwill Industrial Services is an excellent resource for businesses with packaging, assembly, and contract manufacturing needs. Goodwill program participants, in turn, receive valuable preparation for employment opportunities with local manufacturing companies. Photo by John Nienhuis

Goodwill has been successful in its efforts. In 1995 alone the organization provided an array of services to more than 12,000 people and placed 2,418 men and women into community employment. This effort has earned Goodwill Industries of Southeastern Wisconsin the distinction of being the largest of the 185 Goodwill organizations in North America.

Boys & Girls Clubs of Greater Milwaukee

In an age of difficult challenges for youth and families, Boys & Girls Clubs of Greater Milwaukee has expanded its facilities to meet the needs of 45,000 Milwaukee youths each year.

At six sites, the Clubs focus on combating youth delinquency by instilling positive values that help prevent problems from taking root, and preparing children for responsible, productive adulthood.

"The children we serve are Milwaukee's future," says R. Wallace Watson, executive director. "The majority of them will grow up here, work here, and raise families here. That's why what we do is so important not only to each individual child but also to the community as a whole."

Photo by Andrea Weiner

The Boys & Girls Clubs of Greater Milwaukee has served the community since 1887 and has become the city's largest neighborhood youth guidance organization. It also has been recognized as one of the top five Boys & Girls Club organizations in the nation.

One of the main reasons the Milwaukee Clubs are emulated is their innovative programs like the Truancy Abatement/Burglary Suppression (TABS) program. Milwaukee launched the citywide collaborative program in late 1993, becoming only the third city in the United States to do so—and the first to include a Boys & Girls Clubs component.

"Until TABS, the authorities really didn't have authorization to do much about truancy, so there was a lot of loitering and daytime crime by juveniles," Watson recalls. "This program allows parents, police, and other authorities to direct truants to us, so it addresses the problem at the same time that it becomes a positive influence in the kids' lives."

Since TABS began, nearly 8,000 truant students have been counseled, more than 60 percent were attending school 30 days after TABS contact, and juvenile crime dropped nearly 19 percent during TABS hours.

Courtesy of WITI-TV SIX IS NEWS

Overall, Boys & Girls Clubs are the largest source of support and guidance for central city children, helping them resolve crises and eliminate obstacles that prevent them from planning a productive and successful future. Value-based programs teach self-respect, caring for others, respect for the community and nature, and a strong work ethic.

The Clubs also applaud achievement—and thus create more excitement for learning—by means such as "Youth of the Year" and "Citizen of the Month" awards. And they teach skills ranging from life skills like parenting and nurturing to school- and job-related skills and recreational and creative skills.

The organization opens up whole new areas of opportunity that Club members otherwise wouldn't be able to experience, including summer camps, field trips, college scholarships, job training and placement, trips to leadership conferences, and international youth-exchange programs.

When it comes to results, the facts speak for themselves: Nationwide, 87 percent of Club youths graduate from high school compared with the national average of 66 percent; 25 percent finish college, compared with a national average of 16 percent. Another indication that participants truly assimilate the Clubs' values is that teen pregnancy and arrests related to substance abuse have decreased as much as 50 percent in neighborhoods with Clubs.

Says Watson, "How we touch kids' lives, and how that helps kids make more of their lives, encourages people to provide tremendous support to our agency."

Right: Photo by Nicholas Patrinos

St. John's Home of Milwaukee

Milwaukee, like America itself, is maturing. St. John's assures that Milwaukee's residents can do so with grace, nurturing, independence, and certainty that they will receive care when they require it.

That's what St. John's has been doing since 1868, when it was founded by a group of Episcopal Church women. Now, St. John's—headquartered at 1840 North Prospect Avenue—comprises St. John's Tower Apartments, Canterbury assisted care center, St. John's Home skilled nursing facility, home health services, rehabilitation services, and Sunrise Care Center skilled nursing facility.

St. John's Tower Apartments provide comfortable and secure apartment living for Milwaukee's independent seniors.

Right: St. John's has developed a winning combination of care, convenience, and security for its residents.

The wide range of facilities and services owned and operated by St. John's attests to how seriously it regards the philosophy of providing a "continuum of care" for its residents. "Our array of services is rare in a retirement community," says Dennis Gralinski, St. John's president. "We believe we have developed the perfect combination of care, convenience, and security on which our residents have come to rely."

St. John's Tower provides comfortable and secure apartment living for Milwaukee's independent seniors. When residents select an apartment they have two financial arrangements—Life Care or Rental. "The philosophy behind St. John's Tower Apartments is that life begins at retirement. That's why many of our retired residents are more active than before they came here to live. People come here because they want to enjoy life to the fullest, without all of the demands that come with home ownership," according to Gralinski.

Canterbury assisted care center provides for those who can live independently but may need some help with demanding daily tasks. St. John's Home is a skilled nursing facility providing private rooms and special programming for those with Alzheimer's disease or related impairments. St. John's Home Health Services cares for people in their homes across southeastern Wisconsin while St. John's Rehabilitation Agency provides physical, occupational, and speech therapy at St. John's and at several adult day care centers in and around Milwaukee. Finally, Sunrise Care Center, an affiliate of St. John's, provides skilled nursing to residents of Milwaukee's south side.

"With the increased focus on health care and fitness, people live longer and healthier lives. At the same time, hospitals are providing less and less of a harbor for people to recover from illness and injury," explains Gralinski. "So we offer a warm, caring atmosphere along with highly skilled health care to return someone to independence after illness and injury." Also, a wide variety of cultural and social activities is available to all residents, including the acclaimed Uihlein-Peters Art Gallery and the Flagg Theatre.

Photo by Eric Oxendorf/Third Coast Stock Source

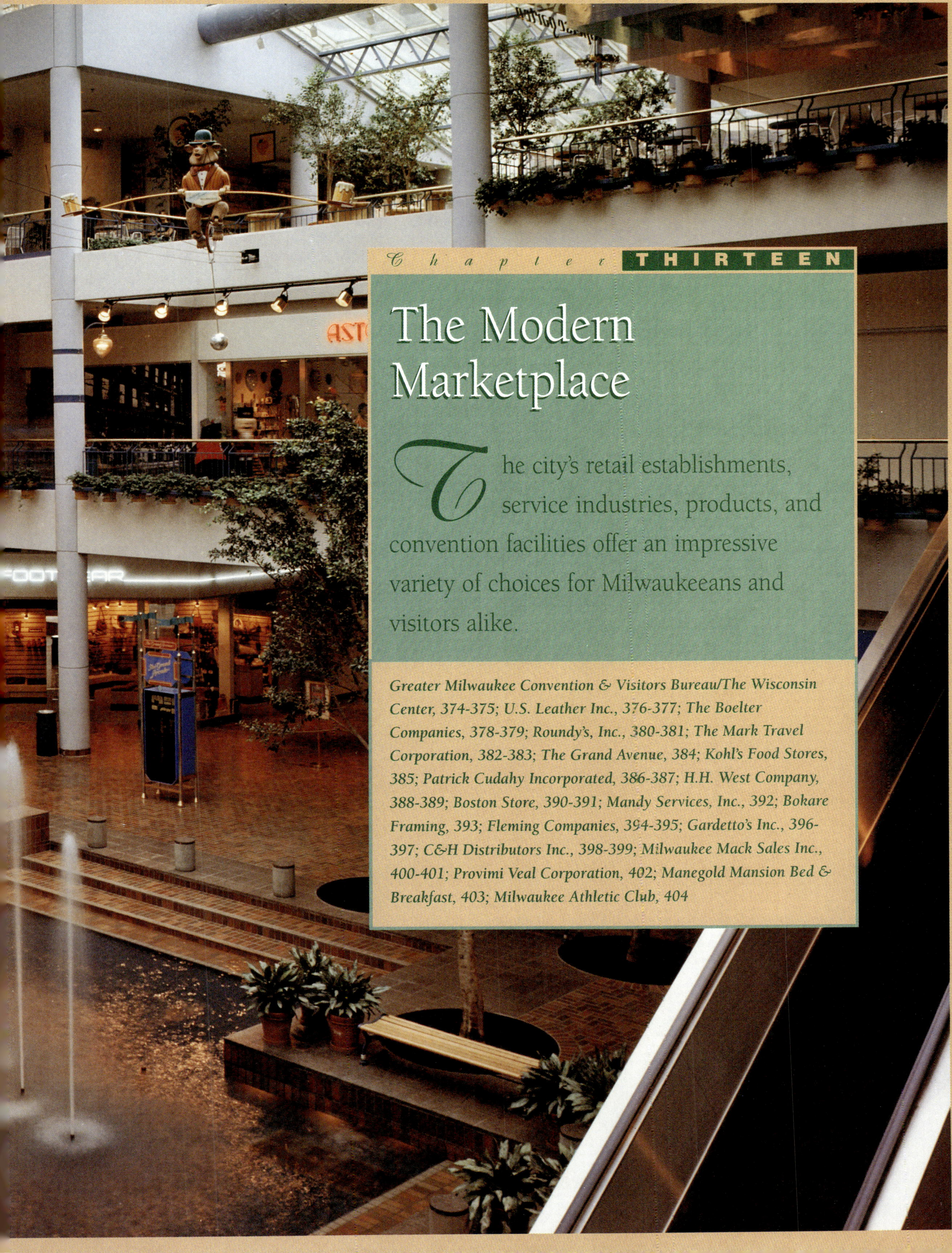

Chapter THIRTEEN

The Modern Marketplace

The city's retail establishments, service industries, products, and convention facilities offer an impressive variety of choices for Milwaukeeans and visitors alike.

Greater Milwaukee Convention & Visitors Bureau ~ The Wisconsin Center

The forces that propel conventions and tourism in Greater Milwaukee have begun a strong push that they believe will raise the city's national profile significantly by the turn of the century.

With a new slogan and logo for Milwaukee, a new director of the Greater Milwaukee Convention & Visitors Bureau (GMCVB), and a new state-of-the-art convention complex in the works, city convention and tourism executives are optimistic about grabbing more "share of mind" for Milwaukee over the next few years and about garnering a larger share of the booming meetings market.

"We consider ourselves an emerging national tourism and convention destination, a vital, dynamic, *new* destination that can be competitive with the St. Louises and Indianapolises of this country," says William A. Hanbury, president of the GMCVB. "And we're willing to concede that we have not been that until now."

Hanbury, who took the reins of the bureau in 1994, is optimistic about Milwaukee's emerging higher profile for several reasons in addition to the new marketing effort and the expected opening of the Wisconsin Center convention complex in 1998.

He also points to the city's retention of the Milwaukee Brewers with a $250-million new stadium and to the ongoing physical renaissance of downtown Milwaukee, including the new Betty Brinn Children's Museum in the Pavilion at O'Donnell Park on Lake Michigan, the $170-million Wisconsin Center convention facility, the $27-million Milwaukee Art Museum expansion, the $10-million Riverwalk project and the new IMAX Theater complex connected to the Milwaukee Public Museum, and the new Discovery World Museum of Science, Economics and Technology.

"All those elements give this period an exciting feel sort of like a decade ago, when the Grand Avenue Mall was opening and the Bradley Center was being built," says Mary Denis, the director of tourism for the GMCVB.

The GMCVB is an independent sales agent responsible for promoting and marketing metro Milwaukee as a tourism and convention destination. Established in 1967, the bureau is a private, nonprofit coalition of business, industry, and organizations; it is not a government agency. It is funded primarily by a percentage of the room tax levied by hotels and motels in Milwaukee, Wauwatosa, and Glendale.

The biggest recent initiative by the bureau itself was the initiation in late 1995 of a new slogan and logo for Milwaukee: "Genuine American." In replacing the previous theme, "Great City on a Great Lake," the GMCVB was seeking to reflect the ethnic diversity of Milwaukee; its hardworking, industrial heritage; and a

Milwaukee is an emerging national tourism and convention destination, in large part due to the efforts of the GMCVB. Courtesy, Dave La Haye

contemporary, energizing attitude.

"Milwaukee: Genuine American" immediately became the focus of the GMCVB's advertising campaign in its key markets of the Fox Valley of Wisconsin, central Wisconsin, and Chicago and northern Illinois. The bureau launched a new toll-free number (1-800-554-1448) for the "Genuine American Getaway," which supplies callers not only with up-to-date information about the city, its accommodations, and attractions, but also gives them the capability to make reservations, buy tickets, and order an individualized travel itinerary during the same phone call.

The bureau has conducted a benchmark study of perceptions of Milwaukee by outsiders in its key regional tourism markets and plans to check for any changes periodically. Another new initiative tied to the slogan is first-ever international advertising for Milwaukee as a tourist destination. The bureau took out ads in travel-trade journals in Germany. The city's tie-in via its German heritage made that country a natural, of course, but there's more.

"Germans have a lot of vacation and expendable income, and many of them have seen all the big U.S. cities," Denis explains. "They like water, good food, golfing, and the Native American culture, so it seems natural for tour companies there to offer, say, shopping in Chicago and then the ability to come to Milwaukee and Wisconsin for an additional escape."

By far the biggest addition to Milwaukee's national and international image will be the Wisconsin Center. Convention executives expect the completed structure, along with the planned addition of 500 rooms by adjacent hotels, to leapfrog Milwaukee over many other similar-size cities in the intensifying derby to land meetings business. One reason Hanbury expects the opening of the complex to have immediate impact is that no other new convention center will be opening in a major American city for another two years after the Wisconsin Center debuts.

Another reason for high hopes surrounding the Wisconsin Center is that it will be "an information superhighway marvel," according to Hanbury. "The spine of the building will include every technological whistle and bell imaginable, from fiber optics to state-of-the-art audiovisual capabilities. It will all be adaptable. The Wisconsin Center will be a tremendous asset for the entire area."

The completed complex will provide 700,000 square feet of combined space, with 200,000 square feet of exhibit space built to convention-industry standards. A 40,000-square-foot ballroom will hold 3,200 people. Forty meeting and breakout rooms will include more than 50,000 square feet of space for groups ranging from 150 people to more than 10,000 at a time.

The Wisconsin Center will replace the Milwaukee Exposition and Convention Center and Arena (MECCA), which has its own storied heritage. It hosts national conventions such as that for sales agents for Northwestern Mutual Life Insurance Co., and many local and regional events including the auto and sports shows, the annual Holiday Folk Fair, and even wedding receptions. Before the Bradley Center opened in 1987, the Milwaukee Bucks played in MECCA.

But, says Hanbury, the relatively small size and limited flexibility of MECCA, as well as an inadequate number of hotel rooms, have handicapped Milwaukee's convention business, especially as competing U.S. cities have overhauled and expanded existing facilities or built new centers.

The Wisconsin Center should bring a dramatic jump in visitors to Milwaukee, both because of its attributes as well as the fact that the convention business continues to surge by about 20 percent a year in this country, creating more and more opportunities to land bookings. Already, Hanbury says, the Wisconsin Center has been able to book the national conventions of the International Association of Chiefs of Police for 2000 and the American Jail Association in 2001.

"There's a new energy and confidence among community leaders that we need to be more proactive about the Wisconsin Center and everything else we've got to offer," Hanbury says. "There's a lot to offer about Milwaukee, and more is coming fast."

The Wisconsin Center, slated to open in 1998, is expected to bring a dramatic increase in convention business to Milwaukee.

U.S. Leather Inc.

Pfister & Vogel is an allegory for many Milwaukee companies: a successful enterprise in a traditionally American industry that is, by pluck and determination, continually overhauling itself to remain a strong player in the newly globalized economy.

Founded in 1848 by German immigrants Guido Pfister and Frederick Vogel, the company is the oldest tanner in Milwaukee, traditionally one of the nation's tanning centers. The business is headquartered at a half-million-square-foot plant on North Water Street, the nation's largest tannery under one roof, and annually produces 45 million square feet of leather while employing some 500 people.

In 1988 Milwaukee-based U.S. Leather Holdings, now U.S. Leather Inc., purchased P&V and A.L. Gebhardt and assembled them under one corporate umbrella. U.S. Leather's worldwide annual sales exceed $340 million.

Pfister & Vogel is the leading domestic producer of finished leather used in high-quality men's casual shoes.

Top right: The company annually produces 45 million square feet of leather while employing some 500 people.

P&V produces more than 100 lines of shoe leather as well as "wet-blue" hides and "splits," leather products that it markets to other leather-processing plants worldwide. The leading domestic producer of finished leather used in high-quality men's casual shoes, P&V counts among its customers practically every maker of such shoes in the United States and many around the world, including Sebago, Bass, L.L. Bean, Timberland, Florsheim, and Cole-Haan.

Milwaukee-based A.L. Gebhardt, the second-largest U.S. Leather operation, is a world leader in specialty leathers for personal accessories, sporting goods, and shoes and work boots. Its division in Berlin, Wisconsin, processes gameskins. Gebhardt also processes unfinished and finished split leather.

Some of Gebhardt's products go into garments such as high school letter jackets and other items including Amity and Prince Gardner wallets, and the tags on the waistline of Lee jeans. The company also supplies seats and saddlebags for Harley-Davidson motorcycles, a boom market if ever there was one.

Now Gebhardt is in the midst of a drive to expand its presence in high-volume footwear leather, though in end markets not as upscale as those of its larger affiliate. Gebhardt already has succeeded to a significant extent: For example, it is producing the uppers for the popular Doc Martens style manufactured by Ehrwehr of Great Britain.

The market battle is epic for Pfister & Vogel. Maintaining production in America, with high labor and other costs compared with overseas manufacturing, has meant that P&V has had to successfully market high-margin products to ensure continued profitability.

That strategy, in turn, has meant having some staffers whose lucky jobs are globetrotting major fashion centers to keep up on international fashion trends so that the company can make its most informed, most sophisticated product pitches to shoe manufacturers.

Such proprietary intelligence, for instance, helped Pfister & Vogel identify the trend toward business-casual dress around the world several years ago—long before it became a staple look in the United States. In turn, the company was able to develop and market leather varieties appropriate for loafers and other casual styles.

Another challenge is that, because more and more shoes sold in the United States are made abroad, particularly in the Far East, the company's base of end customers is dwindling. A similar shakeout among shoe companies in this country occurred in the early 1980s before leveling off around 1984, but the process seems to have begun again.

One of the first international leather companies to recognize the importance of exports—more than two decades ago—P&V now exports about 70 percent of its production, more than double the level of exports just five years ago.

At the same time, while it's been many years since most shoes sold in the United States were made here, to date Pfister & Vogel has stayed ahead of foreign tanneries in terms of product development and sophisticated technological applications. But Asian companies are getting closer to matching P&V's franchise products and the firm is trying to develop products that stay one step ahead of them.

Indeed, the company is intent on keeping its technological leadership and continues to devote significant resources to the goal of keeping a five-year edge on the rest of the industry. That's how P&V managed to lead most of the market with leathers for hiking-style ankle boots several years ago and, more recently, with its versions of the specially treated water-resistant leathers that have become popular.

P&V has needed technology and much more to meet the twin challenges of its significant continuing role as an industrial and social anchor in north-central Milwaukee: environmental cleanliness and employee satisfaction.

For two decades the firm has worked closely with regulators to maintain a state-of-the-art waste-management system, assuring that the water used in the plant is carefully purged of tanning toxins and other manufacturing byproducts before it is released into the Milwaukee sewer system. (Though it's adjacent to the Milwaukee River, P&V discharges no wastewater into the river.)

Pfister & Vogel and A.L. Gebhardt are spending a great deal of money to be exemplary environmental citizens. They are collecting, dampening, and reflecting everything they can, and are continually striving to meet the steadily increasing expectations of the company's performance by regulators and environmental activists in a neighborhood that, while once almost completely industrial, gradually has converted to a community of service businesses.

The firm maintains a state-of-the-art waste-management system, discharging no wastewater into the Milwaukee River.

The company even is trying to turn its leather scraps into an environmental plus. It has developed a golf-course fertilizer out of proteins derived from the scraps in a process that also recovers and reuses processing chemicals. The goal is to market this product to the point where demand could consume all of the Milwaukee-produced scraps, which right now go into the landfill.

Despite hourly wage and benefit levels that average about $18, the company has managed to keep its tannery cost competitive and highly productive through the extensive use of automation including robots, automatic stackers, electronic measuring equipment, infrared dryers, and bar code readers. In fact, Pfister & Vogel produces about 50 feet of leather per manhour compared with an industry average in the high 30s and low 40s.

At the same time, however, the company knows well that in some tasks, there is no substitute for human eyes and hands, including inspection and grading of hides during the tanning process. Any employee has the right to reject a flawed hide at any point of production.

P&V and Gebhardt extend their good citizenship by continually renewing their commitment to employ inner-city residents in well-paying manufacturing jobs. About 60 percent of the bigger company's work force is minority members, and that percentage is even higher at Gebhardt.

In many other ways, the company long has contributed to the community; for example, the Vogel family built Milwaukee's Vogel Recital Hall. This group of companies likes being here in Milwaukee and would like to stay here.

Left: P & V produces about 50 feet of leather per manhour compared with an industry average in the high 30s and low 40s.

The Boelter Companies

Some chief executive officers only talk the talk.

But when William Boelter tells an interviewer that the supportive "culture" of his privately held restaurant-supply enterprise, The Boelter Companies, is the most important contributor to its impressive growth, his customers—and his associates—back him up.

"We consider The Boelter Companies far, far more than just an equipment supplier," says Ron Hamel, director of development for Cousins Submarines, a fast-growing Menomonee Falls, Wisconsin-based chain. "We consider them a valuable resource."

Adds Dolores Juergens, associate restaurant director for Northwestern Mutual Life Insurance Co. in Milwaukee: "They really do put their heart and soul into helping a person succeed."

Boelter says that this sort of service-oriented approach pays off in optimal relationships with customers for Boelter's contract restaurant equipment, food-service supplies, industrial products, food and beverage promotional products, and food-facility design services. It also makes for happy company associates.

Bill Boelter (left), president of The Boelter Companies, presents a book on Milwaukee to Moscow's Mayor Popov in Brussels, Belgium, in 1993.

"Because our people in sales, for instance, know that they've got the whole company behind them, they've got an entirely different attitude," explains Boelter, whose father, Fred W. Boelter, Sr., founded the company in 1929. "They have tremendous confidence because they know they're not just out there alone.

"And our customers get to know that, unlike our competitors who may have one lone representative, we have a whole team of people to help them. It's difficult for them to compete with our whole company instead of just one person. Everyone in the industry has similar products; it's strictly the relationships you build that make the difference."

Over each of the past seven decades, in fact, The Boelter Companies has been a continually greater success. Sales have about doubled in the past five years; the firm employs more than 170 people at its locations in Milwaukee, Chicago, Detroit, Minneapolis, and the Fox Cities. In 1986 Boelter moved into a newly remodeled, 105,000-square-foot headquarters at 11100 West Silver Spring Road, formerly occupied by General Electric.

And even with the extreme competitiveness that is the rule in its markets, Boelter has distinguished itself by being named Dealer of the Year by *Foodservice Equipment and Supplies Specialist* magazine. The Boelter Companies' leaders have also been invited to speak before numerous industry groups and conventions.

One of the company's fastest-growing businesses currently is its promotional beverage products division, which provides printed glassware, coasters, and related items for brewers, national restaurant chains, and other major accounts. Boelter says that because the American restaurant business has become so competitive, many of this division's new accounts are cost-sharing "cooperative marketing" ventures between, for example, Chili's restaurants and Oscar Meyer or Lone Star Steak House, Molson beer, and, of course, The Boelter Companies. In 1994 Boelter received Miller Brewing Company's prestigious "Partner in Excellence" award from Miller's Promotional Products Division.

Boelter's food-facility design division continues to grow as well. Company design specialists provide comprehensive, start-to-finish food-facility development in a unique service that combines computer-aided design

Right: Eagan's on Water Street in downtown Milwaukee is a new and popular dining establishment for young and young-thinking adults in the Milwaukee area. Owner Jim Pandle says, "The Boelter Companies is very organized, runs smoothly, and really comes through when you're in a jam."

Far right: It takes top quality and superior service to become a Miller Brewing Company "Partner in Excellence" award winner. The Boelter Companies won this award in 1994 from the Miller Promotional Products Division for attaining the highest level of perfection.

Above: Chicago's famous Watertower Place on Michigan Avenue features "foodlife," a totally unique, upscale food court offering many ethnic entrées. The Boelter Companies had a key role in the design and installation of this outstanding concept.

Above left: The prestigious Onwentsia Country Club in Lake Forest, Illinois, did a recent kitchen remodeling to bring everything up to current codes. According to chef Ben Muhl, local health department officials said it was the finest remodeling job they had ever seen.

(CAD) technology and front-to-back interior design capabilities. The division, together with the contract-equipment division, has supervised the design and installation of food-service facilities for establishments as diverse as railroad dining cars for Charter Wire and Quad/Graphics, Milwaukee's gleaming Bradley Center, Cousins Submarines outlets, Northwestern Mutual Life, Children's Hospital of Milwaukee, and Westmoore Country Club.

The company's bread-and-butter business, so to speak, long has been its food-service supplies division, which carries complete lines of competitively priced tablesetting, kitchen, disposable, and janitorial products. Product line specialists offer customers extensive product knowledge and fresh ideas. A unique showroom that comprises the front of the corporate headquarters, unrivaled in the industry, displays a wide assortment of easy-to-find product samples across Boelter's various lines, on display in realistic settings.

This operation demonstrates the firm's philosophy of responsiveness to customers' needs in every area. The outside sales force carries laptop computers to begin information processing immediately and pagers to keep in touch with the office and with customers. A sophisticated inventory-control system and a fully computerized warehouse at the Silver Spring complex allow orders to be filled, loaded, and shipped usually within 24 hours. Customers are surveyed on an ongoing basis to determine their needs.

Boelter augments customer service by staying up to date on the trends shaping an industry that is moving faster and faster and by making sure that it disseminates the most current information thoroughly among its associates. "Building trust among our customers is a product of character and competence," Boelter says. "Integrity and honesty are important, but you have to couple them with providing the best possible expertise."

Another reason that continually building competence is crucial: In a business changing so quickly that "three- or five-year plans aren't useful anymore," says Boelter, his company is counting mainly on performing better and better in its current primary markets for future growth. For example, while Boelter already is a dominant presence in the Milwaukee-area restaurant market, it is garnering significant business in food-facility design from the many Native American-run casinos that are opening and expanding across Wisconsin and elsewhere in the Midwest. And while its Minneapolis-based operation offers only food-facility design and food-service equipment integration, Boelter believes that the company can grow significant business in both areas in that local market.

The company's fastest-growing and most recent major strategic gambit was the 1991 purchase of E.A. Hinrichs, a distributor of china and glassware for the white-tablecloth restaurant market that had offices in Chicago and Detroit. The Boelter Companies has fully integrated the former Hinrichs operations and broadened its lineup of products and services so that it now addresses a much fuller range of market opportunities. In metro Detroit, for example, Boelter has added customers like the Henry Ford Museum, General Motors, and The Palace pro basketball arena; in Chicago, the company's focus has been the many hotels that serve the local convention and tourist trades.

"We've only touched the tip of the iceberg in those markets because they're so big," William Boelter says.

Roundy's, Inc.

Roundy's, Inc., always focused its business around Milwaukee. From the day in 1872 when Smith, Roundy & Co. began business as a wholesale grocery distributor downtown, to the opening of its first Pick 'n Save warehouse supermarket on Bluemound Road a little more than a century later, Roundy's has understood its market—and prospered in it.

That's what Roundy's will continue to do for a long time to come as well. At a time of tremendous consolidation in its industry and unprecedented pressures to broaden its scope both geographically and structurally, Roundy's plans simply to get better and better at what it still does best: providing an expanding variety of high-quality, reasonably priced foodstuffs, delivered with maximum convenience, to member and other grocery stores in key markets in its home region.

"We're committed to the Upper Midwest," says David Busch, corporate vice president for administration. "All our focus is on development of that region. We want to be the number one wholesaler in the markets where we're already doing business."

A new model Roundy's tractor and trailer.

But that doesn't mean sitting still for Roundy's, which is the sixth-largest food wholesaler in the United States, generating revenues of nearly $2.5 billion in fiscal 1994 by supplying more than 1,400 supermarkets in 12 states. From its headquarters at 23000 Roundy Drive in Pewaukee, the company's nearly 5,000 employees are "constantly seeking opportunities to fill in the holes in our target area," Busch says. The company is experimenting with new store formats, tweaking its level of involvement in retailing, pioneering applications of data base marketing, and streamlining its cost structure.

Roundy's has always been a dynamic force in an industry where success is made difficult by a blur of change as well as by the constant of low margins compared with most other businesses. The company has deftly adjusted to—and often anticipated—new realities, dating back to 1892, when it burned to the ground during the Third Ward fire; Roundy's was back in business at another site within one week of the blaze.

The business formally incorporated as Roundy, Peckham & Dexter in 1902. In 1929 Roundy's introduced the "food studio," where women's club members flocked for a cooking demonstration followed by a free lunch and were sent home with a cookbook full of recipes using Roundy's products.

In 1953 a new corporation, Roundy's, Inc., owned cooperatively by hundreds of retail grocers throughout Wisconsin, bought the business; today the company still operates on a cooperative basis in Wisconsin, where it garners more than 40 percent of food purchases through its Roundy's Member and Pick 'n Save stores, and on a traditional supplier basis elsewhere. The new Roundy's built up-to-date warehouse facilities at a site on 113th and Burleigh, where many Milwaukee-area divisions are still housed today.

Roundy's began a growth spurt 20 years ago when it launched the Pick 'n Save format, which correctly anticipated that shoppers would be more than willing to bag their own groceries in a relatively spartan store setting in exchange for value. Soon Roundy's was taking the Pick 'n Save concept on the road, expanding it through company-owned and independent operations to outlets in Ohio, Illinois, Indiana, Michigan, and West Virginia.

The firm's latest adjustment phase began about five years ago, when the wholesale food-distribution industry began shrinking into two major players, Fleming Companies and Super Valu Stores, and a second tier consisting of Roundy's and a handful of other stalwarts in various regions of the country. The entire industry also saw completely new forms of competition such as warehouse buying clubs.

But while the two giants are increasing their presence in grocery retailing and expanding geographically, Roundy's management plans to focus on its historical roots in wholesaling in the Upper Midwest and, Busch says, "using our flexibility to best fit the needs of our independent-retailer customers."

Gold's East Pointe Market Place Pick 'n Save.

To that end, Roundy's has been boosting the efficiency of workflows in its 10 distribution centers in five states, in part by adopting "cross-docking," in which goods essentially move from the supplier's truck to the retailer's back room without idle warehousing in between. "It's a way to drive down costs in a big way without requiring a lot of capital investment," Busch explains.

At the same time, in an increasingly competitive environment, Roundy's and its labor unions have begun working to shave costs by redesigning work procedures and job responsibilities. Effective wage rates have risen along with a performance-oriented pay system. "We're accomplishing a lot by working together," Busch says.

Roundy's approach to retail operations continues to evolve as well. Its own, and many independent, Pick 'n Save stores have moved to a more upscale format that emphasizes greater variety and more service than in its original concept. To ensure that the company and the stores it supplies remain in the forefront, Roundy's also plans to introduce retail outlets with expanding fresh formats.

One concept under development is called Roundy's More for Less stores: low-price, limited-assortment outlets that could be established in smaller-population areas, like rural towns, or locations that are economically stagnant. Another concept is Roundy's Express convenience-type stores. A third under consideration is a perishables-only store.

Target marketing has emerged as another significant aspect of Roundy's strategy. Its innovative Advantage Plus Savers Club now has more than one million customer cards in distribution. Competitors have testified to its effectiveness by copying Advantage Plus.

During the past two years Roundy's has been rolling out a new wrinkle through more than 60 Pick 'n Save and Roundy's stores: The Advantage Rewards Program. Roundy's checkouts at each participating store record volume and frequency of purchases in tightly defined categories, and customer-activated kiosks print a list of discount offers targeted at each customer.

Advantage Plus and other technology-based efforts are helping Roundy's maximize use of narrower and more effective marketing. "The days of huge newspaper ads, and our not knowing who we're enticing, are over," Busch says. "We're improving our return on sales because we know what our customer base is buying, and we're better able to market to them."

The Mark Travel Corporation

When William La Macchia eagerly bought out the travel operation that he ran in 1974 on the strength of a bold idea about how to transform the leisure-travel business, he dreamed of having a successful company. But he never imagined that the business would grow into the huge enterprise that it has, The Mark Travel Corporation.

Frustration with the level of service he was receiving as a travel agent when he ran the travel subsidiary of Manpower Inc. was what originally motivated La Macchia to establish his own company as Funway Holidays Funjet. Its emphasis on service began to garner significant business, which allowed La Macchia to form The Mark Travel Corporation in 1983.

The Mark Travel's Diversity Initiative is aimed at providing a cohesive and multicultural work environment.

From there, the company has built tremendous economies of scale and has become an even stronger competitor in an intensely competitive industry.

After The Mark Travel established its own brand-name vacation company, now named Funjet Vacations—and known for its packaging and automation expertise in the travel industry—airlines and hotel chains began to look to the company to operate their leisure vacation packages.

In addition to Funjet Vacations, The Mark Travel has contracted with major industry powers to operate Southwest Airlines Fun Pack Vacations, USAir Vacations, United Vacations, Funjet Express, Vacations by Sheraton, and Mountain Vacations.

The Mark Travel, located at 8907 North Port Washington Road, has become a major corporate force in Milwaukee as well as a travel-industry leader. Employing more than 1,000 people in the city alone, La Macchia's notion has become one of the 10 largest privately held companies in the metro area, according to rankings by local media.

During the 20-plus years it has been in business, The Mark Travel has grown from 10 employees to more than 1,700, with 13 offices in the United States and in London, Jamaica, and Australia. The company also has distributors in Japan, Germany, and Italy.

With over $600 million in sales in 1995, The Mark Travel served more than 1.5 million vacationers. Its tour operations offer vacation packages to the United States, Hawaii, Canada, the Caribbean, Mexico, Latin America, Europe, the South Pacific, the Orient, and the rest of Asia. The Mark Travel Corporation has become one of the largest U.S. companies in the industry and is recognized for innovation, growth, strength, and the contributions it has made to the industry.

Each of its tour operations is a separate strategic business unit within The Mark Travel and is responsible for its own bottom line but draws upon the overall strength of the parent corporation and its shared operational departments. The corporation has built such a reputation that it has the buying power to negotiate large blocks of hotel and airline seats. In 1995 it controlled more than 15,000 hotel rooms every night.

It is one of only 43 travel businesses in the country that have the strength and financial stability to belong to the United States Tour Operators Association's $1 Million Consumer Protection Plan. The corporation actually must post a million-dollar bond and meet a long list of financial and management requirements to be accepted in the plan, which is proof positive to travel agents and vacationers that they can depend on all of

Funjet Express

Mountain Vacations

Funjet Vacations

USAir Vacations

Vacations by Sheraton

United Vacations

Southwest Airlines Fun Pack Vacations

Left: The company has more than 700 reservationists located in four call centers—Milwaukee, Denver, Orlando, and Salt Lake City.

The Mark Travel's companies to deliver.

The strength and success of the organization is the result of dedicated employees who have developed a knack for superior customer service. All vacation packages are backed with special services to agents and travelers.

For example, so it can provide complete time-zone coverage to travel agents across the country, The Mark Travel has more than 700 reservationists located in four call centers in Milwaukee, Denver, Orlando, and Salt Lake City. And the company has 24-hour traveler-assistance representatives to help vacationers with a variety of situations.

Other factors that have enabled The Mark Travel to assume industry leadership are its grasp of the importance of technology and La Macchia's recruitment of talented people, from reservationists to top management.

The company has built and maintains one of the largest and most advanced travel-product data bases in the industry. Designed by in-house programmers and technicians, the system meets The Mark Travel's changing needs and enables immediate availability and confirmation of hotel rooms and airline seats among all reservations centers, electronic distribution systems, and direct-access links in many travel agencies nationwide.

According to La Macchia, the company has been able to capitalize on industry relationships that have come its way because it was able to develop the specialized technology necessary. Its technology development has stayed on the cutting edge of the industry, particularly with electronic distribution systems. About 30 percent of the company's business now is handled through electronic distribution connections.

"Our greatest opportunity for the future is with technology," La Macchia says. "Our mission is to stay at the head of our industry with it. Our objective is to link our data base globally to create even more purchasing power in the United States and abroad.

"The trend toward more international travel is growing. And we're prepared to be a part of that."

La Macchia gives credit for The Mark Travel's success to its staff of creative and innovative individuals. It has retained high-caliber employees by empowering workers at all levels to make decisions, creating job satisfaction. The company's mission statement and guiding principles focus on outstanding people caring about the people they serve and promoting creativity, teamwork, and professional growth.

The Mark Travel also has pioneered its industry's involvement in building a multicultural work force. A committee of employees has been shaping The Mark Travel's Diversity Initiative, which is aimed at providing a more cohesive and multicultural work environment. Though The Mark Travel is large, it maintains a family-like work atmosphere and recognizes the needs of working parents and the demands of continuing education.

The Mark Travel's support also extends to the Milwaukee community. It has maintained its headquarters in the area for more than 20 years and strongly supports the services of other companies in the state. In addition, the corporation gives generously to numerous fund-raisers in Wisconsin and around the country every month. The Mark Travel Corporation strongly believes in enhancing the quality of life of its employees, customers, and their communities. And it has become a world leader with that dynamic philosophy.

The Mark Travel has taken the lead in technology and electronic distribution systems. Travel agents have direct access to vacation packages 24 hours a day, seven days a week.

The Grand Avenue

Since its opening in 1982, The Grand Avenue has become one of the economic anchors of downtown Milwaukee, a destination attraction, and a symbol of the persistent vitality of life in the middle of the city.

With some of the major new developments that now are reshaping its neighborhood, the fresh ideas being developed by its management, and the hope of greater cooperation with other business stakeholders in the city, The Grand Avenue is anticipating an even more significant future.

"It remains the focal point of downtown and an important catalyst to downtown development," says Andrew Tilmont, the general manager of The Grand Avenue for The Rouse Company, which owns and operates similar retail-and-marketplace centers in major cities around the country. "It simply represents a lot of what is great about this city."

Hopes were raised for Milwaukee's beleaguered downtown when Francis E. Ferguson, who was chairman of Northwestern Mutual Life Insurance Co., spearheaded the creation of the limited-profit Milwaukee Redevelopment Corporation in 1974, and the new entity then conceived The Grand Avenue project in 1976.

The major revitalization of Milwaukee's historic shopping district enveloped but preserved the architectural character of five historic buildings from the turn of the century and created 245,000 square feet of enclosed retail space in two arcades between the major department stores, Gimbel's (now Marshall Field's) and Boston Store. Connected structures provided 1,800 parking spaces with direct access to both arcades.

"A new day for Milwaukee's Downtown," then-Mayor Henry Maier said. *Business Week* called The Grand Avenue "a dazzling new inner-city shopping mall," and *Forbes* marveled at its "merchandising magic."

Many individual stores have come and gone in the past decade or so, but several important characteristics of The Grand Avenue have remained constant: It offers not only top-notch anchor department stores but a rich variety of big-name national chain outlets; its independently owned specialty shops, and cart and kiosk retailers, lend a particular Milwaukee flair to the site; and the top-floor Speisegarten food court sports a changing, appealing mix of ethnic fast foods.

While The Grand Avenue has remained a crucial economic boon for downtown, Tilmont and others are counting on major new developments nearby to provide more support for the retail center that, in turn, will make the entire area more appealing to metro Milwaukee residents and visitors alike.

The major such development will be the Wisconsin Center that is to open just a few blocks away beginning in 1997, but new building blocks also will include expansion of hotel space, the construction of a new apartment complex nearby, and The Humphrey IMAX Dome Theater. The Milwaukee Public Museum and The Discovery World Museum will also be housed in a brand-new facility adjacent to the IMAX.

Tilmont believes that greater cooperation among The Grand Avenue and other businesses with stakes in downtown will maximize the advantages these new developments will bring to the entire area, such as the attraction of more out-of-town visitors.

As for The Grand Avenue itself, Tilmont says the complex may add new amenities like full-scale restaurants and retail outlets whose wares could add to the unique local feel of the center.

Top: The Grand Avenue offers top-notch department stores as well as a rich variety of big-name national chain outlets.

Below: Since its opening in 1982, The Grand Avenue has become one of the economic anchors of downtown Milwaukee.

Kohl's Food Stores

Kohl's Food Stores offers appealing combinations to customers of its 51 supermarkets in southeastern Wisconsin—and that doesn't just mean crackers and cheese, or bananas and strawberries.

Providing service to the Milwaukee customers started when the first Kohl's store opened in 1927 on the corner of East Lincoln and South Kinnickinnic Avenue. Max Kohl arrived in the United States a few years earlier with a dream and a vision. With the help of his family and dedicated employees, his vision evolved as he developed additional store locations. In 1946 the first modern self-service Kohl's supermarket opened at 4623 West Burleigh Street and continues to provide a neighborhood shopping opportunity.

Yesterday's Kohl's store had a familiar arch-type roof.

Today the company combines an old-fashioned approach to quality and service with the conveniences created by the latest technology. It presents the price-consciousness that consumers demand as well as the constant marketing and merchandising innovation that is necessary to make the grocery-shopping experience enjoyable and even exciting.

And Kohl's Food Stores enjoys the trust generated by its venerable local brand name along with the backing and experience of one of the biggest names in the worldwide grocery business.

Since the Great Atlantic & Pacific Tea Co.—A&P—acquired Kohl's Food Stores in 1983, the company has been continually reshaping itself to compete at the front edge of a business that is notorious for being brutal on participants who don't prove worthy.

Over the past several years Kohl's also has been implementing its new Food Emporium format in all stores that it opens as well as reformatting as many older stores as possible. The Food Emporium concept offers full-service departments that are targeted to the demands and life-styles of Kohl's customers. That means amenities and even entire product categories that shoppers previously weren't used to seeing in supermarkets, including salad bars and in-store bakeries, fresh fish, and flowers.

Food Emporiums continue to evolve, too. For example, new grab-and-go deli meals at some locations fit nicely with Wisconsinites' fast-paced life-styles. Many produce departments are gaining a farmer's market approach to merchandising, which will inject more variety—and fun—into shopping for fruits and vegetables.

Kohl's private-label brands—America's Choice, Master Choice, Health Pride, and Eight O'Clock Coffee—are recognized as among the best in the industry. America's Choice was acclaimed recently by *The New York Times* as presenting a great value in an independent comparison between private-label and major brand products.

The company has been among area leaders in establishing point-of-purchase, value-added electronic marketing programs. The Kohl's Bonus Savings Club card entitles shoppers to save extra on items in every aisle and automatically deducts coupon values at the checkout. By allowing Kohl's to learn more about its customers' shopping preferences, the Bonus Savings Club card also is a powerful marketing tool.

Kohl's Food Stores believes strongly in promoting from within; nearly all of its store managers started as clerks or in other entry-level positions at a Kohl's. To help ensure that employees continue to find a Kohl's career interesting and rewarding, and to raise the level of customer service even higher, the company is installing state-of-the-art interactive-training systems in many of its stores.

Today's newest Food Emporium is at Riverpoint Shopping Center in Fox Point.

Patrick Cudahy Incorporated

Patrick Cudahy, the founder of Patrick Cudahy Incorporated, knew what hard work and effort meant in achieving a goal. Among other things, it sometimes meant that his pride would have to take a back seat to good business. Cudahy was known to ask for what he wanted, and he never lost sight of the initial good that it would do.

For example, in order to start the project of building a meat-packing plant, he had to ask for loans from local businessmen to purchase the 700-acre plot of land where the company is still located. Slowly, but surely, his dream grew from working at the Plankinton and Armour meat-packing plant to owning (in partnership) his pride and joy: Cudahy Brothers Company, which started in 1888. The name changed to Patrick Cudahy Incorporated in 1957.

The corporate headquarters of Patrick Cudahy is located in Cudahy, Wisconsin.

Business grew to include trade connections in every important city in the United States, Canada, and the overseas markets of Liverpool, Hull, Bristol, Glasgow, Dublin, Hamburg, Stockholm, and Christiania. Because many of his most popular products originated in Europe, Cudahy recruited many professional procurers from Germany, France, and Italy so that he could supply North American and European markets with authentic cured-pork specialties.

Not only did Patrick Cudahy support the growth of his company, he also supported Cudahy and Milwaukee. His firm made many donations to the Milwaukee County Park System and seeded new business ventures with capital, including Ladish Company, Helmholz Mitten Company, and the Vinegar Works and Red Star Yeast Company.

Alongside his business, Cudahy had a love for people. Some of his first employees were immigrants, many of whom he helped to purchase their own land and housing in Cudahy for a mere $2.50 to $3 in the form of a regular payroll deduction. Additionally, during World War II he sponsored families of deceased veterans with $1,000 grants and generously gave $100 to each returning veteran in his employ.

Cudahy made an early commitment to the best-available technology that has persisted to this day. The company always implemented the latest innovations. For example, in 1928 it established a government-certified laboratory and test kitchen. In 1930 Cudahy installed the first of a new wave of highly effective freezers. Furthermore, in 1960 the American Humane Association honored Patrick Cudahy Incorporated for adopting humane methods of hog slaughter that used an electric stun gun. The company closed its slaughterhouse in 1988, moving from the "packinghouse" era into its current niche as a meat processor preparing foods for the ever-growing foodservice and delicatessen trade.

Patrick Cudahy Incorporated has become an integral link in the food chain that fulfills consumers' needs. The items it produces are sold to foodservice distributors, wholesalers, and retailers, who make them available to end users.

The company long has been identified as the "Home of Sweet Apple-Wood Smoked Flavor." The products have a distinct taste, especially the Patrick

Right: Founder Patrick Cudahy's portrait hangs above his original desk and chair.

Cudahy Bacon, which is naturally smoked with sweet apple-wood chips. Patrick Cudahy Bacon is the number-one-selling bacon in the Milwaukee metro market, but a far greater share of bacon produced today is sold to foodservice and is available at restaurants, hotels, casinos, and hospitals.

Cooked hams have become an important segment of Patrick Cudahy Incorporated's business as well. The company's ham-processing department produces many different varieties, including low-sodium, low-fat, honey- and maple-cured, and smoked hams.

The firm's product line also includes pepperoni, hard salami, genoa salami, deli hams, pork sausage, bologna, cooked salami, braunschweiger, mortadella, luncheon loaves, lard products, vegetable oil, bacon bits, precooked bacon, and meat toppings. New value-added lines of presliced meats, precooked bacon, and preportioned products continue to provide the company with what it will take to succeed in the twenty-first century.

Award-winning Wisconsin products made by Patrick Cudahy include natural smoked maple ham, German bologna, natural smoked bacon, braunschweiger, hard salami, and boiled ham.

Today Cudahy's mainstay processed meat brands include Patrick's Pride, a line of smoked meats such as ham. Other brands that continue to filter throughout national markets include Agar, Golden Crisp, Appleblossom, Cebeco, Pavone, Royalean, Danzig, Bremen, Monte Rosa, Venicia, Flavortainer, and Portion Perfect. One thing that the company strives to ensure across its product and brand lineups is superior quality and consistency. Numerous awards for quality and taste profiles in every category grace the company's office walls.

Prosperity hasn't been its consistent companion, however. In its 108-year life, Patrick Cudahy Incorporated has endured not only two wars and the Great Depression but also serious fires, devastating labor shortages, strikes, government takeovers, and bankruptcy. But shutting the doors forever was never an option to the founder or his successors in top management.

Roger R. Kapella, president and chief operating officer, put the firm back on its feet after a strike in 1987. He continues to see innovation as the cornerstone of future prosperity. For example, the current expansion was part of Cudahy's response to the market's strong demand for high-quality meats produced by state-of-the-art methods.

"We recognize the importance of reliable service and a consistent quality product, competitively priced," Kapella says. "We have dedicated ourselves to be worthy of our customers' trust and confidence."

H.H. West Company

H.H. West Company continues to prosper by keeping one axiom central to its business: Think big and act small.

For the premier local supplier of office products and furniture and computer-installation services, that has meant paying close attention to the individual needs of its business customers while bringing to bear the most sophisticated approach to its own operations.

And it has meant a steady emphasis on growth, so that H.H. West could compete effectively in a rapidly consolidating industry while still maintaining its particular identity as a Wisconsin-based company that understands the business climate in which its customers are operating.

After nearly 150 years in business in Milwaukee, H.H. West has enjoyed unprecedented growth and success during the past several years even as competition in its two markets, from "big-box" retailers and others, has become fiercer than ever. In fact, since Marvin Cooper acquired the family-owned venture in 1972, H.H. West's sales have zoomed from less than one million dollars to about $70 million for fiscal 1995-1996.

The company's approach and its prolific growth also resulted in another major natural step in its evolution in 1995. After a fast-paced string of acquisitions over the past several years that saw H.H. West take over 18 smaller office-products dealerships around the state, the firm joined forces with Capitol Heights, Maryland-based U.S. Office Products Corp. and became part of a $2-billion alliance of local office-products leaders around the nation.

"We're operating H.H. West the way we always have, with an ultimate eye out for our customers and how we can uniquely fill their needs, and continued local identity and leadership because we know our market best—and our name and reputation have substantial equity here," says Cooper, who remains president of H.H. West.

"Yet now we're affiliated with a huge company that affords us the economies of scale and sophisticated management-information systems that can be supported by its size, as well as strong new connections with a network of local and regional dealers like ourselves across the country."

The affiliation also offers H.H. West's employees the opportunity to participate, through stock-purchase options, in the rapid growth of U.S. Office Products. In fact, H.H. West associates' overall participation in purchases of its parent company's stock has been the highest of any affiliate of U.S. Office Products: That's how much confidence H.H. West's people have in their own future in the business.

H.H. West operates 14 retail stores throughout Wisconsin and central operations in Milwaukee and Madison from which it delivers supplies and provides services to customers. From pens to modular office furniture, H.H. West's product line meets virtually every supply need that arises in offices around the state.

Yet the essence of the firm's relationship with its customers stems as much from its approach as from its products. H.H. West offers a number of services ranging from delivering supplies to customers' offices—right down to the level of individual desktops—to providing computerized tracking of requisitions and usage.

And, of course, service is at the core of H.H. West's other major division, Business Technology, which sells, installs, and services a wide variety of PCs, faxes, copiers, and other office equipment for customers across the state.

H.H. West is one of the oldest

companies in Milwaukee in continuous operation. Samuel C. West founded it in 1847, renting a small store on the corner of Michigan and Water streets, purchasing a small stock of stationery, and proudly announcing to a very young city the birth of his own new business. Samuel's brother, Harry E. West, took over management in 1860.

Ownership of the firm passed occasionally over the next several decades, always to families that were careful to continue to nurture its reputation and other assets. For 36 years Dorothy Gill, who started out as an employee of the company, owned H.H. West. In 1972 Cooper purchased H.H. West and its single location.

From 1972 to 1986, through increased sales from operations and acquisitions of office-supply competitors, H.H. West expanded to 10 locations and nearly $10 million in annual sales. The expansion included opening retail locations in strip mall centers and diversifying into office-equipment sales and service.

In the late 1980s another string of major acquisitions expanded H.H. West dramatically, including the 1988 purchase of Modern Business Machines, which represented the most significant business diversification in the company's history. From about $5 million in annual sales then, West's Business Technology Division has grown to about $30 million.

H.H. West's last acquisition before its affiliation with U.S. Office Products also was its largest and most ambitious geographically: the 1994 purchase of Madison-based Office Express Inc.

The reason for the consolidation in the industry is that office products has become an increasingly competitive arena. Nationally, the number of office-supply firms has decreased from 11,500 in 1986 to 6,800 in 1994, according to an analysis by business-research

firm Dun & Bradstreet.

The proliferation of the so-called office "superstores" has been one major new factor in the industry. Because H.H. West's principal clientele has always been commercial clients, most of whom have shunned the superstores, the company has never faced the competitive threat that some have perceived.

But H.H. West has been more than willing to tackle the superstores head-on. Cooper and his employees are fond of noting the assistance that H.H. West provides to its customers in understanding best how to purchase and use supplies—in marked contrast to the hands-off, no-service approach used by the "big boxes." And he notes that, on a "market basket" of representative office products used by its customers, H.H. West's prices are competitive with those of the superstores anyway.

H.H. West also is pursuing more vigorously than ever the small-business and home-office markets that weren't major factors in its traditional market mix. Overall, those companies are providing the most growth in the modern economy, in Wisconsin and nationwide.

One never knows: Another century and a half from now, or even much sooner, one of those small accounts could evolve into H.H. West's largest customer. "We're treating smaller businesses now like we've always treated our customers," Cooper says. "We don't take them for granted."

Boston Store

Its name may suggest otherwise, but Boston Store is the essence of Milwaukee retailing.

Since the founding of its first store downtown in 1900, Boston Store has been the preferred destination for Milwaukee shoppers—a full-line, traditional department store that has always offered one-stop shopping for apparel, accessories, home goods, gifts, and more.

"We represent the standard of the full-service department store experience in Wisconsin," says Stanton J. Bluestone, chairman and chief executive officer of Carson Pirie Scott & Co., the Milwaukee-based parent company of the Boston Store chain.

"We've grown up in this city, and while many retailing trends have come and gone —and indeed, many of our competitors—shoppers here still know that they can count on finding the up-to-date variety, timeless values, and genuine customer service they want at the Boston Store."

The stores offer full lines of women's, men's, children's, and infants' apparel and shoes as well as jewelry, accessories, cosmetics, fragrances, luggage, gifts, housewares, furniture, and a wide variety of other items. The company specializes in high-value brand-name merchandise, implements ambitious promotional activities, relies on behind-the-scenes technological improvements to boost productivity and service—and emphasizes complete customer satisfaction.

Boston Store has six locations and about 2,600 employees in Greater Milwaukee, including anchor stores at The Grand Avenue mall downtown, Mayfair Mall, Northridge and Southridge malls, Brookfield Square, Bayshore, and the newly opened Brookfield Furniture Gallery. The other Boston Stores scattered around Wisconsin are in Green Bay, Racine, Janesville, and two stores in Madison.

One of the largest department store retailers in the Midwest, with $1.1 billion in annual sales, Carson also owns 31 Carson Pirie Scott stores and 12 Bergner's locations, as well as three Furniture Galleries throughout Illinois, Indiana, and Minnesota.

Carson's ownership of the Boston Store chain has coincided with a period of renaissance for Boston Store as well as for department store retailing in general.

"Seven years ago department stores generally were thought of as dinosaurs that were about to be overrun by discounters on one side and specialty stores on the other," Bluestone recalls. "But today consumers are rediscovering the department store—and in Wisconsin, that means us—as the retail outlet that can provide the best answers to their needs for quality merchandise, convenience, and saving time."

When Julian Simon opened his first dry-goods store downtown, he chose a corner of Fourth and Grand (now Wisconsin Avenue) because of its accessibility to carriage, trolley, and train and appropriately adopted the slogan, "The Heart of Milwaukee."

As business improved, Simon opened a variant of the department store, a concept popularized by a Massachusetts retailer who offered many goods and services under one roof. Simon leased space to other merchants, including the Stone Brothers of Chicago. In 1900 Milwaukee Boston Store opened with 30 different departments. (Like the owners of many other unrelated stores around the country at the turn of the century, Simon also chose the name "Boston Store" because Boston was considered the nation's fashion center.)

Management changed hands in 1906, and the Boston Store Company chose Nat Stone as president. The new store motto, which lasted for decades, was "Fair, Square and Liberal." The company forged ahead as a leading retailer and in 1934 joined the Associated Merchandising Corp. In 1948 Boston Store was purchased by giant Federated Department Stores. Formed

Boston Store—Milwaukee's fashion leader for nearly 100 years.

in 1929, Federated consisted of Lazarus, Shillito's, Filene's, Abraham & Straus, and Bloomingdale's.

Throughout its years of expansion, Boston Store was a leader in retailing methods. It introduced a bargain basement to offer fine-quality goods at reduced prices. Sales promotions became an integral part of the store; there were "half-price" sales, "mill end" sales, and "Double Our Business" days.

All were forerunners of the current "Capacity Days," Boston Store's biggest annual sales event. The first Capacity Days sale, organized by Nat Stone as a one-day event, witnessed a sales volume four times larger than normal.

Boston Store has never hesitated to try new and different ideas to improve its service to customers and employees. The store had the first complete escalator service in Wisconsin and air conditioning on three floors of its downtown location as early as 1936. A decade later it established "Night Owl Service" so that customers could place phone orders during non-business hours.

The company also instituted the Thrift Association credit union, beginning in 1927; a shorter working day (9:30 a.m. to 5:30 p.m.), as early as 1937; and the world's first regular department store air-delivery service, in 1945.

A recent innovation, begun in the fall of 1994 and held twice a year, is The Goodwill Sale. The items collected, then donated to Goodwill Industries had a value of more than $1.8 million by the fall of 1996.

Boston Store's advance into Milwaukee's suburbs began with the opening of a Bay Shore location by 1958, and the 1967 opening of the store in Brookfield Square, Wisconsin's first enclosed mall, marked the beginning of Boston Store's most dramatic growth period; that same year the company constructed a 750-space parking garage adjacent to its downtown store.

By 1972 Southridge and Northridge stores had opened, and in 1982 Boston Store opened its first location in Green Bay. The company's geographic development came full circle in 1982, when a newly renovated and redesigned Boston Store anchored the opening of The Grand Avenue mall downtown, the linchpin of the city's urban revitalization efforts.

P.A. Bergner & Co., owned by the Maus and Nordmann families of Switzerland, purchased Boston Store from Federated in 1985, and the new company's sales volume ranked it in the top third of retail department stores nationwide. In 1987 Bergner acquired three former Gimbels' locations in Milwaukee and Madison.

The company opened a new distribution center in Rockford, Illinois, in 1988, which was regarded by retailers nationwide as an example of the best modern technology for retail distribution. "That continued this company's historical record of being on the cutting edge of new retail technologies," Bluestone says.

In 1989 Bergner acquired Carson Pirie Scott & Co. After a rocky start brought on largely by the recession of the early 1990s, the new, merged company survived a bankruptcy period from 1991 to 1993 by streamlining operations and recovering its marketing momentum. Upon its emergence from bankruptcy in October 1993, P.A. Bergner & Co. became Carson Pirie Scott & Co. By 1996 the company was making a strong bid to catapult into a position of regional department store leadership. By the end of 1997 all Milwaukee area Boston Stores will have been renovated under a multimillion-dollar program that demonstrates Boston Store's commitment to the community.

Through it all, Boston Store's focus has remained on Milwaukee—not just as a market, but as a partner. It gives amply of financial resources and employees' time to causes that center on improving children's lives, positive social action, and maintaining the arts in the city.

"Our legacy has been to be more in touch with Milwaukee's wants and needs than anyone else," Bluestone says. "That means what they want to buy, yes—but it means a lot more as well."

BOSTON STORE
THE HEART OF MILWAUKEE

"I will be sure to use (Boston Store) as an example of a firm that is able to do well in the marketplace and, at the same time, act ethically."

—Michael L. Rothschild
Chair, School of Business,
University of Wisconsin

Mandy Services, Inc.

"Mandy Services made the difference between finding a satisfying career and finding just another job," states a client. "I finally found my dream job." That's how Jan Mandy's customers respond after working with her company.

Jan Mandy owns and operates Mandy Services, Inc., an outplacement company that has one of the highest re-employment rates in the country. Centrally located at 11430 West Bluemound Road, Mandy Services is an outplacement and résumé resource center for all levels of personnel. The company enjoys a diverse clientele, drawing customers from all areas of the community. "I make it my business to know what's happening in the business community," says Jan. "By keeping close tabs on the market, I can best guide my clients to career opportunities."

Jan Mandy, owner of Mandy Services, Inc.

Right: Mandy Services is the premier outplacement center in the Milwaukee area, offering clients customized job search assistance.

As the premier outplacement provider in the Milwaukee area, Mandy Services is unique in the way it helps its customers. Every client presents a unique set of circumstances. It's like a puzzle, and Mandy's job is to find the solution. Working closely with clients to identify transferable skills—each client's professional and personal abilities that can be applied to new positions—and, most importantly, determining how that client can position and use those skills in the most satisfying and productive way, provides the personal touch to her services.

When working with Mandy Services, individual clients can expect that by defining their skills, knowledge, and interests, their personal advisor will help them to find the best career match possible.

The next step is developing a *marketing campaign* to get the job. This means producing a top-quality résumé and cover letter—*the marketing tools*—that catch the attention of employers and get interviews. Jan Mandy's team of writers creates résumés that paint a "word portrait" of each client, so prospective employers get an instant understanding of how the clients will apply their skills and strengths on the job. This successful résumé strategy emphasizes how the client is different and better suited for the job than every other applicant.

According to Jan, "The résumé is like a critical leg of a three-legged stool. A well-written and formatted résumé gets a client in the door. From there, the résumé continues to represent clients until they have the opportunity to present their qualities in person during the interview." Mandy Services prepares its clients not only with a concise and yet comprehensive résumé, but also with advice and counsel for succeeding in the interview process. It is the counseling throughout the *entire* process that creates the results.

In addition, if a client is interested in starting a business, Mandy Services provides assistance with feasibility/marketing studies, business planning, and "incubator" type services, such as office space, phone, fax, and administrative support. Jan Mandy is proud to have assisted many successful entrepreneurs.

To corporate clients, Mandy Services offers pre-termination counseling to help define severance pay levels, outplacement, and other benefits that can be provided on a group or individual basis. Jan works closely with corporate human resource representatives or small business owners, especially during terminations, restructuring, and reorganizations. Many outplaced clients are so thrilled with their new positions that they write to their former employers, thanking them for the opportunity to have been outplaced with Mandy Services.

When you work with Mandy Services, the results exceed your expectations.

Bokare Framing

When the Katz women established Bokare Framing in 1982, their admittedly modest intentions were to run a small retail shop together and have some fun. Pam Katz Bogan and her mother Elayne Katz are still enjoying the business after 14 years and the addition of a second location in Mequon.

The partners also have turned Bokare Framing into a growing operation with a reputation for high-quality products and services, a loyal and burgeoning clientele, and two locations in suburban Milwaukee.

"We just do quality work," says Pam, "and customers expect perfection from us."

Adds Elayne, "Some customers even have their framing done here and shipped to their homes in other states."

Elayne's art background and sales experience, combined with Pam's bookkeeping knowledge and winning ways with customers, have made their business grow. They have expanded from their 2,400-square-foot, two-level site at 6936 North Santa Monica Boulevard in the Fox Point Shopping Center to follow the new growth northeast to Mequon. There Bokare Framing has operated in the Mequon Pavilion, at 10972 North Port Washington Road, since 1990. Helping Pam and Elayne at Bokare's two locations are four experienced and talented employees.

Because nearly every piece brought in requires a customized frame, Bokare Framing provides its clients with insight and experience as well as with the materials themselves. Each store has a unique atmosphere that serves as a creative catalyst to employees and customers alike. For instance, at the Pavilion site, Bokare offers more than 700 frame and matte samples covering the walls and a living room-like setting for discussing ideas—as well as a play area to keep accompanying children engaged.

"Everyone who works here has a good eye with impeccable taste, and that means we can always suggest ideas that we think would best present the piece that is being framed," says Pam. "But it's the customer's ultimate decision.

"And when they pick it up, and it's finished, they love it," she adds.

"People realize that you can't be both the best and the cheapest—that you have to be one or the other," Elayne says. "But once you have something done really right, you can't go back to anything less."

Another of the advantages of choosing to service the high end of the framing business, they say, is that they aren't being faced with competition from the mass discounters that are beleaguering so many other small retailers. However, cost issues have posed a challenge, particularly in the past few years, as the price of paper, wood, and glass supplies has risen sharply. The continued satisfaction and steady growth of their customer base has helped the partners overcome those obstacles.

They also enjoy extending themselves and their stores to the community. For example, each spring Bokare Framing hosts 150 kindergarten children from the area for three days of fun and framing. Bokare donates time, advice, space, mattes, and other materials, and the students each frame a special piece of art they have produced for Mother's Day. The children get to see each step from beginning to end—from picking out the best mattes and frames to mounting, cutting glass, and putting together the actual frame. Bokare plans to extend this event to schools throughout the Milwaukee area.

Top: Pam Katz Bogan (left) and Elayne Katz established the company in 1982.

Bokare Framing's second store was opened at 10972 North Port Washington Road, Mequon, in 1990.

Fleming Companies

Food shoppers in metro Milwaukee think of two names when it comes time to get out their grocery lists: Sentry and SuperSaver.

The stores operate under somewhat different concepts, including their price orientation and size, with Sentry being the smaller, more traditional, service-oriented setting and SuperSaver presenting everyday low prices in more contemporary larger stores.

Their corporate ownership has evolved from that of a Milwaukee-grown company to their current status as a division of the world's largest food wholesaler. Formerly Godfrey Co., the operation is now supplied by the Milwaukee division of Fleming Companies with the Sentry franchise being managed by the Marketing Group of Fleming and the company-owned chain of SuperSavers being managed by the Fleming Retail Group.

But both Sentry and SuperSaver are solely dedicated to providing the utmost value in food retailing as they continue to meet the fast-changing needs of Wisconsin's modern families.

"Each concept has been developed to the point that they're a leader in the local market as well as a leader within Fleming Companies as a whole," says Ronald Henningsen, advertising manager for Fleming's Milwaukee Marketing Group. "They're each doing very well standing on their own two feet, plus they're supported by Fleming's distribution expertise and efficiency."

Godfrey was founded in 1870 in the city's historic Third Ward by Edwin R. Godfrey. By 1890 E.R. Godfrey & Sons Co. was operating as a dry-goods wholesaler. In 1925 the firm became one of three wholesalers in the country to join the Independent Grocers Alliance, and in 1936 became one of the nation's first wholesalers to enter the frozen-foods business.

Godfrey relocated to Glendale in 1949. Shortly thereafter, it broadened operations to include the provision of fresh meat to its clients. The Sentry Markets retail division was formed in 1953 to meet the challenge of national chains that were steadily encroaching upon Godfrey's traditional markets. Eleven years later Godfrey relocated to Fleming's current 112-acre site in Waukesha.

In November 1987 Godfrey was purchased by Fleming, the Oklahoma City-based, world-class food-marketing and distribution company. Fleming services more than 10,000 stores, including 3,700 supermarkets in 43 states and several foreign countries.

Fleming supplies its own stores and other retail customers with virtually every national-brand grocery product as well as high-volume private-label items. It also provides full lines of perishables, including meats, dairy and delicatessen products, frozen foods, and fresh produce along with a variety of general merchandise. The company offers its retailers a complete range of services to enable them to compete more effectively.

Fleming/Marketing has devoted much of its attention recently to refining the Sentry retailing concept, while the Retail Group is working to expand the SuperSaver retail format and strategy.

Sentry focuses on serving grocery shoppers in more traditional, service-intensive ways, such as extensive in-store bakeries and delicatessens. In the most evolved Sentry locations, such as those in Delafield and Muskego, levels of selection and service are offered in the meat and produce departments that are unmatched in the entire metro Milwaukee area.

Fleming Companies began to operate the SuperSaver format in 1992 and by the end of 1993 the company had 13 of these large super stores operating in Wisconsin. The format has evolved since the initial store openings into a contemporary food and drugstore format that features everyday low prices throughout the store and deep discounts for customers who participate in the format's "frequent shopper program." By using the "Card," customers are given more convenience and flexibility. The company then utilizes the purchase information from the customers using the card to reward even more special values to its best customers. The format also features top-quality branded fresh departments such as S.S. Brothers produce, Champion Quality meat, Crestwood bakery, City deli, and Sentry Floral, Wisconsin's largest full-service floral retailer. Most stores offer a large video department that utilizes the frequent shopper card for more customer convenience.

The SuperSaver format bywords are "Buy More For Less," but service is not sacrificed. The format provides full service at the checkouts with bagging and carry-out, and most stores offer a pharmacy that provides lower prices on drugs than the national drugstore chains, staffed by friendly professionals who utilize the latest in health care technology for consumer safety and convenience.

Today there are 19 of these stores in operation and according to Doug Sumpter, president of Fleming's Milwaukee Retail Group, plans call for a more aggressive roll-out of the format over the next several years.

Another area of emphasis for Fleming/Milwaukee these days is more fully integrating into the parent company's overall system of transporting and distributing food items to continually reduce costs to end consumers.

That thrust includes cost-efficiency measures such as eliminating as much "deadheading"—in which trucks come back empty from stores—as possible. Instead, Fleming has been finding ways for more and more retail-transport trucks to stop at food manufacturers and other suppliers on the way back to the distribution center; in Wisconsin, for example, that might mean stopping at a paper-products supplier in the Fox Valley.

Fleming also is doing more "cross-docking" at its facilities, in which computerized tracking of shipments helps goods move out of an incoming truck and nearly directly onto an outgoing vehicle—without the traditional but costly step of having the goods sit on a warehouse shelf for a time.

Also posing a challenge to Fleming to become even more cost-efficient is the growing trend of manufacturers toward evening out their previous wide swings in production and emphasizing "just-in-time" inventory control.

Those developments put a premium for Fleming on maximizing usage of its distribution space by, for instance, operating more of them around the clock. "We know that these methods are benefiting manufacturers," says Michael George, operations manager for Fleming/Milwaukee Distribution. "It's up to us to make sure that we can operate efficiently and pass the savings through to our customers."

Under the Fleming banner, the operation has continued to maintain its various commitments to Milwaukee-area causes ranging from the National Football League Alumni Golf Tournament that benefits Big Brothers/Big Sisters to sponsorship of events such as the Waukesha Riverfest and Milwaukee's Summerfest and Winterfest.

"I only see our presence expanding in the Milwaukee market," says Ron Lusic, president of the Milwaukee division, Marketing & Product Supply. "Sentry and SuperSaver are two very good nameplates in the eyes of consumers here, and Fleming has become a good corporate citizen much in the tradition of Godfrey. We plan to keep building on all those positives."

Gardetto's Inc.

Over the past six decades, during its evolution from a beloved neighborhood bakery to an efficient wholesale breadstick supplier to a consumer-driven niche salted snack manufacturer and marketer, Gardetto's has relied on innovative and progressive decision making as the core of its success.

Today, headquartered at 4625 South Sixth Street, Gardetto's employs more than 200 Milwaukeeans in developing, manufacturing, and marketing its unique snack mixes and distributing them to eager consumers throughout the United States and in a growing number of foreign markets.

As the firm's mission statement declares, "Gardetto's purpose is to provide the world with unique, superior-tasting snacks, and it is committed to profitable growth while maintaining the sensitivity, simplicity, and agility of a small company."

The key to fulfilling Gardetto's mission is maintaining the family ownership with its entrepreneurial spirit that has continued into the third generation. Moving forward on that basis is challenging because the company's main competitors are huge, well-known giants of the salted snack industry.

But private ownership also gives Gardetto's an edge. "What makes us unique is that we have a long-term vision for the company and we base our daily decisions on these desired results," says Nan Gardetto, executive vice president. "In our long-range planning, we focus on being progressive in our strategy and proactive tactically in whatever we do. This helps to insulate us from our bigger rivals."

Gardetto's Bakery on Howell Avenue in the heart of Bay View, 1949.

Competing with multinational corporations was the last thing on their minds in 1932 when Baptiste and Diane Gardetto founded Gardetto's Bakery in Milwaukee. At first, the Gardettos made bread and delivered it door to door throughout the city.

In 1938 they moved the bakery to a Howell Avenue location in the heart of Bay View, where it remained until 1970. Impressed with the strong work ethic of the area's residents, the Gardettos put them to work baking bread, rolls, breadsticks, cakes, doughnuts, and pies and staffing a full-line deli counter as well.

After sons John and Richard joined the business, Gardetto's made another in a series of strategic business decisions: focusing on breadsticks instead of a neighborhood-oriented retail operation that increasingly was being threatened by supermarket bakeries. Beginning in 1968, first at a Howell Avenue facility and later on South Sixth Street, the firm built a national reputation for the fine breadsticks it sold to restaurants and grocery distributors.

Gardetto's SNAK-ENS® were born in 1980. John's wife, Judy, had begun making a snack mix from her home that included baked breadstick pieces with a "special" seasoning for family and friends. Due to outstanding feedback from all who tried the recipe, their daughter, Nan, approached her father about making the product commercially. She proved its commercial

Left: Nannette Gardetto, executive vice president; Greg Gardetto, director of marketing; John Gardetto, Sr., president (seated); and John Gardetto, Jr., materials manager.

Far left: Gardetto's corporate headquarters at 4625 South Sixth Street, Milwaukee.

appeal and potential by loading up the family station wagon and selling one-pound bags of the special mix to local bars and restaurants. And in 1981, using an old mixer and the bakery's breadstick ovens, the first large-scale batch of SNAK-ENS® was produced. By 1988 Gardetto's began selling nationally through the vending class of trade with its SNAK-ENS® product. In 1990 son Richard retired and moved to Florida while John Sr. continued as president and owner of the company.

Today, with its product available nationwide in grocery, convenience, mass merchant, drug, and club stores, as well as in vending machines and on U.S. military bases worldwide, the company is setting the stage for expansion into the rapidly Americanizing cultures of Europe and Asia.

Another key to maintaining the company's leading-edge position is its employees. Some have been with Gardetto's in one capacity or another for as long as 40 years. In addition to receiving competitive pay and benefits, employees are encouraged to enhance their job skills and flexibility as well as achieve a degree of personal growth. "Our employees are truly committed to our company; they not only help create but also share in our growth," says John Sr., who along with third-generation Nannette, Greg, and Johnny Gardetto provides the family leadership.

The firm also remains dedicated to the community that created its success, contributing to a wide variety of Milwaukee-area charities.

From today's perspective, Gardetto's growth has been phenomenal: from fewer than 50 employees in 1987 to more than 200 today; and from 40,000 square feet of facility space to today's total of 185,000 square feet. The company now can manufacture in less than a minute what it produced in that original batch of SNAK-ENS® in 1981.

"Our goals continue to be focused on aggressive growth through strategic innovation, planning, and execution," says Nan Gardetto. She continues, "I'm confident that with vision, leadership, and just plain hard work, we can create our own successful destiny."

John Gardetto, Sr., in the company's production area.

C&H Distributors Inc.

For nearly 60 years C&H Distributors Inc. has focused intensively on serving its customer base: thousands of companies nationwide that order from the company's vast and varied inventory of industrial supplies and have come to expect fast delivery and the utmost in service.

It's one mark of the firm's success that, in September 1996, C&H finally made a major move that really *doesn't* have to do with pleasing customers. It moved from its longtime headquarters at 400 South Fifth Street in Milwaukee to a brand-new, 68,000-square-foot headquarters office in West Allis. The new facility will provide a pleasant and efficient environment, a central location, and ample room for growth on 10.5 acres.

The firm's distribution centers maintain high levels of inventory for products offered in its catalog.

"This is really something we're doing for our employees, because very few of our customers ever have a reason to visit us," says David Stark, president and chief executive officer of C&H, which employs about 275 metro Milwaukeeans. "Our employees deserve a facility like this. They've built quite a company."

From its headquarters and from its distribution centers in Milwaukee, Dayton, Atlanta, Dallas, and Reno, C&H processes more than 450,000 orders a year for customers who want the gamut of industrial supplies, including cabinets and lockers, shelving and racks, material storage and material-handling equipment, shop equipment, shipping supplies, dock equipment, safety products, maintenance supplies, and office equipment.

C&H's industry-leading brand-name suppliers contribute over 28,000 items to the company's nearly 500-page catalog, of which it distributes more than three million copies each year.

Want a ramp so that your forklifts can load and unload goods from a semi trailer? Look for seven different options on page 227 of C&H's catalog. Need shelving or storage cabinets? C&H has over 40 pages of options. Interested in a gross of disposable respirators to protect workers from a nasty environment? Check page 348. How about a precision vise? Three different sizes on page 127. Office chairs? More than a dozen choices on pages 444-445.

C&H has become the natural choice for so many industrial companies because of its attitudes about the importance of reliability and of keeping customers number one. It takes on a partnership role with its clients.

The firm's distribution centers maintain high levels of inventory for products offered in its catalog, and ships more than 90 percent of its stock orders, complete, within 24 hours. Prices are consistently competi-

C&H Distributors' new corporate headquarters is at 770 South 70th Street, West Allis.

The C&H family of catalogs has a combined circulation of more than 15 million each year.

tive, in part because as one of America's largest industrial distributors, C&H purchases in volume and can offer lower selling prices.

Customer-service personnel are efficient and responsive, using C&H's proprietary computer software to inform customers quickly and accurately about availability of supplies, shipping costs, and other relevant information—as well as to counsel them, when necessary, about alternative products that might better fit their needs. And most orders reach nearly any location in the United States within just a couple of days.

Because of this outstanding customer service, C&H's customers don't miss a beat. In fact, the company is a much-relied-upon ally of many purchasing managers. "The convenience and economics work in the customers' favor," Stark says. "Most purchase orders that we receive are in the $500 to $1,000 range, and for those kinds of routine orders, it's more efficient for a purchasing manager to call us than to try to locate everything himself. He satisfies his people, and he can go on to something more pressing where he can really have an impact on his operation."

Stark says that C&H has pushed its service to levels comparable to those achieved by the top-notch consumer mail-order companies. "Business customers are entitled to the same level of convenience, service, and courtesy that they receive when they order items for their personal use."

Another part of C&H's philosophy is to know thoroughly what it's selling and to understand its customers' needs. That's why the company is constantly testing catalog items for quality and integrity and scouring markets for new products. C&H's technical-support group helps customers find solutions to their purchasing problems—even if that sometimes means finding a product that isn't in the catalog.

For high-volume customers, C&H account representatives routinely search for better pricing, coordinate volume discounts, and research client industries for developments that help the firm's partners stay ahead of the competition.

Avenue Industrial Supply, a wholly owned subsidiary of C&H, serves all of Canada out of its facility in Toronto, offering the same philosophy and services that have helped C&H grow in the United States. Dozier Equipment and Direct Safety, two of the company's recent catalog acquisitions, specialize in material-handling equipment and industrial safety products. Another C&H division, BrownCor, is a catalog operation that offers packaging, shipping, and warehouse products, from cartons to packaging tapes.

The C&H of today has evolved in many ways from the partnership that was begun in 1937 by Charles Clark and Otto Henke, who formed their company to wire houses. In 1941 they purchased a motor-repair business and then branched into the sale of electric motors, fans, and other electrical equipment.

After World War II the company began to purchase government industrial surplus and, in order to sell in large quantities, expanded its market area by using catalogs and direct-mail pieces. When surpluses tightened up several years later, Gordon Henke, who was then president, moved the company into the wholesale distribution of industrial lines and built the foundations for the present-day company.

In 1988 the Henke family sold its controlling interest in C&H to Kaiser and Kraft GmbH of Stuttgart, Germany. With K&K's support, the company's growth continued to accelerate, and the German parent's commitment to Milwaukee has deepened. "We've had great support for our company's goals and culture; it's been a wonderful relationship," Stark says.

The new headquarters building is symbolic of C&H's commitment to the metro area, which also includes substantial corporate support for local charities and community groups.

"This city," says Stark, "is home to us."

C&H's early home, at 436 Juneau Avenue, was later razed to make way for the Fourth and Broadway freeway spur.

Milwaukee Mack Sales Inc.

Directed by confident management, capitalizing on industry trends, and fueled by the increasing reputation of its Mack Trucks product line, Milwaukee Mack Sales approaches its 50th anniversary in 1997 on the heels of the largest growth period in its history.

Sales more than doubled in 1995 from five years earlier, nearing the $50-million mark. Employment grew to about 90 people overall, 70 at the Milwaukee Mack headquarters at 4444 West Bluemound Road and the remainder at the company's Mack Sales of Fond du Lac division, in Fond du Lac, Wisconsin.

"We have an extremely talented sales force that goes out and lets our story be known. Our work force is very experienced and stable, and our parts and service are open 24 hours a day to meet our customers' needs. The privilege of selling our products has become synonymous with heavy-duty quality," says Roger Kriete, president and second-generation owner of Milwaukee Mack.

Milwaukee Mack's management team (left to right): David Haertl, general manager-Milwaukee; Roger Kriete, owner and president; and Jeff Martell, general manager-Fond du Lac.

The company's market area is southeastern Wisconsin ranging from Appleton south to Illinois and from Lake Michigan west to halfway between Milwaukee and Madison. It sells and services a broad line of diesel and medium-duty trucks.

The rugged Mack chassis is on the job at nearly every heavy-duty job done in southeastern Wisconsin, including those by county and city municipalities, fire departments, refuse companies, bulk haulers, dump trucks, and concrete mixers. Milwaukee Mack also supplies city delivery units and huge plows that keep runways open at Mitchell International Airport.

While each vehicle is designed for a specific task, they share common values that set Mack Trucks apart: advanced engineering, a comfortable, productive driving environment; low life-cycle costs; and high resale value.

And while it's a vastly larger and very different enterprise than it was then, Milwaukee Mack is headquartered in the building that bears its bulldog trademark, standing at the west end of the Wisconsin Avenue Bridge. Mack Trucks Inc. was established in 1927 in the very same building, but the company relocated to 37th and Lisbon streets in 1938.

Top: The Mack bulldog trademark has become synonymous with heavy-duty quality.

Henry Kriete, who had started as a floor sweeper for Mack Trucks Inc. in New York in 1924 and had risen to the level of head of the corporate parts department, purchased the business in 1951. Roger, Henry's son, purchased the business in 1973; one of the first decisions he made was to "go home again" by moving back into the bulldog building.

One major contribution to Milwaukee Mack's growth was the acquisition of the Fond du Lac's Mack sales organization in 1993. This purchase enlarged its territory and added employees and other assets.

The increasing popularity of truck leasing has also become a prominent growth catalyst for Milwaukee Mack. The company currently has on lease about 500 trucks; four years ago that number was only about 100. Kriete says that more and more customers prefer leasing to outright ownership in large part because it gives them more control over their cash flow and operating expenses.

A tribute to the quality of Mack products is the fact that, even at the end of the typical five-year lease, many Milwaukee Mack customers still seek to purchase the vehicle they'd been leasing. "That says a lot about customer satisfaction with the Mack product," Kriete says.

Rising customer appreciation of the Mack product

One of the challenges of the business is handling its lopsided seasonality. Most construction-industry customers order trucks for spring delivery, naturally, wanting them to be delivered right after the frost leaves the ground—but not a moment sooner so they're not paying for a new truck that is just sitting idle.

Another reason that Milwaukee Mack's production scheduling is a demanding discipline is that most trucks it produces are ordered with plenty of custom options. "If you're buying a $100,000 truck, you want it to be *your* truck," Kriete says.

"Between the weather factor and our customized approach, we try to do a lot of educating of our customers about the advantages of ordering ahead," Kriete says.

Kriete and his employees are big backers of the Vince Lombardi Cancer Clinic at St. Luke's Medical Center, including the annual Lombardi Classic celebrity golf tournament at North Hills Country Club in Menomonee Falls. The Rawhide Boys Ranch is another major recipient of resources and attention by Milwaukee Mack Sales.

The company also donates engines and scholarship funds to the Milwaukee Area Technical College for degree programs such as diesel mechanics. One benefit of that, of course, is that Milwaukee Mack Sales is possibly helping to prepare future members of its own work force.

"It's a good cause, because our business is very sophisticated today, and not just anyone can come in and understand it," Kriete says. "We want to ensure that the type of quality employees we've had over the years just keep coming to us."

The rugged Mack chassis is at work on nearly every heavy-duty job done in southeastern Wisconsin.

line, which is built in plants in Pennsylvania and North Carolina, also has been a boon. The company's overall U.S. sales have risen to number three in the industry.

"What makes Mack unique is that it's a totally integrated truck; we manufacture our own engines, transmissions, and rear ends, and no one else in the industry does that," says David Haertl, general manager. "They're all designed specifically for each other, while our competitors must put separate components together from a number of manufacturers."

Milwaukee Mack employs 70 people at its headquarters at 4444 West Bluemound Road.

Provimi Veal Corporation

Provimi essentially created the veal-processing industry in this country. Now, more than three decades later, the company is redefining that business and continuing its market leadership.

Provimi Veal Corporation is the country's most recognized packer of veal products, specializing in supplying distributors, clubs, supermarkets, restaurants, and specialty markets with first-quality veal products tailored to the needs and desires of its customers. Adding each step of the way to a record of innovation unsurpassed in the industry, Provimi has evolved from a supplier mainly of commodity products into the most prolific supplier of value-added veal specialties.

Aat Groenevelt, founder, chairman, and chief executive officer of Provimi Veal.

"We made special-fed veal into a vibrant food business in this country, and we're continuing to lead the industry in new directions," says Aat Groenevelt, chairman and chief executive officer. "We never want our heritage to become only a legacy."

The company began operations in 1962 when Groenevelt, a native of The Netherlands, introduced the Dutch method of producing milk-fed veal to the United States. This type of veal is distinguished by its light pink color, firm texture, and even marbling throughout the meat.

By 1974 Provimi had developed a viable supply network among the dairy farms of the state and opened its first slaughter and packaging facility in Seymour, Wisconsin. Soon the company came up with the innovative approach of selling veal freshly vacuum packaged in select pieces, rather than the standard method of selling full carcasses. It also originated color grading of veal. Both methods now are industry standards.

Provimi developed stringent quality and grading standards, assuring customers of consistent satisfaction. It also became the only American veal packer to meet the extremely stringent manufacturing standards that enable it to ship to member countries of the European union, and Provimi now exports nearly one-quarter of its production to Europe, Asia, Mexico, and Canada.

Top: Provimi is the only American veal selected by world-renowned French chef Paul Bocuse for use in his exclusive culinary competition in Lyon, France.

Headquartered in Waukesha, Provimi employs nearly 200 people at its production facility in Seymour and operates a facility in suburban Toronto that conducts research, development, and small-batch manufacturing.

The corporate headquarters is located in Waukesha and the two production facilities, which employ nearly 200 people, are in the northeast section of the state in Seymour. The Green Bay area is home to many other meat packers and provides an opportunity to hire and retain workers with generations of experience in the industry. This stable job force helps maintain the high standards set many years ago by Groenevelt.

There are also many dairy farms in the immediate vicinity. These farms supply local calf raisers with a consistent supply of the special type of calves needed by Provimi. Most of these Wisconsin growers enjoy a long-lasting relationship with the company and also take pride in being a vital part of the Provimi success story.

Provimi continues to adapt to the changing needs and desires of both the food-service and retail markets by introducing new products that make preparation easier and fit into today's healthy life-styles.

"We were thrilled that an American company was being recognized in this manner," says Groenevelt. "It was extra special that it occurred right in the heart of where the veal industry began."

Manegold Mansion Bed & Breakfast

Combine a spacious Victorian setting with good home cooking, gracious amenities, and an unbeatable location barely minutes away from every major Milwaukee tourist attraction and from most companies as well, and you have a dream spot for a business trip or a respite.

Actually, you have the Manegold Mansion Bed & Breakfast. Located at 3009 West Highland Boulevard just minutes from downtown Milwaukee, Manegold Mansion only became a vacation spot this year. Even after Katherine Bailey moved into the century-old mansion in 1995, it took her a few months to realize the potential of the 5,700-square-foot house.

The charming inn combines the comforts of home—including breakfasts cooked by owner Katherine Bailey—with the efficiencies of the modern office.

"I noticed I was having guests every weekend, and I even had people stop in and ask if it was a bed and breakfast," Bailey recalls. "So I did some checking and found out that there were only two existing bed and breakfast places in the whole city. I thought, my house is gorgeous; I have 10 bedrooms. So why not give it a try?"

The rest, as they say, is a success story. Manegold Mansion is becoming one of the more distinctive tourist landmarks in all of Milwaukee, as well as a charming alternative to a typical hotel stay.

The three-story, 17-room Victorian was built in 1897 by William and Mathilda Manegold, according to Bailey. William was in several businesses, including quarrying, milling, and brewing. He died in 1936, and Mathilda sold the house shortly thereafter.

The house bears all the hallmarks of classical Queen Anne Victorian architecture, including a turret in front. Its light-colored brick has endured remarkably well. In fact, Manegold Mansion still bears about 98 percent of its original materials and pieces right down to the woodwork, eight-foot double doors with leaded glass, and the original gaslight fixtures. It also features a third-floor ballroom with a fabulous circle room in front.

"We have done practically nothing to refurbish it; the house was in great shape when we bought it," Bailey says.

Manegold Mansion, which began with two guest bedrooms, has great appeal to weekend tourists as well as to "business travelers who are looking for something different than the hotel scene," Bailey says. From breakfasts cooked by the owner herself to the availability of a copier, computer, and fax services and a fully equipped exercise room on the first floor, the mansion provides the comforts of home and the efficiencies of the office.

Bailey has enjoyed her guests at Manegold Mansion so much—and vice versa—that she briefly considered buying another nicely aging mansion across the street and converting it to a second bed and breakfast. But the demands of running the mansion properly convinced her otherwise.

"Part of what makes this business so enjoyable is interacting with people," she says. "I love getting to know the people who come to stay with me. To do that, you need to be there and unfortunately you can't live in two mansions at once."

Right: Manegold Mansion Bed & Breakfast bears all the hallmarks of classical Queen Anne Victorian architecture, including a turret in front.

Milwaukee Athletic Club

Like a stalwart isle amid the ever-changing sea of downtown, the Milwaukee Athletic Club has always served the business, social, and athletic needs of its members on a daily as well as a special occasion basis.

Yet so it can always do so effectively, the MAC has continued to alter its approach to fulfilling those needs. That's why it remains the most distinctive and distinguished such club in Milwaukee. In fact, from its 12-floor site at the corner of Broadway and Mason, the MAC does business as the only private club in Milwaukee that offers dining, meeting rooms, guest rooms, and full athletic facilities.

The Milwaukee Athletic Club, at the corner of Broadway and Mason, circa the 1920s.

Right: The MAC's present-day lobby.

"Our pledge has been, and always will be, to stick with our core mission, but we must also respond to the changing needs of our members," says Charles Crosse, a local attorney who is the president of the MAC. "That way, the club can continue to play an important role in their lives."

The club is governed by a 12-member board of directors that sets policy and directs the general manager. Membership is by invitation from a current member and approval by the board.

The club was established in 1882 as the Milwaukee Athletic Society by eight young men for the purpose of "development of the bodily powers" through exercise. In 1898 the organization changed its name to the Milwaukee Athletic Club.

Nine buildings housed the MAC before it moved to its present site in 1918. Within its walls are a formal dining room, sports bar and restaurant, game room, 17 private meeting rooms including the Grand Ballroom, 65 overnight guest rooms, cocktail lounge, library, barbershop and styling salon, child care room, racquetball courts, hardball and softball squash courts, golf practice range, and private men's and women's athletic facilities, each with its own pool.

Although its focus has always been athletics, the MAC now provides a broader range of services and opportunities for its membership that make the club a much greater whole than the sum of its parts. The club's facilities, management, and staff of about 270 full- and part-time employees work together to provide members with a home away from home, a social venue, a freshening-up stop before downtown activities, and a business networking arena.

The MAC also has been the site of a number of historically important events in Milwaukee, ranging from a campaign stop by then presidential candidate Bill Clinton and a visit from Vice President Al Gore to the 1993 press conference at which future Hall-of-Famer Paul Molitor announced he would be leaving the Milwaukee Brewers.

Adaptation has managed to keep the club central to the downtown life of Milwaukee's business community. A driving range replaced a rifle range. Pool tables once anchored a recreation area; then they disappeared as the game fell out of favor; now they're back. Wine-and-cheese tastings and ski trips are more common club outings now than the dinner dances of yore. Casual wear has replaced dress attire at many MAC functions.

Perhaps the most exciting recent innovation is the MAC's arrangement with The Bog, a striking new golf course in Ozaukee County, to give MAC members the opportunity to purchase all rounds through at least 1999. Intrigued by how popular the program is with MAC members, other downtown clubs across the country are interested in trying to duplicate it.

Entering its 115th year, the Milwaukee Athletic Club is on target to serve the ever-changing needs of the Milwaukee community into the twenty-first century.

About Milwaukee Publishing Group

Milwaukee Publishing Group is a joint venture headed by David Turner and Don Toohey, both of whom have extensive experience in the specialty book publishing industry. David Turner is a longtime Milwaukee resident and Don Toohey lives near Kenosha, Wisconsin. The MPG staff is comprised of dedicated publishing professionals who have worked in all facets of the book publishing industry for more than 15 years and who have helped to develop, produce, and market hundreds of illustrated hardcover and softcover publications for economic development groups, chambers of commerce, historical societies, museums, and trade and professional organizations throughout North America.

Above: Co-publisher David Turner (right) shows some sample layouts of Milwaukee 150 *to Mayor John Norquist. Photo by Milwaukee DCD/ Dave La Haye*

Left: Participants in the Milwaukee 150 *project included (left to right) corporate historian Dale Buss, illustrator Lynn Casper, illustrator Steve Slaske, co-publisher Don Toohey, co-author Ellen Langill, co-author Dave Jensen, corporate historian Linda Duczman, and photo researcher Carlen Hatala. Also part of the team but not photographed were editorial director Karen Story, design director Ellen Ifrah, photo editor Patty Salkeld, and editorial assistant Kathy Peyser. Photo by Khris Erickson*

Notes on Sources

The following books and publications have been the most helpful in pulling together the first three chapters of this overview of Milwaukee's 150-year history. Of these books, the Bayrd Still volume still stands out for its thoroughness and breadth. Robert Wells' book has value in its humor and detail, and the work of Harry Anderson and Fred Olson is comprehensive and insightful. The Aderman volume is also an excellent resource. I used its chapters by Fred Olson, Donald Vogel, Steven Avella, Harry Anderson, and Harold Mayer. The other materials, listed below, provided valuable additional information from which I was able to draw. I also acknowledge with gratitude the assistance of David Turner in uncovering corporate biographies for use in this narrative and Karen Story for her skillful editing of the manuscript.

Alderman, Ralph M., ed. *Trading Post to Metropolis, Milwaukee County's First 150 Years*. Milwaukee: Milwaukee County Historical Society, 1987.

Anderson, Harry H., and Frederick I. Olson. *Milwaukee at the Gathering of the Waters*. Milwaukee: Milwaukee County Historical Society, 1981.

Commercial Milwaukee, Yearbook 1909. Milwaukee: Merchants and Manufacturers Association, 1909.

Conrad, Will C., Kathleen Wilson, and Dale Wilson. *The Milwaukee Journal: The First Eighty Years*. Madison: University of Wisconsin Press, 1964.

Drew, William Ryan. *Built in Milwaukee, An Architectural View of the City*. Milwaukee: Department of City Development, 1980.

Filardo, Gregory. *Old Milwaukee, A Historic Tour in Picture Postcards*. Vestal, New York: The Vestal Press, 1988.

Fromstein, Ruth. *Milwaukee: The Best of All Worlds*. Chatsworth, California: Windsor Publications, 1990.

Hoeveler, Diane L., ed. *Milwaukee Women Yesterday*. Milwaukee: Milwaukee Humanities Program, 1979.

Jakubovich, Paul J. *As Good As New: A Guide to Rehabilitating the Exterior of Your Milwaukee Home*. Milwaukee: City of Milwaukee, 1993.

Jakubovich, Paul J., and Les Vollmert. *Good For Business: A Guide to Rehabilitating the Exteriors of Older Commercial Buildings*. Milwaukee: City of Milwaukee, 1995.

Langill, Ellen D. *Foley & Lardner, Attorneys at Law 1842-1892*. Madison: The State Historical Society of Wisconsin, 1992.

McBride, Genevieve. *On Wisconsin Women: Fighting for Their Rights from Settlement to Suffrage*. Madison: University of Wisconsin Press, 1993.

Maier, Henry W., selected articles on. *The Milwaukee Journal*, July 18, 1994, p.1; *The Milwaukee Sentinel*, July 18, 1994, p. 11A, July 19, 1994, p. 1, 10A.

Maier, Henry W. *The Mayor Who Made Milwaukee Famous, An Autobiography*. Lanham, Maryland: Madison Books, 1993.

Mariner, Mary. *The Woman's Club of Wisconsin, 1876-1976*. Milwaukee: The Woman's Club of Wisconsin, 1976.

Milwaukee: More Than a City. Milwaukee: Department of City Development, 1985.

Milwaukee, 100 Photogravures. Milwaukee: The Milwaukee Real Estate Board, 1892.

Milwaukee's Great Industries. Milwaukee: The Association for the Advancement of Milwaukee, 1892.

Perrin, Richard W.E. *Milwaukee Landmarks*. Milwaukee Public Museum Publications No. 9, 1966.

Still, Bayrd. *Milwaukee: The History of a City*. Madison: The State Historical Society of Wisconsin, 1948.

Wells, Robert W. *This Is Milwaukee: A Colorful Portrait of the City that Made Beer Famous*. Garden City, New York: Doubleday & Company, Inc., 1970.

Wells, Robert W. *Yesterday's Milwaukee*. Miami, Florida: E.A. Seemann Publishing, Inc., 1976.

Acknowledgments

A special thanks to Victoria Soukup and Nancy Raabe for their research and editorial contributions, to the Metropolitan Milwaukee Association of Commerce for statistical data, and to all of the individuals, companies, and organizations who graciously supplied information and comments for this book.

Patrons

The following individuals, companies, and organizations have made a valuable commitment to the quality of this publication. Milwaukee Publishing Group and the City of Milwaukee Department of City Development gratefully acknowledge their participation in *Milwaukee 150: The Greater Milwaukee Story.*

ABB Flexible Automation Inc.*
ABB Industrial Systems Inc.*
Allen-Edmonds Shoe Corporation*
Ambrosia Chocolate, A Grace Cocoa Company*
Arthur Anderson
ArcRon, Ltd.*
Aurora Health Care*
Badger Meter, Inc.*
Beck Carton Corporation*
Bentley & Son, Inc.*
The Blood Center of Southeastern Wisconsin*
The Boelter Companies*
Bokare Framing*
Boston Store*
Boys & Girls Clubs of Greater Milwaukee*
W.H. Brady Co.*
Bucyrus International, Inc.*
Busch Precision Inc.
C&H Distributors Inc.*
Catalyst International, Inc.*
Charter Manufacturing, Inc.*
City of Milwaukee Department of City Development*
The W. Clasmann Corp. 1916-1996
Community Newspapers Inc.*
Patrick Cudahy Incorporated*
Dawes Rigging and Crane Rental, Inc.
Delzer Lithograph Company*
Downey Inc.*
EBI Companies*
Eppstein Uhen Architects, Inc.*
Ernst & Young, LLP
The Falk Corporation*
Family Health Plan*
Firstar Corporation*
Fiserv, Inc.*
Fleet Mortgage Group*
Fleming Companies*
Froedtert Malt Corporation*
Galland Henning Nopak, Inc.*
Gardetto's Inc.*
GE Medical Systems*
General Mitchell International Airport*
Russell T. Gilman Inc.*
Godfrey & Kahn, S.C.*
Goodwill Industries of Southeastern Wisconsin*
Gossen Corporation*
Graef Anhalt Schloemer & Associates, Inc.*
The Grand Avenue*
Greater Milwaukee Convention & Visitors Bureau/The Wisconsin Center*
Grede Foundries, Inc.*
Camille Haney
Harley-Davidson, Inc.*
Harnischfeger Industries, Inc.*
Harris Classical Broadcasting Inc.*
Hatco Corporation*
Helwig Carbon Products, Inc.*
Hispanic Chamber of Commerce of Wisconsin*
IDI Corporation*
Johnson Brass & Machine Foundry Inc.*
Johnson Controls Inc.*
Kalmbach Publishing Co.*
Kendall Packaging Corporation*
Kohl's Food Stores*
Koss Corporation*
Mandy Services, Inc.*
Manegold Mansion Bed & Breakfast*
The Mark Travel Corporation*
Marquette Medical Systems
Marshall & Ilsley Corporation*
Master Lock Company*
Metropolitan Milwaukee Association of Commerce*
Midland Paper Company
Midwest Distribution Systems
Midwest Express Airlines*
Milliman & Robertson, Inc.*
Milwaukee Area Technical College*
Milwaukee Athletic Club*
Milwaukee Black Pages*
Milwaukee Boiler Manufacturing Co.*
The Milwaukee Community Journal*
Milwaukee Electronics Corporation*
Milwaukee Mack Sales Inc.*
Milwaukee Tool & Equipment Company*
Mutual Savings Bank
New England Financial Services*
Nordberg Inc.*
Northwestern Mutual Life Insurance Co.*
Oldenburg Group Incorporated*
Opus North Corporation
Overton Consulting
Paper Machinery Corporation*
Pelton Casteel, Inc.*
Penfield Children's Center*
Phoenix Products Company Inc.*
Precision Woodwork Inc.
Principal Financial Group, Eastern Wisconsin Agency
Provimi Veal Corporation*
Radyne Corporation
RE/MAX Lakeside Realtors
Rockwell Automation/Allen-Bradley*
Roundy's, Inc.*
St. John's Home of Milwaukee*
St. Luke's Medical Center*
St. Mary's Hospital of Milwaukee*
C.G. Schmidt, Inc.*
Siemens Power Corporation*
Sinai Samaritan Medical Center*
A.O. Smith Corporation*
Smith & Nephew Rolyan Inc.*
W.G. Strohwig Tool & Die Inc.*
Superior Services, Inc.
Tecumseh Products Company*
Thompson Consulting, Ltd.
Time Insurance Company*
Tool Service Corporation
Trammell Crow Company
U.S. Leather Inc.*
Wacker Corporation*
Warner Cable*
Waukesha County Technical College*
Wauwatosa Realty Company*
H.H. West Company*
Keith C. Winters & Associates, Ltd.
Wisconsin Energy Corporation*
Wisconsin Gas*
Wisconsin Paperboard Corp.*
WITI-TV SIX IS NEWS*
Zigman Joseph Stephenson*

*Participants in Part Three, "Greater Milwaukee's Enterprises." The stories of these companies and organizations appear in chapters 7 through 13, beginning on page 214.

Directory of Corporate Sponsors

ABB Flexible Automation Inc., 271
2487 South Commerce Drive
New Berlin, WI 53151
414/785-3400
Ann Smith

ABB Industrial Systems Inc., 270
16250 West Glendale Drive
New Berlin, WI 53151
414/785-3200
Hubert Schlegel

Allen-Edmonds Shoe Corporation, 258-259
201 East Seven Hills Road
P.O. Box 998
Port Washington, WI 53074
414/284-3461

Ambrosia Chocolate, A Grace Cocoa Company, 284-285
12500 West Carmen Avenue
Milwaukee, WI 53225
414/358-5700
Mary Rosenthal

ArcRon, Ltd., 268-269
West 141 North 9501 Fountain Boulevard
Menomonee Falls, WI 53051
414/255-4150
Ron Wilfer

Aurora Health Care, 360-361
3000 West Montana Street
Milwaukee, WI 53215
414/647-3020
Diane De La Santos

Badger Meter, Inc., 248-249
4545 West Brown Deer Road
Milwaukee, WI 53223
414/355-0400
James L. Forbes, President/CEO

Beck Carton Corporation, 244-245
311 East Chicago Street
Milwaukee, WI 53202
414/273-2552
Thomas Wamser

Bentley & Son, Inc., 348-349
8970 North 55th Street
Milwaukee, WI 53223
414/365-6000
Thomas Bentley III

The Blood Center of Southeastern Wisconsin, 364
638 North 18th Street
Milwaukee, WI 53233
414/933-5000

The Boelter Companies, 378-379
11100 West Silver Spring Road
Milwaukee, WI 53226

Bokare Framing, 393
6936 North Santa Monica Boulevard
Milwaukee, WI 53217
414/351-1092
414/351-2017 fax

Boston Store, 390-391
331 West Wisconsin Avenue
Milwaukee, WI 53203
414/347-5191
Roger Gaston
Executive Vice President of Human Resources

Boys & Girls Clubs of Greater Milwaukee, 370
1437 North Prospect Avenue
Milwaukee, WI 53202
414/274-6100

W.H. Brady Co., 272
6555 West Good Hope Road
Milwaukee, WI 53223
414/358-6600
Daniel Wink, Corporate Relations Manager

Bucyrus International, Inc., 290-291
1100 Milwaukee Avenue
South Milwaukee, WI 53172
414/768-4000

C&H Distributors Inc., 398-399
770 South 70th Street
West Allis, WI 53214
414/443-1700

Catalyst International, Inc., 274-275
8989 North Deerwood Drive
Milwaukee, WI 53223
414/362-6800
Renée Truttmann

Charter Manufacturing, Inc., 266-267
1212 West Glen Oaks Lane
P.O. Box 217
Mequon, WI 53092
414/243-4700
John A. Mellowes

City of Milwaukee Department of City Development, 320-321
809 North Broadway
Milwaukee, WI 53202
414/286-5830
Martha L. Brown

Community Newspapers Inc., 228-229
640 East Ryan Road
P.O. Box 7
Oak Creek, WI 53154
414/938-5000
Thomas H. Krekel

Patrick Cudahy Incorporated, 386-387
3500 East Barnard Avenue
Cudahy, WI 53110
414/744-2000

Delzer Lithograph Company, 250-251
510 South West Avenue
Waukesha, WI 53186
414/542-5791
Eric Delzer

Downey Inc., 354-355
2207 West Wisconsin Avenue
Milwaukee, WI 53233
414/933-3123
Gregory Coffman

EBI Companies, 336-337
325 North Corporate Drive, Suite 100
Brookfield, WI 53045
414/879-0463
Jon Gice

Eppstein Uhen Architects, 346-347
P.O. Box 92728
Milwaukee, WI 53202
414/271-5350
414/271-7794 fax

The Falk Corporation, 304-305
3001 West Canal Street
P.O. Box 492
Milwaukee, WI 53201
414/937-4386
Michael Blomgren

Family Health Plan, 358-359
11524 West Theodore Trecker Way
Milwaukee, WI 53214
414/256-0040
Marketing Department

Firstar Corporation, 332-333
777 East Wisconsin Avenue
Milwaukee, WI 53202
414/765-4321
Anne Curley

Fiserv, Inc., 334
255 Fiserv Drive
P.O. Box 979
Brookfield, WI 53008-0979
414/879-5000
Kevin Kasper

Fleet Mortgage Group, 331
11200 West Parkland Avenue
Milwaukee, WI 53224
414/359-9300
Richard J. Franas

Fleming Companies, 394-395
1200 West Sunset Drive
Waukesha, WI 53186
414/542-9311

Froedtert Malt Corporation, 262
3830 West Grant Street
Milwaukee, WI 53215
414/671-1166

Galland Henning Nopak, Inc., 294-295
1025 South 40th Street
West Milwaukee, WI 53215
414/645-6000
414/645-6048 fax
Hermann Nunnemacher

Gardetto's Inc., 396-397
4625 South Sixth Street
Milwaukee, WI 53221
414/483-6000
Nannette Gardetto

GE Medical Systems, 273
3000 North Grandview Boulevard
Waukesha, WI 53188
414/544-3556
Wendee Puccetti

General Mitchell International Airport, 222-223
5300 South Howell Avenue
Milwaukee, WI 53207
414/747-5300
Patricia Rowe

Russell T. Gilman Inc., 277
1230 Cheyenne Avenue
P.O. Box 5
Grafton, WI 53024
414/377-2434
Paul Haas

Godfrey & Kahn, S.C., 340-341
780 North Water Street
Milwaukee, WI 53202-3590
414/273-3500
414/273-5198 fax

Goodwill Industries of Southeastern Wisconsin, 369
6055 North 91st Street
Milwaukee, WI 53225
414/252-6400
Cheryl Lightholder

Gossen Corporation, 276
2030 West Bender Road
Milwaukee, WI 53209
414/228-9800
Bob Simon

Graef Anhalt Schloemer & Associates, Inc., 350-351
345 North 95th Street
Milwaukee, WI 53226
414/259-1500
Harold Farchmin, Vice President

The Grand Avenue, 384
275 West Wisconsin Avenue, Suite 5
Milwaukee, WI 53203
414/224-0384

Greater Milwaukee Convention & Visitors Bureau/The Wisconsin Center, 374-375
510 West Kilbourn
Milwaukee, WI 53203
414/273-3950

Grede Foundries, Inc., 306-307
9898 West Bluemound Road
Milwaukee, WI 53226
414/257-3600
W. Stewart Davis

Harley-Davidson, Inc., 252
3700 West Juneau Avenue
P.O. Box 653
Milwaukee, WI 53201
414/343-8300

Harnischfeger Industries, Inc., 302-303
414/797-6626

Harris Classical Broadcasting Inc., 226-227
West 172 North 7348 Shady Lane
Menomonee Falls, WI 53051
414/255-3100
Randall Harris

Hatco Corporation, 253
635 South 28th Street
Milwaukee, WI 53215
414/671-6350
Ronald Halverson

Helwig Carbon Products, Inc., 246-247
8900 West Tower Avenue
Milwaukee, WI 53224-0400
414/354-2411

Hispanic Chamber of Commerce of Wisconsin, 339
816 West National Avenue
Milwaukee, WI 53204
414/643-6963
Maria Monreal-Cameron

IDI Corporation, 335
20875 Crossroads Circle
P.O. Box 888
Brookfield, WI 53008-0888
414/798-3000
Robert Agnew

Johnson Brass & Machine Foundry Inc., 286
270 Mill Street
P.O. Box 219
Saukville, WI 53080
414/377-9440
Lance Johnson

Johnson Controls Inc., 264-265
5757 North Green Bay Avenue
P.O. Box 591
Milwaukee, WI 53201-0591
414/228-1200

Kalmbach Publishing Co., 230-231
21027 Crossroads Circle
Waukesha, WI 53187
414/796-8776

Kendall Packaging Corporation, 280-281
633 West Wisconsin Avenue
Milwaukee, WI 53203
414/276-4770
Eric Erickson

Kohl's Food Stores, 385
11100 West Burleigh
Milwaukee, WI 53222
414/771-8000
Tim Wade

Koss Corporation, 263
4129 North Port Washington Road
Milwaukee, WI 53212-1029
1/800/USA-KOSS or
414/964-5000

Mandy Services, Inc., 392
11430 West Bluemound Road
Milwaukee, WI 53226
414/453-8682
Jan Mandy

Manegold Mansion Bed & Breakfast, 403
3009 West Highland Boulevard
Milwaukee, WI 53208
414/344-5655
Katherine Bailey

The Mark Travel Corporation. 382-383
8907 North Port Washington Road
Milwaukee, WI 53217
414/228-7472

Marshall & Ilsley Corporation, 330
770 North Water Street
Milwaukee, WI 53202
414/765-7809
Michael A. Hatfield

Master Lock Company, 260-261
2600 North 32nd Street
Milwaukee, WI 53210
414/444-2800

Metropolitan Milwaukee Association of Commerce, 322-323
756 North Milwaukee Street
Milwaukee, WI 53202
414/287-4100

Midwest Express Airlines, 224-225
6744 South Howell Avenue
Oak Creek, WI 53154
414/570-4000

Milliman & Robertson, Inc., 326-327
15800 Bluemound Road, Suite 400
Brookfield, WI 53005
414/784-2250
414/784-4116 fax

Milwaukee Area Technical College, 366
700 West State Street
Milwaukee, WI 53233
414/297-6322

Milwaukee Athletic Club, 404
758 North Broadway
Milwaukee, WI 53202
414/273-5080
Mark W. Guirlinger, CCM
General Manager

Milwaukee Black Pages, 237
3009A West Highland Boulevard
Milwaukee, WI 53208
414/344-1111
Katherine Bailey

Milwaukee Boiler Manufacturing Co., 299
1101 South 41st Street
Milwaukee, WI 53215
414/645-0068
Richard Stevens

The Milwaukee Community Journal, 236
3612 North Martin Luther King Jr. Drive
Milwaukee,WI 53212
414/265-5300
Mikel Holt

Milwaukee Electronics Corporation, 254-255
5855 North Glen Park Road
Milwaukee, WI 53209
414/228-5000

Milwaukee Mack Sales Inc., 400-401
4444 West Bluemound Road
Milwaukee, WI 53208
414/258-8484
Roger Kriete

Milwaukee Publishing Group, 405
P.O. Box 780
Milwaukee, WI 53201
414/671-3555
David Turner

Milwaukee Tool & Equipment Company, 296-297
2773 South 29th Street
P.O. Box 2039
Milwaukee, WI 53201
414/645-0200
Tom or Dick Gutenkunst

New England Financial Services/ The Marris Group, Inc., 342
300 North Corporate Drive,
Suite 250
Brookfield, WI 53045
414/792-1680
William C. Marris, CLU

Nordberg Inc., 292-293
3073 South Chase Avenue
Milwaukee, WI 53201
414/769-4300

Northwestern Mutual Life Insurance Co., 324-325
720 East Wisconsin Avenue
Milwaukee, WI 53202
414/271-1444

Oldenburg Group Incorporated, 240-243
8600 West Bradley Road
Milwaukee, WI 53224
414/357-8600
Wayne Oldenburg

Paper Machinery Corporation, 298
8900 West Bradley Road
Milwaukee, WI 53224
414/354-8050
John P. Baumgartner

Pelton Casteel, Inc., 314-315
2929 South Chase Avenue
Milwaukee, WI 53207
414/481-3400
Michael Gwyn

Penfield Children's Center, 368
833 North 26th Street
Milwaukee, WI 53233
414/344-7676

Phoenix Products Company Inc., 256-257
6161 North 64th Street
Milwaukee, WI 53218
414/438-1200
George Wordingham

Provimi Veal Corporation, 402
20800 Swenson Drive, Suite 440
Waukesha, WI 53186-4044
414/784-8520
Aat Groenevelt
Chairman and CEO

Rockwell Automation/Allen-Bradley, 300-301
1201 South Second Street
Milwauke, WI 53204

Roundy's, Inc., 380-381
23000 Roundy Drive
Pewaukee, WI 53072
414/547-7999

St. John's Home of Milwaukee, 371
1840 North Prospect Avenue
Milwaukee, WI 53202
414/272-2022

St. Luke's Medical Center, 367
2900 West Oklahoma Avenue
Milwaukee, WI 53201
414/649-6000

St. Mary's Hospital of Milwaukee, 362
2323 North Lake Drive
Milwaukee, WI 53211
414/291-1000

C.G. Schmidt, Inc., 353
4199 North Richards Street
P.O. Box 11609
Milwaukee, WI 53211
414/332-1177

Siemens Power Corporation, 317
1040 South 70th Street
Milwaukee, WI 53214
414/475-3600
Cynthia Phillips

Sinai Samaritan Medical Center, 363
945 North 12th Street
Milwaukee, WI 53233
414/219-2000
William I. Jenkins, President

Smith and Nephew Rolyan Inc., 278
One Quality Drive
P.O. Box 1005
Germantown, WI 53022
414/251-7840

A.O. Smith Corporation, 310-311
11270 West Park Place
P.O. Box 23971
Milwaukee, WI 53201
414/359-4000

W.G. Strohwig Tool & Die Inc., 282-283
3285 Industrial Road
Richfield, WI 53076
414/628-4477
Wolfgang Strohwig

Tecumseh Products Company, 312-313
900 North Street
Grafton, WI 53024
414/377-2700

Time Insurance Company, 328-329
501 West Michigan
Milwaukee, WI 53203
414/271-3011

U.S. Leather Inc., 376-377
1531 North Water
P.O. Box 745
Milwaukee, WI 53201

Warner Cable, 235
1610 North Second Street
Milwaukee, WI 53212
414/277-4000
Jacqueline Janz

Waukesha County Technical College, 365
800 Main Street
Pewaukee, WI 53072
414/691-5566
414/691-5593 fax
http://www.waukesha.tec.wi.us/

Wauwatosa Realty Company, 352
17450 West North Avenue, 2nd Floor
Brookfield, WI 53008
414/827-4200
John Horning, Sr.

H.H.West Company, 388-389
505 North 22nd Street
Milwaukee, WI 53233
414/344-1000
Marvin Cooper

Wisconsin Energy Corporation, 216-219
231 West Michigan Street
Milwaukee, WI 53203
414/221-2146
Corporate Communications Department

Wisconsin Gas, 220-221
626 East Wisconsin Avenue
Milwaukee, WI 53202

Wisconsin Paperboard Corp., 308-309
1514 East Thomas Avenue
Milwaukee, WI 53211
414/271-9000

WITI-TV SIX IS NEWS, 232-234
9001 North Green Bay Road
Milwaukee, WI 53217
414/355-6666
Patti Gorsky

Zigman Joseph Stephenson, 338
100 East Wisconsin Avenue,
Suite 1000
Milwaukee, WI 53202
414/273-4680
Linda Stephenson

Index

Italicized entries indicate illustrations.